Google®
SECRETS

Enjoy This Book!

Manage your library account and explore
all we offer by visiting us online at
www.nashualibrary.org.

Please return this on time, so
others can enjoy it, too.

If you are pleased with all that the
library offers, tell others.

Google®
SECRETS

DO WHAT YOU NEVER THOUGHT POSSIBLE WITH GOOGLE

Yvette Davis

WILEY

John Wiley & Sons, Inc.

EXECUTIVE EDITOR: Robert Elliott

PROJECT EDITOR: Charlotte Kughen, The Wordsmithery LLC

TECHNICAL EDITOR: Todd Meister

PRODUCTION EDITOR: Rebecca Anderson

COPY EDITOR: Kim Cofer

EDITORIAL MANAGER: Mary Beth Wakefield

FREELANCER EDITORIAL MANAGER: Rosemarie Graham

ASSOCIATE DIRECTOR OF MARKETING: David Mayhew

MARKETING MANAGER: Ashley Zurcher

BUSINESS MANAGER: Amy Knies

PRODUCTION MANAGER: Tim Tate

VICE PRESIDENT AND EXECUTIVE GROUP PUBLISHER: Richard Swadley

VICE PRESIDENT AND EXECUTIVE PUBLISHER: Neil Edde

ASSOCIATE PUBLISHER: Jim Minatel

PROJECT COORDINATOR, COVER: Katie Crocker

COMPOSITOR: Craig Woods, Happenstance Type-O-Rama

PROOFREADER: Jen Larsen, Word One New York

INDEXER: Johnna VanHoose Dinse

COVER DESIGNER: Ryan Sneed

COVER IMAGE: © Chad Baker/Lifesize/Getty Images

Google® Secrets

Published by

John Wiley & Sons, Inc.
10475 Crosspoint Boulevard
Indianapolis, IN 46256
www.wiley.com

Copyright © 2012 by John Wiley & Sons, Inc., Indianapolis, Indiana

Published simultaneously in Canada

ISBN: 978-1-118-02665-6

ISBN: 978-1-118-19370-9 (ebk)

ISBN: 978-1-118-19371-6 (ebk)

ISBN: 978-1-118-19372-3 (ebk)

Manufactured in the United States of America

10 9 8 7 6 5 4 3 2 1

For general information on our other products and services please contact our Customer Care Department within the United States at (877) 762-2974, outside the United States at (317) 572-3993 or fax (317) 572-4002.

Wiley also publishes its books in a variety of electronic formats and by print-on-demand. Not all content that is available in standard print versions of this book may appear or be packaged in all book formats. If you have purchased a version of this book that did not include media that is referenced by or accompanies a standard print version, you may request this media by visiting http://booksupport.wiley.com. For more information about Wiley products, visit us at www.wiley.com.

Library of Congress Control Number: 2011926331

As always, this book is dedicated first to my children: Crystal, Nicole, Aj, Justin, Jennifer, and Bryanna. You are the reason for my being. Second, to my husband, Allan. Without your loving support I would not be who I am today. Finally, for their impact on my young impressionable mind, this book is also dedicated to Kathryn Eckel and Marilyn Buehler.

Acknowledgments

I'd like to acknowledge and thank Jerri Ledford Whatley and Lynn Haller for bringing this project to my attention. A huge thank you goes out to Joe Teixeira for his much-appreciated assistance.

And of course, the staff at Wiley, especially Robert Elliot and Charlotte Kughen, without whom this book would never have been completed.

I'm sure there are others whose names should appear on this page. Their omission is more a sign of my failing memory than lack of appreciation. Thank you to all who had a hand in making this book happen.

About the Author

Yvette Davis is an avid supporter of open source software, which is why she uses Google products on a Linux operating system. She has been helping users learn and understand technical topics for almost 18 years through articles, books, and workshops. As the former managing editor of BrightHub.com's Google Channel she has a deep understanding of Google's wide range of services as well as the needs of the users utilizing them. In her off time, Yvette enjoys learning new Linux distros and experimenting with programming languages. She plays saxophone in community orchestra and is studying to become a Traditional Naturopath. Yvette lives in the middle of the U.S. with her husband, their six children, and assorted fur-kids.

About the Contributor

Joe Teixeira is currently the Director of Web Intelligence at MoreVisibility, a Google Analytics Certified Partner (GACP). Joe is a leading expert in the field of Web Analytics, as he is Google Analytics Individually Qualified (GAIQ), and Google AdWords and MSN AdCenter Certified. Joe has presented over 200 online webinars in a variety of topics, including web analytics, pay-per-click marketing, search engine optimization, as well as webinars focusing on user experience and web site testing. In addition, Joe frequently trains and educates companies on all aspects of web analytics and search engine advertising via online conferences and in-person, face-to-face meetings. Joe co-authored *Google Analytics*, Third Edition, authored *Your Google Game Plan for Success*, and has appeared as a guest blogger on the official Google Analytics Blog.

About the Tech Editor

Todd Meister has been working in the IT industry for more than fifteen years. He's been a technical editor for more than 75 titles ranging from SQL Server to the .NET Framework. Besides being a tech editor, he is the senior IT architect at Ball State University in Muncie, IN. He lives in central Indiana with his wife, Kimberly, and their four lively children.

Contents at a Glance

Contents

Read This First

Thank you for purchasing Google Secrets! This book will
serve as your ultimate "go-to" guide for all programs, tools, and resources on the Google
ecosystem. You can read this book from cover to cover like a traditional novel, but
you're also more than welcome to start from any chapter and jump between sections
to retrieve the insights for the product that you're looking for.

Who This Book Is For

Google Secrets is a book perfectly suited for web developers, web site marketers,
Internet analysts, fans of all things Google, and CEOs (not Chief *Executive* Officers. . .
Chief *Everything* Officers).

If you're a web developer, you'll really enjoy the chapters that focus on collaboration and productivity. If you're a website marketer, you'll love the chapters that dive
deep into your Google experience and building a web site with Google. If you're an
Internet analyst, you'll appreciate the chapters that deal with data, measurement,
and insights. If you're a fan of all things Google, you'll love the chapters focused on
using Google's robust product suite. If you're a Chief Everything Officer, you'll like
just about everything this book has to offer!

Regardless of whom you are or what your professional duties include, *Google
Secrets* is suited for you.

What This Book Covers

Google Secrets covers more than twenty of the most popular and widely used products in the Google family. Google has an extremely large ecosystem of free products
and services that fulfill the needs of anyone, from the most casual to the most entre-
preneurial user.

Just take a peek at some of the amazing Google products that are covered in this
book and you'll be wanting more:

- ▶ Android
- ▶ Blogger

- ▶ Buzz
- ▶ Gmail
- ▶ Google Analytics
- ▶ Google Calendar
- ▶ Google Docs
- ▶ Google Reader
- ▶ iGoogle
- ▶ Image Search
- ▶ Knol
- ▶ Local Search
- ▶ Orkut
- ▶ Picasa
- ▶ YouTube
- And much, much more!

How This Book Is Structured

Before you get started, let's review how this book is structured so that you know what to expect as you start flipping through pages. *Google Secrets* is organized into eight separate parts:

- ▶ **Part I: Customizing Your Google Experience.** Google is one flexible stream of products and features. At your fingertips, you can edit your Google profile, increase your knowledge with programs such as Google Reader, and you can build your own Google experience with an iGoogle page. Part I contains three chapters full of creative and insightful ways to optimize how you use and interact with Google products.

- ▶ **Part II: Google Search Secrets.** Google is, by far, the giant in the search industry. No one does search better than Google, and no one has more hidden treasures and secrets waiting to be shared! In Part II, you find six chapters chock full of surprises, gems, insights, and advanced functionality. You learn how to use Google search like a Google engineer, how to take advantage of Local Search, how to find people using Google, how to enhance your next presentation with Image Search, and much more.

- **Part III: Google Gmail Secrets**. Using e-mail is no longer a chore—it's an art form! With Gmail, you can completely revolutionize the way you think about e-mail with awesome built-in features, functionality, and available apps. In Part III, you are exposed to two full chapters that dive into detail on the ways to improve your Gmail productivity, how to manage, label, and sort messages, and writing filters to organize your e-mail.

- **Part IV: Secrets for Sharing Content with Google Applications.** Sharing content goes beyond opening up a Facebook account and posting random 140-character thoughts on Twitter. Google lets you share written, photographed, and video-recorded content with the masses by offering free, powerful applications. Part IV features four chapters showcasing the powerful and advanced ways that you can share blog content, upload and manage pictures, and host videos. In Part IV, you learn how to build a custom blog, how to manage that custom blog, and how to syndicate your blog via Really Simple Syndication (RSS) with Blogger; you see how to crack open YouTube to "force" your way into high-quality video uploads and customization options; and you get to know Picasa and Picnik, two Google image-sharing platforms.

- **Part V: Google Social and Collaboration App Secrets.** Google has made an incredibly strong push into the social media world, so this part of the book is your guide to how you can leverage the Google ecosystem to make it work for you, socially. In Part V, six secret-filled chapters await you on some of Google's best social networking and social sharing platforms, including Google Groups, Orkut, Knol, Google Buzz, Google Voice, and Google Talk. You don't just learn how to use these programs, you learn the powerful secrets that only very few people know about how to customize and maximize your Google social experience.

- **Part VI: Google Productivity App Secrets.** Google isn't just about entertainment. You can actually be very productive and get a lot of work done by utilizing Google's robust productivity suite. Google Docs and Google Calendar provide users with a large number of product offerings, which allow you to work online and "in the cloud," without having to install expensive software and be tied to your physical computer to do work. In Part VI you learn how to build better presentations, how to work with and create templates, how to design spreadsheet formulas, forms, and drawings, how to sync multiple calendars, and more.

- ▶ **Part VII: Google Website Secrets.** It's no secret that Google wants website owners to deliver the most appropriate, most refined, best-looking, and fastest-loading websites to visitors. A good website is good for both Google and the website visitor, so Google provides users with tools to build, add on to, and analyze their website performance. In Part VII, you learn the secrets behind using Google Sites, Google Apps, and Google Analytics.

- ▶ **Part VIII: Secrets for Sharing, Syncing, and Working from Your Computer or Mobile Device.** Google Android is one of the world's most-used mobile interfaces, with a large market share and growing popularity. In this last section of *Google Secrets*, you learn about the inner workings of the Android system, and how to customize your Android-based mobile device to perform the tasks that you want.

What You Need to Use This Book

With technical books, most people find it helpful to sit in front of their computers or mobile devices so that they can follow along while reading through each chapter. Others find it helpful to use it as a resource guide, highlighting and making their own margin notes in specific sections.

You probably won't go wrong by having any or all of the following at the ready with your copy of *Google Secrets*:

- ▶ Your computer (with an Internet connection)

- ▶ Your mobile device

- ▶ Pen or highlighter

- ▶ Notebook (for additional notes)

- ▶ Your favorite beverage and snack

> **NOTE** Google is constantly tweaking, updating, and testing features throughout all of their platforms within their network of tools. Because of this fact, it is nearly impossible to replicate in our screenshots the exact screen that you might see if you're following along on your computer. Therefore, it is perfectly normal and should be expected that you will see slight variances between the screenshots in this book and your online version.

Features and Icons Used in This Book

The following features and icons are used in this book to help draw your attention to some of the most important or useful information in the book, some of the most valuable tips, insights, and advice that can help you unlock the secrets of Google.

▶ Watch for margin notes like this one that highlight some key piece of information or that discuss some poorly documented or hard to find technique or approach.

SIDEBARS

Sidebars like this one feature additional information about topics related to the nearby text.

TIP The Tip icon indicates a helpful trick or technique.

NOTE The Note icon points out or expands on items of importance or interest.

CROSSREF The Cross-Reference icon points to chapters where additional information can be found.

WARNING The Warning icon warns you about possible negative side effects or precautions you should take before making a change.

Part I

CUSTOMIZING YOUR GOOGLE EXPERIENCE

Starting Strong: Google Account and Profile Secrets

IN THIS CHAPTER

▶ Administrating multiple Google accounts simultaneously

▶ Managing your Google dashboard effectively

▶ Reviewing Google Voice call log and Google search histories

▶ Utilizing your Google profile in an effective, beneficial manner

Quite a few Google Apps are available, the most common of which is Gmail. Google Apps are a versatile collection of applications that give you the flexibility you need to be your most productive at home and in the office. To get the most out of your Google Apps, though, you first must know where to manage your settings, how to use the Dashboard, and how to set up your public profile, if you decide to use one.

CONNECTING GOOGLE ACCOUNTS

One great thing about Google Apps is that all your applications are connected to one another and convenient to access. At the same time, each application has individual customization settings. For example, your Gmail Chat picture can be different from your Google profile picture. You can configure Gmail to send appointments to your Google Calendar, or embed a calendar into your Google Sites website, or even onto your iGoogle homepage. And, when you use multiple sign-ins, you can easily move data from one account to another. Truly, the possibilities are endless.

Using Multiple Sign-ins

If you're like me, you have several Google accounts. I have a personal account, one for my business, and a third to collect professional newsletters and group mail. Some people use Google Apps for business at work and have a personal Gmail account. No matter how you use your multiple Google accounts it's always a time-saver to be able to log in to more than one Google account at a time. You have several ways to do this.

SIGNING IN USING DIFFERENT BROWSERS

One way to log in to more than one account at a time is to use different web browsers for each account (see Figure 1-1). For example, say you have three Google accounts and regularly use Microsoft Internet Explorer, Google Chrome, and Mozilla Firefox. Open Internet Explorer and log in to your first Google account. Next, open Google Chrome and log in to your second Google account, and finally, open Firefox to log in to the third account. You can use all Google services for each account, just as if you were logged in to just one. I find this method useful when I need to move information from my Gmail inbox of one account to my Google website on another account.

> **TIP** If you use Google Chrome, the Incognito window acts as a separate browser. But, be aware that your history won't be saved when you're using the Incognito window.

USING MULTIPLE INBOXES

If you want to access e-mail for all your Gmail accounts from only your main Gmail account, you can use the Multiple Inboxes feature from Google Labs. Log in to your Gmail account and go to Gmail Lab and find Multiple Inboxes about three-fourths down the page. Select Enable and remember to save your settings (usually a button on the bottom of any editing screen).

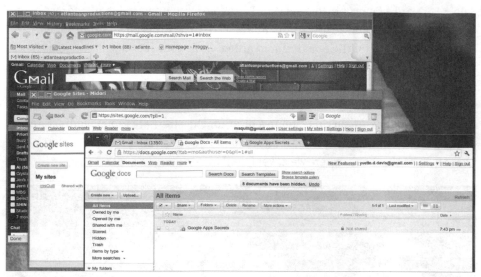

FIGURE 1-1: Logging in to your Google accounts with different browsers is a simple and effective way to get the job done.

FIGURE 1-2: With a little tweaking, the Multiple Inboxes feature enables you to access e-mail from your other Gmail accounts.

Now, log in to the Gmail account you'd like to access from your main account. Click Settings in the upper right, and select the Forwarding and POP/IMAP tab. Select Forward a Copy of Incoming Mail To and enter your main Gmail address using the button marked Add a Forwarding Address. Use the drop-down menu to tell Gmail what to do after the e-mail is forwarded. Save your settings. Now, go back to the Settings page of your main Gmail account and select the Multiple Inboxes tab. Type **to:yourothergmailaddress@gmail.com** in the text box marked Pane 0. Go to Settings and set up a filter so that e-mails in your new inboxes don't show up in your main Inbox. To do this, create a filter for the alternate e-mail address and check the Skip the Inbox option. If filters sound good to you, you should check out Chapter 11 of this book, where we cover Gmail filters more in depth.

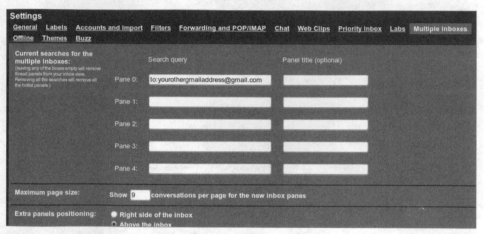

FIGURE 1-3: Tell Gmail for which e-mail addresses to create inboxes.

USING MULTIPLE SIGN-INS

The final way to sign in to multiple Gmail accounts, called Multiple Sign-in, is a newer feature of Gmail. Using the Multiple Sign-in feature enables you to access more than one account for Gmail, Voice, Sites, Reader, Calendar, and Code from within the same web browser.

To turn on Multiple Sign-in, go to the Settings page for your main Google account. (Access this page from Gmail by clicking Settings → Accounts and Imports → Google Accounts Settings.) Under the heading Personal Settings, you'll find the Off - Edit setting for the Multiple Sign-in feature, if it's available for your account. Click Edit and select On. You'll need to read and click each of the checkboxes to say you've read and agree to the warnings.

> **NOTE** When you use Multiple Sign-in, your Offline Mail and Offline Calendar are disabled, and any unsent mail may be lost.

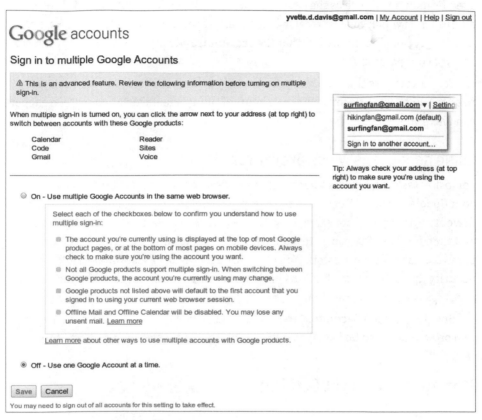

FIGURE 1-4: Turn on Multiple Sign-in.

Recovering Passwords and Lost Accounts

It's inevitable—at some time you will forget the password for your Google account. If you've paid attention to the Google security nag screens that periodically remind you to update your Google records with secondary e-mail and cell phone information, forgetting your password is no big deal. Simply click the link that says Can't Access Your Account?, and follow the on-screen directions. You'll be back up and running in no time. But, a lot of people get in a hurry and ignore that nag screen. Or, what if you accidentally delete your Google account? Then what do you do?

USING THE GOOGLE HELP FORM

You could go to the online Google help forum at www.google.com/support/accounts/ bin/answer.py?answer=48598 to fill out a support request form. The form will ask you specific questions, such as the date you opened your Google account, and the e-mail address from which you last received an e-mail. If you can answer those questions, and satisfy Google tech support that the account is indeed yours, you may be able to recover your password.

You can also use this form if you accidentally delete your account. However, you need to submit the help form within 24 hours of the accidental deletion, or tech support can't help you.

USING GOOGLE PASSWORD DECRYPTOR

For lost passwords, there is a handy little third-party program that can recover your Google password from saved password and cookie information on your hard drive. This is useful if, for example, you save your Google Docs password in Firefox and then forget it. Say you go to sign in one day and for whatever reason the saved password auto-fill doesn't work. You can download Google Password Decryptor by Security Xploded. You can find this handy program here: www.securityxploded.com/googlepassworddecryptor.php.

Google Password Decryptor can retrieve your saved Google password from your web browser, or from Google Apps information you have saved using offline tools.

Managing Account Settings

Google makes it easy to manage all your personal information and Google Apps from one page. Log in to your Google account. In the upper right, next to your login address, is the link for My Account. This is where you find everything you need to remove Apps, manage your personal settings, and even change your name. Take some time to look around a bit, and you may discover some exciting new Apps.

One of those new Apps is 2-step verification. For those of you who are concerned about your account's level of security, 2-step verification might be something that can soothe your concerns a bit.

Basically, the way that 2-step verification works is that you configure a mobile phone number to receive a verification code a minimum of once every 30 days. You need to enter that verification code immediately after typing in your Google username and password (and, before you can access your Google account). Enabling 2-step verification also means that your mobile phone Apps or other non-browser methods of accessing your Google account do not function unless you sign-in and configure each device separately.

2-step verification for Google accounts is, ironically, a three-step process:

1. Set up your primary phone. First, on your Google account settings page, click Using 2-step Verification. Then, click on Set Up 2-step Verification. From this point, you need to stop what you're doing without closing your desktop browser window to get your mobile device. At this point in time, you have two options to consider. Option one entails selecting your mobile device and then, on your mobile device, downloading a free app called Google Authenticator (available free on the Android App market, the Apple App Store, or from your BlackBerry, m.google.com/authenticator). This App takes you through the necessary first steps of configuring your primary phone; there is a point during this process where you will receive a code on your mobile phone and are asked to enter and verify it on your desktop computer.

   Option two involves receiving an SMS text message instead of downloading the Google Authenticator App. To do that, you select None - Show Me More Options instead of selecting your mobile device. Google sends you a code to verify on your desktop computer.

2. Add a backup phone. This ensures that you are still able to access and verify your account using 2-step verification, even if you lose your primary phone or get a new phone. Google recommends that the backup phone you enter should not be the same number as you entered for your primary phone.

3. Record your backup codes. You are provided with 10 backup codes after you complete the 2-step verification set-up process. You can use the 10 backup codes once each instead of using the aforementioned verification code to sign-in to your Google account. Backup codes can come in handy if you don't have access to your primary phone and need to access your Google account (travelling internationally, on vacation, or a dead phone battery are some good reasons to keep these backup codes handy on paper, in your wallet or in your purse).

ADDING AND REMOVING APPS

Whether you use Google Apps for business or personal use, you have the flexibility to add and remove individual applications from your account. If, for example, you know you will never use Google Health, you can simply remove it from your Google Apps collection. Likewise, if you know that eventually you'd like to try Google Analytics, you have the freedom to add it to your Dashboard as a reminder to try the program.

Using the Google Dashboard

When the Google Dashboard was rolled out, Google stated that the intention was to improve transparency and give users more control over their data. And, it has accomplished that goal. Google Dashboard (www.google.com/dashboard/) lists every piece of information Google has collected about you and your web usage. Here you find links to every Google App you have ever used, along with all your personal and security information. Google Dashboard is the place to go if you want to access settings for any of your Google Apps, read privacy information, access your Google Voice call log, or see and view your web history. Plus, you can see alerts of any suspicious activity on your Google Account when you view your Dashboard.

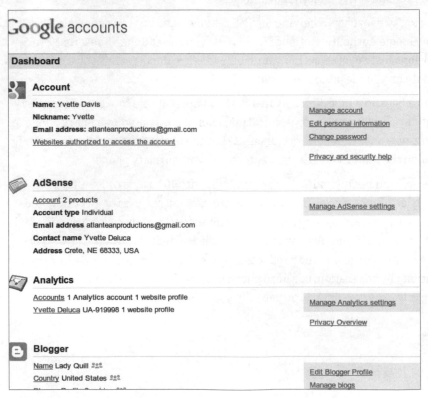

FIGURE 1-5: Google Dashboard gives you access to all your Google settings from one page.

UPDATING PERSONAL AND SECURITY INFORMATION

When you open the Google Dashboard, the first item you see is your account information. Your name, nickname, and e-mail address are listed. Under your e-mail address is a link to Websites Authorized to Access the Account. This is where you find out which websites have access to your Google account. For example, if you use the reminder program Remember the Milk (RTM), it is possible to allow RTM to access your Google Calendar and put your RTM tasks on your calendar.

▶ Check your personal and security information often to ensure you have authorized all access to your account.

To the right, you'll see a link to Edit Personal Information. This is where you can change your name, time zone, ZIP code, and set an alternate e-mail address with which to log in to your various Google Apps. Remember, though, any changes made to your personal information on this page will be effective throughout all your Google Applications.

REVIEWING PRIVACY INFORMATION

It is a smart idea to review the privacy policies of every website where you store information on a regular basis. Google Dashboard gives you one-click access to the privacy policy for every Google App you use. Simply scroll down until you see the App you're interested in, and click the link that mentions privacy.

ACCESSING GOOGLE VOICE CALL LOG

Have you ever wondered about a missed call? Or maybe you suspect someone is using your Google Voice account without your permission? The fastest way to find out is to use Google Dashboard to access your call log. You can see a call history, and how many phones are being forwarded—all at a glance. Of course, if you want more detailed information you can get that too. You learn more about Google Voice in Chapter 17.

REVIEWING WEB HISTORY

For me, one of the most useful features of the Google Dashboard is the Web History section. Here, you find listed all of your search history for

- ▶ Web browsing
- ▶ Images
- ▶ News Products
- ▶ Video
- ▶ Maps
- ▶ Blogs
- ▶ Books

This is helpful when you've been researching a topic and just can't remember where you found a vital piece of information.

RECEIVING SUSPICIOUS ACTIVITY ALERTS

If Google detects a login to your account from a location very different from your usual location it automatically generates an alert in red at the top of your Google Dashboard. So, if you usually log in to your Google account from somewhere near California, and someone in China logs in to your account, a notice appears on your Google Dashboard. This feature is enabled on every Google website to help alert you in the event your accounts are hacked.

Deleting Accounts

I can't imagine why you'd want to, but if for some reason you want to delete your Google account, it's easy.

Go to your accounts page (www.google.com/accounts) and select Edit next to My Products List. You see several choices for deleting your Google accounts. Select your desired option, click the confirmation box, and enter your password. Click Remove. That's all there is to it.

> **WARNING** Remember, deleting a Google account or service is most likely a permanent action. There are a few exceptions (for example, if you can contact Google tech support within 24 hours of the Google account deletion), but for the most part you cannot get your account or your data back.

CREATING A GOOGLE PROFILE

The Google Profile is your opportunity to tell the world about you. List contact information, birthday, career and school information, and create a bio. Google automatically suggests links to your Picasa Web Album or your Blogger blog to include on your profile. This makes it easy to share those things that are important to you. Use your Google Profile to receive messages from friends and strangers alike without ever revealing your e-mail address, and let people know where you have lived in the past and where you are now. You can even present yourself as a creative geek by listing your superpower.

Because Google really does care about your privacy you have the option of making part, or all, of your profile private.

Benefits of Public Profiles

Many people shy away from using the Public Profile page Google provides. I admit, I'm one of them. I value my online privacy, and don't necessarily want anyone with a web connection to have access to my personal information. On the other side of that coin lies the fact that I run a business, have old friends I'd like to find, and have a solid need to network.

I merge these two needs by being selective as to what information I include on my Google Profile. With careful planning on my part, I can use my Google Profile to attract new clients, point established clients to my new ventures, maintain an online presence that allows old friends to locate me, and even provide a central location so that far away family can see what I'm up to.

Building and Modifying Your Profile

Access your Google Profile here: www.google.com/profiles. Click Create My Profile and log in to your account, or create a Google account if you don't already have one. Select Edit Profile in the blue stripe under the Picasa box.

ABOUT ME

The first tab you'll see is the About Me page. This is where you enter your name in all its various forms, specify your gender, and enter the cities and/or states in which you have lived. This information is especially important if you want childhood friends or teachers to be able to find you. You can specify how you prefer people to contact you and enter the appropriate information. You can also include all the different names by which people might search for you.

Fill in your profession, current employer, and past employers. This allows old co-workers to find you. List your current and past schools.

The Introduction and Bragging Rights sections gives you space to create a witty and personal biography.

In the Links section, Google suggests websites to include in your profile. If you have a Blogger, YouTube, or Picasa account, they are listed here. Blogs hosted with other services and your personal website may also be in the list. Click Add for the site to which you'd like to link, and just ignore the others.

You can add your own custom links to your Google Profile as well. There is a space for this directly below the auto-list.

Use your Profile URL to point others directly to your Google Profile. Some potential uses may be to include it in your e-mail signature, Facebook page, Twitter account, LinkedIn, or even on your business cards.

Deleting and Hiding Your Profile

To delete your Google Profile, simply select Delete Profile and Disable Google Buzz Completely. The next screen is the confirmation screen. If you're sure you want to delete your profile, select Yes, I Want to Delete My Profile.

WARNING   Remember, after you delete your Google Profile you cannot get it back (and even if you contact Google tech support within 24 hours, you most likely will still permanently lose the account). It is removed from your list of Google services, and you are no longer able to use Buzz. However, if you create a new profile, you can simply use Google Buzz again and any other option that you choose.

There is no easy way to hide your Google Profile. This is an important point to consider before you create one. You can, of course, decline to display specific information, such as your display name, e-mail address, IM names, and contact list, but there's no way to hide your profile as a whole. You always have the option, as discussed earlier, of deleting your Google Profile.

Sharing Your Profile

Google makes it easy to share your profile. Near the bottom of the About Me page is a link to your Google Profile. Copy that link to include in your e-mail, on business cards, or on your website. Give your personal URL to anyone whom you wish to see your profile.

SUMMARY

The launch pad for customizing your Google experience however you want is through your Google account settings. If you've been following along on your own account with this first chapter, you have already experienced the labyrinth that the Google ecosystem can be. Although you can modify the way you access accounts, your profile information, and your Google Buzz, you need to be able to find where these are in the first place!

Chapter 1 is designed to start you off strongly and confidently because there are more than 30 more chapters chock full of secrets left to discover!

CHAPTER 2

Customizing Your Google Experience with iGoogle

IN THIS CHAPTER

▶ Making your iGoogle page your own

▶ Getting some style with themes

▶ Creating gadgets and themes

I use my iGoogle page as my centralized information point. Everything I need, or want to keep track of, is organized and available in one click. I can embed Gmail and Google Docs to access them from my iGoogle page. I use gadgets to pull in news, shopping, and weather, and tabs to keep those all organized and easy to find. Themes let me customize each page so I always know where I am within my iGoogle page. Tens of thousands of gadgets are available to connect you with services such as CNN, Google Translate, NYTimes, time trackers, and current weather. Play a game of chess, Scrabble, and checkers while keeping up with Facebook and Twitter, all without leaving your iGoogle page. The Google teams and private developers are creating more gadgets every day. iGoogle gives me all these things and the ability to create my own theme, too! What more could a girl want?

CUSTOMIZING YOUR IGOOGLE PAGE

Gadgets are mini-programs that embed in your iGoogle page. If you're like me and want to use your iGoogle page as a sort of home base, gadgets are an invaluable tool.

Adding and Removing Gadgets

It's much easier to remove a gadget than it is to add one. Both tasks are completed with only a few clicks, but adding a gadget requires going through the gadget library to find the gadget you need, and with so many great gadgets to choose from it's easy to get side-tracked.

"To add a gadget, first log in to your iGoogle page (go to www.google.com/ig). Now, click the Add Stuff link," as shown in Figure 2-1.

FIGURE 2-1: Add Stuff is the door to greater productivity with gadgets.

You can sort gadgets by category, see the newest gadgets, or browse the gadgets that boast the most users. For those who don't want to get caught up in the gadget library there is a search bar so you can get in, get what you need, and get out again.

> **NOTE** Keep in mind when using the gadget search bar that if you enter a search term and then decide to view a category instead, the search term you entered will still be valid, even if you delete the term from the box. To clear your entered search term either refresh your browser, or perform a blank search.

When you find a gadget you want to add, simply click the Add It Now button. When you're finished adding gadgets, click Back to iGoogle Home. You'll find this link at the top of the page.

Thousands of gadgets are available, but Google realizes that you may want to add a web page or RSS feed to your iGoogle for which there is no gadget. There is an easy way to do this. At the bottom of the left navigation bar is a link entitled Add Feed or Gadget. Its exact location is shown in Figure 2-2. Click Add Feed or Gadget and enter the URL of the web page you want to add. Click the Add button and the desired page is embedded in your iGoogle page like any other gadget.

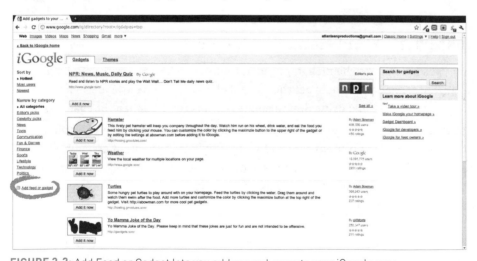

FIGURE 2-2: Add Feed or Gadget lets you add any web page to your iGoogle page.

To remove a gadget, click the downward-facing arrow icon in the gadget's title bar as shown in Figure 2-3 and select Delete This Gadget from the drop-down menu that appears. A confirmation box pops up. Select OK and the gadget goes away. Just in case you change your mind, an information bar appears below the search buttons in your iGoogle header. To bring the gadget back, click Undo. If you're sure you want to remove the gadget, you can just ignore the information bar. It goes away the next time your iGoogle page refreshes.

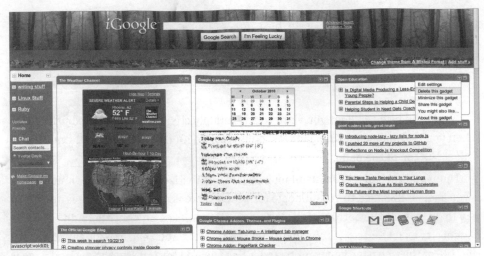

FIGURE 2-3: The gadget toolbar is on the right side of the gadget's title bar.

Customizing and Managing Gadgets

The next section talks about changing your theme, and how to create your own theme, but for now you should get the hang of changing the page layout, moving things around a bit, and using Greasemonkey scripts to customize your gadgets.

Some people prefer their iGoogle pages to have the same layout as their blogs, with a small left-hand content area and a larger right-hand content area. Others prefer all three content areas to be the same size. And still others like to position gadgets with specific functions, such as Google Calendar or Gmail, in a larger, center content area. Whatever your preference, there is a page layout to meet your needs. To change the layout of your iGoogle page start by clicking the tab for the page you want to change. Right-click the downward-facing arrow to the right of the tab's name, as shown in Figure 2-4, and select Edit This Tab from the drop-down menu.

This page is called the General Settings page, and from here you can change the language and default location of the tab, and turn Google Chat on and off within the tab. The Content section enables you to change the tab's name and delete gadgets. You can change your theme from this page, as well.

What you're looking for, though, is toward the bottom. The Layout section enables to choose your page layout. Pick between one, two, three, or four columns of varying width (see Figure 2-5). Select the layout that works for you, and click Save at the bottom of the page.

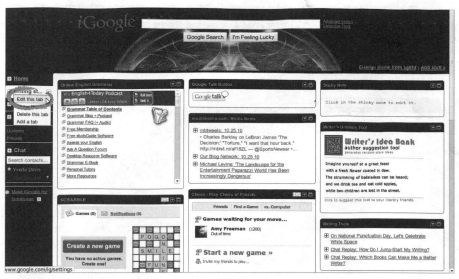

FIGURE 2-4: Use Edit This Tab to change the page layout.

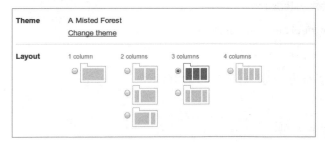

FIGURE 2-5: With multiple options, you should find one page layout you like.

Now that you've chosen your page layout, it's time to move gadgets around the page so you can find what you need, when you need it.

Place your cursor in the title bar of the gadget you want to move and simply drag and drop it to the desired location. When you drop a gadget into a slot, it automatically moves the gadget currently occupying that space down one spot.

If you're using the Firefox web browser you have the option of using Greasemonkey scripts to customize your iGoogle page. Most Greasemonkey scripts work in Google Chrome and Opera. A few even work in Internet Explorer. If you're not a programmer, or don't know much about JavaScript, the best way to use Greasemonkey code is to install it from a library, such as userscripts.org. Just type **iGoogle** into the search bar at http://userscripts.org as shown in Figure 2-6.

▶ Each page layout has predefined spaces in which to drop gadgets. Gadgets are laid out one below another. You can't leave space between gadgets.

▶ Chrome calls these little JavaScript gems "User Scripts" instead of Greasemonkey scripts. But they are essentially the same thing.

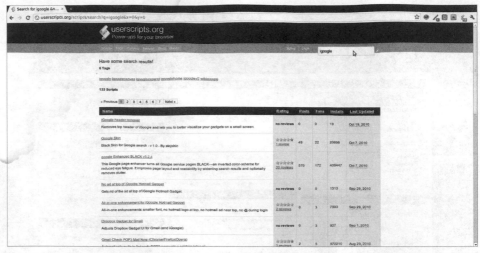

FIGURE 2-6: Userscripts.org is one user script library available online.

You can use Greasemonkey scripts to make changes to your iGoogle page such as:

▶ Cleaning up the page for a sleek look

▶ Placing gadgets closer together to conserve screen space

▶ Taking out the header and/or footer

▶ Changing out the Google logo with a photo of your choice

▶ Resizing columns

▶ Just about anything you want!

> **NOTE** The procedure for installing Greasemonkey scripts is browser- and operating system–dependent. In general, you create a directory called user scripts in the Chrome folder on your hard drive. It looks something like this: C:\Documents and Settings\[User_Name]\Local Settings\Application Data\ Name of Browser\User Data\Default\User Scripts.
>
> When you create a script by hand, save it in this folder with the extension `.js`.
>
> Some of the script libraries, such as the one I mentioned earlier in this section, include a handy Install button that removes the need to install by hand.

Figure 2-7 shows an example of one user script in use. This script was developed by Richard Coombs and is available as an open-source script posted on userscripts.org under the name Super iGoogle. The script removes the iGoogle header and makes your page more compact by moving your left tabs, header, footer, and other nonessentials to a menu in the upper right. Hidden elements are also accessible through keyboard shortcuts. This one is ideal for Netbook users.

> **WARNING** Always be cautious about installing scripts, regardless of the source. Most script developers are honest people who just like to tinker around with code to improve an already good product. However, some use Greasemonkey and user-scripts.org to upload viruses. If you install a script, be sure you understand what you are doing. Read the discussions and pay attention to reviews, the number of installs, and the overall popularity of a script. These are important tools in determining the trustworthiness of the script.

FIGURE 2-7: The Super iGoogle script in use on my iGoogle homepage.

Organizing Interests with Pages

iGoogle pages are great because you can use them to organize your gadgets into related groups, making it easy to find all those gadgets you just installed. To add a page to your iGoogle home page, select an existing page tab and click the downward-facing arrow. Click Add a Tab and a window pops up. Type your desired tab name in the textbox. Uncheck the box if you don't want your page to be automatically populated with gadgets based on your tab name. Click OK. Your new page takes on the theme of your Home tab.

▶ If you're at a loss as to what to name your tabs, Google can help you with auto-complete in the drop-down menu. Just click the title that best matches your subject.

As you move gadgets and dedicate pages to specific topics, you may find it necessary to remove a page. To do so, click the tab to make the desired page active. Click the downward-facing triangle next to the name of the tab you'd like to remove and select Delete This Tab. As when you remove a gadget, iGoogle gives you the option to change your mind after deleting a tab by providing an Undo link under the search buttons.

> **NOTE** You can move any gadget to an existing tab by placing your cursor on the title bar of the gadget you're relocating. Then, simply drag and drop the gadget to the left-hand navigation tab of your desired tab.

THE GOOGLE CONTACTS PAGE

I have a difficult time keeping my address book current. I tend to write addresses and phone numbers on random scraps of paper and paper clip them to my paper calendar. That's fine, until something gets lost. The Google Contacts page helps eliminate this problem. It's available through Edit This Tab on every iGoogle tab.

Choose the tab you want to work with, click the downward-facing triangle, and select Edit This Tab. At the top are two tabs: General and Contacts. Click Contacts.

You can add people from your Gmail address book, import comma-separated value (CSV) and vCard files, or input contacts by hand. And because it's part of the iGoogle page, you can access it from anywhere, including a mobile device.

TURN A PAGE INTO AN EFFECTIVE PLANNER

Here's a straightforward way to turn an iGoogle page into an effective planner and note-keeping tool. You see a visual of a project planner on iGoogle immediately following these instructions in Figure 2-8:

1. Create a new tab. Name it Planner, Scheduler, or something similar.

2. Add six copies of the To-Do-List or To-Do-List + gadget.

3. Name the gadgets as follows:

   ▷ **Do This**—Tasks that take less than two minutes

   ▷ **Inbox**—Unassigned tasks

   ▷ **On Hold**—Tasks that are waiting for someone else

   ▷ **Time Sensitive**—Items with a specific due date

▷ **Actions**—Tasks that take longer than two minutes

▷ **Projects**—List of projects

4. Add one copy of your Google Calendar.

5. Add one sticky note.

FIGURE 2-8: Project Planner on iGoogle.

STYLING IGOOGLE IN YOUR THEME

Installing a theme in iGoogle is similar to installing a gadget. Click the Change Theme From link, right from your iGoogle homepage. You find this under and to the right of the search bar.

As you can see in Figure 2-9, you have the option of sorting themes by category, or you can choose to view only those themes filed under the Hottest, Most Users, or Newest links.

For those who don't like the side scrolling view, click the More Options link and you see a list view with the same sorting options.

When you find a theme you like, click Add It Now and your selected theme is applied to your page.

▶ It is important to note that the theme you select is applied only to the active page. You must select themes for each tab. When you add a page to your iGoogle, it automatically takes the theme of your Home page.

FIGURE 2-9: Sort themes in one of several ways or simply scroll through.

Finding Easter Eggs and Surprises (3:14 a.m. Surprise)

Google programmers seem to have a sense of humor, and seem to enjoy leaving surprises for their users. These gems take the form of hidden games that occur when you use a specific keystroke combination, or at a specific time programmed into the application.

In the case of iGoogle pages, every theme except the Bus Stop and Classic themes contains a surprise that activates at 3:14 a.m. every day. Every theme is different; for example, the theme named Beach shows a silhouette of the Loch Ness monster, and Sweet Dreams displays the Pi symbol.

The Bus Stop theme doesn't include the 3:14 a.m. surprise. However, this theme has a surprise of its own. Bus Stop changes depending on your current regional weather.

> **NOTE** In earlier iGoogle times, it used to be that it was impossible to remove the Home tab from your iGoogle page. The application treated your homepage like it was a permanent fixture. However, that has changed, and you can now remove the Home tab just like any other tab.

Adopting the iTwitter Tab

The iTwitter tab gives you full access to your Twitter account through your iGoogle page. You can send and receive Twitter feeds, access Twitter links, Twitter Search, Tips and

Help, and even your Twitter Tools, just as if you were logged in to your Twitter page, all without ever leaving your iGoogle page. The iTwitter tab was developed by Dan Hollins, creator of Twittin Secrets: 100 World's Greatest Twitter Tips & Twitter Secrets.

▶ Dan's website is http://twittinsecrets.com.

To install iTwitter to your iGoogle page go to the iTwitter page at `http://twittinsecrets.com/twitter-links/itwitterhelp.html` and click the link listed under "Step 2" of the instructions. You are taken to a page that contains instructions and an Add to iGoogle button.

FIGURE 2-10: Add iTwitter to your iGoogle page.

CREATING YOUR OWN GADGETS AND THEMES

Building a gadget by hand requires a functional understanding of XML, HTML, and JavaScript. But many tools are available to help you build gadgets, even if you don't know these languages.

The most important aspect of programming is to have a clear understanding of what you want your program to do. The second most important programming aspect is be sure the language you are using, and your available server resources, can handle the project at hand.

For gadgets this means you must have one specific function that can be carried out within a small web page without leaving a large footprint on the Google servers.

You can use two tools to write your gadget. First, and most difficult for new gadget creators, is to type the code in a text editor, such as Microsoft Notepad. Linux users

▶ You must be logged in to your Google account to save your gadget. To save your gadget select File → Save and enter your gadget's name.

can use Tomboy Notes, gedit, or something similar. Or you can use the Google Gadget Editor. If you use the Google Gadget Editor it checks your code for errors as you type and saves and hosts your gadget on the Google servers. You can access Google Gadget Editor here: http://code.google.com/apis/gadgets/docs/gs.html.

After you've designed and written your gadget you must test it before you can use it. Google provides a tool for this, called the Gadget Checker.

Gadget Checker embeds in your iGoogle Homepage and verifies code on gadgets stored on a web page, local file on your computer, or written and stored via the Google Gadget Editor. You can see the Gadget Checker in action in Figure 2-11. To add Gadget Checker to your iGoogle Homepage go to www.google.com/ig/adde?moduleurl=www.google.com/ig/modules/codechecker/codechecker.xml and click the Add Gadget Checker to iGoogle button.

> **NOTE** I tested the Gadget Checker on Windows and Ubuntu Linux in different browsers. It embedded and worked perfectly on Windows, regardless of the browser used. However, on my Linux machine, the Gadget Checker did not embed when I used Google Chrome. The Gadget Checker embedded correctly when I used Mozilla Firefox, and after it was on my iGoogle page, Gadget Checker worked correctly in Google Chrome.

FIGURE 2-11: Gadget Checker finds a variety of coding errors.

When you're finished creating your gadget, you must submit it to the Gadget Directory so that you, and the world at large, can embed and use your Google Gadget. The Directory Submission page is located at www.google.com/ig/submit.

Now that you've created a gadget, you can look at how to create your own theme.

You can always hand write your iGoogle theme using HTML, XML, and JavaScript, but if you're not a web developer that isn't very time effective. For those not well versed in writing web pages by hand, there is Google Theme Maker. You can find this gem at www.google.com/ig/tm.

This one is pretty straightforward. Click Upload an Image. You can use images stored in your Picasa account, on the Web, or stored locally on your computer. Your image choices are shown in Figure 2-12.

> **WARNING** Make sure you own copyrights to any image you use in your theme. You can get into legal trouble if you snag an image from the Web without the owner's permission.

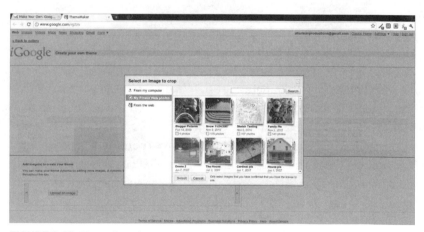

FIGURE 2-12: Chose from images stored in Picasa, the Web, or on your computer.

Use the cropping tool to choose a section of your image that measures 690 pixels by 185 pixels. Then, click Select. Your image is applied to the header, and the page colors change to match. To change theme colors, select from the Theme Color menu near the bottom of the page.

► Create a theme that changes pictures by repeating this process up to sixteen times.

When you're finished loading images and changing theme colors, click the Add Theme Details button at the bottom of the page. Enter the title of your theme, your name, and any description you want to include. Click Submit Theme. Figure 2-13 shows a completed theme in use.

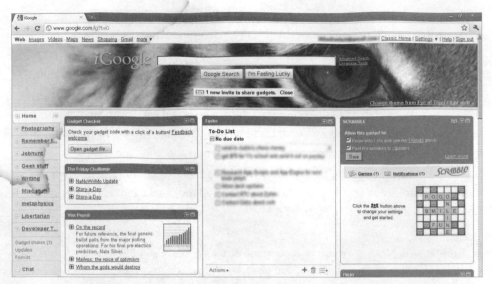

FIGURE 2-13: Eye of Tiger theme created by Allan Davis, Jr.

SUMMARY

Whether you're customizing your iGoogle page to be more useful to you from a productivity or a pleasure standpoint, you now know that you can accomplish one or both of those tasks. Most people who use iGoogle get hooked on it, and, like me, use it as a central information point. Most iGooglers have their iGoogle pages set as their default browser homepages, so the information that you've read in this chapter is going to go a long way in letting you configure your important central hub for your specific needs.

CHAPTER 3

Increasing Your Knowledge with Google Reader

IN THIS CHAPTER

► **Configuring RSS feeds with Google** Reader

► **Applying keyboard shortcut commands for increased productivity**

► **Additional Google Reader** customizations with Greasemonkey scripts

► **Customizing Google Reader** with advanced settings

Google Reader is a straightforward application that brings all your RSS feeds together in one place for quick and convenient reading. Mobile access means you can keep up with your favorite blogs on the go, and user scripts give you the ability to customize Reader. There's something for everyone.

WORKING WITH RSS FEEDS

The acronym RSS has different meanings across the World Wide Web. In this chapter and in this book, we're talking about Really Simple Syndication. These types of RSS feeds give writers a fast way to get their content out to the people who want to read it. For readers, RSS means being able to read your favorite newspaper, blog, or other online content from one web page.

Google Reader (www.google.com/reader) gives you a central location to manage and read all the RSS feeds to which you subscribe. After you've set up your RSS feeds in Google Reader, you might be receiving massive amounts of information in one place, and you might want to learn the keyboard shortcuts for the tasks you perform most. Tables 3-1 through 3-4 list the keyboard shortcuts to perform general navigation, perform specific actions, jump between items, and control the application. Keyboard shortcuts with Google Reader work for both Windows and Macintosh operating systems.

TABLE 3-1: Keyboard Shortcut Commands—General Navigation

KEYBOARD	ACTION
=	Zooms in
-	Zooms out
Shift + O	Opens subscription folder, or currently selected folder
Enter	Expands or collapses selected item in list view
O	Expands or collapses selected item in list view
Shift + X	Expands or collapses selected folder in navigation
Shift +N	Selects next subscription in navigation
Shift + P	Selects previous subscription in navigation
Space	Moves page down
Shift + Space	Moves page up
J	Selects next item on list
K	Selects previous item on list

TABLE 3-2: Keyboard Shortcuts—Acting on Items

KEYBOARD	ACTION
S	Toggles star on or off selected item
L	Toggles Like or Un-like for selected item
Shift + S	Toggles Share or Un-share for selected item
Shift + D	Shares selected item with a note
V	Opens article's original source in a new window
T	Opens the tagging field for the selected item
M	Toggles between Read and Un-read
Shift + A	Marks all items in current view as Read
E	Opens new e-mail to send as e-mail

TABLE 3-3: Keyboard Shortcuts—Jumping Between Items

KEYBOARD	ACTION
G then D	Shows recommendation page; browse page if no recommendations
G then Shift + T	Switches to Trends view
G then Shift + F	Shows all friends' shared items
G then F	Navigates to a friend's shared items when you enter the name of friend
G then T	Navigates to a tag by entering name of tag
G then U	Navigates to subscription by entering subscription name
G then Shift + S	Switches to Your Shared Items view
G then S	Switches to Starred Items view
G then A	Switches to All Items view
G then H	Goes to Google Reader homepage

TABLE 3-4: Keyboard Shortcuts—Application

KEYBOARD	ACTION
R	Refreshes unread counts in navigation
F	Toggles in and out of fullscreen mode
U	Toggles list of subscriptions on and off
1	Displays subscription as expanded items
2	Displays subscriptions as list of headlines
/	Moves cursor to search box
A	Opens Add a Subscription in the sidebar
?	Opens quick guide to shortcuts

If you're using Google Reader, you probably know how to add, share, and read your feeds. But, do you know you can use JavaScript to make Google Reader even better?

Chapter 31 talks about Greasemonkey scripts (I also refer to it in Chapter 2). I show you how to find them and how to install them. The Google Chrome Extensions Marketplace is where you can find officially supported JavaScript extensions for every Google App, including Google Reader. You can find the Google Extensions Marketplace at `https://chrome.google.com/webstore`. Type **Google Reader** into the search bar to find extensions to customize Google Reader to your needs.

MANAGING FEEDS

Managing and keeping up with your RSS feeds doesn't have to be complicated or take a lot of time. A lot of tools can help.

Keep up on your feeds when you're on the go with Google Reader mobile. Access Google Reader mobile at `www.google.com/reader/m/view`.

Or, if you prefer, be notified on your desktop when a new RSS feed comes in to Google Reader. Google-reader-notifier-qt sits quietly in your system tray and monitors Reader's unread feeds. It notifies you when you have new, unread feeds. You find Google-reader-notifier-qt here: `code.google.com/p/google-reader-notifier-qt/`.

Gears users used to have the ability to read RSS feeds with Google Reader while offline. Of course, Gears is no longer supported, making offline use impossible. However, several good programs are available that synchronize with Reader to provide offline support. These programs link up with your Google Reader account and download your feed items so that you can read them later or while "on-the-go" without Internet access (which is perfect for anyone using a tablet without having access to the Web). Windows users have FeedDemon. For Mac OS X users, there is NetNewsWire, and Linux users can get offline support from Liferea.

▶ Some programs that provide offline support for Reader are FeedDemon (www.feeddemon .com), NetNewsWire (netnewswireapp.com), Liferea (liferea .sourceforge.net).

Tagging Feeds

When you're following a large number of blogs and websites, keeping track of them all and finding the information you need when you need it can get a little difficult. That's where tags come in.

At the bottom of every preview window is a link called Add Tags that allows you to add tags to the feed. Just like in other Google Apps, tags are short labels that act as keywords, helping you search for what you need. Clicking on Add Tags enables you to type in your tags, comma-separated, into a small pop-up window that appears next to the Add Tags link. When you create tags, those tags appear in the search drop-down menu, allowing you to search all saved feeds by tag.

Sometimes, after you've spent time tagging items, you may find that you need to change the name of a tag. It's a simple process. First, click Settings at the top of the page, next to your e-mail address, and select Reader Settings from the drop-down menu, as shown in Figure 3-1.

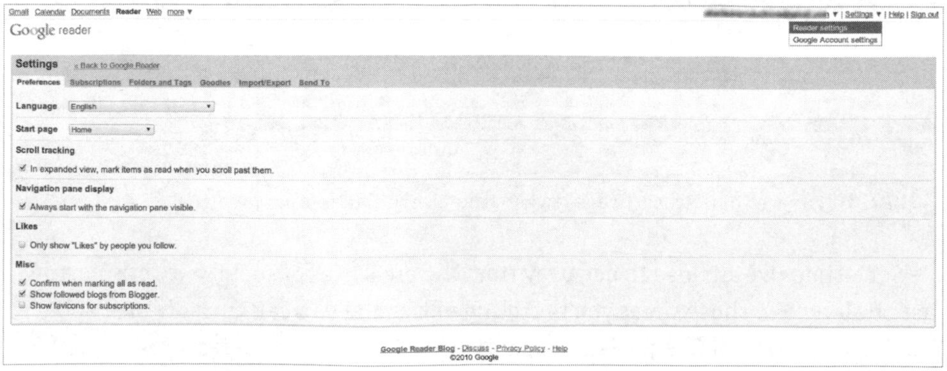

FIGURE 3-1: Access Google Reader's Settings page to change the name of a tag.

Now, click Folders and Tags. Scroll down until you see the tag you want to change. Click Rename and enter the new tag. Click Save.

Sharing Feeds

Sharing feeds is a quick way to share important information or fun blogs with your friends. You can do it right from your browser without ever opening Google Reader. If you're logged in to your Google account (which you have to be in order to use Google Reader), in several places within the Google ecosystem you see your Gmail contacts and their online/offline status. You also see people you follow on Google Buzz. (Read more about Gmail and Google Buzz in later chapters.)

Navigate to your Google Reader Settings page and click Goodies. Drag and drop the Note in Reader button to the bookmark bar of your web browser. (If you're using Google Chrome, you need to change the default settings of Chrome so your bookmark bar is always visible.)

When you visit a website you'd like to share with those who follow you on Google Reader, simply click the Note to Reader link on the bookmark bar. As shown in Figure 3-2, a box opens where you can add a note or tags before sharing the link with your friend list.

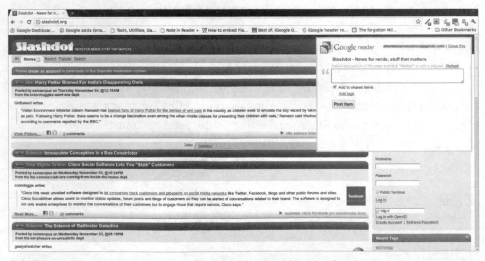

FIGURE 3-2: Share your favorite websites with friends without leaving the page.

Sometimes we all need to get away from the pressures of social networking and just be alone. For those times you're feeling antisocial you can turn off the People You Follow section of Google Reader. This turns off all the social features. Type the following simple JavaScript line into the address bar of your browser:

```
javascript:antisocial ('true')
```

Press Enter on your keyboard to activate the JavaScript. When you decide you're ready to follow people again, you can turn the antisocial feature off by typing the following in the address bar:

```
javascript: antisocial ('false')
```

SUMMARY

Google Reader is the best way to aggregate all of your blog, feed, and news website subscriptions into one centralized location. Knowing the secrets within Google Reader (as you do now) helps you to take advantage of the program and customize it to your exact needs. With Google Reader, you never need to visit your favorite news or blog websites again.

Part II

GOOGLE SEARCH SECRETS

CHAPTER 4

Using Your Words: Natural Language Searches

IN THIS CHAPTER

▸ Editing your search results by using advanced functionality
▸ Configuring Google to search in another language
▸ Accessing Google's cache and viewing saved web pages
▸ Modifying your search results with several advanced navigation options

It would be nice to be able to type any question into the search bar and have the natural language program understand exactly what you were asking. It would then display only the results that answer your question. Google Search is good, but it's not like talking to a person.

To get the most relevant results possible it's necessary to learn and use tools that help the search engine understand exactly what you want. This chapter talks about how to tell the Google search engines exactly what you want to know, and just as importantly, exactly what you don't.

OMITTING SEARCH RESULTS

When you're searching for specific information, understanding how to omit unwanted or irrelevant results saves you time and frustration.

Depending on the purpose of your search, you may want to omit results that come from a specific web domain. For example, say you're writing a college paper on Galileo and you need Internet sources that you can cite. Most colleges teach that .com sites are, for the most part, unreliable sources of information and encourage students to use .gov or .org sites instead, so you need to know how to tell Google to not return any results from a .com site.

> CROSSREF Web domains are explained in more depth in Chapter 5.

You can easily omit all .com sites from your search results by entering a minus sign (-) in the search box before the phrase .com. For example, the phrase I entered for the Galileo example is **Galileo -.com**. Figure 4-1 shows the first page of results from this search.

FIGURE 4-1: Omit all the .com results from your search.

Sometimes you know which website contains the information you need before you start your search. For example, you might need to find out if your child's school has called a snow day, or you might be searching for a specific news article from your local newspaper's online edition. Save time by searching that website directly from your Google search bar by typing the search term as **site:*website*.com**, where *website* is the name of the site you want to search.

Quotation marks tell the Google search engine to return only results that contain the phrase exactly as it appears between the quotation marks. A search for **galileo rocks** returns different results than for **"galileo rocks"**.

When you're shopping it's helpful to know which stores in your hometown carry the item you want. Do a quick search using the name of the item and your ZIP code to find places to shop. Figure 4-2 shows the results from a simple search executed on the keywords "music store piano 85032".

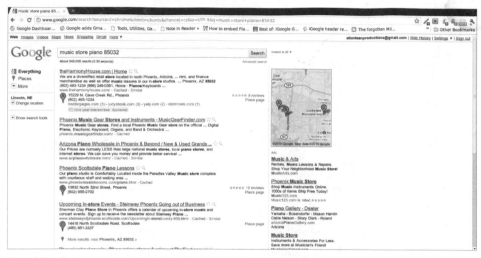

FIGURE 4-2: Music stores that sell pianos in the 85032 ZIP code.

While you're shopping online, you may want to do some price comparisons. Even though most symbols and punctuation are ignored by the Google search engine, you can use the dollar sign ($) to indicate that the following number is a monetary amount. So, if you want to search for pianos in the $900.00 range, search for **piano $900**.

When you use Google Search, results are automatically expanded to include variations of the word(s) for which you search. When you search for cat, Google returns results that include cat, cats, catty, CAT, and C.A.T. If you want to see search results for cat without the variations you must omit all related search results. Tell Google Search to return only those results for cat by placing quotation marks around the word, for example, "cat".

The Google search engine allows the use of synonyms, so a search for philosopher might also turn up results for thinker. If you don't want to search for synonyms then type a **+** before the word to turn off synonyms for that word.

For the most precise search query, consider combining these techniques, but remember that it is possible to narrow your search too much. If your query does not return any results, widen your search by removing quotation marks, allowing synonyms, or reducing the number of words in your query.

Natural language searches allow you to find often-needed information quickly and easily. Package tracking calculators, ZIP codes, weather, and more are at your fingertips.

- For package tracking, type the FedEx, UPS, or USPS tracking number directly into your search bar for a link to tracking information.

- Enter a ZIP code into the search bar to instantly find out where the ZIP code is located.

- Type mathematical equations into the search bar to activate Google's calculator function.

- Enter the word **time** followed by the city to find out the current time in many cities.

- Type a company's ticker symbol into the Google search bar to get up-to-the-minute stock information.

- Find out the weather in any location by entering **weather** followed by the ZIP code or city name.

- Track airline departure and arrival times in the United States by typing the airline name and flight number in the Google search box.

- Get instant dictionary definitions by typing **define** *word* into the search box.

- To find current earthquake activity, type **earthquakes** in the search box.

- Access public data, such as city population or current unemployment rates, by entering the data you want in quotation marks followed by the city name or state, for example, **"unemployment rates" Maine**. [1]

EXPANDING SEARCH RESULTS

Sometimes, you need to widen your search results to find the information you need. Google offers several tools to make this easier.

If you want to receive the widest range of results, keep your search terms broad and use as few words as possible. Remember that each word you type into the search bar is used to filter search results.

Use Google Instant to help you expand search criteria. Google Instant shows a drop-down menu with instant-fill search phrases as you type. To turn on Google Instant, click the Google Instant link to the right of the search bar. Figure 4-3 shows Google Instant suggestions when I typed Galileo into the search bar.

FIGURE 4-3: Google Instant gives search suggestions that you may not have considered.

When you perform a standard Google search the search engine automatically gives you related, but different, search suggestions in the left navigation bar. Use these suggestions to expand your search and find related information.

> ► These search suggestions are listed under the heading Something Different.

By default, the Google search engine searches for all the words in your query. Change this by using the Boolean operator OR. By typing a search query that includes the OR operator, you're telling the search engine to find instances of either search term instead of instances of both terms. So, if you search for **galileo OR copernicus** you get results that include either person, but if you type **galileo copernicus** your search results are pages on which both men appear.

> ► You can use the pipe symbol (|) in place of the word OR.

When you're looking for a world-wide view on a topic, sometimes it helps to see results from other countries. View results that have been translated from languages other than English to get a broader view of the subject at hand. In the left navigation bar, click More Search Tools → Translated Foreign Pages.

Also in the left navigation bar is the option to view related searches. The Related Searches link gives a list of popular search terms to help you gain information that is related to your search topic.

VIEWING CACHED PAGES AND SIMILAR RESULTS

Sometimes web pages are removed by the owner. When that occurs the web page becomes unavailable online. However, you may still view it by choosing the cached version of the page. Cached pages also enable you to view the last previously saved version of a web page by Google. This can be useful if you want to compare a recently updated page against its previous version. To access a cached page, click the blue word Cached after the URL in any Google site listing.

When you click the Similar link that follows a page's URL, Google lists all the pages related to your search that are similar to the page you select.

NARROWING SEARCH RESULTS WITH SHOW OPTIONS

When you perform a Google search, you are getting everything that the Google system has as results in return. Sometimes, depending on what you're looking for, you're no better off than when you started, as you are in front of several million different results. However, you can narrow your search results with the Show Options filter tools. For example, you can view search results for all media, or choose to view only specific types. You can choose from web pages that have been on the Web forever, view only the most recently uploaded results, or choose your own custom time range; it's up to you which search results you see and how you see them.

The Show Options filter tools are located in the left navigation and change based on the search you perform. As shown in Figure 4-4, the Show Options tools are divided into three separate sections. The top section lets you filter results by the type of media. By default, only some of the more popular media types are displayed, but you can select from the following:

- ► News
- ► Videos
- ► Images
- ► Shopping
- ► Books
- ► Places
- ► Blogs
- ► Updates
- ► Discussions

FIGURE 4-4: The Show Options filters let you customize search results in many different ways.

Each media type has specialized options to help you narrow your results further. When you choose to see only Image results, you can specify the image size, type of image, choose between black-and-white or color images, and even choose a specific color that must be in the image. Figure 4-5 shows all the options for filtering images.

FIGURE 4-5: Choose the size, type, and colors of the images you see in the results.

When searching for only video media, you have the option to filter by duration, time frame in which the video was uploaded, and video sources. You also have the option of viewing only those videos that are closed captioned. See Figure 4-6 for option details.

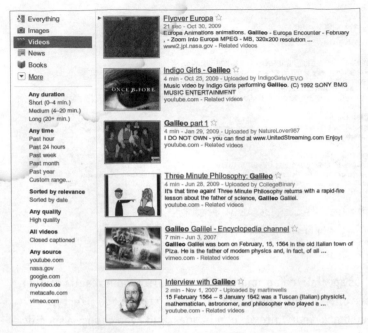

FIGURE 4-6: Select video duration, source, and upload time frame to find the video that best meets your needs.

If you are searching for news sources, you have the option of filtering for

▶ Top Stories

▶ Images, Blogs, or All News

▶ Items in the past hour, past 24 hours, past week, or past month

▶ 2008–2010

▶ 2007

▶ 2005–2006

▶ 2002–2004

▶ 1989

▶ Archives

▶ Custom Range

You can also sort news results by relevance or date.

Filter Book results by century, type of book, level of view available online, and books or magazines. Browse books that are related to your search topic that are available online and add them to your reading list through Google Books.

The Shopping search lists things you can purchase that are related to your search query. Compare prices, stores, and items easily. You can choose to see only those items with free shipping, or online stores that offer Google Checkout. Sort by price, brand, or store. Figure 4-7 shows the Shopping options for the search on Galileo.

FIGURE 4-7: Shopping options for Galileo.

Places shows physical locations related to your search. Locations are shown on Google maps where possible.

When you select Blogs, you see results for every blog indexed by Google that contains your search term, along with information about when that blog was last updated. You can filter the blogs by when they were last updated. You can choose between blogs updated in time periods ranging from the past 10 minutes to the past year. You can also specify a custom range.

The Updates filter returns results of Twitter updates, along with a time line for your search terms.

The final media type option is Discussions. This directs you to places on the Web where people are talking about your search topic. Filter by time of last discussion, relevance or date, forum discussions or Question and Answer formats, and the location of results in relation to your physical location.

The middle section of the left navigation lets you customize results by location. If you're signed in to your Google account you see location information. Results are filtered to be most relevant to your location. Your location is auto-detected based on your IP address and your Google Toolbar's My Location feature, if you have that installed and enabled. To change your location, click the Change Location link. There is no way to turn the location detection off; Google claims it is necessary to provide the most relevant search results. However, if you're concerned about privacy you do have the option of manually setting your location as broadly as you'd like within the domain of the Google site you're using for your search. So, for example, if you're conducting a search through Google.com, you can't set your location to Spain because in Spain they use Google.es.

The last section of the left navigation enables you to set publication date, type of results, method of viewing results, and image and language filters. You should see something like Figure 4-8 at the bottom-left of your Google search result pages.

Choose to view the latest media, media published within the past week, month, year, or set your own publication date range. This is useful if you know the time frame in which the information you're looking for was published, or if you need only the latest information published on your subject.

Choose to view all media, only media recommended by your social network, or media with relevance to your local area.

Decide if you'd like to see only those pages you have not yet visited, only those pages you have visited, or all results. This is one of my favorites, because it helps me keep track of which websites I have visited as I'm researching a topic.

The next group of filter choices are related to how information is presented. I discuss the Timeline and Wonder Wheel in depth in Chapter 5.

The final group of choices enable you to display only sites with images or pages that have been translated from non-English sites. This is a great feature if you want to see what people in other countries are saying about your topic.

Any time
Latest
Past 24 hours
Past week
Past month
Past year
Custom range...

All results
Sites with images
Related searches
Timeline
Dictionary
Reading level
Social
Nearby
Translated foreign
  pages

Fewer search tools

FIGURE 4-8:
Expanded filtering options for Google search results.

SUMMARY

Entering a few words into the Google search bar and scanning through the results is only one of the many things that you can do within Google's powerful search application. You can modify your search results based on your criteria, you can search for Images, Places, or for Realtime results, and you can customize Google to only show what's relevant to you.

When it comes to search results, it's not what Google wants to show you—it's what you can do to those results.

CHAPTER 5

Refining Your Search

Sometimes natural language searches don't do the trick, and you need a search with a little more power. Use the Advanced Search page to locate specific file types, information on specific websites, or even little-known domain names. Learn about using wildcards for those times you're just not sure exactly what you're looking for. Examine your web history to learn how past web searches affect your current search.

Refine and polish your search parameters until they shine. Doing so puts the power of Google to work for you.

UNDERSTANDING SEARCH LANGUAGE

The key to finding exactly the information you need quickly is to use the correct search tools, in the right combinations. Combining natural language search tips from Chapter 4 with the search tools in this chapter yields results you can count on.

Using Common Words

▶ These spiders crawl the Web and make records of almost every web page in existence. When you perform a search using Google your search criteria is compared against the indexes to return your results.

When you're looking for something on the Web, it's vital to search for the words most commonly used on the websites from which you hope to find information.

Google Search is effective because it's based on indexing performed by Google spiders. Using common words increases your search results and ensures your search criteria are matched correctly.

Google spiders are also known as crawlers or bots. Google (and the major search engines, such as yahoo.com and bing.com) have developed spiders in an effort to build their search indexes without having to visit websites manually in order to record data. Spiders have been used all throughout Google's history; it's an extremely effective way of collecting information on new web pages and new websites, as well as collecting updated information on web pages and websites already indexed by Google.

Therefore, if a web page makes use of your search query, chances are good that that web page will be returned in a search result. The Google system places high emphasis on web pages designed with relevant, meaningful content. The more meaningful the content, the more likely a web page will appear in Google's search results when you search for any common term or phrase on Google.

Executing Stop Words

Common words that are needed for grammatical correctness, but that don't add anything to a search query, are called stop words. Stop words include *a*, *and*, *the*, and *for*. Stop words can be omitted from your search query. If you choose to include *the*, the search engine will usually ignore it. In some cases including stop words is vital to obtaining the correct results. For example, if you are searching for the term "who," stop words will help the search engine determine if you want to see results for the rock band The Who, or if you're looking for information on the World Health Organization, abbreviated as WHO.

Matching with Exact Phrases

Searching for an exact phrase returns only those results that contain the phrase you are looking for. You have two ways to accomplish an exact phrase search.

The first method is to type the phrase for which you want to search in the standard Google search bar between quotation marks. An example looks like this: "Galileo in England." The Google Search engine returns only those results that contain that exact phrase, as shown in Figure 5-1. The exact words of your search appear in bold within the title and descriptions (the text you see within the search result pages).

▶ This search returns only this exact phrase. So websites that include the phrase "Galileo was in England" or anything similar are ignored.

FIGURE 5-1: Search for the exact phrase "Galileo in England."

For a more specific exact phrase search, use the Advanced Search page. A link for the Advanced Search page is located to the right of the search textbox. Notice that under the first bold heading, Find Web Pages That Have, the second text entry box is labeled This Exact Wording or Phrase. Enter your desired search phrase in this box. If you want to further narrow your search, include words or phrases that should not be included in the appropriate box.

Expanding Results with Similar Words

Many times you can improve your search results by using synonyms or related searches. Enter your desired search term in the search bar and click More Search Tools in the left navigation bar to expand your search choices. Now, select Related Searches from the list. Google offers a list of possible searches that are related to the keywords you typed. Click any (or all) of these links to expand your search. Figure 5-2 shows the related search results for the keywords "philosophers from 300 BC."

▶ Related searches are derived from your search query and are based on some of the more popular search results that closely resemble what you entered for your search query. Google uses an algorithm to deduce what the related searches should be.

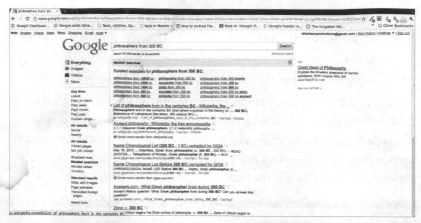

FIGURE 5-2: Related search gives you suggestions to expand and improve your search.

Taking Advantage of Wildcards

You may remember wildcard searches from the Commodore 64 days. To find a file on disk, we used BASIC to type a command that resembled "dir work*." This query returned all directory (folder) and file names that started with *work*. So, your search returned the directories for workforce, workschedules, workphonenumbers, worklocations, and so on. This wildcard search approach was great if you couldn't remember the exact name of the directory or file you needed. The asterisk could be placed at the beginning, the middle, or the end of your search query.

Luckily for us, the asterisk is still recognized today by most search systems, including Google Search. Wildcard searches through Google help you form your query as an open-ended statement. If you want to find out what Galileo discovered, you would type **Galileo discovered *** into the Google search box. Figure 5-3 shows the results of this wildcard search.

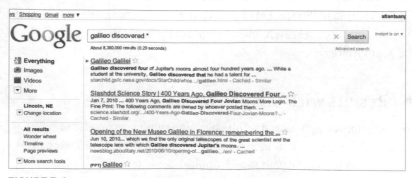

FIGURE 5-3: All results with the phrase "Galileo discovered" are included in this wildcard search.

NARROWING RESULTS WITH ADDITIONAL SEARCH TRICKS

If you perform a search while signed in to your Google account, the Google Search engine uses your search history to help narrow search results to items in which you have shown an interest. This feature can indeed help you get more relevant data, but if you're looking for a wide range of information, it may hinder your search as well. Figures 5-4 and 5-5 show the differences in the Galileo -.com search from Chapter 4 with web history tailored search and a search that does not take web history into consideration.

▶ Google has a huge database of indexed pages, images, videos, and other content. Enabling search history allows Google to exclude potentially irrelevant search results and also return fewer results, which usually means you get better quality results.

FIGURE 5-4: Galileo search with web history.

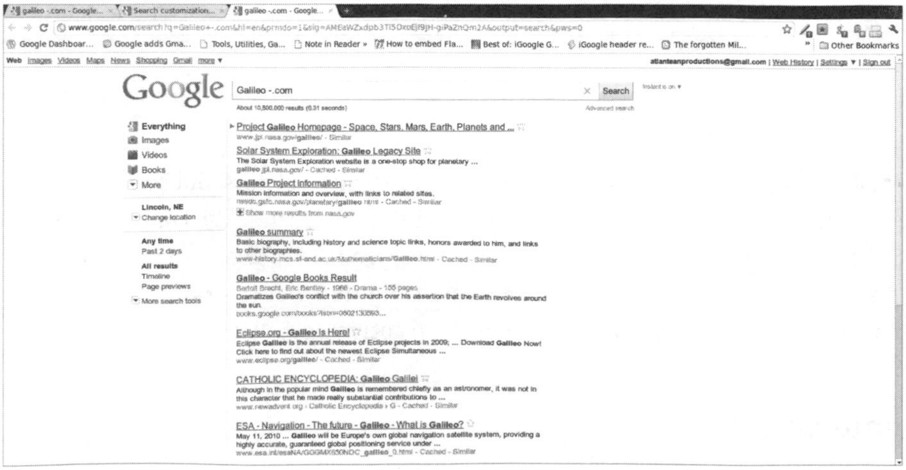

FIGURE 5-5: The same search without web history.

To view your web search history, click Web History to the right of your e-mail address in the top right of the window." From here, you can view every Google search you have executed while logged in to your Google account. Use the Remove Items link in the left navigation bar to remove items from your search history to alter your search results.

When you want your search to return only results that contain a specific word or phrase, type the word or phrase enclosed in quotation marks, like this: "Galileo's discoveries." The quotation marks tell the search engine to look for that exact phrase.

Another feature of Google searches that can help you narrow results is SafeSearch. If you would rather not return search results containing sexually explicit material, turn on SafeSearch to omit these results. First, from the Settings drop-down menu to the right of your Google login information, click Search Settings, which is about halfway down the page. You can see what they look like in Figure 5-6. Select the SafeSearch setting you'd like and save your changes at the bottom of the page.

▶ You can also access Subscribed Links from this page. I talk about those next.

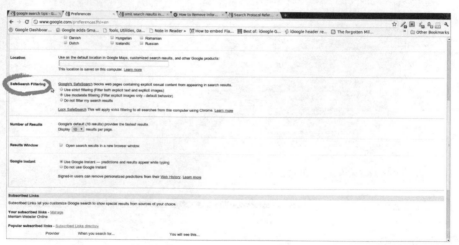

FIGURE 5-6: SafeSearch excludes potentially offensive material from search results.

▶ Activate Subscribed Links from the Subscribed Links Directory: www .google.com/coop/ subscribedlinks/ directory/All_ categories. You must be signed in to your Google account for changes to take effect.

Another way to narrow search results is with Subscribed Links. Subscribed Links let you tailor your searches to find very specific information quickly." For example, the Subscribed Link called Color Swatch causes search results to return with a color sample when you search for a hexadecimal value. Figure 5-7 shows results of a search for hexadecimal code #330066 with Color Swatch activated.

Google Squared

A new Google search tool designed to help you find and organize the most relevant search results is Google Squared. Google Squared is still in testing and development in Google Labs, so it's not perfect. It's open for public use at www.google.com/squared. Google Squared takes your search results and places them in a table for easy comparison. The results in the table, called a "square" by Google, aren't sorted, but columns are automatically created. These columns provide additional information about the subject. Figure 5-8 shows a Google Squared search result for the search term "philosophers from BC." The columns titled Date of Birth, Place of Birth, Date of Death, and Place of Death were auto-generated. Obviously, Died and Date of Death are the same piece of data. To remove one of these values, click the X in the right corner of the column you want to remove.

▶ This is useful for comparing any list of items. Enter real estate you're interested in, or items you're thinking about buying. You can even use Google Squared to compare political candidates.

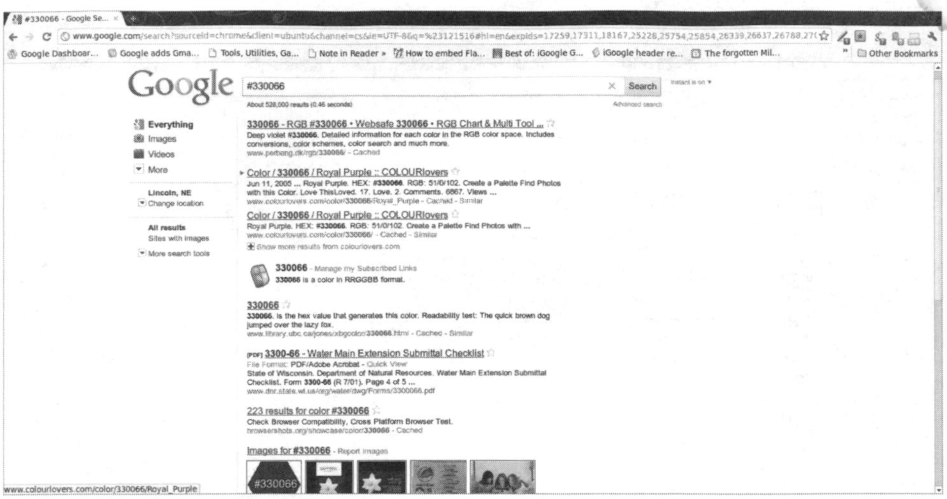

FIGURE 5-7: Results of search for #330066 with Color Swatch Subscribed Link turned on.

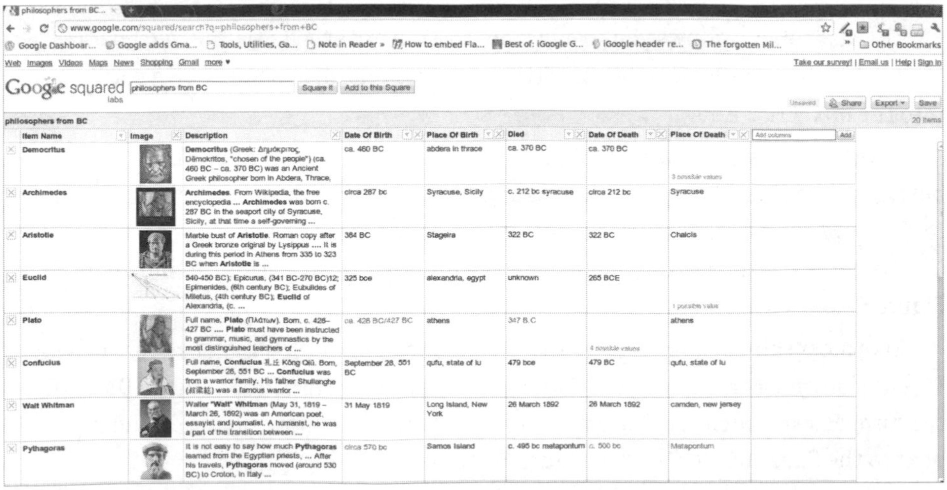

FIGURE 5-8: Google Squared results for philosophers from BC.

Likewise, you can remove a row if the results in that row are irrelevant. In the results in Figure 5-8 Walt Whitman is listed; however, according to the Date of Birth column, he was born in 1819, so this is an irrelevant result in relation to our search. Click the X to the left of Walt Whitman to remove that result.

Click the downward-pointing arrow in any column head to sort search results based on that column. At the time I'm writing this, results are limited to sorting each column by alphabetical order, or reverse alphabetical order. But because Google Squared is a Google Labs project, that could change at any time. Figure 5-9 shows results sorted by Place of Death in alphabetical order.

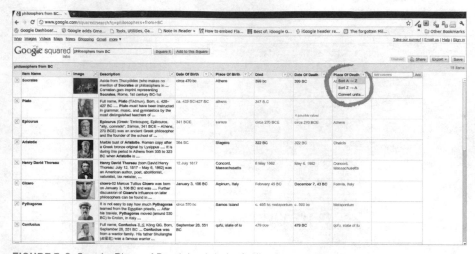

FIGURE 5-9: Sort by Place of Death in alphabetical order.

The last column allows you to add more sorting criteria. Click the textbox to choose from a drop-down menu of sorting suggestions, or type your own sort term into the box. Click Add.

Save your Google Squared search table for future reference by clicking the Save button on the right. If you're not signed in to your Google account, you are prompted to sign in. Access saved Google Square searches by clicking the Saved Squares link underneath and to the right of your Google login information, as shown in Figure 5-10.

▶ The default setting is Public. Click the Share button to share via Email, Buzz, Facebook, or Twitter, or to copy the direct link to the Square you created. Select Private if you'd rather not share.

Like most things Google, you can choose to share your Square, or keep it private. In addition, you can export your Square to either a CSV file or your Google Docs, in the form of a spreadsheet. The controls for sharing and exporting are on the right next to the Save button (refer to Figure 5-9).

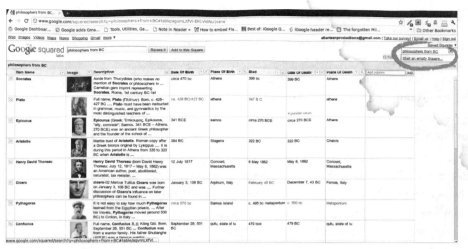

FIGURE 5-10: Choose Saved Squares, or start a new Square from the Saved Squares drop-down.

TIMELINE SEARCH

Pare down search results by time period by using the Timeline. From the main Google search page (or your iGoogle page) type your search term and click Show Search Results in the left navigation bar. Under Standard view, click Timeline. A timeline displays above the search results. To narrow search results, mouse over the timeline until a square appears around the era in which you're interested, as shown in Figure 5-11. Click the timeline and search results are limited to the selected era.

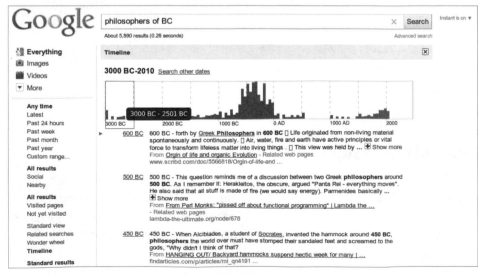

FIGURE 5-11: Limit results to 3000 BC to 2501 BC.

Using the Advanced Search Page

Google's Advanced Search page is available from either the classic Google search page or an iGoogle page. You can use the Advanced Search when you are logged in to your Google account, or when you are not logged in. Remember from our earlier discussion on search history that your web searches are saved when you are signed in. So, if you are concerned about privacy issues, be sure to log out of your Google account.

Regardless of how you use Google Search (logged in, or not) and whether you use a classic Google search page or iGoogle to perform your search, the link for Advanced Search is located to the right of the search box. Some of the iGoogle themes make it hard to see the link, but it's there. Figure 5-12 shows the Advanced Search page with the bottom link, Date, Usage Rights, Numeric Range, and More selected.

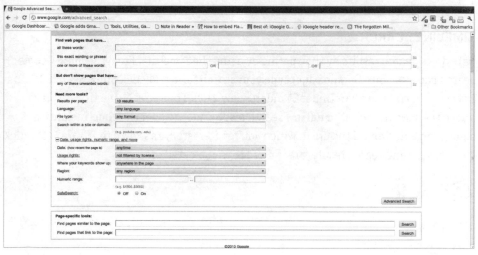

FIGURE 5-12: Google Advanced Search page.

Restricting Results

One of the most important Internet search skills is knowing how to eliminate the results you don't want. Millions of websites are on the Internet, and for any search you run you get thousands of hits. Not all of those hits are relevant to what you need to know. Restricting results helps you get a handle on those thousand hits so you can find what you need.

TO A DOMAIN OR WEBSITE

Restricting your search to a specific domain type, or even a specific website, is a great technique to find relevant results for a specific purpose. You could use the general search bar and type your search query using the minus sign (-) to eliminate all the .com sites as discussed in Chapter 4, but you would still be left to wade through the thousands of sites that do not have a .com suffix.

INTERNET DOMAIN SUFFIXES AND THEIR DEFINITIONS

- ▶ **.edu**—Academic sites

- ▶ **.ac**—British academic sites

- ▶ **.gov**—United States government sites

- ▶ **.gb**—Great Britain

- ▶ **.coop**—Business cooperatives and organizations

- ▶ **.biz**—United States business sites

- ▶ **.int**—International institute sites

- ▶ **.info**—United States information with no restrictions

- ▶ **.jobs**—Employment and job related

- ▶ **.mil**—United States Military

- ▶ **.museum**—Museums around the world

- ▶ **.name**—Family and individual names

- ▶ **.nato**—NATO site

For a complete list of Internet domain suffixes, go to **www.computerhope.com/jargon/num/domains.htm**.

Instead, use the Advanced Search page. Enter your search term in the textbox labeled All These Words. Look under the heading Need More Tools? and find the textbox with the label Search Within a Site or Domain. Type the domain suffix in which you want to search. For example, if you want to search academic web sites in Great Britain for philosophers from the previous examples, your search query would look like Figure 5-13.

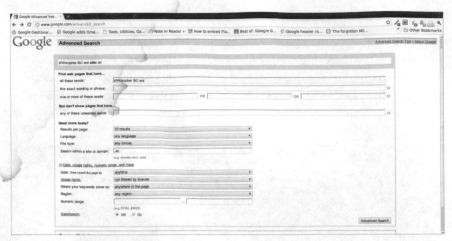

FIGURE 5-13: Search all academic sites in Great Britain for philosophers who lived in the BC era.

Restrict your search to any single website on the Web: Use the same textbox to enter the URL of the website to which you'd like to confine your search. For example, you could modify the previous search to return results only from the Doane College website by entering "doane.edu" in the Search Within a Site or Domain box."

TO WORDS IN SPECIFIC LOCATIONS

You can use the Advanced Search page to search for words that appear in specific areas of the web page. Enter your search terms in the correct textboxes. Below the textbox labeled Search Within a Site or Domain there is a link entitled Date, Usage Rights, Numeric Range, and More. Click here to reveal more search options. The third option is Where Your Keywords Show Up. The default is Anywhere in the Page. Click the downward-facing arrow to open the drop-down menu, shown in Figure 5-14. Select the option you need, and click the Search button.

TO PAGES LINKED TO A SPECIFIC PAGE

To locate all the web pages that are linked to a specific web page, use the Find Pages That Link to the Page textbox on the Advanced Search page (you might have to expand the options by clicking Date, Usage Rights, Region, and More in order to see this textbox). This is a great feature if you're trying to find out how many times your website has been linked to from outside sources. It's also useful to know if a website you're planning on using for reference has been linked to by others and to check the quality of those links. Just enter the domain name of the site to which all results must be linked and then click Search.

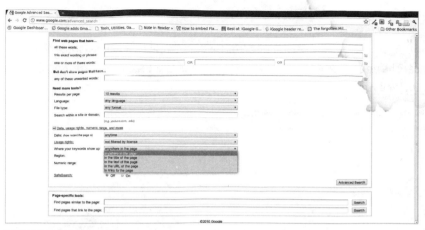

FIGURE 5-14: Determine where your search words should be located on the page.

TO SPECIFIC FILE TYPES

To search the Web for an article that contains a set of keywords and is in a specific file format, type your search keywords in the appropriate textbox(es). Under the heading Need More Tools is a drop-down menu labeled File Type. Click the downward-facing arrow and select the desired file type. Included file types are

- ► **.pdf**—Adobe Acrobat
- ► **.doc/.docx**—Microsoft Word
- ► **.rtf**—Rich Text Format
- ► **.ps**—Adobe Postscript
- ► **.swf**—Shockwave Flash
- ► **.ppt/.pptx**—Microsoft PowerPoint
- ► **.xls**—Microsoft Excel
- ► **.kmz**—Google Earth
- ► **.klm**—Google Earth
- ► **.dwf**—Autodesk

Saving Your Search Results

Whether you perform a Google search from the standard search bar or from the Advanced Search page, your search results are automatically saved to your Google web history, if you are signed in to your Google account. Google saves the parameters of your search, along with any links you click from the search. Figure 5-15 shows a web history. To get to your web history, go to the Google.com homepage and click on your name at the upper-right corner of the page (log in if it reads Sign In). You should see a link for Web History under the My Products portion of your account's page.

FIGURE 5-15: Use Google Web History to access saved searches.

Manage your search history by using the links in the left navigation bar. Click the Remove Items link to permanently remove items from your web history. Select the item you want to remove by clicking the box in front of the search and then clicking the Remove button. Or, if you'd like to remove all items in your web history, click Clear Entire Web History.

To view statistics about your saved web searches, click Trends in the left navigation bar. The Trends page gives you information about which websites you visit the most, which links you click the most, and which sites you search the most. There is also a summary of your monthly and daily search activities.

SUMMARY

Searching Google isn't a chore—it's an art form! It's also extremely productive and beneficial for end-users like you who need to be able to maximize Google's powerful search engine for business and academic needs. As you've read in this chapter, you can also take advantage of Google's flexibility using features such as Google Squared and Advanced Search to accomplish your tasks.

CHAPTER 6

Staying Close with Local Search

Everyone needs a little help finding what they need. Whether it's a new doctor for the kids, a knock-out restaurant to impress a date, or a hotel in the middle of the night, Google Search and Place Pages help you find the businesses and services you need. And now, with Google Product Search, you have the ability to see which local store has the item you need in stock, so you can get it when you need it.

FINDING LOCAL BUSINESSES AND RESOURCES

When you need to find a local business fast, Google provides several tools to help you. The simplest way to locate a business near you is to type the service you need in the standard Google search bar.

Google Search automatically tailors search results to your local area. You may remember from Chapter 5 that Google Search uses your IP address to determine your location. You can, of course change your location. Click Change Location in the left navigation bar and enter your ZIP code. For a wider search, you can enter your city, county, state, region, or country.

Do keep in mind that matching an IP address to a geographical location is not an exact science. You can live or do business in one location, but when you use Google you might receive results for another location. Part of this discrepancy lies in the fact that your IP address originates from your Internet Service Provider (ISP). If your ISP is in another city (or state), you see results on Google from that city or state. Mobile devices, dynamic (non-static) IP addresses, and ISPs who cloak or mask users' IP addresses are other reasons why you may see results from a different geographical location than your own. Remember that you can always manually change your location on the left-hand navigation menu of a Google search result page.

When you type **pizza** into the search bar and click Search, the returned results include the names and addresses of restaurants that serve pizza in your area. Figure 6-1 shows the results of a simple search for pizza when the location is set to Rapid City, South Dakota (Notice the "Google Doodle" on the top-left, denoting Robert Louis Stevenson's 160th Birthday; Google is constantly using their logo to celebrate holidays or remember special historical figures). If restaurant reviews have been entered you see a link to those reviews to the right of the entry. Some results also show star ratings.

Notice the teardrop-shaped markers to the left of many of the entries. These markers correspond to the map on the right side of the page. Click the marker for any listed restaurant and you are taken to the Google Place Page, which gives the address, telephone number, and website URL, along with a detailed map of the restaurant's location. Also on this page are user reviews, and in some cases a star rating system. Further down the page you find a list of Related Places—in this case, other restaurants and a section entitled More About This Place, which links to other mentions around the Internet. Figure 6-2 shows the Google entry for Piesano's Pacchia, a pizza restaurant in Rapid City, SD.

Notice that in Figure 6-2, the second section is titled Details. It is in this section that you may find a link to the restaurant's listing on allmenus.com, along with more reviews and a line graph of the restaurant's reputation from judysbook.com." Not all restaurants are listed on these two websites, of course, but I have found this information very helpful in deciding to try new restaurants when it is included.

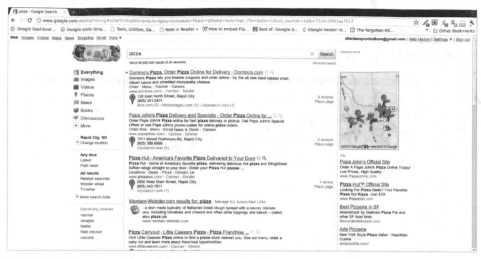

FIGURE 6-1: Search results for pizza in Rapid City, SD.

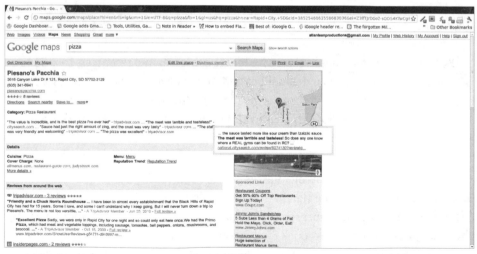

FIGURE 6-2: Piesano's Pacchia, Rapid City, SD.

Click the map embedded in the business entry and the exact location is shown in Google Maps. The map information includes a link to written directions, nearby searches, and the option to save the map.

CROSSREF I talk more about Google Maps in Chapter 27.

Another example is in the case of doctors in Rapid City, SD, the teardrop map marker takes you to the business' official website. To browse the Google reviews and details page click the link for the Place Page to the right of the entry. Figure 6-3 shows the search results for the keyword "doctors" for Rapid City, SD.

FIGURE 6-3: Doctor listings for Rapid City, SD. Notice the link for the Place Page.

You can use Google Maps to search for local businesses and resources, too. Go to maps.google.com and set your default location, if you have not already done so. Type the name of the business or the type of business you're looking for and click Search Map. Every business that Google can find of the specified type appears on the map, and is listed in the left navigation bar with contact information. Figure 6-4 shows the results for a search on hospitals when the default location is set to Omaha, NE.

You may be wondering how businesses get a Google Place page. It's simple, really. Go to google.com/places and sign in to your Google account. Click the List Your Business button. Select your country from the drop-down menu, and enter your business phone number in the textbox. Click Find Business Information.

Google searches its database for your business phone number. If your phone number is found, you are asked to edit or verify your business listing information. If your business phone number is not listed in the Google database, you are directed to a page to enter your business information. Figure 6-5 shows the data entry page.

After you enter location and category information, the form asks for Service Area and Location Settings. It is here that you specify the areas for which your business entry appears in the search. You have the option of stipulating your service area without showing your business address on the map. That's a great feature for home-based businesses. When you've completed the form, click Submit.

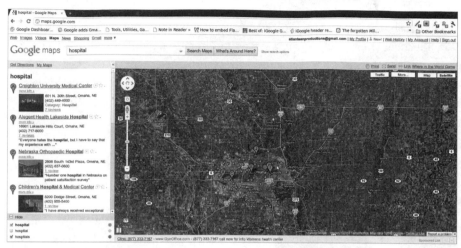

FIGURE 6-4: Map and details for every hospital in and near Omaha, NE.

FIGURE 6-5: Enter details about your business.

The next step is to verify that this is a legitimate business entry. Select between phone or postcard verification and click Finish.

If you've selected phone verification, a Google computer calls within seconds with a PIN number. Enter that PIN in the box that appears on the subsequent page following your verification choice and click Go. When you see a verification page, you are finished.

If you select postcard verification, you receive a postcard in the mail that contains further directions for verifying your business account.

It takes approximately 24 hours after you complete the verification process for your business to appear in local searches.

When I'm shopping for a specific item I usually research it online to find the best price. Sometimes the best price is in a store right in my backyard. Of course, the next step is to call the store and ask if the item is in stock. It is at that point where frustration usually sets in as I am passed from one associate to another. Typically, this procedure ends with someone asking me to call back, or telling me he/she thinks it's in stock, but I should come down in person to find out for sure.

Google has given us a solution to this problem. It's called Google Product Search. At the time I'm writing this, Google Product Search is still in beta. You can find it at www.google.com/products. Product Search has been around for a while, but the ability to see which items are in stock in your local stores is new.

Like most things Google, it's fairly straightforward to use. Type the name of the item in the search bar and click Search. On the results page, check the In Stock Nearby box in the left navigation bar. Figure 6-6 shows my search for Vitamix. Notice the In Stock Nearby checkbox on the left.

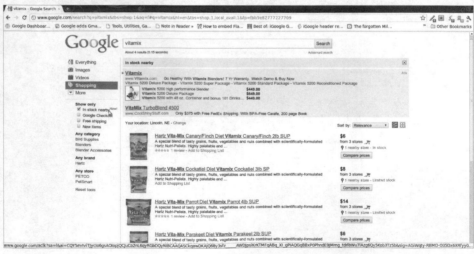

FIGURE 6-6: Search for Vitamix.

When you check the box, results automatically update to show only those items that are in your local area. To change your location click Change toward the top of the item list and enter your ZIP code or city/state information.

FINDING BUSINESSES IN OTHER AREAS

When you're traveling it can be difficult to find the businesses and services you need. Google can help.

You can use the standard Google search bar to find what you need when you're away from home or searching for a friend. Just enter the business type, along with the ZIP code or city and state information, in the search bar and click the Search button, or press Enter on your keyboard. You get the same kind of results as you would for your local area.

If you're traveling for an extended period, you may consider changing your local area settings.

"Google Maps is a terrific resource for locating businesses when you're away from home. You have two methods for finding the information you need.

First, type the category of the business or service you need, along with your location information. For this purpose use either ZIP code, city/state, or even the street name." Figure 6-7 shows a search query for a hotel near I-295 in Cherry Hill, NJ.

FIGURE 6-7: Search for hotels near Interstate 295, near Cherry Hill, NJ.

If I were traveling down I-295 and nearing Cherry Hill, NJ I could easily locate a nearby hotel. And, because nightly rates and reviews are right there in the left navigation bar, it's easy to choose a well-rated hotel in my price range.

"But, what if you've already checked into your hotel and want to find an activity to pass the time? For this, try using Google's What's Around Here? feature."

Type your current location into the search bar, and click What's Around Here? (which is the second button to the right of the search bar). Google Maps locates all the businesses in your area. Figure 6-8 shows the search results when you type the address for Holiday Inn Philadelphia Cherry Hill.

Points of interest   Location of the hotel

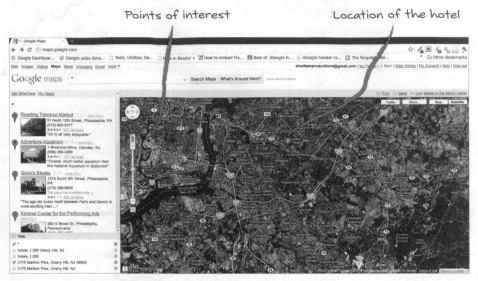

FIGURE 6-8: What's Around Here? results for 2715 Marlon Pike, Cherry Hill, NJ.

As you can see in Figure 6-8 the location of the hotel is marked with a purple marker to help you determine which businesses are closest. Use the zoom bar on the left side of the map to resize the map. Click the markers on the map to see address information for the locations you select, and click Directions to get directions from where you are to where you would like to go.

SUMMARY

You may have heard of the saying: "Think Globally—Act Locally." This now-popular catch-phrase fits the theme of this chapter well. Google, as powerful as it is, can be customized for local searches with the help of Google Maps, Google Places, Google Product Search, and some other features to turn the world's most powerful search giant into a local version of your neighborhood bulletin board.

You can also find just about anything in other areas outside of your own, which is perfect for business people who are on the go, and anyone planning a vacation.

CHAPTER 7

Learning More with Informational Searches

Over the course of a day you need many types of information. Whether you're shopping, managing your finances, keeping up on world events, or expanding your horizons through education, information at your fingertips saves you time and money. In order to bring you up-to-the-minute information, Google has created Google Scholar, Google Books, and Google Finance so you can get what you need and be on your way.

DISCOVERING GOOGLE SCHOLAR

▶ Find Google Scholar at scholar.google.com."

Google Scholar is the online equivalent to a world-wide card catalog. It brings books, court opinions, court rulings, academic papers, professional journal articles, theses, abstracts, and other scholarly works together in one place. Documents are evaluated similarly to the way researchers rank research. The full text of the document is evaluated and weighted, along with where the document was published, credibility of the author, how often the document is cited by other scholarly writers, and how recently.

After you type in your search criteria and click Search, the next page shows results. Use the first drop-down menu to choose the type of academic work you'd like to see. Choose between

- ▶ Articles and patents
- ▶ Articles excluding patents
- ▶ Legal opinions and journals
- ▶ Federal cases
- ▶ Local cases
- ▶ Advanced Search

The second drop-down menu lets you choose the time period in which to search. Choose to begin your search in any year from 1991 to the current year.

The final drop-down menu gives you the option of viewing those academic articles that include only summaries, or those that have been cited.

If you're doing ongoing research on a topic, the Create Email Alert link is especially useful. With just two clicks you can be alerted when new academic articles that are relevant to your keywords become available.

Sometimes you need more search power than basic search can give you. You can access Advanced search in two ways. Choose Advanced Search from the first drop-down menu, or click the link to the right of the Search Button.

As you can see in Figure 7-1, you have many options to help narrow your search. Like a simple Google Search, you can search for an exact phrase, many words, exclude words, and specify where your search term appears on the web page. In addition, choose to return articles by a specific author, or those articles published through a certain journal. Choose a date range in which to search. These search options help when you know the information was published in, for example, *The Journal of Biological Chemistry* sometime in 2009.

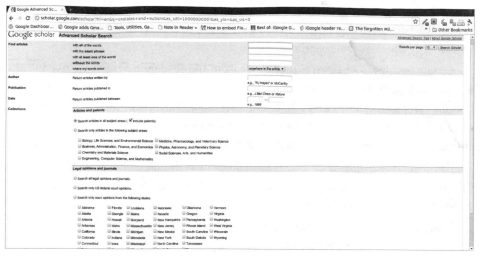

FIGURE 7-1: Google Scholar Advanced Search page.

The next area of search specification is Articles and Patents. Here you choose to search within all subject matters and subjects. Deselect the box if you don't want to include information on patents.

If you want to search only specific subjects, you can check as many subjects from the list as apply to your search.

The final section, Legal Opinions and Journals, is where you customize a legal search. Choose between searching

- All legal opinions and journals

- Only U.S. federal court opinions

- Court opinions from individual states

When you choose the last option, you then must select the state(s) from which you want to see results. There is no limit on the number of states you can select.

Some papers have restrictions on who may access them, but you can read access-restricted papers through your local college, high school, or public library. For example, many libraries subscribe to multiple professional and academic journals. This enables members of the library to gain access to articles published through those journals. Set your local library through the Scholar Preferences page. You can access Scholar Preferences from the link at the top, next to your login information.

Library Links is the fourth section from the top on the Scholar Preferences page. Type the name of your college, high school, or local library in the search box, and click Find Library. Google Scholar limits you to three libraries. When you've finished adding the libraries to which you belong, save your preferences. Now, when you search through Google Scholar, you are alerted to articles you can read in full through the libraries you specified.

Google Scholar is a powerful tool for locating the academic papers you need. Make it even more powerful with user scripts. One such script is the Google Scholar Citation Explorer available on userscripts.org. Created by Mayank L, this script lets you choose documents across your searches and then cross-reference the "Cited By" list so you can easily see which documents have been most cited, and by whom.

Users of the service CiteULike may find the Post Google Scholar Citations to CiteULike user script handy. Created by Ted Kandell, this popular script adds academic papers to your CiteULike library with one click.

Many more user scripts are available for Google Scholar, and of course, if you're a JavaScript whiz, you can always create your own.

While we're talking about works cited, you should know that under many results entries is a link for Cited By, followed by a number. That number tells you the number of times this academic paper has been cited in other people's work. In other words, how often it has been used as a reference. Click the Cited By link to see a list of the publications that have cited this work.

BANKING ON GOOGLE FINANCE

Google Finance is a one-stop shop for all your financial information needs. Follow financial news, up-to-the-minute stock prices and currency rates, see trends, sector summaries, and follow markets around the world at a glance. Google Finance gives you all the tools you need to evaluate past performance and make wise investment decisions.

Finding Stocks and Company Information

The first step in finding stock information for any company is to know the stock market symbol for that company. Traditionally, those symbols are hard to find because before you can look up the symbol, you need to know which of the several world-wide stock markets the company is listed on.

Google Finance makes finding a company's stock symbol as simple as typing the company name in the Finance search box. As you can see in Figure 7-2, the auto-complete feature can help you locate the business you're looking for, even if it has branches listed on several different world-wide markets, such as Nissan (www.nissanusa.com).

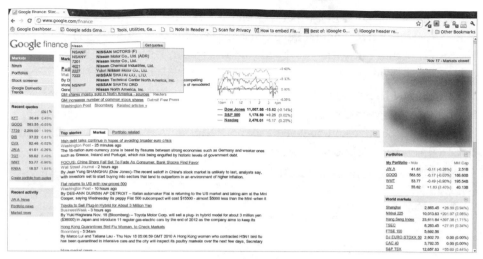

FIGURE 7-2: Choose the Nissan stock you'd like to view.

When you select a company, Google Finance gives you the names of officers and directors, the physical address of the company, along with website, related companies, and company overview information.

> **TIP** You find type of stock, the market name, and symbol in parenthesis next to the company name in the blue stripe.

The stock market information is presented in a graph that you can expand or condense using your mouse, or the time period links directly above the graph. Inside the graph, you find lettered flags. These flags correspond to the lettered news articles to the right of the graph. The news pieces are arranged on the graph in order of date and time, with A being the most recent entry. This helps you see which news events have affected stock prices (see Figure 7-3).

When you've added a stock to your Google Finance portfolio, you can add events, such as quarterly review presentations, from the Events heading. To add upcoming events to your Google Calendar, simply click the Add to My Calendars link.

Managing Your Portfolio

You can review and keep track of all your stocks from My Portfolio. To do so, select Portfolios from the left navigation menu.

By default, the Portfolios link lands on the Overview tab. This is where you manage personal investments. Keep track of the amount of money you invest, and the results of those investments, by using the Deposit/Withdraw links directly under the company listings.

Use the Add Transactions link to record stock transactions. Record the type of transaction, date, number of shares, price, commission, and notes. When you add these transactions to your Google Finance portfolio, you see your daily results in the Day's Gain column of the Overview tab.

You have several different ways to manage your portfolio from within the Overview tab. You can

- ▶ Import Transactions—.ofx or .csv format
- ▶ Edit Transactions
- ▶ Edit Portfolio
- ▶ Delete Portfolio
- ▶ Download to Spreadsheet
- ▶ Download to .ofx

You can also import your Google Finance portfolio information directly to a Google Docs Spreadsheet.

> **CROSSREF** You learn how to import from Google Finance into Google Docs Spreadsheets in Chapter 24.

You can compare the performance of two or more stocks right on the graph. Enter the ticker information into the box on the chart labeled Compare and then click Add.

Figure 7-3 shows the stocks of three well-known auto makers. Notice the stocks are color coded for easy comparison. To change the date range to be compared, type the beginning date in the first box above the graph key, and the ending date in the second box above the graph key.

To share the stock graph click Link To This Chart below the chart. Google Finance generates a link that you can paste into an instant message, e-mail, or website HTML.

The second control tab in the portfolio is Fundamentals. This tab gives you basic information about the performance of each stock in your portfolio over time.

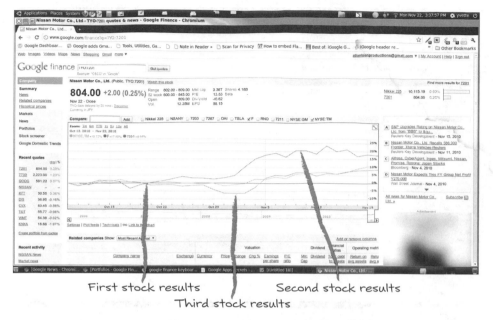

First stock results
Third stock results
Second stock results

FIGURE 7-3: Compare the stock results of three auto makers on the same graph.

The third control tab is Performance. Here, you see how your shares are faring in the market while learning if the shares you hold went up or down in value, and by how much.

The final control tab is the Transactions tab. The Transactions tab lists every transaction you record, the number of shares involved, the price of those shares at the time of the transaction, and the amount of commission.

Many people select the stocks they invest in by specific criteria such as the price change over the last fifty-two weeks, or the company's five-year net income growth rate. You can see this kind of information, and much more, with the Stock Screener. Access Stock Screener from the left navigation bar on any Google Finance page. Enter the criteria you use in your evaluation. If you don't see what you're looking for among the default criteria, click Add Criteria to see the extensive list of options. Figure 7-4 shows the Stock Screener with the price options list open.

As you enter search criteria, the list changes to show only those stocks that meet the criteria you set. Click the column headers to order results. Figure 7-5 shows a search ordered by fifty-two-week high, from highest to lowest.

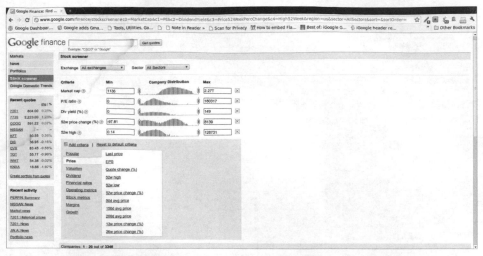

FIGURE 7-4: Stock Screener Price Options.

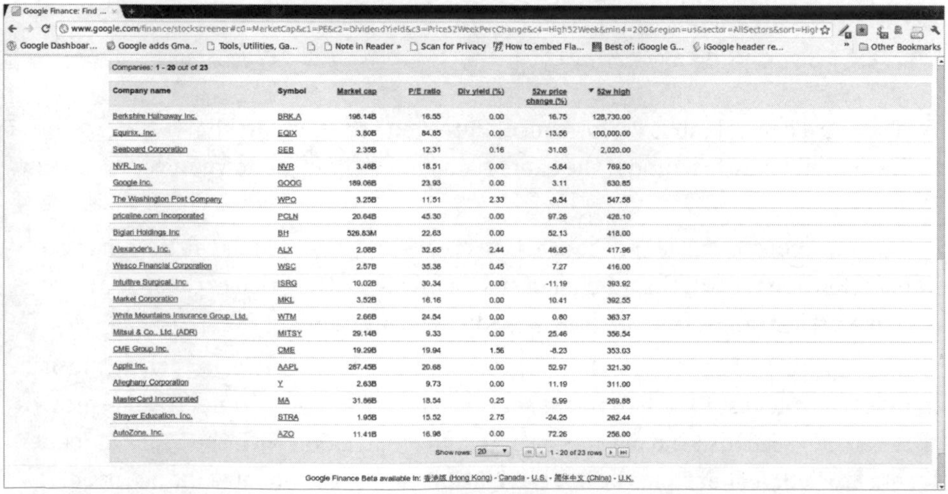

FIGURE 7-5: Criteria search ordered by 52-week high.

NOTE Put your Google Finance information on your iGoogle page for quick and easy access. There is an official Google release of the Finance feed. Search for **Google Finance** in the iGoogle Add Stuff page.

KEEPING CURRENT WITH GOOGLE NEWS

Google News is my favorite news service because it brings world-wide news from many sources together on one page. Google News lets you customize the type of news you see, the topics included, and the page layout. Add that to the ability to embed Google News in an iGoogle or personal website, and it becomes one of the best news services available.

Creating Advanced News Searches

With Google News, you can keep up with and customize news from anywhere in the world. In the U.S. Edition, the country drop-down is located on the right side of the page, just next to the Add a Section link. To select news from a foreign news source, click the downward-facing arrow to open the drop-down menu, and select the country from which you want to read news. To switch back to U.S news, or read news from a different country, look for the drop-down menu at the top of the left navigation bar. Figure 7-6 shows Google News for Chile. Notice the news sources are Chilean sources.

▶ The Google Chrome web browser has Google Translate built in, allowing you to translate foreign news pages with one click.

FIGURE 7-6: Google News as those in Chile view it.

Regardless of which Google News edition you are viewing, you have the ability to add an entire genre of news with two clicks. Click the Add a Section link, found on the right side of the window. This takes you to the Custom Sections Directory. Scroll through available news sections, or use the left-hand sort choices to narrow your search by overall popularity, category, or edition. On the right side of the screen, you can use keywords to search available sections and find what you're looking for quickly. You can also type a ZIP code or city and state information to add a section specific to that local area. Use the drop-down menus to add a standard section from any available edition. This option adds standard sections for any foreign edition to your U.S. Google News page. That's helpful if you regularly follow the news of another country. Finally, you can create a custom search.

Click Create a Custom Search to set your own search parameters. Figure 7-7 shows the Create a Custom Section page.

Refine your search using the techniques discussed in Chapters 4 and 5, such as enclosing exact search terms in parentheses, and using the minus sign (–) to omit specific words or web domains to help you get the news you want and avoid the news you don't.

FIGURE 7-7: Define your own news section.

After you enter search terms and select the news edition and desired language, a preview of your results displays in the space on the right. This preview helps you refine your search terms. If you'd like to share your custom news section with all Google News users, tick the checkbox labeled Publish This Section to the Directory.

Choose your favorite news publishers and let Google News know which news publishers you'd rather not read from the News Settings page. The Settings drop-down is next to your Google login information. Click Settings and select News Settings from the menu. Figure 7-8 shows the News Settings page.

Sorting Results

If you follow many different types of news it can be cumbersome to sort through the Google News main page in search of what you want to read. Sort options on the left side of the screen make this easier. Every time you add a news section to your Google News account, the left navigation bar is automatically updated with a corresponding link. Use these links to see only those headlines that are related to the desired topic. For example, to see only U.S. news, click U.S. in the left navigation bar.

FIGURE 7-8: Google News settings options.

To have all the news you've selected visible on your main Google News page, click All News in the bottom section of links in the left navigation bar.

If you want to see only the most recent headlines around the world, click Headlines in the last section of links in the left navigation bar (see Figure 7-9).

Some people view their news based on the images that accompany news articles. To see only news images, click Images in the last section of links in the left navigation bar.

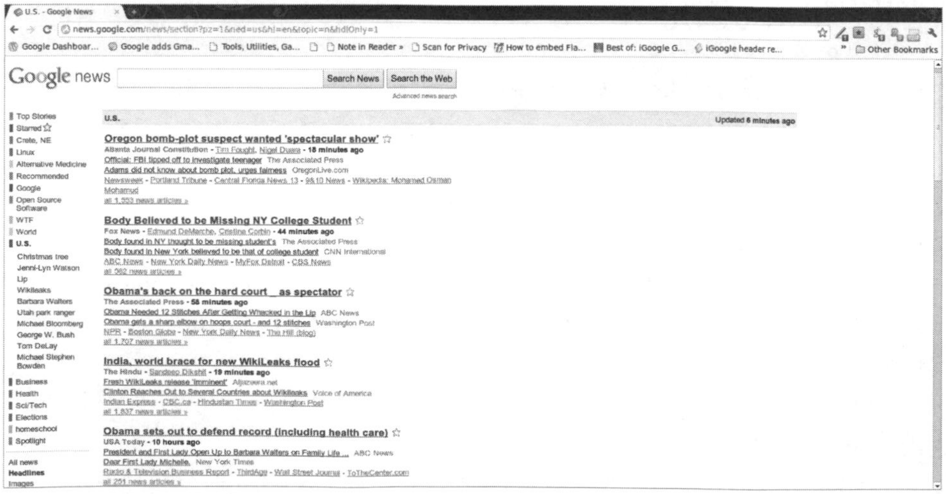

FIGURE 7-9: News stories organized by recent headlines worldwide.

Making News Easy to Find

Stars make finding news articles on Google News easy. Click the star located at the end of the bolded headline, and Google News files it in your Starred links. Later, when you want to read a news item you've starred, just look for the link to Starred articles in the left navigation bar.

Many people like to help friends find news they may want to read. Most of us to do this by posting to Facebook, Twitter, Google Buzz, or by sending an e-mail. One advantage of sharing news is that it helps the posters find headlines quickly when they want to refer to or quote the news article later. Google News makes it easy to share news articles via social networking and e-mail. Located to the right of the star is a downward-facing arrow. Click this arrow, and social networking options are presented in a drop-down menu.

Keep Google News handy by embedding it in your personal web page or iGoogle page.

For news on the go, access your Google News account from your mobile device at `mobile.google.com/news/index.html`.

With some mobile providers you have the ability to set up news alerts through your mobile Google News page. To find out which services are available, go to `www.google.com/mobile` and follow the on-screen directions.

FINDING A GOOD READ WITH GOOGLE BOOK SEARCH

For the unfamiliar, Google Books, at `books.google.com`, offers the ability to search published books and magazines. For books under current copyright, you can view a preview of the book, along with ratings, comments from readers, and a list of places to buy the book online or find it in your local library. Books for which the copyright is expired are usually available for reading online in their entirety.

Books are categorized into subjects such as Cooking, Family & Relationships, Business & Economic, and the like, but they are also listed by general type. For example, you can browse Classics, Trending Topics, Magazines, Religion, Law, Literary Collections. Philosophy, or choose from many other categories. Figure 7-10 shows the basic Google Books page.

When you mouse over a title in the standard view, a summary box appears. Included in the book summary information is the copyright information. Books that have a copyright date of 100 years ago are typically available to read on Google Books.

FIGURE 7-10: Browse books by subject or general category.

After you choose a title you'd like to read, you have several options. For books that are still under copyright you may buy the book from listed sellers, search your favorite book seller for the title, add the title to your Google Books library, or search your local library for the book. Books which are no longer covered under copyright law may be read online or downloaded for offline reading, in addition to the previously mentioned options.

Unearthing Exceptional Titles

Everyone has a different idea about what makes a great book. With Google Books you can find and read books you think are great. Leave a comment and star rating to help other people decide if your favorites are right for them.

You have many ways to find the perfect book. The simplest options are to use either the subject list on the left, or the category list on the main section of the page. These options let you browse books within your selected subject or category. Save books that interest you in your Google Books library by first clicking the book title. Then, from the book page, click the Add to My Library link. A drop-down menu appears that enables you to mark the book as a favorite, add it to your To Read list, mark the book as one you Have Read, or one you are Reading Now. Save your changes. Use the My Library link on the Google Books homepage to come back to your saved selections. Figure 7-11 shows the book page for *Wuthering Heights*, by Emily Brontë. Pay special attention to the drop-down menu shown on the right.

▶ If the selected book is already in your Google Books Library, this link changes to the text In My Library and a link to Change the Designated List appears next to the text.

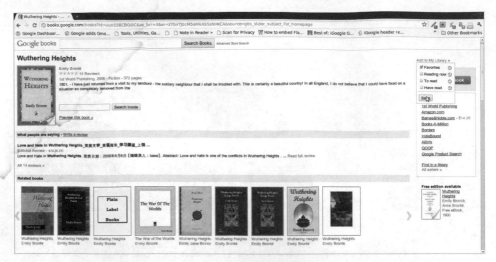

FIGURE 7-11: *Wuthering Heights* by Emily Brontë on Google Books.

Some book listings include a section entitled Related Books. Use this to find books similar to the one you are viewing. Browsing the Related Books section may help you find other books you will enjoy.

At its core, Google Books is simply a Google search engine and as such, all the search tips discussed in Chapters 4 and 5 apply here as well. You can use the search bar to search Google Books for any subject or author you want. Place search terms in quotation marks to find an exact match, use the minus (–) sign to exclude words, or use AND or OR to help focus your search. Review Chapters 4 and 5 for more search tips.

After you've entered your search terms click Search Books. Now, you can use the options on the left to narrow your search and find the book you're looking for. Choose to view books that are offered in either Full View, Preview and Full View, or Any View. If you're looking for a book that you are certain is in the public domain, choose Full View. This eliminates all books for which Google Books cannot display the full text. In contrast, if you know the book you are looking for is not in the public domain, or you want to find a recently published book on your topic, select Preview and Full View to eliminate all books for which the copyright has expired.

Now, choose between viewing those works that are books or magazines. If you're unsure, choose Any Document.

Decide how you would like to view the results. List view is the default. Grid view displays results photos of the cover along with title, author, publication date, and number of pages. This view gives less book information, but lets you see more books per screen.

Next, choose a time period for the book you're looking for. Was the book published in the 19th, 20th, or 21st century? If you have more specific publication date information, you can use the Custom Range option. And, if you don't know the publication date, simply leave the date range set to default setting, which is Any Time.

Tell Google Books how you want results sorted. You can sort by keyword relevance or sort by publication date.

Finally, choose the general subject your desired book falls under. In the example in Figure 7-12, the search criteria are as follows: Keyword – Yoga, show books with Preview and Full View, Books only, Grid View, 19th century, sorted by relevance.

FIGURE 7-12: Books published in the 19th century about Yoga. Results in Grid view.

Using Advanced Book Searches

Use Advanced Search when you want to narrow search results even further. Access Advanced Book Search by clicking the link below the Search Books button. Figure 7-13 shows the Advanced Book Search page.

The blue highlighted section of the Advanced Book Search page is just like any other Google advanced search page. This is where you enter your desired search terms, and specify which phrases should be exact and which words should be included or omitted. The rest of the page is specific to Google Books.

The Search and Content headings are simply another way to tell Google Books what level of preview should be available for the works returned by the search, and whether those works should be in the form of books or magazines.

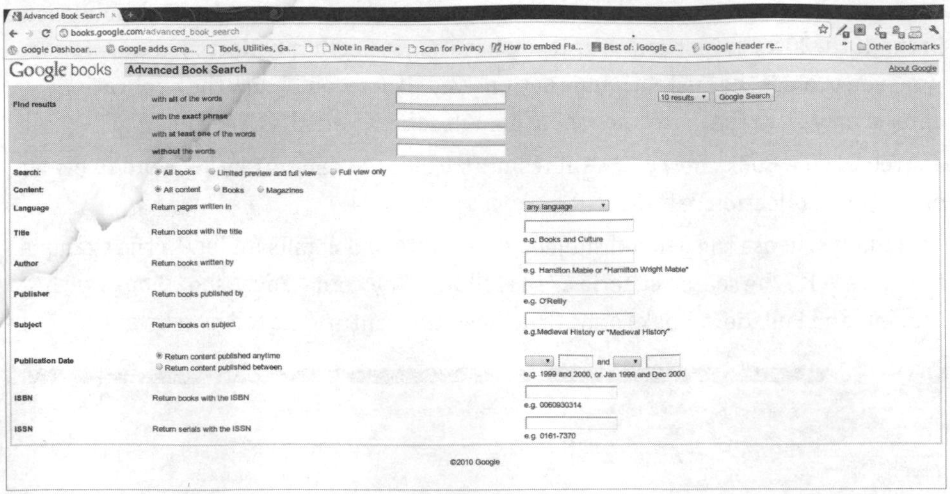

FIGURE 7-13: Google Books Advanced Book Search page.

The Language section lets you choose in what language the books or magazines should be published. Use the drop-down menu to select your desired language.

The next section is Title. Use this only if you know the title of the book. Otherwise, leave it blank.

Do you know the author's name? If you have the exact name, put it in parentheses, otherwise, you can include just the author's last name, or even just his/her first name, if that's all you know.

The next section lets you return books and magazines for a specific publisher. Not only is this useful for finding books on specific topics by a certain publisher, but if you enter only publisher information, you can see all the works released by the publisher you enter.

The Subject section is helpful if you are looking for resources on a subject for work, school, or personal reasons. Enter the subject in the textbox with or without parentheses.

If you know the approximate publication date of the work you're looking for, use Publication Date to enter that information.

Most books have an ISBN. If you know the ISBN of the book you're searching for, enter it here.

Sister to the ISBN is the ISSN. The International Standard Serial Number is issued to print and online magazines. If you know the ISSN of the magazine you want to find, enter it in the last search box.

▶ ISBN is an acronym for International Standard Book Number. This is a unique number assigned to books for identification purposes. All books released by major publishers carry an ISBN. Every country has its own ISBN issuing agency.

When you've entered all the search information you can, use the drop-down menu in the blue highlighted section to set the number of search results per page, and click the Google Search button. Figure 7-14 shows an Advanced Book search for all books on Yoga that were published in the German language between January 1966 and January 1970. Figure 7-15 shows the results of that search.

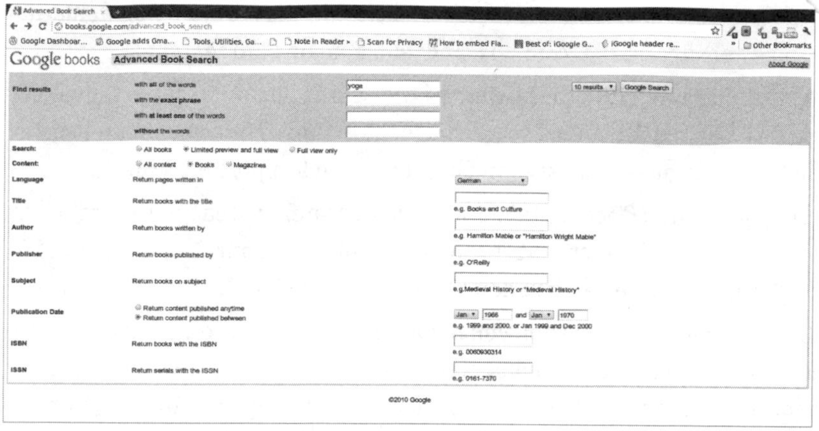

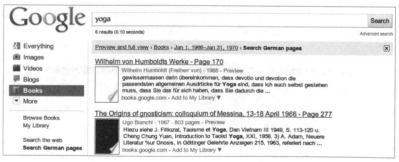

FIGURE 7-14: Completed Advanced Book Search form.

FIGURE 7-15: Results of search on keyword Yoga published in German between January 1966 and January 1970.

ACCESSING ADVANCED AND SPECIALTY SEARCHES

Sometimes you need a more specific search to quickly locate the information you need. That's where Specialty Searches come in. Specialty Searches enable you to search specific databases, such as the USPTO database, or a database of U.S. government resources. Some of these search resources, such as Google Blog Search, are available through both the standard Google Search page and a specific page, and others, such as Technology Search, require specific techniques be employed.

▶ USPTO is the acronym for the United States Patent and Trademark Office. Its website is available at www.uspto.gov.

Using U.S. Government Searches

▶ Keep in mind that all the natural language techniques discussed in Chapters 4 and 5 apply here as well.

When you're looking for information from U.S. government sources you can use the Advanced Search on the standard Google Search page, as discussed in Chapter 5, or you can use www.google.com/unclesam to access the U.S. Government Search engine. Use the textbox to enter your desired search terms and click Search. Google's U.S. Government search locates your search term across websites in the .gov and .mil domains. In addition, some websites on the .com, .us, and .edu domains are searched.

Use the Advanced Search link to the right of the Search button to access advanced searching options. Use the Advanced Search page to further define your search criteria. Again, all the techniques discussed in Chapters 4 and 5 apply here as well.

The real benefit of using Google's U.S. Government search instead of the standard Google Search page lies in the fact that the Government search automatically eliminates all non-government sites, so you don't have to do it by hand.

If the U.S. government information you're looking for is public data such as state unemployment rates or population numbers from the last census, you can use the standard Google Search page to locate the information. Just type the information you seek, along with the abbreviation of the state for which you want the information, and click Search. Figure 7-16 shows the results for a search on "unemployment rate" Az. As you can see, the first link is the U.S. Department of Labor, Bureau of Labor Statistics chart listing the "Arizona Economy at a Glance."

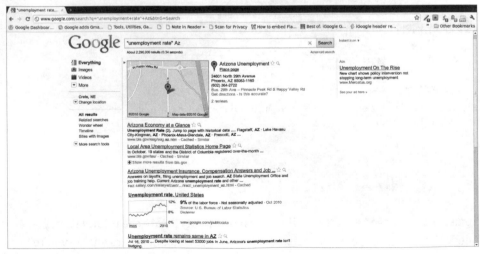

FIGURE 7-16: A simple search for public information returns U.S. government websites containing the desired information.

Advancing with Technology Searches

Keep abreast of new technological advances with focused Google searches. I use a combination of Google News, RSS feeds on my iGoogle page, and Google Blog Search, which is covered later in this chapter, to keep on top of the latest technology and gadgets.

"To use Google News to follow technology topics, start from the Google News homepage. In the left navigation bar, look for the red-tagged Sci/Tech link. This takes you to the general Science and Technology news feed."To further narrow your search, click one of the links under the Sci/Tech heading in the left navigation menu. Figure 7-17 shows the Sci/Tech page for Gadgets. Notice the button that reads Add to My Personalized News Page. Click this button if you want Google News to keep you informed of your chosen Sci/Tech news on your Google News homepage.

"To add this same Sci/Tech news to your iGoogle homepage, copy the link from your browser's address bar. Open a new tab, or use your current tab to open your iGoogle page. Click Add Stuff and look for the link to Add Feed or Gadget in the left navigation bar. Click Add Feed or Gadget, paste your copied link into the box provided, and click Add. Your selected Google News Sci/Tech feed is now available from your iGoogle page. Remember, you can do this with any website or news feed."

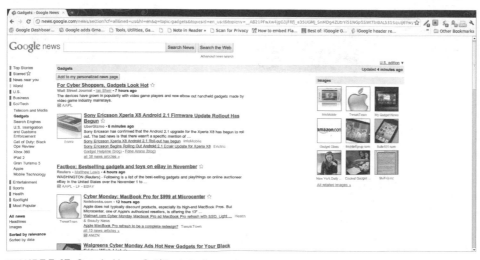

FIGURE 7-17: Google News Sci/Tech Gadgets news page.

Finding Patent Searches

Google and the USPTO have partnered to allow access and free downloading of the several million patents issued by USPTO. Patent information falls within the public domain, and is available through the U.S. Patent and Trademark Office website. The advantage of using Google Patents Search at www.google.com/patents is that you can download and print patent information in bulk, or individually for free. There is a charge to obtain this information through the U.S. Patent and Trademark Office. Google Patent Search hosts the patent pages on Google servers, allowing for faster searches. At this time, only patents issued in the United States are available through Google Patent Search. Those looking for patents issued in other countries should contact the patent office of the issuing country.

To use Google Patent Search simply type your search term into the text bar and click the Search Patents button. Google searches the patent database and returns all matches. Chose the patent you want to view from the results. Figure 7-18 shows the Overview page for the Mobius strip puzzle, owned by Daniel L. Morris. From this page you may choose to read the Abstract, view the Drawing, read the Description, read the Claims, Read the entire patent, or Download the entire patent in PDF so you can read it later. You also have the option of viewing the patent at the USPTO website.

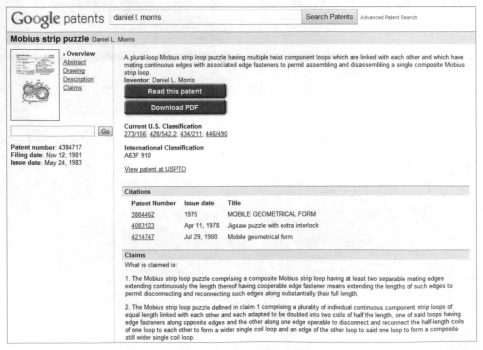

FIGURE 7-18: Google Patents overview page for the Mobius strip puzzle by Daniel L. Morris.

For a more exact patent search, use Google Patents Advanced Search. The link for the Advanced Search page is directly to the right of the Search Patents button. Figure 7-19 shows the Advanced Search page for Google Patents.

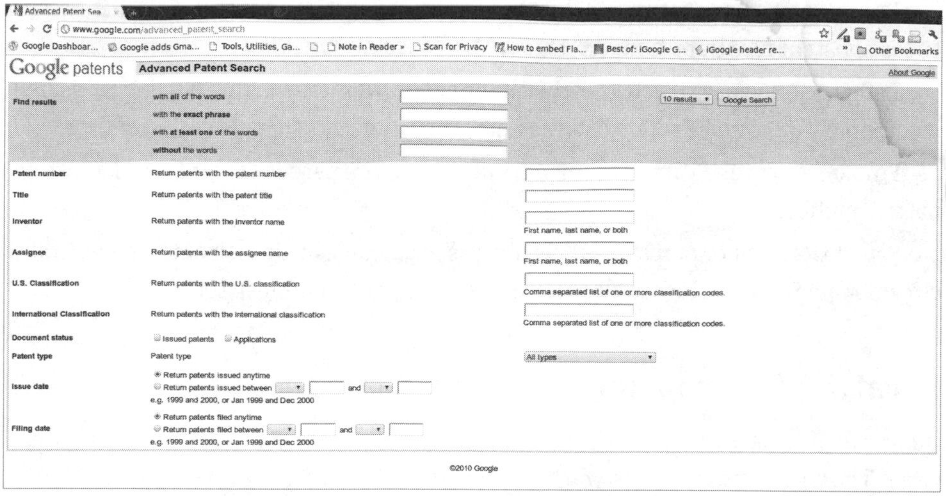

FIGURE 7-19: Google Patent Search—Advanced Search Page.

As you can see, the blue highlighted section of the Advanced Search page is the same as any other Google Advanced Search page. The options that follow are specific to Google Patents Search.

Search by patent number, if you know it, by entering the official patent number in the box.

Type the title of the patent in the box labeled Title.

If you know the name(s) of the person or people to whom the patent is assigned, enter it in the box labeled Assignee. This is especially useful if you want to know all the patents held by a particular person or group.

Every issued patent carries classification numbers. On the Google Patents Overview page, these classification numbers are listed directly below the Download PDF button and are labeled U.S. Classification. Classification numbers are predetermined and assigned based on the category of materials, and the purpose of the item that is patented. If you know the U.S. Classification number, enter it in the box labeled as such.

International Classification codes have the same purpose as the U.S. Classification codes, but the codes are not the same. Enter the International Classification code, if you know it.

Check Issued Patents, if you are looking for a patent that has already been issued. Check Applications if you are searching for a patent application that has not yet been granted.

Use the drop-down menu to select the Patent Type, if you know it. Ten different types of patents are listed. If you're unsure, choose All Types.

Enter the Issue Date if you know when the patent was issued. This is a helpful search if you simply want to see which patents were issued during a specific period of time.

Finally, enter the Filing Date, if you know when the patent owner filed the initial patent application.

Select the number of results you want to see per page at the top of the page, and click Google Search to locate all patents that meet your search criteria.

Locating Information with Blog Searches

Blogs can provide up-to-the-minute updates in a way that news and e-zine websites can't. The trick is finding trustworthy blogs from which to get your information." You have two ways to search blogs using Google.

The first technique involves using the Blog link on the main Google Search page and using the options under that link to define your search. Go to the main Google Search page and type your search term into the search bar. Click Google Search. Look for Blogs in the first section of the left navigation bar. Click this link." Search results are limited to blogs about the topic, or blog posts in which your search terms appear. Use the links on the left to further refine your search. Choose between instances where your search terms are part of the posts, or restrict the search to blog homepages. Choose the how recently the blog post was posted. Chose from posts within the last 10 minutes, past hour, past 24 hours, past week, past month, past year, or enter your own custom date range. Finally, choose to sort results by date or by relevance.

" The second blog searching technique is to use Google Blog Search at blogsearch .google.com." Like all Google search services, enter your desired search term, including any exact phrases or word omissions, and click Search Blogs or press the Enter key on your keyboard. Alternatively, use the topic headings on the Google Blog Search homepage to browse popular blog posts and topics.

After you have entered your search term and clicked Search Blogs, further narrow your results by choosing the date range for results.

FINDING PEOPLE WITH GOOGLE SEARCH

At some point, just about everyone wants to find someone else. Whether it's an old flame, your high school English teacher, or your best friend from third grade, finding people you've lost contact with can be difficult.

"The first step in finding anyone online is executing a Google search. From the main search page, use either the standard search bar or the Advanced Search page to enter as much information as you know. Include first and last name within quotes as the primary search term. Then, include city and state information. If you're using Advanced Search the city and state information are best placed within the line that asks for One or More of These Words. Use this section to include school or career information, if you know it. Click Search." Further refine your search, if necessary.

" For more information about the person, use the Blogs, Updates, or Discussion links in the left navigation bar to see if the person is mentioned in a blog, discussion group, or through Twitter. "

" Use Google's U.S. Government search to see if there is information about the person on any U.S. government websites, and search for the person's name on Google Calendar's public calendars." Many people make their Google Calendars public and you'd be surprised at what you can find.

"A search for the person's name on Google Groups lets you see all public Google Group discussion boards and Usenet archives for the past twenty years." That's a lot of information to sort through, but if you really need to find the person, it's a great resource.

" If you know what the person does for a living, or what his or her interests are, sometimes a search related to their interests or career field may prove fruitful." Google provides information about those people in your social group when you execute a Google search about a topic in which that person in active. While researching something for my daughter on Google, I noticed a section toward the bottom of the page labeled From Your Social Contacts with links to articles, blogs, and a website authored by my friend on the topic.

" If those searches turn up nothing, the next step is the Google Phone Book." Google Phone Book is discussed in depth in Chapter 4.

If you still don't find the information you need, the last resort is to use Google to find an online service dedicated to finding people."

— https://groups.google.com

SUMMARY

No matter what your search needs, Google offers a specialized search engine to help you find what you need quickly. Google Scholar is the perfect starting tool to find academic work, and Google Finance gives you the tools to maximize your investments and track your money. When you're looking for a great book to settle in with, try Google Book Search. Google puts United States government information, including patent and trademark information, at your fingertips. Finally, you can use Google to keep on top of the latest technology and cool gadgets as well as find long lost friends. When you use these tools together, there is nothing you can't find.

CHAPTER 8

Using Multimedia Search to Find Entertainment

Google knows how to do search — it's just what Google does best. So, it makes sense that if you want to find images, videos, or audio files that you should use Google's specific search engines to find the media file that you're looking for. Whether you're in need of a media file for a presentation, for a college class project, or just for fun, it's critical to know how to use Google's search engines like an expert.

In this chapter, you discover some tips and techniques to find the image, video, and audio files that you're looking for. You also learn how to tag videos for inclusion, how to use Advanced Search, and how to find audio files using text.

GETTING THE PICTURE: GOOGLE IMAGE SEARCH

When you're looking for that perfect image for your website or presentation, Google Image Search can help you comb through every image on the Web to find exactly the right one. Google spiders crawl the Web and catalog every image they find. Then, Google search algorithms analyze any captions and other text surrounding the image to determine which keywords apply to the image. When you execute a Google Image Search, your search terms are compared against the image keywords, duplicates are removed, and matching results are returned to you.

> **WARNING** Just because an image appears in Google Image Search does not automatically mean it is legal for you to use it. Before using any image you find through Google Image Search, or anywhere else on the Web, it's wise to familiarize yourself with copyright laws.

► Access Google Images from your mobile device by surfing to www .google.com/xhtml, which takes you to the Google Mobile homepage. Access Image Search from this page.

To use Google Image Search go to images.google.com. The basic Google Image Search operates just like the standard Google Search. Type your desired keywords into the search bar. All defining operators valid in a standard search are also valid here, including the ability to search one specific website. For example, to search for images of a toy fox terrier on the website dogster.com, you type **"toy fox terriers"site:dogster .com** into the search bar. Of course, you can use the Advanced Search page to do the same thing, but I talk about that later in this section. Figure 8-1 shows the Google Image results from the toy fox terriers search.

Notice the sorting options in the left navigation menu. Choose to see only large, medium, or icon-sized images. Or, click Larger Than to access a drop-down menu where you choose an image size. Figure 8-2 shows the drop-down menu associated with the Larger Than link.

Specify the precise width and length, in pixels, of the image you need by using the Exactly link.

► You can also access Google Image Search from the standard Google Search page, www .google.com. Type in your search criteria, press Enter, and click Images in the left navigation bar. You have the same sort options and the same Advanced Search page as you do if you start from images.google.com.

If you want to see the size of each image as it is displayed in the search results, click Show Sizes. This is located under the color picker, in the left navigation bar.

Choose the type of image you are looking for. Select Face to see only headshots of humans. Select Photo to return only those results that are photographs. Choose Clip Art if you only want to see images of that sort, and select Line Drawing to view drawings within your search criteria.

FIGURE 8-1: Google Image results for the search "toy fox terrier" site:dogster.com.

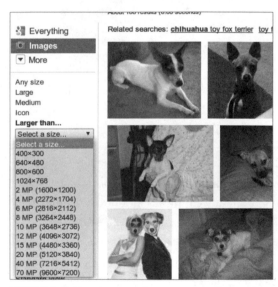

FIGURE 8-2: Use the drop-down menu to choose the smallest image size you want to see.

Finally, use the color picker to choose the dominant color within the image. This is a great feature if you are trying to color-coordinate a website or slide presentation. The color picker isn't a text link; it's a few rows of colors on the left-hand navigation menu that you can click on to filter your image search results by the chosen color. You can also choose to view only full color or black-and-white images.

For more in-depth sorting, use the Google Images Advanced Search page. You can access Advanced Search through the link under the Search button. When you're at the Advanced Search screen, you have a slew of options to refine your search, as you can see in Figure 8-3.

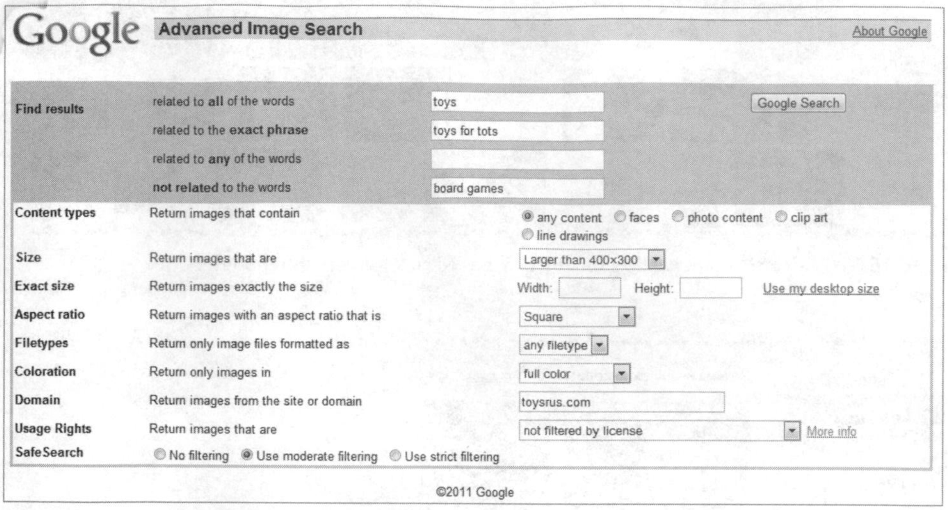

FIGURE 8-3: Google Advanced Image Search.

Like most Google Advanced Search pages, the highlighted lines are the area in which you enter your desired search terms. The rest of the form is specific to Google Images.

Content Types lets you choose not only line drawings, clip art, photos, and faces, but you can choose to view only news content, as well. News content includes those images that appear in a newspaper. Choosing News Content from the Advanced Search page shows you only those images that are in the news that day.

As a general rule, news content is searched when you do any Google Image Search. If news images match your keywords that day, they are shown at the top of the image results because they are time-sensitive images. It is possible to return news content one day, but not the next on the same keywords.

The Size drop-down menu gives the same size options as the heading of the same name in the left navigation bar of the Google Image Search homepage.

Use the Exact Size boxes to enter the exact size of your desired image, or click Use My Desktop Size to let Google Images read the size of your computer's desktop.

Aspect Ratio means the shape of the image. Use the drop-down menu to choose between Tall, Square, Wide, and Panoramic.

Use the Filetypes drop-down to specify the type of image file you want to see. Choose between JPG, GIF, PNG, and BMP files.

Coloration gives fewer choices than the color picker on the Google Image homepage. The drop-down menu on Advanced Search enables you to choose between black and white or full color.

The next line, Domain, is where you enter the domain name(s) of the website(s) you want to search. Leave this blank if you are searching the entire Web.

The Usage Rights option is probably the most important option on the Advanced Image Search page. This filter helps you find images that you can legally use. Copyright is an important issue, and so it is vital that you use only images for which you have the legal right to do so. Usage Rights is a great tool to ensure you don't accidentally get yourself into copyright problems. Use the drop-down menu to select from the following license types:

▶ **Labeled for Reuse**—This means you can copy and/or modify the image and reuse it for your purpose.

▶ **Labeled for Commercial Use**—You can copy and use the image as-is for your own commercial use.

▶ **Labeled for Reuse with Modification**—You can copy and use the image, but you must change the image in some way.

▶ **Labeled for Commercial Use with Modification**—You can copy and use the image for your own commercial use, but you must change the image in some way.

> **WARNING** Every image you find online is owned by someone and falls under copyright law. Be sure you read the license and understand exactly what you are legally permitted to do with the image you plan to use.

Finally, tell Google Image Search how to use SafeSearch for this Image Search. Your settings here override your global SafeSearch settings for only this search. Choose from No Filtering, Moderate Filtering, or Strict Filtering.

> **CROSSREF** SafeSearch is discussed in depth in Chapter 9.

LOCATING VIDEOS WITH VIDEO SEARCH

In today's multimedia-centric world online videos are used to teach, share, and entertain. Online videos hosted on YouTube, Metacafe, Hulu, or any website on the Net are quickly becoming the world's newest and best medium for sharing information. Videos are so popular that several websites boast complete K–12 curricula through video.

So, how do you go about finding all this great content? That's where Google Video Search comes in. Google Video Search gives you several ways to locate and put the world's best videos to work for you.

> **WARNING**   Every video on the Internet is owned by the creator(s). Just like books, music, and movies, the videos you find online are covered by copyright law. If you search for video with the intention of embedding that video into your website, you must be mindful of the copyright requirements.

Using Google Video

Google Video was Google's answer to YouTube, allowing users to upload and host their own videos on Google servers. However, when Google bought YouTube in 2006 it found itself with two services that did about the same thing. The smart business move, of course, was to focus energy on the more popular service. So, Google Video was closed in 2009 in favor of expanded YouTube services. I explore YouTube in depth in Chapter 15.

Videos previously hosted with Google Video are still available to view through Google Video Search. The owners have access to those videos just as they did before Google closed Google Video. This section focuses on Google Video Search.

You can access Google Video Search in one of two ways. First, you can go to the standard Google Search page and enter your keywords into the search bar and click Google Search. Then click Videos in the left navigation menu. Or, you can head to the official Google Videos homepage at http://video.google.com.

The only real difference between these two routes is that when you use the Google Videos homepage you can access the most current news and entertainment videos directly from there. Figure 8-4 shows what the Google Videos homepage has to offer.

On the Google Videos homepage, enter your keywords into the search box and then click Search Videos. Figure 8-5 shows the results page you receive regardless of your preferred method of accessing the page.

FIGURE 8-4: Google Videos homepage.

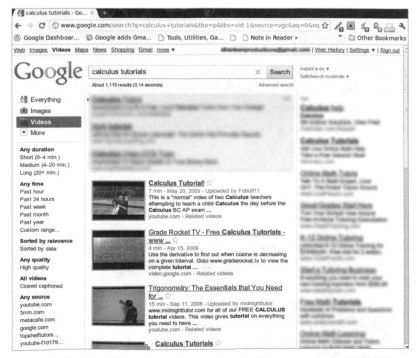

FIGURE 8-5: Google Videos Search results for the keywords calculus tutorials.

Use the sort options in the left navigation bar to find the exact video you need.

The first block of choices allows you to view only those videos that are within a specified duration. Choices are Short (0–4 minutes), Medium (4–20 minutes), and Long (20 or more minutes). To see all available videos, regardless of runtime, choose Any Time. Sorting by video length is helpful when you are working to get a message across, or learn a topic in a specified amount of time.

Sometimes you need to find the most recently uploaded videos on a topic. Google video gives you two ways to find the most current videos. Select videos that were uploaded in the past hour, 24 hours, week, month, or year, or click Custom Range to enter your own date range. Or, choose to sort all videos By Date instead of By Relevance to find the most recently published videos.

▶ To get more relevant results, use the By Relevance setting and use the time frame choices to determine the publish date; this method returns only those videos with your keywords in the title. When you sort by date, Google looks at all the keywords in your search terms and then orders those by date.

> **TIP** Many video listings tell you exactly how long the video is. This information is typically found on the first line after the video title. The published date is usually found in the same line, directly after length information. If you need a new video of a certain length, simply sort by publish date, and look for the length information in the first line.

For higher quality videos suitable for work or school project presentations, click High Quality, otherwise, leave this set to the default Any Quality to expand your search results.

Choose to view only those videos that are closed captioned by clicking Closed Captioned. Captions aren't only for individuals who are deaf. Hearing people can use closed captions when viewing a video in a setting where they don't want to make a lot of noise, like a library or crowded conference room. Captioned videos are also a great way to encourage young children to practice newly acquired reading skills.

> **TIP** Be wary of defining your search parameters too much. If you use too narrow a search you may not find what you're looking for. If you don't get good results, try expanding your search a bit.

▶ Selected search options are highlighted between the search bar and the upper paid advertising area. Turn off all sort options at once by clicking the X on the right side of the highlighted area.

Choose the source of videos returned in the bottom block of choices. Instead of surfing to each of the six listed sources, simply click the site from which you prefer to see results.

Defining the hosting source of any video you use has several practical applications. For example, you may remember posting an instructional video to Google Video, but for some reason can't access your Google Video account. You could type the topic keywords along with the username you used to upload the video, and then choose to see only Google Video videos. Or, maybe you are preparing a video presentation for work or school and know YouTube is the only video hosting site not locked behind your company's fire-wall. Search only YouTube videos to find one you are sure to be able to access when giving that big presentation. The hosting sites accessible through Google Video Search are

- ▶ bukisa.com
- ▶ metacafe.com
- ▶ google.com (this shows only videos uploaded to the old Google Video hosting service)
- ▶ 5min.com
- ▶ topshelftutors.com
- ▶ youtube.com

Google Video Search Advanced Search page offers the same sort and search options as the left-hand navigation and standard search bar with one addition. Use Advanced Search to find videos recorded in languages other than English. The Language drop-down enables you to choose from 33 different languages, or Any Language. Figure 8-6 shows the Advanced Search page for Google Video Search.

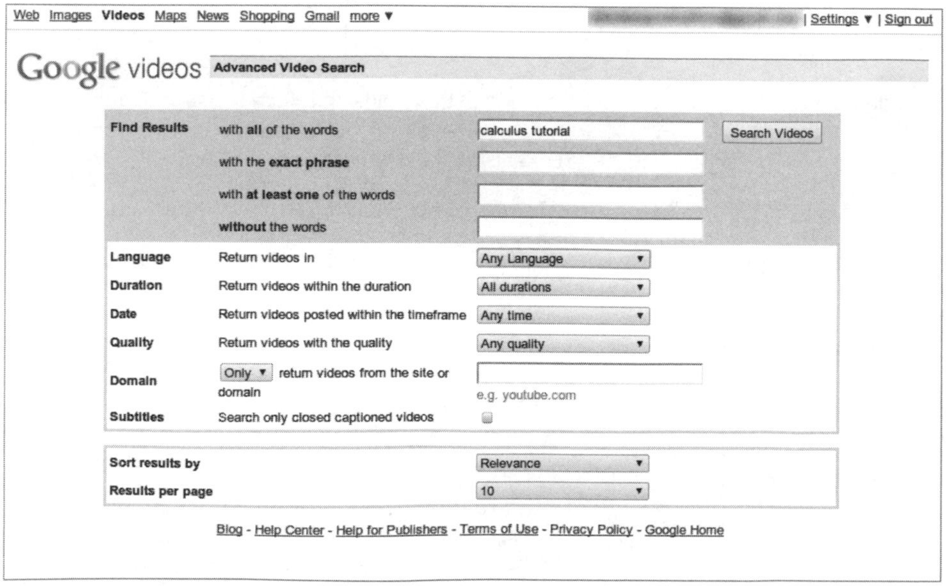

FIGURE 8-6: Google Video Search, Advanced Search Page.

If you're a video creator, you may be wondering how to get your videos into Google Video Search quickly. Sure, you can wait for the Google web crawlers to find and catalog your video on their own, but there is a faster way.

Submit a video sitemap to Google and tell the Google-bots about your video. First, create your sitemap using Sitemap Protocol 0.9. Include information on your video. Table 8-1 lists the sitemap tags Google requires for video. Table 8-2 lists the video tags that Google recommends, but does not require, and Table 8-3 shows all optional video tags. Then, submit your sitemap to Google via Google Webmaster Tools.

▶ Sitemap Protocol is defined at sitemap.org.

> **NOTE** Learn more about sitemaps, and read detailed directions for creating your sitemap and submitting it to Google through Google Webmaster Central. The direct link to sitemap information is **www.google.com/support/webmasters/bin/answer.py?answer=183668**.

TABLE 8-1: Required Video Tags for Sitemaps

TAG	DEFINITION
`<loc>`	URL of the page the user lands on when he or she clicks to play your video.
`<video:video>`	The filename of the video itself.
`<video:thumbnail_loc>`	URL of the video's thumbnail image. Thumbnails must be in either .jpg, .png, or .gif format, and must be at least 160x120 pixels.
`<video:title>`	Title of the video. No more than 100 characters.
`<video:description>`	Description of the video. Descriptions longer than 2048 characters are shortened.
`<video:content_loc>`	URL points to the video to be played. The URL must specify the video file type. This tag is required unless the `<video:player_loc>` tag is used.
`<video:player_loc>`	This tag may be used in place of the `<video:content_loc>` tag. This URL specifies the video player to be used. Example: www.anywebsite.com/swf/nameofvideo.

TABLE 8-2: Recommended Sitemap Tags for Video

TAG	DEFINITION
`<video:duration>`	Length of video in seconds. Must be between 0 and 28800 seconds.
`<video:expiration_date>`	Date the video will no longer be available online. Date must be in the format stipulated by the W3C. This applies only to videos that are time sensitive.

TABLE 8-3: Optional Sitemap Tags for Video

TAG	DEFINITION
`<video:rating>`	Video rating, if any. Value must be between 0 and 5.0.
`<video:content_segment_loc>`	Used only with the `<video:player_loc>` tag. This is used when you have posted video in segments.
`<video:view_count>`	Number of times video has been viewed.
`<video:publication_date>`	Date video was first published. Must be in W3C format.
`<video:tag>`	Short, descriptive tag(s) associated with the video. Example: family. Use a new `<video:tag>` for each tag to be included, with an upper limit of 32.
`<video:category>`	General category of video. Example: Persian is a valid category for a website about cats.
`<video:family_friendly>`	If the video should not be available to users with SafeSearch turned on, set this tag to NO.
`<video:restriction>`	List of countries where video may or may not be played. List using ISO3166 format.
`<video:gallery_loc>`	Link(s) to gallery or galleries where the video appears.
`<video:price>`	Cost required to download or view video. Use ISO4217 format for currency.
`<video:requires_subscription>`	State whether the user needs a subscription of any type to view the video.
`<video:uploader>`	Name of the video uploader.

USING AUDIO SEARCH

Google used to have a separate search page for audio files. However, it has integrated this service into the standard Google search bar.

Whether you remember the name of the song, only the artist name, a handful of lyrics, or some combination of these, you can find the song and artist name by typing what you remember into the standard Google search bar and clicking Search. Google returns sites where you can listen to and purchase the song, along with any music videos, links to lyrics, links to information about the artist, and the song's Wikipedia page, if applicable. Figure 8-7 shows results for a search of the lyrics "dancing queen."

FIGURE 8-7: Search results for the lyrics "dancing queen."

If you enter the name of a musical group, the top search results are links to listen to the most popular tunes recorded by that group. Figure 8-8 shows results from a search for the Celtic group Great Big Sea.

All the standard search tips apply to music searches as well.

Some people feel more comfortable searching from a search page that seems dedicated to the content for which they are searching. For those people there is www.google.com/landing/music/. Type your keywords into the search bar and click Search for Music. You get the same results either way.

> On www.google
.com/landing/
music/ you also
find a Google
instructional video.
This video shows how
to search for music
from the standard
Google search page.

FIGURE 8-8: Search for Great Big Sea.

Finding Audio Clips

You can use Google in many ways to locate audio clips. The most straightforward method is to enter your desired person or subject, along with the words *audio clip* into the search bar. For example, if you want an audio clip of former President Ronald Reagan talking about the economy use the keywords economy, Ronald Reagan, audio clip. Figure 8-9 shows the results of this search.

Finding Podcasts

Finding the podcasts you want is just as easy as locating your favorite song. Type the name, subject matter, or author of the podcast, along with the word **podcast** into the standard Google search bar, and click Search. Google returns only those podcast results that match your query. Figure 8-10 shows the results for a search for podcasts that talk about the dental health of dogs.

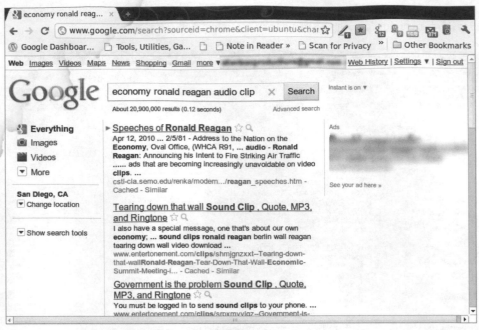

FIGURE 8-9: Results for a search with the keywords economy Ronald Reagan audio clip.

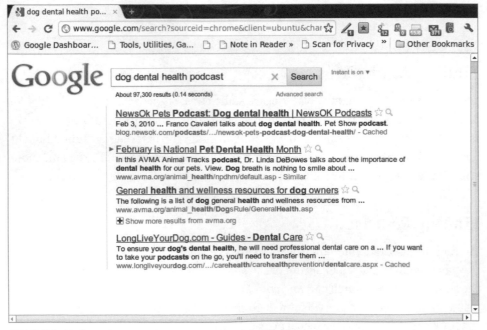

FIGURE 8-10: Search results for dog dental health podcast.

SUMMARY

Searching like an expert enables you to find the media content that you need, without having to stumble and struggle through options, features, or segments. Google has indexed several million images, videos, and audio files, and has integrated functions within its search engines to refine your search to enable you to get exactly what you want.

After reading this chapter, you should have a strong grasp of how to search for media files for your next business presentation, internal company meeting, or school project, as well as how to include a video via a sitemap for inclusion.

Customizing Search to Your Needs

No matter what your search needs, Google makes it easy to customize your search experience. Use Custom Search Preferences to help you get the results you want. SafeSearch lets you eliminate the results you don't want to see, and Google Labs expands your entire Google experience with access to functions and apps that are in the late developmental stages. Have the latest information delivered right to your inbox with Google Alerts, and even search individual websites for what you need. With so many ways to customize your search experience, Google always gives you exactly what you need, when you need it.

CUSTOMIZING YOUR SEARCHES

Google Search is a powerful search engine that goes a long way to helping users find what they need on the Internet. But, as great as Google is on its own, you can help make it better by customizing your search preferences and taking advantage of Google's SafeSearch options.

Setting Custom Search Preferences

Access Google Search preferences by first surfing to the main Google Search page at www.google.com. If you are not already logged in to your Google account, do so now. Click the downward-facing arrow for Settings. This is located in the top-right section of the window, next to your login information. Select Search Settings from the drop-down menu that appears.

After you've logged in to your Google account you can set your global search preferences. Figure 9-1 shows the top half of the Google Search Preferences page.

> ► You can also access the Google Search Preferences page directly by typing www.google.com/preferences into the address bar of your web browser.

WARNING Changes you make on the Google Search Preferences page are global. They affect every Google product you use anytime you are logged in to your account. If you want to make a one-time change, use the tools on the Advanced Search page of the search service you're using.

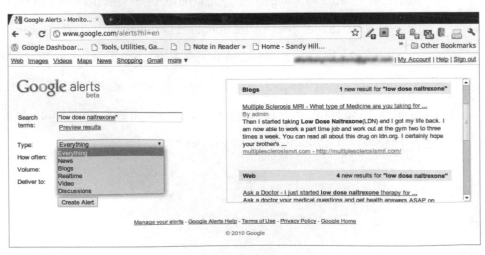

FIGURE 9-1: The top half of the Google Search Preferences page.

Use the first section, entitled Interface Language, to set the language in which messages and tips are displayed. This only changes the language of the left navigation bar, top of screen links, and displayed search tips and suggestions. It does not change the language of search results. All the world's major languages are included in the list, along with a couple of fun choices for the computer geek in us all. Some examples include the following:

▶ English

▶ French

▶ Greek

▶ Albanian

▶ Afrikaans

▶ Klingon

▶ Pirate

▶ You must have cookies enabled for customized settings to take effect.

The section called Search Language lets you choose the language of the returned search results. This does not change the language, but instead searches for results to your search query that are published in the language you specify.

The next section is where you set your Location. This tells Google where you are when you execute a local search. Location is used by Google Product Search, Google Maps, and anytime you search for an item within the standard Google Search page. Google also may use this information to help target the paid advertisements you see.

The SafeSearch Filtering section lets you set image filtering. I talk about this in depth in the following section of this chapter.

The next section is called Number of Results. This sets the number of results you see per page. The default number is 10, and this gives you the fastest search. But you can use the drop-down menu to set the number of results per page to see 10, 20, 30, 50, or 100 results per page. Remember, the more results shown per page, the longer the initial search time.

If you prefer to have the results page open in a new window, check the box labeled Open Search Results in a New Browser Window. You find this checkbox in the section labeled Results Window.

And, finally, the last section is Google Instant. Google Instant is the feature that predicts your search terms and results as you type into the search bar. You can alter or eliminate the predicted results by removing items in your web history. I discuss this in a minute.

Below the Global Settings you find Subscribed Links. Subscribed Links give you increased customization through specialized search sources. Google suggests Subscribed Links based on your common searches and the popularity of certain Subscribed Links. You can subscribe to the suggested options or look through the Subscribed Links directory and choose for yourself.

Two links take you to the Subscribed Links Directory. Each link lands on a different page of the directory. The first link is next to the heading Your Subscribed Links. If you are currently subscribed to any links your subscriptions are listed under this heading and you can click Manage to go to a page from which you can view all the links to which you have subscribed. You can unsubscribe from any or all with one click. If you are currently not subscribed to any links, the Manage link takes you to a page from which you can set up your subscriptions.

If you prefer, you can choose from these suggested, top-rated links or use the links in the left navigation bar to explore the many categories and find the perfect match for how you use Google Search.

The second link from the Preferences page is Popular Subscribed Links. The link appears to the right of this heading, and under this heading are subscription buttons to the three most popular subscribed links. Click Subscribed Links Directory to surf to an uncategorized list of all available Subscribed Links. (See Figure 9-2.)

FIGURE 9-2: All categories list of Subscribed Links.

To see a detailed explanation of what each Subscribed Link does, simply click its title. Many links have an associated website for even more in-depth information. Click the Subscribe button to add a Subscribed Link to your Google Search. Some Subscribed Links that I have found helpful include the following:

- **unix manpages**—Gives direct links to online documentation for specific Unix and Linux distributions.

- **Weather Radar**—Lets you type **weather** followed by city name or ZIP code. You get a radar map of the designated area in your search results.

- **TrainCheck**—Find out the timing of the next few trains at your stop. Know if your train is on time before you go out to meet it.

- **GasBuddy**—Up-to-date gas prices for your local area. Helps you find the lowest gas prices.

- **Merriam-Webster Online**—Save time when you need to look up a word. Just type the word into Google Search. This Subscribed Link automatically checks the dictionary.

- **Flight Status/Flight Tracker**—If you have a frequent flyer in your life this helps you know if their flight is on time or delayed.

- **CalorieLab**—Automatically returns nutritional values when a food item is entered into the Google search bar.

- **CheatCodesGuides.com**—Find the most recent cheat codes available on the Web.

Editing Auto-Complete Settings

As I mentioned earlier in this section, you can optimize your search results and make auto-complete more accurate by altering your saved web history. Access your web history from the Preferences page by clicking the link called Web History within the Google Instant section.

The Google search engine uses the information on this page to predict your intended search phrase while you type in the search box. By removing search history items, you change the data that is available and, therefore, alter the auto-complete predictions. To remove items individually, click Remove Items in the left navigation bar. Tick the checkbox immediately in front of the item you want to remove. Click the Remove button toward the top of the page. You can remove more than one item at a time. Figure 9-3 shows an example.

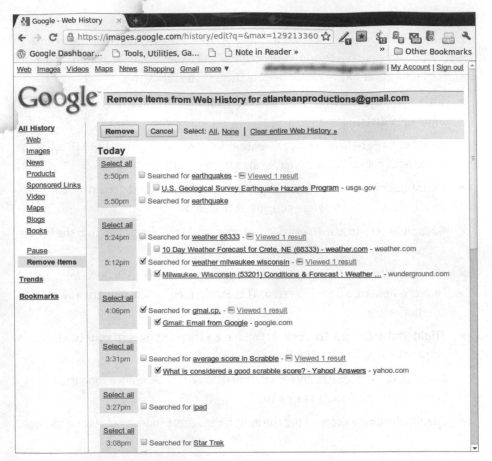

FIGURE 9-3: Remove web history items individually.

You can repeat this process for each type of Google search (Images, News, Products, and so on). Select the search type from the left navigation bar, and tick the checkboxes associated with any searches you want to remove. Or, select All History and edit the history of all your Google searches at once.

When you want to execute a Google search but don't want that search recorded in your history, click Pause in the left navigation menu. This suspends web history collection until you log back in to the web history page and click Resume.

To completely turn off search customization, go to the standard Google Search page. Execute a search. Find the link for Web History on the top right side, next to your login information. From here, you can turn off search customization, but you can always turn it back on by following the same steps as described in the last sentence.

Using SafeSearch

It's a fact: Sexually explicit material is easily available on the Internet. It's also a fact that it is easy to block that type of content if you would rather not stumble across it. Google's SafeSearch feature allows you to block sexually graphic materials with one click. Google's SafeSearch tools also enable you to lock your settings, so that those settings are inaccessible to anyone who does not have your password. As an added layer of protection, there is a graphic cue, visible from across the room, that lets you see at a glance if your filters are still active.

Turn on SafeSearch from the Search Preferences page, www.google.com/preferences. You find SafeSearch directly under the Location section. To block all sexually explicit images and text, select the first option, Strict Filtering. The second option, Moderate Filtering, blocks only images. This is the default setting. To turn off filtering completely, choose the last option, Do Not Filter My Results.

Your selection is saved both in your Google account and on your computer as a cookie. This gives you protection regardless of whether you are signed in to your Google account. However, if you are not logged in to your Google account, simply clearing your cookies removes your filter choices. Filter protection resumes while you are logged in to your Google account.

SafeSearch Lock enables you to lock your Strict Filter settings with a password. To lock your settings, select Use Strict Filtering. Now, click the link under the filtering selections entitled Lock SafeSearch. Enter your account password when prompted. Click the button labeled Lock SafeSearch. Google now strictly filters every search across all Google search services. With SafeSearch locked, your search pages now show several colored balls in the upper-right corner of the screen. This is your visual indication that SafeSearch strict filtering is active and locked. See Figure 9-4 for an example.

> **WARNING** If you use more than one browser, the lock takes effect only within the browser you used to make the change. You must go through this process from within each browser for which you want SafeSearch to be effective. Additionally, you must follow these steps for each profile on the computer.

Google Labs Search Experiments

Google Labs is the place to find the next great Google feature or application. This is where Google programmers release features and applications that are still under development. Google users who choose to use the items in Labs serve as beta testers, and provide feedback to the Google programmers. Sometimes Labs experiments become full-featured applications. Google Docs is one such application. Other times there is not enough interest and the project is discontinued, like Google Notes.

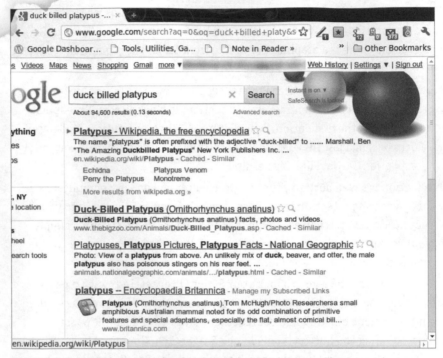

FIGURE 9-4: Visual indication that SafeSearch is locked in strict filtering mode.

▶ Be sure to
poke around
Google Labs at
www.googlelabs.com
to see what the
Google programmers
are up to. I'm sure
you can find some-
thing new and cool
every time you visit.

▶ You can join only
one experiment at
a time.

NOTE Keep in mind that all Google Labs projects, including the Search Experiments, change often as Google programmers add features and fix bugs. Anything in Google Labs can disappear at any time without warning.

Search Experiments are search functions that Google releases within Google Labs. Search experiments range from the Indic Music Search, which searches the Web for Hindi music, to Gesture Search, which enables you to control your Android device by drawing alphabet gestures on your screen. See for yourself the cool Search Experiments Google Lab has for you at www.googlelabs.com/?tags=search. This takes you to Search Experiment applications like Google Squared. To access search experiments that affect the way basic search works, click the link for Search Experiments in the right naviga-tion menu. See Figure 9-5 to help you locate the link.

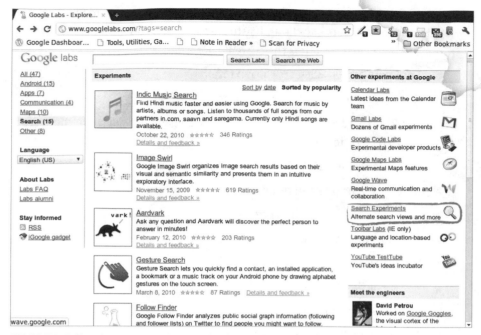

FIGURE 9-5: Try alternate search views, keyboard shortcuts, and more with Google Search Experiments.

Aside from increasing productivity and making searches more effective, using Google Search Experiments, and Google Labs in general, is simply fun. Here is a list of my current favorite Google Search experiments. The first two are found on www.google.com/experimental/ and the rest are apps from www.googlelabs .com/?tags=search.

▶ **Keyboard Shortcuts**—Lets you navigate your search pages with minimal mouse use. When Keyboard Shortcuts is activated you can use the following shortcuts:

  ▷ **J**—Selects the next result

  ▷ **K**—Selects previous result

  ▷ **O**—Opens selected result

  ▷ **Enter**—Opens selected result

  ▷ **/**—Places cursor in search box

  ▷ **Esc**—Removes cursor from search box

- **Accessible View**—Gives you all the functionality of the Keyboard Shortcuts, with added shortcuts and the ability to magnify items for easier viewing. Currently Accessible View offers the current shortcuts:

  - ▷ **J** or **Down arrow** — Selects the next item

  - ▷ **K** or **Up arrow** — Selects previous item

  - ▷ **L** or **Right arrow** — Moves to the next search page section (from sponsored ads to results, for example)

  - ▷ **H** or **Left arrow** — Move to previous search page section

  - ▷ **Enter** — Opens selected result

  - ▷ **/** — Places cursor in search box

  - ▷ **N** — Moves to next result

  - ▷ **P** — Moves to previous result

  - ▷ **=** — Magnifies current item

  - ▷ **–** — Shrinks current item

  - ▷ **A** — Turns on Accessible Search Results

  - ▷ **W** — Turns off Accessible Search Results and returns to standard results

- **Aardvark**—Ask questions within a network. Type your question, and Aardvark finds a real person to answer your question. You receive an answer in a couple of minutes.

- **Image Swirl**—Organize results of image search based on how similar the images are. Images are presented in a mind map form.

- **Google Squared**—Organize search results in a grid for easy comparison. Google Squared is discussed in Chapter 5.

- **Google Code Search**—Find sample code and definitions of functions easily.

- **DataWiki**—Structured data in the form of a wiki.

CREATING A GOOGLE CUSTOM SEARCH

▶ The CSE homepage is www .google.com/cse/.

Together, Google search tools provide a powerful way to find the information you need. But, sometimes the information you're looking for is very specialized, obscure, or just plain hard to find. That's when a Google Custom Search Engine comes in handy.

Custom Search Engine, or CSE, puts to use Google's powerful search technologies you've come to rely on such as the following:

► Auto-complete functions

► Website ranking

► Google indexing

► Synonyms

These technologies, when combined with the ability to search exactly the pages or websites you want, provide more relevant search results in less time than using Advanced Search. And, after you create a CSE it is there for you to use until you decide to remove it. When you use Google's Advanced Search Page, you must redefine your search each time you use it.

How does CSE help you complete your work faster? Say you're an undergraduate college student studying biochemistry and you are writing a paper on plant viruses. You could search 50 different scientific websites individually, and do a Google Scholar search to find relevant papers, but, really, who has that kind of time? It's faster and easier to set up a CSE to search those 50 websites and Google Scholar for your search terms at the same time. Then, later when you have another paper to do, you can use the same CSE to search those same 50 websites and Google Scholar for the topic of your next paper.

Using a CSE isn't limited to college research. If you search any website or group of websites on a regular basis, CSE can save you time.

Creating a Customized Search Engine

Google provides a handy wizard for CSE creation. This wizard is at www.google.com/ cse/manage/create. This page, shown in Figure 9-6, is all you need to create a powerful Custom Search Engine.

First, give your search engine a name. Because the CSE you create is saved in your profile for later use, be sure the name is something you'll recognize later.

Next type in a description of the search. Define what the search is about.

Use the Language drop-down to select the language in which results should be written.

The next box, called Sites to Search, is the important part. This is where you tell the search engine exactly what websites or web pages to search. Only those URLs listed in this box are searched. List only one URL per line. Enter URLs using the following formatting guidelines: ʹ\

▶ To include an entire domain use **thisdomain.com**.

▶ If you type **www.thisdomain.com/nameofpage.html** that is the only page on that website that will be searched.

▶ Use wildcards to search specific parts of a website. To search all pages on a website that have plant in the page name, you would type **www.thisdomain.com/*plant***.

▶ To search a whole website use **www.thiswebsite.com/***.

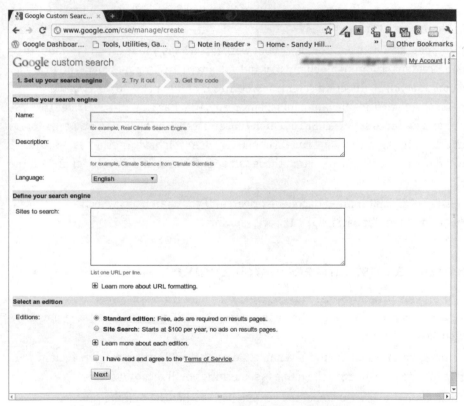

FIGURE 9-6: The Google Custom Search Engine setup page.

When you have finished entering the URLs of websites and web pages you want to search, use the following section to choose between the free and paid editions of

Google Custom Search Engine. The free version displays ads on search results, and the paid edition removes the ads.

Read the terms of service and, if you agree, tick the checkbox.

Finally, click the button labeled Next.

On the following page, you can choose a style and customize the look of the page. Use the tabs to change the color and font of the different page aspects. Use the Results tab to determine how the URL of result websites are displayed. Choose between full URL and domain name only.

When you're satisfied with the look of your search page, click Next.

The next page contains the JavaScript code created to run your new search engine. Figure 9-7 shows the final page of the CSE creation wizard.

Copy all the code in the box and paste it into the page where the CSE is to run. This can be your website or simply an HTML file stored on your computer. You can even save it as HTML in your Google Docs account. When you want to run this search engine, just open the page, enter your desired search words, and click Search.

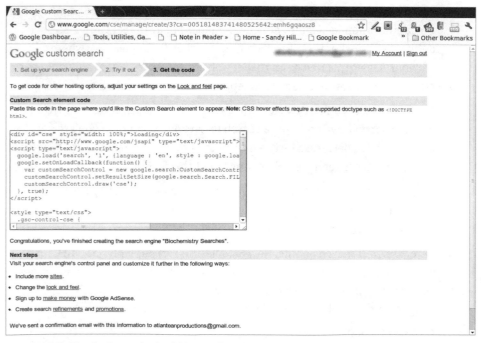

FIGURE 9-7: The final page in the CSE creation wizard.

Configuring Google Site Search

Google Site Search is a specialized CSE. With Google Site Search, visitors to your website can search within your site and find the information they need quickly. Google Site Search is a paid service for business websites. Because Google Site Search is a paid service, ads are not displayed on the search results page. Pricing is based on the number of search queries you expect users to execute. The Google Site Search homepage is at www.google.com/sitesearch/.

Google Site Search is not available in as many languages as the traditional Google search is, so you need to visit the previously mentioned URL and check the top-right corner for available languages.

Configuring Google Site Search is a process that involves four major steps; be sure to sign in to your Google account first before proceeding. On www.google.com/sitesearch/, click on the large Add Google Site Search button on the right side and follow these four steps:

1. Set up your search engine. Here, you need to provide Google with some basic information about the kind of search engine you want to build for your website. Google asks you for a name and a description of your search engine, as well as the language (again, not all languages are available). You also need to define the sites that this search engine searches (the domains), where you can list your website, as well as any other website you want your search engine to crawl through. You also need to accept the Google terms of service.

2. Try it out. Here, you can preview what your search engine looks like from both a design perspective and from a search results perspective. If you are not satisfied after you perform a test search on the provided search bar, go back to Step 1 and modify your search engine to get the desired results.

3. Provide contact information. Google needs to collect some basic personal information to be able to provide technical support for you in the future, if necessary. Enter in all requested information here.

4. Purchase your search engine. Now it comes time to put your hand in your pocket and bring out your credit card. As mentioned earlier, Google charges you based upon your search query volume. At the time of this writing, Google's current pricing model looks like this:

   ▷ Up to 20,000 queries per year: $100

   ▷ Up to 50,000 queries per year: $250

   ▷ Up to 150,000 queries per year: $750

   ▷ Up to 500,000 queries per year: $2,000

Choose the plan that you think works best for your website, and proceed to purchase your search engine (Google provides you with a shopping cart via Google Checkout to make your purchase).

After you make your purchase, you can install the Google Site Search on your website.

SEARCHING AUTOMATICALLY WITH GOOGLE ALERTS

Google has its own automatic search alert service. Like all Google search-based services, Google Alerts is free. You have two ways to access Google Alerts. First, you can surf there directly at www.google.com/alerts. Or, if you'd rather, you can surf there through Google Account Settings. From your main Google search page, click the Settings arrow. Select Google Account Settings from the drop-down menu. On the resulting page, look for Alerts in the My Products list. If you don't see a link for Alerts, scroll down the page and find the Try Something New section. Look for the Alerts link there and click it.

> **NOTE** There has been a bit of confusion regarding the service known as Google Alert. The website parked at the URL **www.googlealert.com** is owned by Indigo Stream Technologies, the same company that owns Copyscape. At this web address Indigo Stream Technologies operated a fee-based service it called Google Alert. This service enabled users to create ongoing and automatic searches on a topic. When new results were located for the user's keywords, the user received an e-mail alert. In August of 2009 Indigo Stream Technologies changed the name of its alert service to GigaAlert. It still operates GigaAlert at the URL **www.googlealert.com**. The service hosted at this website is not now, nor ever has been, owned by Google.

Creating Alerts

After you navigate to the Google Alerts homepage, type the search term for which you would like to set alerts in the box labeled Search Terms. Click Preview Results to see a sample of results returned by your search term. Using search preview is optional, but it is extremely helpful in ensuring that you receive the type of results you desire.

> **TIP** All previously discussed search techniques are valid here as well.

When you find the search term that returns the results you want, use the drop-down menu labeled Type to select the type of information you need. Figure 9-8 shows the Google Alerts page with this drop-down menu expanded.

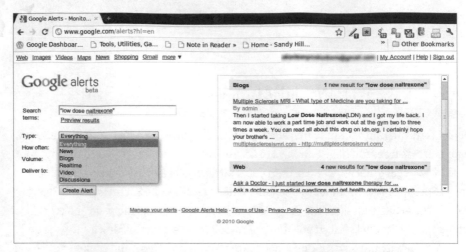

FIGURE 9-8: Google Alerts homepage with the Type drop-down menu expanded.

With the second drop-down menu, set the frequency of alerts. Choose from once a day, once a week, or as it happens.

The drop-down labeled Volume enables you to decide if you want to be alerted to all the results, or only the best results. Here, the best results seem to be defined as the most popular and most relevant to your search term.

Finally, decide if you want to receive alerts in your e-mail inbox or as an RSS feed.

When you're finished, click Create Alert. You are taken to the page titled Manage Your Alerts where you can see all of your Google Alerts at a glance.

Changing and Managing Alerts

Managing Google Alerts is as easy as setting them. Now that you have an alert set you can access the Manage Your Alerts page in three ways. First, simply go to the Google Alerts homepage as described earlier and look for the link that reads Click Here to Manage Your Alerts. Or, go to your Google Account Settings page and look for Alerts in the My Products list. If you prefer, you can type `www.google.com/alerts/manage` into your browser's address bar. Figure 9-9 shows this page.

To change an alert, click Edit at the right side of the screen. Use the drop-down menus on the resulting page to alter the type, frequency, volume, and delivery method of the alert. If you must alter the search terms, type the new search term in the textbox. When you're finished making changes, click Save.

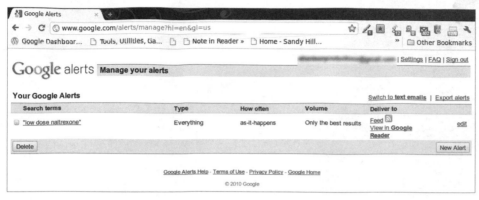

FIGURE 9-9: Managing Google Alerts.

To delete an alert, tick the checkbox in front of the alert you want to remove, and click the Delete button under your last alert.

Use the link above your alerts to switch between receiving alert e-mails in HTML or plain text.

SUMMARY

With Google you have access to some of the most powerful search technology available. Specialized tools such as Customized Search Engine and Google Alerts help you to keep on top of the latest important-to-you information without spending a lot of time searching. Custom search preferences and Google's SafeSearch help keep you and your family feeling safe and comfortable with online content. Google Labs Search Experiments continues to push the limits of what is possible with search and provides users with cutting-edge search technology. All these features make Google Search the most personalized search engine available.

Part III

GOOGLE GMAIL SECRETS

Harnessing the Power of a Gmail Account

Sure, Gmail is a great e-mail server. Very little down-time and super-effective SPAM filters make Gmail one of the best mail servers available. But, have you ever thought about Gmail as your primary mail client? Gmail has all the functionality of expensive e-mail programs with none of the hassle. You can change your signature, use multiple signatures, and even import e-mail from any existing email accounts, all from the comfort of Gmail. Labels, multiple views, excellent search abilities, and enhancements from Google Labs are only some of the features that make Gmail not only my e-mail server, but also my preferred e-mail client as well.

RATCHETING UP PRODUCTIVITY WITH GOOGLE LABS AND GADGETS

▶ The URL for the Google Labs site is simple: googlelabs.com. Bookmark it and start playing with Google's experiments!

As I mentioned in Chapter 9, Google Labs is where you find new and experimental add-ons for various Google services. You can find Gmail-specific labs through either the Google Labs homepage or through your Gmail homepage.

From the Google Labs homepage, click the link for Gmail Labs in the right-hand section entitled Other Experiments at Google. From your Gmail page click the green beaker icon in the upper right, directly between your login information and the Settings link.

Because so many cool Labs are available, Google makes it easier to keep track of which Labs you've installed. Labs that you've enabled are listed first under the heading Enabled Labs. Those Labs that you are not using are found further down the page under the heading Available Labs.

The Google programming team adds new toys regularly. Here are some of my current favorites:

- **Send & Archive**—Adds a button that sends your e-mail and then archives the conversation.

- **Google Calendar gadget**—Adds your Google Calendar to the bottom of the left-hand navigation bar.

- **Got the wrong Bob?**—Confirms you are including the correct person when you have people with the same first name. This works only if you are e-mailing two or more people.

- **Create a Document**—Open a Google Docs document from your Gmail. You must have keyboard shortcuts enabled. Press G, then W.

- **Auto-advance**—Shows the next message in your Inbox after you delete, archive, or mute a conversation.

- **Custom keyboard shortcuts**—Enables you to define your own Gmail keyboard shortcuts.

- **Superstars**—Add more icons for organizing your Gmail. Enables you to sort and search by icon.

- **Nested labels**—Organize e-mail using labels with the hierarchy method. For example, you can use the label Work, and then place the labels Meetings and Paperwork within the Work label.

These are only a few of the Gmail Labs available. Sometimes a Labs feature may graduate to become a built-in feature; others may simply go away. Still others remain in Labs indefinitely, operating as opt-in features of Gmail. To activate any Lab, click its corresponding Enable button. Be sure to save your changes.

Always keep in mind that the toys in Google Labs are still in the experimental stages. As with any experiment, sometimes things can go wrong. If one of the Google Labs selections misbehaves and makes it difficult to load your Inbox, use the following URL to get past the problem so you can disable the offending Lab: `https://mail .google.com/mail/u/0.?labs=0`. (Be sure to be logged in to your Google account prior to using this URL).

As if Google Labs alone doesn't give you enough cool things to play with, you can also add any Gadget to your Gmail page by simply entering the URL of the Gadget into the Gadget tab.

To activate the Gadget tab, click Settings from within Gmail, and then click Labs. Look for the Lab project called Add Any Gadget by URL. Select Enable, and save your settings.

As discussed in Chapter 2, you can find ready-to-go Gadgets at `www.google.com/ ig/directory`, or you can make your own using the instructions in Chapter 2.

Though not a Lab feature or a Google Gadget, every Gmail power user needs the list of keyboard shortcuts handy. Before you can use keyboard shortcuts in Gmail, you must enable them in your Gmail settings. From within Gmail click Settings. The controls for keyboard shortcuts are three sections down from the top. Turn on shortcuts and save your changes. And, remember you can designate your preferred keyboard shortcuts with Custom Keyboard Shortcuts in Google Labs. For your convenience, Table 10-1 provides a full list of Gmail keyboard shortcuts for you.

▶ Keyboard shortcuts work in most browsers and on most operating systems, but not all. For example, Gmail keyboard shortcuts do not work in the Chromium web browser on Ubuntu Linux. However, when using Firefox on the same Ubuntu system, keyboard shortcuts work fine.

TABLE 10-1: Gmail Keyboard Shortcuts

KEY COMBINATION	ACTION
C	Composes new message.
Shift C	Composes new message in a new window.
/	Places cursor in the search box.
K	Moves cursor to a more recent conversation.
Enter or O	Opens the selected message. Also closes the message in Conversation view.
J	Moves cursor to the next oldest conversation.

continues

TABLE 10-1: *(continued)*

KEY COMBINATION	ACTION
N	Moves cursor to the next message. Available only in Conversation View.
P	Moves cursor to the previous message. Available only in Conversation View.
U	Refreshes page and returns to Inbox.
E	Archives conversation. Works in any view.
M	Archives conversation and all future messages; skips the Inbox unless addressed directly to you.
X	Selects conversation so that you can work with it.
S	Applies Star to message or conversation.
+	Marks as important.
_	Marks as unimportant.
!	Marks message as spam and removes it from conversation list.
R	Replies to message sender.
Shift R	Replies in new window.
A	Replies all.
Shift A	Replies all in a new window.
F	Forwards message.
Shift F	Forwards message in new window.
Esc	Removes cursor from current input field.
Ctrl S	Saves to Drafts when composing a message.
#	Deletes.
L	Opens the Labels menu so you can label a conversation.
V	Moves conversation to a different folder/label.
Shift I	Marks message as read.
Shift U	Marks message as unread.
[	Archives current conversation and moves to previous one.
]	Archives current conversation and moves to next one.

TABLE 10-1: *(continued)*

KEY COMBINATION	ACTION
Z	Undoes last action. Works only for actions that have an "undo" link.
Shift N	Updates current conversation when there are new messages.
Q	Moves cursor to chat search box.
Y	Removes message from current view. Moves messages from Inbox to Archive, from Starred to Unstarred, from Trash to Inbox, or makes a labeled message unlabeled.
.	Displays drop-down menu titled More Actions.
Ctrl down arrow	Opens Chat options.
?	Displays keyboard shortcuts help.
K	Moves up a contact in contact list.
J	Moves down a contact in contact list.
O or Enter	In contact list, opens contact with cursor next to it.
U	In contact list, refreshes page and returns you to contact list
E	Removes selected contacts from the currently displayed group.
X	Selects contact so you can work with entry.
#	In contacts, permanently deletes contact.
L	Opens groups button to group contacts.
Tab then Enter	Sends message.
Y then O	Archives message, moves to next message.
G then A	Takes you to All Mail.
G then S	Lists all Starred conversations.
G then C	Goes to Contact list.
G then D	Opens Drafts page.
G then L	Moves to search box with "label" search operator filled in.
G then I	Returns to Inbox.
G then T	Takes you to Sent Mail page.
* then A	Selects all mail.

TABLE 10-1: *(continued)*

KEY COMBINATION	ACTION
* then N	Deselects all mail.
* then R	Selects all mail marked as Read.
* then U	Selects all unread mail.
* then S	Selects all starred mail.
* then T	Selects all unstarred mail.

SETTING PREFERENCES FOR POWER USERS

Individual preferences are what make the world go 'round. Google gives users the ability to change the way Gmail organizes and displays messages. Colored and nesting labels help you organize mail in a way that makes sense to you. And mail fetching lets you get mail from other accounts without ever having to leave your Gmail page. If you want individuality, look no further.

Customizing the Way You View and Send Gmail

Threaded message viewing is one of those things that most users love. Or hate. There doesn't seem to be much in between. No matter which message layout you prefer, you can get what you want with Gmail.

Obviously Threaded, or Conversation, view is the Gmail default. Use Gmail Settings to change it to the more familiar "most recent first" view. In the General tab, six entries down, find the heading Conversation View. Select Conversation View Off.

For even more customization in how incoming messages appear, use the Snippets heading on the same page to show the first line of incoming e-mail. Snippets can help you determine if you need to read that e-mail right now, or if it can wait a few minutes.

Gmail also lets you choose an image to display when you send e-mail. Find the section titled My Picture and click the link Select a Picture. Use the resulting window to navigate to the image you'd like to share. You can use images stored on your local system, your Picasa web album, or hosted on a specific URL.

Sometimes you might prefer to designate which photos you see for your contacts instead of seeing the photos they've picked. To avoid seeing that picture of a tipsy Aunt Mabel dancing with the dining room chair last Thanksgiving, you can turn off images other people have chosen to display along with their e-mail addresses. Select Only Show Pictures That I've Chosen for My Contacts in the section named Contacts' Pictures.

DELEGATE OTHERS TO SEND E-MAIL IN YOUR PLACE

Until recently, Gmail Delegation was available only to paid subscribers, but now it's available to anyone who uses Gmail. Gmail Delegation gives you the ability to appoint someone else limited access to your Gmail account. The appointed party can send, delete, and read e-mail for you but has no access to any other Google App you use. The delegate also can't change your account settings or your password. Your appointee does not have access to your Google chat window. You can designate up to ten people as your appointees. To avoid any confusion about who really sent that e-mail, anytime an appointee logs in and sends an e-mail for you. Gmail lists the sender as Account Holder (sent by appointee's Name).

To enable Gmail Delegation, do the following:

1. Access your Gmail Settings. Choose Accounts and Import from the top navigation. Look for Grant Access to Your Account.

2. Click Add Another Account.

3. In the pop-up window, type your appointee's e-mail address. Click the button labeled Next Step.

4. Verify you have typed the e-mail address correctly. Click Send E-mail to Grant Access.

> **NOTE** Appointees must use https to log in to your Gmail account. Additionally, the email address needs to be a Gmail account as well.

Gmail will send your appointee an e-mail asking him or her to confirm the appointment. Access is granted after the appointee responds to the confirmation e-mail.

To take away access, navigate to the Accounts and Imports page, find Grant Access to Your Account, and click Delete next to the name of the appointee you want to remove.

USING MULTIPLE VIEWS, LABELS, AND SIDE-BY-SIDE SEARCHES

One of the most common questions I'm asked about Gmail is how to access the preview pane. Google doesn't have a built-in preview pane like some other e-mail programs do. Personally, I don't miss it, but if you just don't feel complete without a preview pane, Google Labs gives you a couple options.

Auto-advance by Bruce D (found within Google Labs) lets you skip the Inbox completely when you're reading new messages. When enabled, Auto-advance opens the next message after you archive, mute, or delete the message you're currently viewing. The settings let you choose between opening the next message or the previous message or going back to threaded messages.

Also in Google Labs, Message Sneak Peek, by Manu C and Jonathan K, enables you to right-click a message to see a preview. You can archive, delete, or mark the message as read right from the preview window. For threads that contain more than one conversation, use the arrows on the right to read each conversation. Or, click the link View Entire Thread to open the thread. Take a look at Figure 10-1 to see Message Sneak Peek in action.

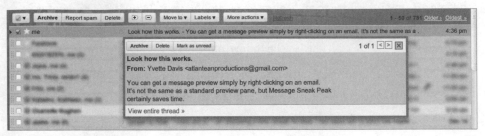

FIGURE 10-1: Message Sneak Peek lets you read e-mails without opening them.

Sometimes you may need to open more than one Gmail component at a time, for instance if you are typing an e-mail and need information located in another e-mail. Press the Shift key and click to open a second (or more) instance of Gmail. A new window opens and takes you directly to whatever you clicked on. See Figure 10-2.

TIP If you need to search more than one folder/label to compare information, Shift-clicking is the fastest way to accomplish the job.

I admit it. I am organizationally challenged. People who can keep their desk, Inbox, and everyday paperwork sorted into neat sections amaze me. But, Gmail helps me keep track of my e-mail and those tasks that are related to e-mails I receive.

Of course you know about labels; they are Gmail's answer to folders and they are used in most Google Apps. Have you ever wished you could label an e-mail with a parent/child label?

Thanks to Google Labs, you can. Navigate to Labs from within Gmail and enable Nested Labels by Manu C. Save your settings. Now, when you add a new label you have

▶ To change the color of a label, click the square directly in front of the label name in the left navigation bar. A menu displays with options for that label, including a color picker.

the option of entering a label nested within another label. Tick the message to which you want to add the new label. Click Labels to open the drop-down menu. Click New. Type in the top-level label followed by a forward slash and then type the second-level label (for example, To Do/appointment). Figure 10-3 shows the New Label window.

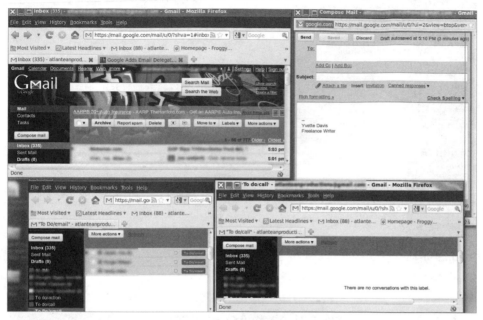

FIGURE 10-2: Four working Gmail windows opened with Shift-clicking.

FIGURE 10-3: Adding a nested label.

Alternatively, click the square in front of the label to which you're adding the child label. From the menu that appears, click Add Child Label. Refer to Figure 10-4 for help finding the menu.

FIGURE 10-4: Use the menu to add a nested label.

Fetching E-mail from Other Accounts

As a society, we're pretty centered around e-mail. Almost every person I know uses more than one e-mail account. Most people have a personal account either through their ISP or a free e-mail service such as Gmail. If you're a college student you probably have an e-mail account through your school, and a good number of employers require their employees to use and maintain a work e-mail. Many computer virus experts recommend keeping a second e-mail account to manage all your e-mail lists and public postings. So, that leaves the average computer-savvy person with at least two, if not three or more, e-mail addresses. Having to regularly check multiple e-mail addresses is a pain, and probably a main reason people use a standalone e-mail client.

With Gmail you can fetch mail from any POP-enabled mail server. Not all mail servers allow POP access, so be sure to check with your system administrator or the FAQ page of your other e-mail accounts.

To set up mail fetching in Gmail, first navigate to the Accounts and Import tab within Gmail Settings.

Look for Check Mail Using POP3. Click the button labeled Add POP3 Email Account.

In the window that opens, enter the e-mail address for which you want Gmail to fetch mail. Gmail can check up to six accounts.

Figure 10-5 shows both the Add POP 3 button and the screen on which you add your first e-mail account.

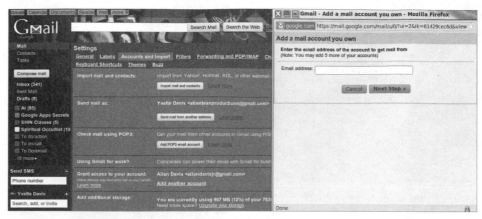

FIGURE 10-5: Add POP3 Email Account, and enter e-mail address to fetch e-mail.

On the next screen, shown in Figure 10-6, enter your password and choose the protocol used by your POP e-mail service. If you're unsure of the protocol, check the provider's FAQ or call tech support. Select the port your computer uses for e-mail.

If you want to leave a copy of retrieved messages on the POP server, tick the box.

The next box asks if Gmail should use a secure connection while fetching mail. Though not a requirement, sticking to SSL is usually a good idea.

Do you want Gmail to apply a specific label to help you identify e-mail that comes from your POP account? If so, tick the box, and use the drop-down menu to choose an existing label, or create a new one.

Finally you can choose to send all e-mails from the POP account directly to your e-mail Archive without having them land in your Inbox.

When you're finished, click Add Account. Depending on your browser and settings you may be asked if your browser should remember the password you entered for your POP e-mail.

The next step is to decide if you want to send e-mail from the POP account from within Gmail. If you Check NO, you are finished. If you check YES, you have a few more steps.

Enter the name you want to appear in the Sent From field when mail is sent from the POP address. You can also change the e-mail address that shows in the Sent From field. Click the blue link to do this. Click Next Step.

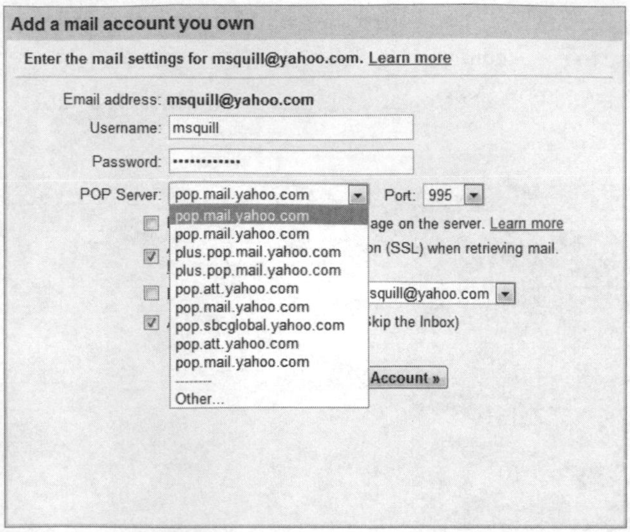

Add a mail account you own

Enter the mail settings for msquill@yahoo.com. Learn more

Email address: **msquill@yahoo.com**

Username: msquill

Password: ••••••••••••

POP Server: pop.mail.yahoo.com ▾   Port: 995 ▾

pop.mail.yahoo.com
pop.mail.yahoo.com
plus.pop.mail.yahoo.com
plus.pop.mail.yahoo.com
pop.att.yahoo.com
pop.mail.yahoo.com
pop.sbcglobal.yahoo.com
pop.att.yahoo.com
pop.mail.yahoo.com
————
Other...

age on the server. Learn more

on (SSL) when retrieving mail.

squill@yahoo.com ▾

Skip the Inbox)

Account »

FIGURE 10-6: Enter mail settings for the account you are fetching.

Complete the verification process, and you're done. If you need to edit or remove the POP account, look for the Edit Info and Delete links on the Accounts and Imports page under the same POP3 heading.

Managing Where Your Messages Are Sent From

Now that you've added a POP account you can send e-mail from either your Gmail account or the POP account(s) you've added. Sign into Gmail and click Compose Mail. Above the To field there is now a drop-down menu. Use this menu to choose the e-mail account from which the e-mail is sent.

Using Multiple Powerful Signatures

Signature lines let you give contact or other information at the bottom of your e-mails. When you use your Gmail account to manage multiple e-mail accounts, you can designate a unique signature for each.

To create an e-mail signature for each of your e-mail accounts, navigate to your Gmail Settings. On the General tab, look for the Signature heading, nine down from the top. Use the drop-down menu to select the e-mail account for which you are creating a signature. Type your signature line in the textbox provided. When you've finished with the first signature, use the drop-down menu to select another account, and create the signature line for that account. Be sure to save your changes when you're finished.

SENDING MAIL FASTER

Some e-mail tasks you repeat weekly, daily, or even several times a day. Things such as meeting RSVPs, weekly reports to the boss, meeting minutes, or even checking in with the family at a certain time each day are routine tasks. Although these tasks are important, they take up time that could be used for more productive (or more fun) endeavors.

There's a saying among database geeks, "Only enter information once. If you have to do it more than once, automate it!"

Gmail lets you automate your e-mail with Canned Responses and e-mail templates. Sure, using canned responses and e-mail templates may only save you few seconds. But, over the course of a day seconds add up to minutes, and minutes to hours.

Sending Mail Faster with Canned Responses

What's a Canned response? It's a message that is programmed into your e-mail or mobile phone. Instead of typing your response, you simply highlight your desired response from the list, and click Send. The response you selected is automatically entered into the body of your e-mail or text message. In the case of Gmail, Canned Responses can be short phrases like, "Okay" or "On my way," or you can write a long e-mail complete with all the formatting options offered by Gmail.

Before you can use Canned Responses, you must enable the add-on in Google Labs. After you've enabled Canned Responses a drop-down menu displays under the address field of all e-mails you compose, whether you are replying to an e-mail or composing a new one.

The first time you use Canned Responses you need to enter your desired responses:

1. Click Compose to write a new e-mail.

2. Type the e-mail that you want to automate.

3. Click the link for Canned Responses. A drop-down menu displays, as shown in Figure 10-7.

4. Select New Canned Response from the menu.

5. Enter a name for this canned response. If you entered a subject line for the e-mail that subject is auto-filled as the title.

> **TIP** When you drop a canned response into an e-mail, remove your signature line, if you have one. Gmail drops the canned response under the signature line.

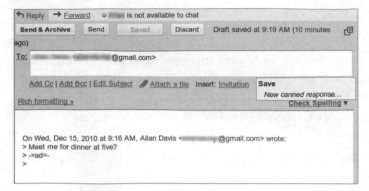

FIGURE 10-7: Canned responses drop-down menu.

To use a canned response, either compose a new e-mail or reply to an e-mail in your Inbox and then click Canned Response. Select the response you want to use from the Insert heading. Note that Canned Response feature does not auto-fill the subject line; you must do that manually. Figure 10-8 shows an inserted canned response after I removed my signature line.

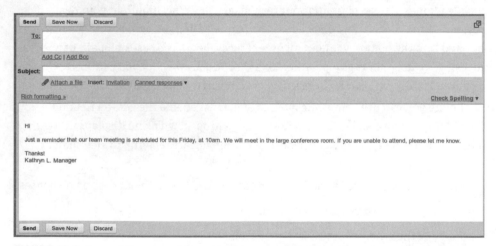

FIGURE 10-8: Canned Response dropped into a new e-mail message.

For a truly automated Gmail, write a Canned Response to be used as an auto-response. Create a new filter to identify the subject, person, or people to whom you auto-respond. On the second page of the Create a Filter process, the option to Send a Canned Response Now appears. Select the response you want to use from the drop-down menu and click Create Filter. Presto!

Creating and Using E-mail Templates

You already know word processing and website templates can save you tons of time. But, have you ever thought about creating e-mail templates? It's easy. Compose a new e-mail and spend some time using Gmail's Rich Formatting tools to get the layout just right. You can add bullet lists, links, images, change the font, add highlighting, change text colors, and so on. Save your formatted e-mail as a Canned Response. All you have to do is drop that response into an e-mail and change the data to suit your needs. Figure 10-9 shows a mock report.

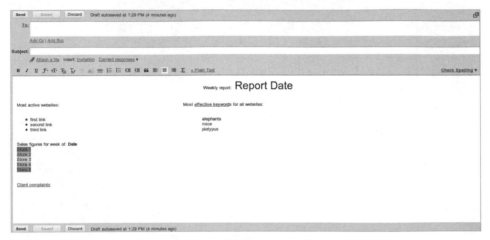

FIGURE 10-9: Use a mock report as a template for your weekly report to the boss.

SUMMARY

With Gmail you can have the space-saving features of web mail without giving up mail client features you've come to rely on. POP mail capabilities combined with color-coded nesting labels eliminates the need to go searching through multiple e-mail accounts to find what you need, which saves you precious time. Canned responses and the ability to use Shift-click to open side-by-side windows help save keystrokes. These features, combined with Gmail Labs, make Gmail a truly powerful e-mail program.

Managing Messages

Gmail isn't just for e-mail anymore. Whether you prefer to communicate by e-mail, chat, video chat, or even telephone, you never have to leave your Gmail page. You can even use Google Talk to ring multiple phones at once, so you never miss an important phone call. Organize e-mail and text messages so you can always find exactly what you're looking for using filters, colored labels, and Superstars. You can even access your calendar and task list from your Gmail page, giving you truly all-in-one communication and scheduling capabilities.

CREATING TASKS AND APPOINTMENTS FROM GMAIL MESSAGES

When you receive an e-mail from your boss or your spouse with an important date or task request it's always a good idea to add the new request to your calendar or Tasks List right away. Save time and keystrokes by adding appointments and tasks to your Google Calendar and Tasks List directly from Gmail.

You have two ways to access your Google Calendar and Tasks List from within Gmail.

The first method enables you to add any appointment mentioned in e-mail directly to Google Calendar with two clicks. When Gmail recognizes appointments in the body of an e-mail it automatically presents you with the option to add that appointment to your Google Calendar. Any time an email's body contains some mention of a date or time (even without other information, such as a location), Google passively scans the e-mail content and there is an option on the right-hand side for you to add an appointment to your calendar. Click Add to open the Google Calendar, Create Event page for the meeting. Enter details, set reminders, make it a repeating event, or share the event, if you desire. Click Save at the bottom of the page. Figure 11-1 shows an e-mail with appointment information, and the Add to Calendar option.

FIGURE 11-1: Add appointments directly from Gmail to Google Calendar with one click.

Or, if you prefer, use the Google Calendar Gadget from Google Labs. This gadget adds a working copy of your Google Calendar to the left of your Gmail Inbox, directly under Chat. To add an event, click the link below the calendar. See Figure 11-2.

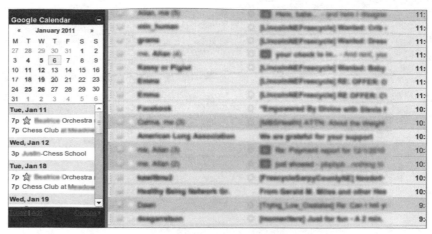

FIGURE 11-2: Embed Google Calendar into your Gmail page.

CROSSREF I talk more about Google Calendar, adding events, and managing tasks in Chapter 26.

Adding tasks to your Google Calendar Tasks list is just as simple. First, open the e-mail that contains the tasks you want to add.

Next, open the Tasks window. To do this, click Tasks in the upper left, just above the Compose Message button. A task window pops up in the lower right of the screen.

Now, in the Tasks window, click the area directly to the right of the first checkbox. This activates the line so you can type. You can either type in the task or copy and paste it from your e-mail into the space to the right of the checkbox.

Click the large plus sign (+) at the bottom of the Tasks window to add another task. The new task is added above any previous entries. Figure 11-3 shows Gmail with the Tasks list open.

You can also add an e-mail to your Tasks list from the More Actions menu. First, select the e-mail you'd like to add. Click More Actions to open the drop-down menu and click Add to Tasks. The subject of the e-mail is automatically added to your Tasks list with a notation that there is a related e-mail.

TIP The Tasks list in Gmail is the same Tasks list you find in Google Calendar. When you add a task in Gmail, it is visible from the Tasks list in Google Calendar, and when you add a task from Calendar, it appears in Gmail Tasks as well. All features and functions are the same regardless of which app you use to add the task.

FIGURE 11-3: Add to your Tasks list directly from Gmail.

LABELING MESSAGES WITH COLOR

Colored labels let you find what you need with just a glance. In most Google Apps labels do the work of folders without the limitations of the standard folder. In Gmail the advantages of using colored labels over folders include the following:

▶ Making it easier to find what you're looking for

▶ Labeling an e-mail in more than one way

▶ Moving labeled e-mails or leaving them in your Inbox for easy reference

To create a new label and give it color, click Labels above your inbox messages. From the drop-down menu, click Manage Labels.

Scroll down to the section named Labels. Click the textbox that contains the text "Create a new label" to clear the default text and type your desired label text in the textbox. Click Create to create the new label. See Figure 11-4 for an example.

▶ If you have shortcuts turned on, type L on your keyboard to open the Label drop-down.

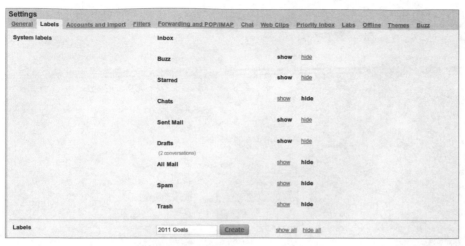

FIGURE 11-4: Create a new Gmail label.

Now, add the color. Find the newly created label in the left navigation bar, under the Compose Mail button. Click the small downward-facing arrow in the box in front of the label you want to color. (See Figure 11-5.) Click the resulting drop-down menu.

Select your desired system color from the color swatches provided. The chosen color appears in the box in front of the label, and every e-mail assigned to that label has a colored tag in front of the subject.

If you'd rather use a custom color, click Add Custom Color from the menu. As shown in Figure 11-6, a pop-up appears that enables you to choose various shades of the standard colors. For more individualization, you can set both background and text colors. So many choices assure you will never run out of color combinations, no matter how many labels you create.

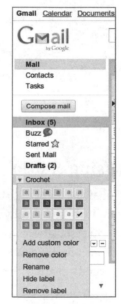

FIGURE 11-5: Open the Label drop-down menu.

NOTE For those who love using labels but use a netbook when away from home or office, you can turn labels temporarily off to conserve screen space. Navigate to your Gmail Labs page and enable the lab entitled Hide Labels from Subject. This hides all labels so you can read the entire subject line. When you return to your larger screened machine, simply return to Google Labs and disable the feature.

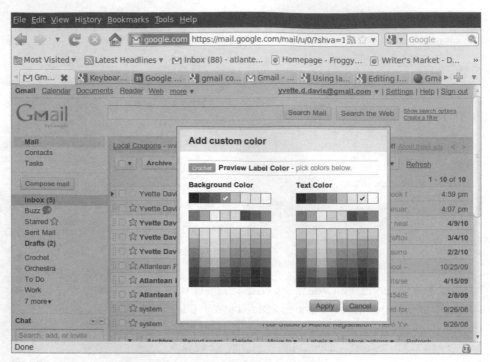

FIGURE 11-6: Custom color picker for Gmail labels.

Using Multiple Labels

Gmail enables you to tag a single e-mail with more than one label. For me, this means the ability to add already tagged e-mail to my To Do list, or mark that e-mail as forwarded to an associate. Multiple Labels is a built-in feature of Gmail. You don't need to enable or add anything; simply add the additional labels as you did the first. Figure 11-7 shows several e-mails with more than one colored label.

FIGURE 11-7: Using multiple colored labels makes organizing e-mails easy.

CROSSREF Don't forget what you learned about using nesting labels in Chapter 10.

Labeling with Drag and Drop

Save time and keystrokes by using drag and drop to label your e-mail. Click the label you want to apply and hold down the left mouse button. Then, drag the label to the e-mail to which you want to apply the label. Position the hand anywhere in the row, and release the left mouse button.

LETTING GMAIL HANDLE YOUR MAIL FOR YOU WITH FILTERS

Filters let you accomplish many things to help keep your Gmail organized. You can use individual filters to

- ▶ Add labels
- ▶ Forward to another e-mail address
- ▶ Star the message
- ▶ Delete the message
- ▶ Archive the message
- ▶ Send an automatic canned response (if enabled)
- ▶ Always or never mark as important (if enabled)

When used together, filters give you complete control over how you manage e-mail. Combine a "family appointment" label with e-mail forwarding to mark appointments and forward them to your spouse. Or use canned responses in combination with message archiving to automatically respond to those weekly reports you keep for reference, but don't actually read regularly.

To set a filter, click the Create a Filter link at the top of the page and to the right of the Search the Web button. Figure 11-8 shows the form you use to create a filter.

Fill in any or all of the filter criteria to define the filter. Use the Test Search button to ensure you return exactly the results you're looking for. When the filter gives the results you expect, click Next Step.

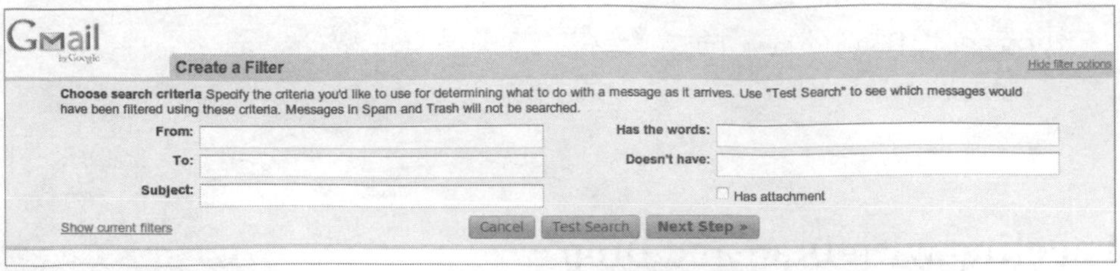

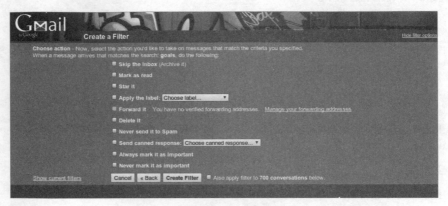

FIGURE 11-8: Use this form to set the filter criteria.

Figure 11-9 shows some of the available filter options. Keep in mind that filter options may change based on your Gmail settings and the labs you have enabled.

FIGURE 11-9: Define the action(s) to be applied to e-mails that meet the criteria.

When you're finished, click Create Filter.

TURNING YOUR GMAIL INTO AN EXTERNAL HARD DRIVE

Have you ever wanted to save a file online in case you need it while you're away from your computer? GmailDrive lets you assign your Gmail account a drive letter so you can easily transfer files to and from your computer. After files are stored on Gmail-Drive, you can access stored files through standard, web-based Gmail.

GmailDrive is freeware and you can download it here: www.viksoe.dk/code/gmail.htm. Be sure to read the install instructions, warnings, and product updates.

After it's installed, GmailDrive creates a virtual drive around your Gmail account. This drive appears under My Computer and on your computer's drive map, so you can store and retrieve files just like you do with your physical hard drive, Flash drive, CD-ROM, or any other storage device on your computer. GmailDrive supports drag and drop.

When you store a file with GmailDrive, the program sends an e-mail to your Gmail account with the file to be stored as an attachment. The file sits in your Gmail Inbox unless you set up a Gmail filter. All files sent by GmailDrive contain the subject GMAILFS. Keep your GmailDrive files out of your way by creating a filter that sends all e-mails with the subject GMAILFS directly to Archive.

> **WARNING** GmailDrive is not supported by Gmail. At the same time, its use is not blocked, either. The creator updates the program when there is a Gmail update that requires a GmailDrive revision. However, he makes no promises or guarantees that the software will continue to work. Someday, Gmail may decide to block the use of GmailDrive, and the software creator has no control over that. This is definitely "use at your own risk" software.

EXPANDING SORTING CAPABILITIES WITH SUPERSTARS

The standard Google star is great when you just want to make one or two e-mails stand out to remind you to take action. Superstars give you custom stars that you can use instead of, or with, labels to make searching easier.

Navigate to your Google Labs page and look for the Superstars Lab by Kal H & Julie W. Click Enable and save your changes.

Now, go to Gmail Settings and look under the General tab. Look for the Superstars section, which is three sections above the Signature section. To use a Superstar, drag and drop the desired star from the row called Not in Use to the row named In Use.

Take the time to learn the names of the Superstars you use by hovering your mouse over the Superstar icons on the General Settings tab. Take a look at Figure 11-10 to see available Superstars.

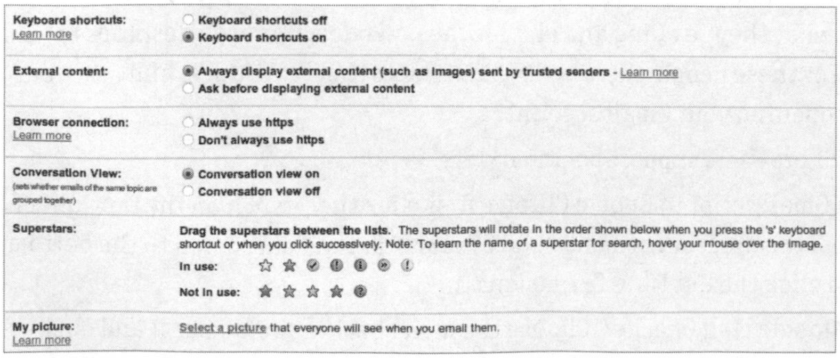

FIGURE 11-10: Superstars are one more tool to help you sort your e-mail.

To apply Superstars to e-mail, click the star icon like you do to add a simple star and then continue clicking until the desired Superstar appears.

> **NOTE** At this time, you cannot add Superstars automatically with filters. You must add each Superstar individually, by hand.

Search for a specific e-mail by entering the phrase **has:star-name** into the search box. Figure 11-11 shows the results of a search for has:green-check.

FIGURE 11-11: Search for all e-mails with the green-check Superstar.

USING BOOKMARKLETS TO NEVER OPEN GMAIL AGAIN

> ► Bookmarklets is another name for userscripts and Greasemonkey scripts.

Some people find all the labs, labels, and sorting options distracting when there is work to be done. Others just like to be able to keep an eye on their Inboxes without having to stop what they're doing and change tabs, windows, or even desktops to check e-mail. For these people there are bookmarklets that let you see, and use, your Gmail without opening your Gmail account.

All the major browsers support bookmarklets.

To install a Gmail script in Google Chrome first click the wrench on the far right of the screen. From the drop-down menu select Tools → Extensions. Scroll to the bottom of the page and click the Get More Extensions link.

Search for Google Mail Checker. Choose the mail checker you like best and click the Install button. My favorite mail checker for Chrome is Google Mail Checker Plus

Classic. Mail Checker Plus Classic adds a small Gmail icon next to the Chrome Omni-bar. Left-click the icon to see your Gmail. As you can see in Figure 11-12, you have a lot of options to choose from.

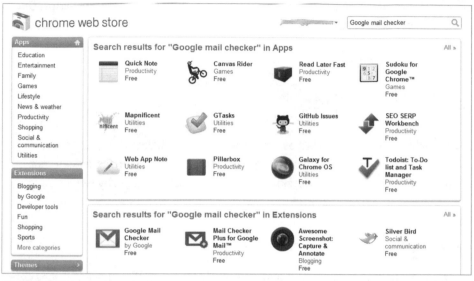

FIGURE 11-12: Searching the Chrome web store for some Google mail checker bookmarklets.

If you use the Firefox web browser go to https://addons.mozilla.org/en-US/firefox and search for Gmail Checker. Find the Gmail script you like, and click Install.

Alternatively, use userscripts.org to locate and install a bookmarklet that lets you check Gmail without actually opening your Gmail account.

Some people find it less distracting to read e-mail through an RSS feed. Instead of opening Gmail, they simply direct e-mails into an RSS feed and read on whatever system they use to receive feeds. I've never tried it, but I'm told it takes away the temptation to answer list and personal e-mails when one is supposed to be working.

First, create an RSS feed address from your e-mail. The URL formula is simple: https://gmailusername:gmailpassword@gmail.google.com/gmail/feed/atom. So if your Gmail user name is whitecat, and your Gmail password is snowy, your RSS feed address would look like this: https://whitecat:snowy@gmail.google.com/e-mail.feed.atom.

Next, head to feedburner.google.com and set up a Feedburner account to host your new RSS feed. Enter your feed address in the textbox provided.

If desired, change the Feed Title and displayed Feed Address, and click Next. Note that you cannot have any spaces in the Feed Address.

▶ Google owns Feedburner, so if you are signed in to your Google account when you head to the Feedburner page, you may not need to sign in to Feedburner.

BOOKMARKING FREQUENTLY ACCESSED MESSAGES

Because Gmail gives each e-mail its own dedicated URL, you can use your browser's bookmarking system to keep frequently referred-to e-mails at your fingertips. Open the e-mail you want to bookmark, and create a bookmark according to your browser's instructions.

MANAGING CONTACTS

You probably receive a fairly large number of e-mails each day. Managing those e-mails and deciding which ones are worth reading now and which ones can wait is an important time-management skill. Use Gmail to sort messages by sender, ignore offensive e-mail, and manage SPAM e-mails.

Sorting Messages by Contacts

When you're looking for an e-mail sent by a specific person, all you need to do is enter the person's name in the search bar and click Search Mail. Gmail locates every e-mail from that person in both your Inbox and message archive.

Muting or Ignoring Contacts

There comes a time in everyone's e-mail experience when they need to put someone on ignore for some reason. Typically the offending person is acting inappropriately in some way. Maybe an e-mail list-mate insists on flaming you offlist because of differing political opinions. Or, perhaps someone doesn't want to take no for an answer and is harassing you in an attempt to get you to change your mind about something. Whatever the reason, you can use Gmail filters to quickly and permanently send the offending e-mails to your Trash without you ever knowing they were there.

Click Create a Filter. Enter the offensive person's e-mail address into the From field. Click Next. From the action list, select Delete It, and click Create Filter. That's it. You'll never see another e-mail from that e-mail address again.

If you ever decide to give the offending person another chance you can remove the filter. From Gmail Settings, select the Filters tab. Locate the filter you want to remove and click Delete at the end of that row.

To mute a conversation that you no longer want to follow, such as a thread on a mailing list that drags on forever, use the keyboard shortcut M. When you mute a conversation it skips your Inbox, and goes directly to your message archive.

If you later want to un-mute the conversation, first use the Gmail search box and search for **is:muted**. This brings up all muted conversations. Then, select the desired conversation and click Move to Inbox. This brings the selected conversation, and all future conversations in that thread, back to your Inbox.

Use Gmail to Manage SPAM on Other Accounts

Gmail's SPAM filter is one of the best. Wouldn't it be nice if you could use Google's SPAM filtering technology with your other e-mail accounts? Well, if your other e-mail account is POP-enabled, you can.

Navigate to Gmail Settings and click the Accounts and Import tab. Use the section titled Check Mail Using POP3 to bring mail from your other account into Gmail.

To do this, click Add POP3 Email Account. Enter the e-mail address you want to add in the pop-up, as shown in Figure 11-13. Click Next Step.

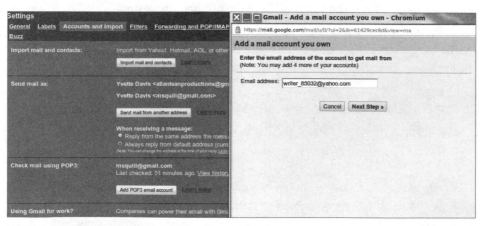

FIGURE 11-13: Add an outside e-mail account to Gmail.

In the next box, enter the password associated with the e-mail address you're adding. Use the drop-down menu to select the POP server and port Gmail should use. If you're unsure, use the default settings. Normally, you use the checkboxes to tell Gmail what to do with the new mail, but in this case there is no need. Take a look at Figure 11-14 to see these options. Click Add Account.

▶ If you decide to leave the incoming mail in your Gmail, instead of forwarding it on, it may be helpful to add a label to identify the e-mail from the outside account.

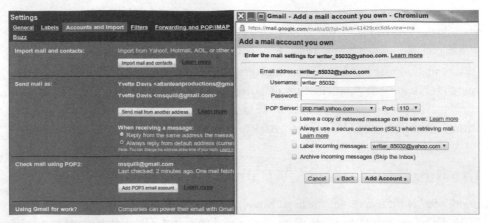

FIGURE 11-14: The second step to adding an outside e-mail address.

Now, all e-mail from your outside account will be pulled into Gmail. As e-mail comes in from this new account it is filtered for SPAM in the same manner as all incoming Gmail. At this point, you can either decide to read e-mails from the outside account in Gmail, or you can forward the e-mail to a different account.

If you want to leave the new e-mails in Gmail, then you're done.

To forward new e-mails to a different account, create a filter as discussed earlier in this chapter. In the form for creating filters, type the incoming e-mail address into the From box. Click Next Step and check Forward It.

> **TIP** You cannot forward the e-mail back to the account it originated from. Doing so creates a never-ending e-mail loop.

> **NOTE** If you have never used Gmail mail forwarding click the Manage Your Forwarding Address link at the end of the Forward It line. On the next screen, click Add a Forwarding Address and enter the address to which you want mail forwarded into the textbox. Click Next. Log in to the account to retrieve the confirmation code, and enter it into the box on Gmail's Forwarding and POP/IMAP tab under Gmail Settings. Click Verify.

Identifying Who's Selling Your E-mail Address

If you get a lot of SPAM, you can find out exactly who is selling your e-mail address by using the plus sign (+) in your Gmail address when you sign up for lists, newsletters, or leave messages on blogs. Assign each blog, list, or newsletter a different identification phrase and enter that phrase with a plus sign (+) after your usual Gmail address.

For example, if you are signing up for a newsletter called Monkey Monday, use the e-mail address yourgmail+monkeymon@gmail.com as your e-mail address. Everything to the right of the plus sign is ignored, so you will receive your newsletter. When you receive SPAM, look at the address to which it was sent. The information to the right of the plus sign tells you exactly where the spammers got your e-mail address.

When you receive a SPAM message, click Show Details to the left of the time sent stamp to see the sender's complete e-mail address and server information.

CHATTING IN GMAIL

In today's world Instant Messaging, text, and chat are a main form of communication. Used for everything from keeping in touch with family, scheduling business meetings, receiving weather and emergency alerts, and even as a meeting room, instant electronic communications are quickly replacing telephone and face-to-face meetings.

With Gmail's integrated chat system, staying in touch with everyone who has claims on your time is easy. Chat, Instant Messaging, computer-to-phone texts (also known as SMS), video chat, and even phone calls from your computer via VoIP are at your fingertips through Google Talk.

Gmail automatically adds Gmail users you email regularly to your chat list. Use the Chat menu to choose whether you see all contacts or only those people you e-mail most often. Also use the Chat menu to sign in to your AIM, add contacts to your chat list, manage chat settings, and set how much screen space the chat list uses. Figure 11-15 shows the Chat menu.

FIGURE 11-15: The Chat menu gives you control over contacts and chat settings.

Using Text Chats

To send a basic Chat message, click the name or Gmail ID of the person with whom you want to chat. Pretty straightforward.

> **TIP** There is a colored dot in front of each chat contact. A green dot means the person is logged in and active. Orange indicates the person is signed in to Gmail, but is inactive, or has the status set to away. Red means signed in, but status is set to busy. If the dot has turned into a camera icon, the person has a webcam installed. A phone-shaped icon indicates the person is using Google Chat with their cell phone, and a gray dot means the person is not signed in to Gmail.

Using Video Chats

Video chat is a great way to attend a meeting or keep in touch with far-flung family and friends. To hold a two-way video chat, both you and the person you're chatting with need webcams. Google Chat uses a video camera icon to indicate the contact has a webcam installed.

To use video chat, first you must install the Google Video plug-in found at www.google.com/chat/video. Follow the on-screen instructions.

After you've installed the plug-in, using video chat is easy. Click the name of the contact you want to video chat with, from the pop-up click Video & More, and then select Start Video Chat from the menu, as shown in Figure 11-16. Your video chat opens in the bottom-right corner of your screen.

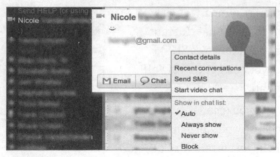

FIGURE 11-16: Access video chat.

Managing Chat Logs

To access your chat logs in Google Chat, click the contact whose logs you want to see. Select Video & More. From the resulting menu, select Recent Conversations. All chats and e-mails with that contact load in the main Gmail window. You can apply labels, archive, and star chat records, just like you can with e-mail.

To stop chat history recording for one contact during a chat, click Actions at the top of the chat window. Now, select Go Off the Record. This turns off chat recording for this contact only.

To turn off chat history for all contacts, navigate to the Chat tab in your Gmail Settings. Here you find controls for chat history, webcam, microphone and speakers, sounds, chat emoticons, AIM sign in, and settings for Google Voice calls.

Making Phone Calls from Chat

Make phone calls from your computer with Google Voice. You can use Google Voice in two ways. The first is from your Gmail page. In your Chat contacts list, look for the entry that reads Call Phone, with a green telephone icon. A small telephone pad opens in the lower-right corner. Figure 11-17 shows the keypad.

Type the number you want to call in the textbox and click the blue Call button at the bottom. Calls throughout the United States and Canada are free. Rates for calls outside those countries are listed at www.google .com/voice/b/0/rates, or click your available amount on the right side. In Figure 11-17, this amount is $0.10. Then click Rates from the drop-down menu.

FIGURE 11-17: Google Voice telephone tools within Gmail.

> **NOTE** Be sure Google Voice is enabled. Go to the Chat tab from within Gmail Settings. Look for the section called Call Phones. Make sure Enable Outbound Voice Calling with Google Voice is checked. This is the default Gmail setting. Also note that you need to download the Google Voice plug-in for your browser before you can make a call.

To add money to your Google Voice account, click the amount available and then click Add Credit. Follow the on-screen instructions.

When you use Google Voice through Gmail, you are assigned a random phone number for that call only. If you want a permanent Google Voice phone number, you need to set up a Google Voice account. To do that, head to https://www.google.com/voice. Click Get a Google Number in the left navigation bar.

Enter the area code or ZIP code you want your Google Voice number to fall under. You do not need to choose the area where you live. Or, type a word or phrase that you would like incorporated into your Google Voice number. Note that not all area codes are supported.

Choose from the available phone numbers by ticking the associated radio button and click Continue.

Enter a four-digit PIN and click Continue. You use this PIN to access voice mail.

In the next screen, enter the phone number to which you want phone calls to be forwarded. You cannot skip this step. Click Continue.

After you complete the phone number verification process, your Google Voice account will be active.

SUMMARY

Gmail gives you true all-in-one communication at your fingertips, with chat, text messaging, telephone, and e-mail all in one place. Use colored labels, filters, and Superstars to keep all your communications organized and easy to find.

Part IV

SECRETS FOR SHARING CONTENT WITH GOOGLE APPLICATIONS

CHAPTER 12

Getting Your Message Out with Blogger

IN THIS CHAPTER

▶ Customizing Blogger for your own tastes and needs

▶ Integrating social media in your blog

▶ Tips and strategies on creating a great blog

▶ Adding images, audio files, and videos in blog posts

▶ Using Search Engine Optimization (SEO) on your blog

Your blog is the world's window into your world. It's where you share your knowledge, experience, and life with anyone who wants to be a part of it. When you invite strangers into your home on the Web, you want the design, colors, images, text, and even the URL to be a reflection of who you are and what you believe. Google Blogger gives you that flexibility.

BUILDING A CUSTOM BLOG

Several components go into making a good blog. The colors, design, and images must work together to create an overall image that is easy on the user's eyes. Content must be interesting and well presented so users can easily understand what you're saying. If you pay attention to these important points, you'll keep your readers coming back for more.

Using Custom URLs

Your blog's web address, or URL, is important. If the URL is too hard to remember new visitors may not be able to find you, and repeat visitors may not find their way back. The official Blogger URL is www.google.com/blogger, which is used by default for every blog created on the Blogger platform. A good blog URL reflects the purpose of the blog. By default, Blogger lets you choose part of your blog's URL. Blogger's standard format is pretty straightforward. When you start a new blog the default URL is http://nameyouchoose.blogspot.com.

It's nice to have that kind of flexibility. But, what if you want use Blogger to host a domain name that you already own, or want to set up a new domain?

Start by creating your blog using the built-in domain tool. Next, choose one of the starter templates and click Continue. Blogger creates your new blog. On the confirmation screen, click Advanced Setup Options to open the menu. Then, click the Set Up a Custom Domain link. Figure 12-1 shows the confirmation screen.

FIGURE 12-1: Use Advanced Setup Options to create a custom domain for your blog.

> **NOTE** To customize the domain of a Blogger blog that you previously set up, go to the Blogger Dashboard. Locate the blog you want to change and click Settings. Click the Publishing tab and then click the Custom Domain link. It's at the top of the page.

The next screen gives you the option to purchase a new domain name. Right now, it costs $10.00. That gets you the domain name for one year and a Google Apps account connected to the new domain. Figure 12-2 shows the form used to purchase a domain name through Blogger.

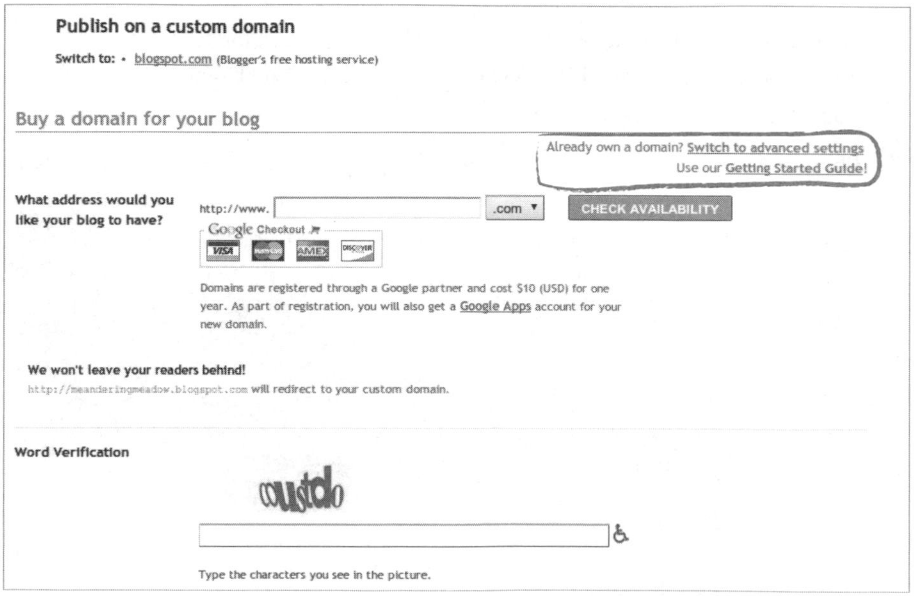

FIGURE 12-2: Purchase your domain name through Blogger.

If you already own the domain, click Switch to Advanced Settings on the right side, as indicated in Figure 12-2.

On the form shown in Figure 12-2, enter your domain name.

Now, go to your domain registrar and configure your DNS information so the Internet servers know where to find your domain. The procedure for configuring DNS information is different for each registrar company, so you need to consult your registrar's FAQ or call tech support for exact instructions.

In general, here's what you need to do:

1. Create a CNAME record for your blog's address. This should be a subdomain of your domain. Example: blog.mydomain.com.

2. Point your naked domain to these IP addresses:

   ▷ 216.239.32.21

   ▷ 216.239.34.21

   ▷ 216.239.36.21

   ▷ 216.239.38.21

3. If desired, enter the URL where you store backup files. Blogger uses this address to locate needed files in the event it cannot find them on the domain you entered in the first section.

4. Complete the word verification for security purposes, and click Save Settings.

▶ Naked domain means your domain without the www. It points users to your blog on Blogger if they type mydomain .com, instead of www.mydomain.com. This step does not apply if you are setting up a subdomain.

> **NOTE** It may take a while for all the DNS servers to get your new information. If it's not working after 48 hours check with your domain registrar.
>
> Your original blogspot address is automatically forwarded to your new blog address.
>
> You can use domains, such as mydomain.com, and subdomains, such as blog. mydomain.com, but you can't use subdirectories, such as mydomain.com/blog, and you can't use wildcards, such as *.mydomain.com.

Using Standalone Pages

In some situations you may want to give readers an introduction to your topic or post important information that won't change very much. This is where standalone pages come in handy. Standalone pages are different from the typical blog page because they don't change when you add a new blog post. You can use a standalone page as a landing page, an About Me page, a map to your business, or anything you want.

To create a standalone page from the Blogger Dashboard, first click Edit Posts. Select the Edit Pages tab from the top navigation bar, as shown in Figure 12-3.

Click New Page. Blogger allows you to add up to 10 standalone pages to your blog. Enter a page title in the space provided and then create your page content using the standard page-editing tools.

FIGURE 12-3: Go to Edit Pages to create standalone pages.

When you create your first standalone page, Blogger asks where it should place the Pages gadget. The Pages gadget links the pages of your blog together and provides navigation links. You can opt to place it in the lower-right corner of your pages, or across the top, under the header like a top navigation bar. You may also opt not to add the gadget. If you do opt out of the gadget you must manually link your pages.

Now, from the Design tab, click the gadget named Pages to determine the order in which pages are listed in the navigation. As you can see from Figure 12-4, you can change the title of the Pages gadget, select whether to have new pages published automatically, rename your Home page, and choose which pages are visible and which are hidden. By default, all pages are visible. To hide a page, click the box in front of the page name to remove the check mark. Save your changes when you're finished.

Creating a Front Page

Depending on your blog's topic, you may find that you want the front page (the home page) to provide a short introduction or welcome message. This can't be accomplished with a blog post because by default the main or first page of a blog is, well, the blog. The order in which blog entries are posted is most recent first. That's the definition of a blog.

But, you can use a Blogger gadget to create a post that acts as a front page for your blog.

First, head to your Design page. Click Add a Gadget. The Text gadget works best for this purpose. Drag the new gadget into the "Body" section of your page layout and position it near the top. The new gadget takes the place of the regular blog page, and the Blog Posts layout section moves down. See Figure 12-5.

In the lower-right corner of the new gadget, click Edit. Expand the window, and look in the URL bar for the Widget ID. You can find it at the end of the URL. You'll need this value in a minute, so make a note of it. Close the editing window. Figure 12-6 shows where to find the Widget ID.

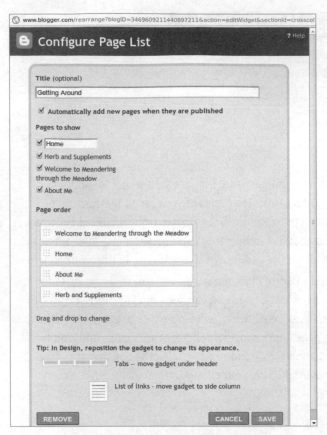

FIGURE 12-4: Control the page order and page visibility.

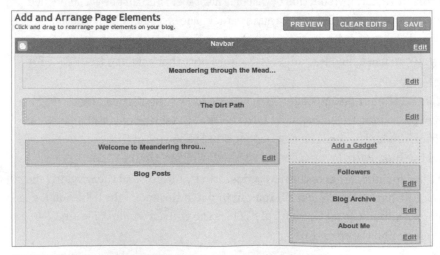

FIGURE 12-5: Place the new gadget in the Body section of your blog.

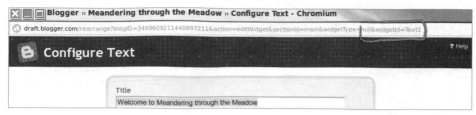

FIGURE 12-6: Write down the Widget ID.

Now you need to edit the template's HTML so that the gadget you just created displays directly above your most recent post, but does not show on older pages.

After you close the widget editing window, the page entitled Add and Arrange Page Elements, shown in Figure 12-7, should be visible again. Click the Edit HTML link in the top navigation bar. Your template's HTML displays in the editing box. Click Download Full Template to save a copy of the template to your hard drive so you can restore the template in case you make a mistake.

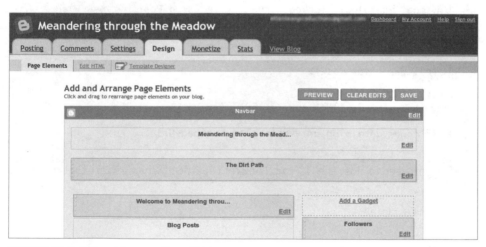

FIGURE 12-7: Add and Arrange Page Elements.

Search the HTML for the Widget ID you wrote down. Make a note of the line after the Widget ID. It looks like this:

```
<b:widget id='Text1' locked='false' title='Welcome to Meandering
through the Meadow' type='Text'/>
<b:widget id='Blog1' locked='true' title='Blog Posts' type='Blog'/>
```

Look directly above the box that contains the HTML. Click the box in front of the words Expand Widget Templates. This enables you to see all the HTML associated with the gadget you placed above the Body section. The exact HTML varies depending on the gadget you chose. If you used the Text gadget you see this:

```
<b:section class='main' id='main' showaddelement='no'>
<b:widget id='Text1' locked='false' title='Welcome to Meandering
through the Meadow' type='Text'>
<b:includable id='main'>
  <!-- only display title if it's non-empty -->
  <b:if cond='data:title != &quot;&quot;'>
    <h2 class='title'><data:title/></h2>
  </b:if>
  <div class='widget-content'>
    <data:content/>
  </div>


  <b:include name='quickedit'/>
</b:includable>
</b:widget>
<b:widget id='Blog1' locked='true' title='Blog Posts' type='Blog'>
```

Within the Widget HTML look for this line:

```
<b:includable id-'main'>
```

On the line after the HTML, type the following JavaScript code:

```
<b:if cond='data:blog.url==data:blog.homepageUrl'>
```

Now you need to close the "if" tag. Look for the line of Widget HTML that reads:

```
<b:include name='quickedit'/>
 <b:includable>
```

Directly in front of <b:includable>, type </b:if> to close the tag.

Click the Preview button before saving your template. If you have made an error, the preview flags the error so you can correct it before the template is saved. When you're satisfied with the result, click Save Template. Figure 12-8 shows the front page with the welcome message. Figure 12-9 shows an older page. You can see the welcome message is omitted from this page.

Hiding or Removing the NavBar

The Blogger navigation bar is the blue toolbar at the top of every Blogger blog. With this navigation bar, Blogger readers can search your blog, follow, share, or report your blog, and move on to the next blog. It's a great little tool, but it's not very attractive, and really, why do you want to give your readers an easy way to read someone else's blog? You can easily use Blogger gadgets to give your readers search, follow, and share capabilities. So, let's get rid of the Blogger navigation bar.

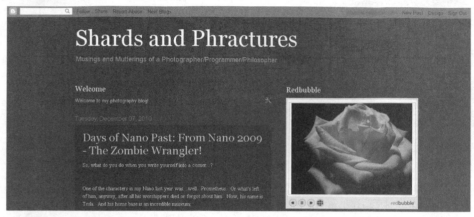

FIGURE 12-8: Front page of blog. Notice the welcome message.

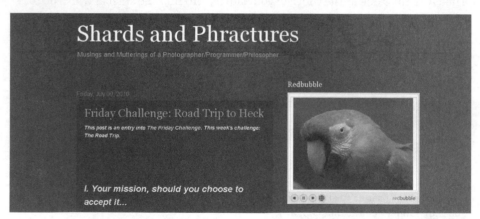

FIGURE 12-9: Individual blog post, without the welcome message.

Insert a CSS definition into your template that sets the height of the navigation bar to zero.

From your Blogger Dashboard, go to the Design tab. Click Edit HTML. Look toward the top of the HTML for the head tag. It looks like this: <head>. When you locate the tag, scroll down until you locate a tag that looks like this: </head>. This is the tag that closes the head section. Anywhere in between those two tags type the following:

```
#navbar {
height: 0px;
```

```
visibility: hidden;
display: none;
}
```

WARNING Blogger Terms of Service prohibit removing the Blogger navigation bar unless you are hosting your blog on your own domain. This trick works on blogs hosted with Blogger.com, but it is a violation of the TOS, and Blogger could shut down your blog for removing the NavBar.

Adding Images above Sidebar Gadgets

Adding an image above the gadgets in your sidebar can help draw your reader's attention to the gadget. Here's how you do it.

This assumes you have an image, and either have that image hosted on your own server, or saved to a free online image storage site, such as Google Picasa or Flickr.

Use your favorite image-editing software to scale the image so that the width of the image is the same as the width of your sidebar. To find the sidebar width go to the Blogger Template Designer. Click Adjust Widths and look for the slider bar titled Right Sidebar.

When your image is the correct size, go to the Design tab, and click Edit HTML. Enter the following HTML before the tag]]></b:skin>:

```
.sidebar h2 {
height: 25px;
width: 260px;
padding-top: 5px;
padding-left: 5px;
margin-top:5px;
background-image: url('Image URL');
background-repeat: no-repeat;
background-color:;
color: #ffffff;
font-size: 12px;
}
```

Adding Social Bookmarking Capabilities

Blogger knows how important social networking is in today's online world. Giving readers the ability to quickly share your blog with social contacts could be the difference between a blog with a readership of thousands, and a blog with a readership of one hundred.

Add social bookmarking from the Design tab. Click Page Elements → Add a Gadget. Use the search bar to locate the gadget named Social Networker. This gadget gives readers access to many social bookmarking sites such as Digg, Stumbleupon, Technorati, Twitter, Facebook, delici.ous, and more, all from one easy box.

Alternatively, you can add buttons for Gmail, Blogger, Twitter, Facebook, and Google Talk automatically. In the Design tab, click Edit in the box labeled Blog Posts. Check Show Share Buttons. This options box is also where you change the date and time format shown on your posts.

You can also use gadgets to give your blog instant message capabilities. Gadgets such as Web and Mobile Messenger Everywhere let you chat with Gtalk, Yahoo! IM, AIM, and others right from your blog. Simply search for any one of these brands with the term "gadget" or "blogger gadget" in your search query to find them. Or, just search for "blogger gadgets" to search through Google's universe of search results for that term.

BUILDING A BETTER BLOG POST

Having a great blog design is only half the battle. To keep readers coming back to your blog, you need great content. Interesting posts on relevant topics, great images, podcasts, and a lively comment board keep readers engaged and interested in what you have to say.

Adding Images

They say a picture is worth a thousand words, but sometimes a well chosen image says it all. Adding images to your posts can help readers feel connected to you, or help them understand your topic better.

To add an image to any post, click the Add Image icon in the toolbar. See Figure 12-10 if you need help finding the icon.

Use the left navigation to tell Blogger if the image is on your computer, stored on Picasa, stored on another website, or stored on the current blog. Then, follow the on-screen directions to tell Blogger exactly where to find the image.

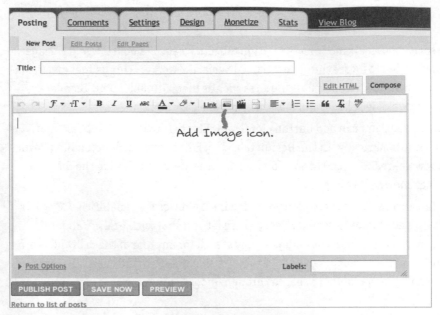

FIGURE 12-10: Find the Add Image icon when composing or editing a post.

Implementing SEO for Blog Posts

SEO, or Search Engine Optimization, boils down to giving the search engines and web crawlers what they need to properly index and rate your blog.

The best way to do that is with frequent posting and relevant tags. Title and tag your posts with phrases you would use to search for the topic your post discusses.

Encourage your readers to subscribe to your RSS feed. The search engines use the number of RSS subscribers to help determine page rank.

Host your blog on your own servers. Blog hosting services are busy places, and that makes it hard to stand out from the crowd. You'll increase your page rankings by purchasing your own domain name and parking your blog there.

Use the online keyword research tool. Sites such as SEOBOOK, Wordtracker, Google AdWords Keyword Suggestion Tool, and Google Suggest analyze the words and phrases your potential readers are searching for so you can incorporate those keywords into your text. However, never randomly insert keywords into your text just for the sake of the keyword. Text should read naturally.

Keep informed about new information within your blog topic. Use Google News, Google Blog Search, and Technorati to stay abreast of new trends.

> **TIP** You can find tools for analyzing keywords and phrases at the following sites:
>
> ► http://tools.seobook.com/keyword-tools/seobook/
>
> ► https://freekeywords.wordtracker.com
>
> ► https://adwords.google.com—Click the Reporting and Tools tab and click Keyword Tool from the drop-down menu.
>
> ► http://tools.seobook.com/general/keyword-information/

Identify popular searches within the past 24 hours with Google Trends. This gives you one more tool to keep on top of current topics.

Place keywords as close to the top of your page as possible. Include the most relevant keywords in the title of your blog post.

Using Alternative Posting Methods

For maximum exposure, it's important to post every day, if at all possible. Blogger knows that can be difficult with a busy schedule, so it offers several ways to publish your posts.

Write posts ahead of time and use Post Options to schedule your post to publish at a future date and time. Click the words Post Options at the bottom of the text editing box. Select Scheduled At on the right and enter the date and time you want the post to publish. When you're finished, click Publish Post. Figure 12-11 shows where to find the scheduling tool.

When you're away from your computer, you can post to your Blogger blog from your mobile phone. To use your mobile phone with Blogger you first have to register the phone so Blogger knows to associate that phone with your account.

To do this, send an e-mail or text message with the subject **REGISTER** to BLOGGR (256447). Blogger responds with the address to your mobile blog and instructions on accessing your mobile blog from your account.

If you ever need to change the settings on your mobile blog, or to set up mobile blogging so that your posts go to your current Blogger blog, go to go.blogger.com.

Mobile Blogger supports text and images that are less than 250k each. Blogger does not charge for mobile blogging service; however, your phone carrier might, so be sure to check with your mobile company.

If you ever want to cancel mobile Blogger, just send a text message to BLOGGR with the subject **STOP.** The command **UNREGISTER** disconnects your mobile device from your Blogger account.

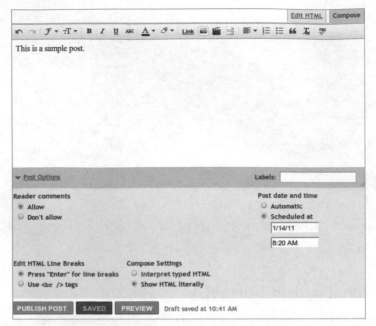

FIGURE 12-11: Plan ahead by writing posts in advance and using the scheduling tool to post at a future date and time.

Adding a "Print This" Option

Give readers a button to quickly and easily print their favorite post.

From the Design tab, click Edit HTML. Type the following code under the `<head>` tag:

```
<style type="text/css" media= "print">
#noprint {display: none;}
//Hide unwanted elements
body {background:fff;color:ooo;}
//Black text on white background
a{text-decoration;underline;color;oof}
//Underlines links in blue
}
</style>
```

Preview to catch any errors. When everything looks good click Save Template.

Now, copy the following code at the bottom of every post to which you want to add a print button:

```
<a href="javascript:window.print()">Print Page</a>
```

If you want a print button on every post, go to the Settings tab and click Formatting. Scroll down to the Post Template and add the code there, instead of in individual posts.

Making Posts Ratable

Give readers a quick and easy way to tell you what they think about your blog posts with ratings. Go to Page Elements on the Design tab. In the box labeled Blog Posts, click Edit. Look for the Reactions check box and check it. Use the textbox to change the name to Ratings, or Opinions, or whatever you'd like to call it.

To change the rating buttons, click Edit. Type your desired ratings in the box. Ratings display on the bottom of each post.

Including PowerPoint and PDF Files

PowerPoint presentations add texture and interest to your blog that you can't get with static photos.

Create your PowerPoint presentation and get it ready to upload. When you're done, log in to your Google Docs account and upload the PowerPoint to Docs. Be sure that Convert Documents, Presentations, Spreadsheets and Drawings to the Corresponding Google Docs Formats is checked.

> NOTE Remember, you can use Google Docs Presentation to create a slide show, as well.

Open the presentation after it uploads. Click Share to open the drop-down menu. As shown in Figure 12-12, select Publish/Embed from the menu.

Click Publish Document. This opens publishing settings and gives you the HTML needed to embed the presentation.

Use the drop-down menus to set player size and slide speed. A medium player size works well for blogs, and the default speed of changing slides every three seconds usually gives readers enough time to read your slide. If you have a lot of text on your slides, consider assigning the slide speed a longer duration. Use the checkboxes to tell Presentation when to start the slide show, and what to do when it is finished. Copy the HTML to your clipboard.

Go back to Blogger to post the HTML on the page where you want to run the slide show. To run the slides within a blog post, use the Posting tab, choose either a new post, or edit an existing one. Click Edit HTML and paste the slide show HTML in the editing box. See Figure 12-13 for an example. Preview the post before you publish.

FIGURE 12-12: Select Publish/Embed from the Share menu.

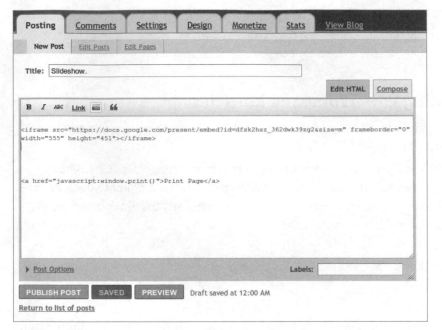

FIGURE 12-13: Paste the presentation HTML into the editing box.

To add your slide show to a gadget, go to the Design tab. Select Page Elements and click Edit within the desired gadget. Click Edit HTML and paste the code in the edit window. See Figure 12-14 for the final result.

Including Podcasts or Audio in Your Post

Adding a podcast or audio file to your blog gives you one more tool to connect with your readers. This assumes you have a media file created, uploaded to your website, and ready to go.

Sign into Feedburner at feedburner.google.com, as discussed in Chapter 11. Type your blog's URL in textbox and check the box labeled I am a Podcaster, as shown in Figure 12-15.

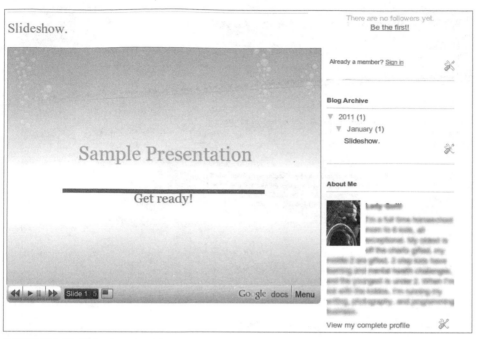

FIGURE 12-14: Slide show in a blog post.

Follow the on-screen instructions to activate your account. You need to choose between an RSS feed or an Atom feed. Regardless of which feed type you choose, your feed is activated, and SmartCast is applied to your blog. SmartCast is a free service that enables you to distribute podcasts.

Use the form shown in Figure 12-16 to describe your podcast. You can select an image to go along with your podcast. Select a category and subcategory so potential listeners can search for your podcast. Enter a summary, type keywords, and if desired, enter an e-mail address where listeners may contact you. In the next section, use the drop-down to indicate whether your podcast contains explicit material, enter any desired copyright information, and click Next.

On the next screen set your statistic tracking. Click Next to complete the setup process.

Now, go back to Blogger. From the Settings tab, click Formatting in the upper navigation bar. Look for Show Link fields and use the drop-down menu to set this value to Yes. Save Settings.

Create a new post. Insert the link to your audio file in the textbox marked Link. It is directly under the post Title box. This redirects the post to your online audio file.

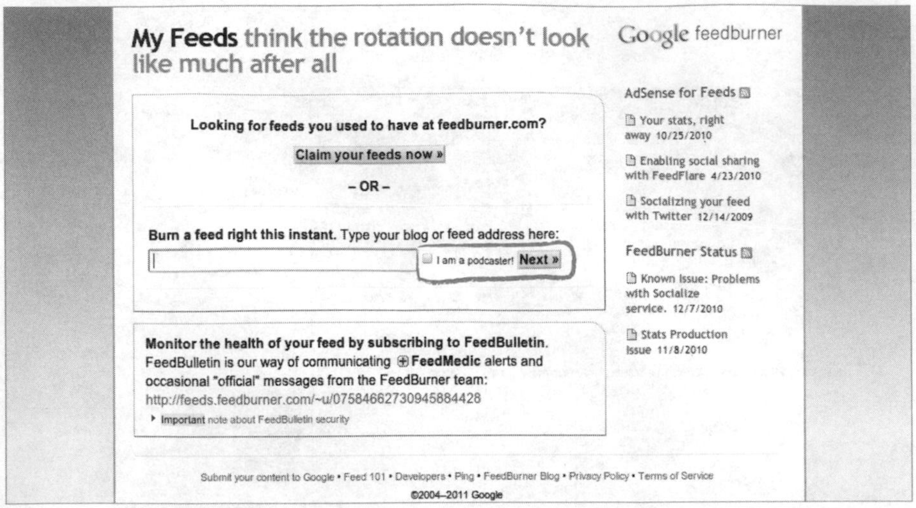

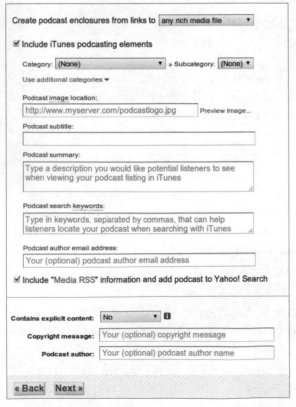

FIGURE 12-15: Tell Feedburner that you are a podcaster.

FIGURE 12-16: Enter information about your podcast.

Locate your Feedburner URL. This was assigned during Feedburner setup. It should look something like `http://feeds.feedburner.com/yourblogname`. Insert this URL into your podcast aggregator. This makes your podcast available for searching.

SUMMARY

Use the tools described in this chapter to make your blog stand out from the crowd. Images, PowerPoint presentations, podcasts, and interesting posts will keep your readers coming back. Use social networking to increase your readership, and make new online friends. And, above all, have fun in your new home on the Web.

CHAPTER 13

Managing Your Blog

Now that your blog is looking good, optimized for the search engines, and contains a couple of posts, it's time to engage your readers with lively discussion to keep them coming back. Comments are the lifeblood of a blog. The comment section turns your blog from "one person talking to themselves" into a community of like-minded individuals discussing a topic. After you've spent some time making the comment section as comfortable as your favorite coffee house, consider setting up an RSS feed to make your blog more accessible to your new friends.

WORKING WITH COMMENTS

An active comment section gives you an opportunity to interact with your readers. That interaction is what keeps some readers coming back. If you take care to police your comment board for spam, respond to posters, and encourage lively discussion, your comment section will help bring people to your blog.

Removing Word Verification from Comments

Word verification has its place. It's a helpful tool to reduce spam, but it can also discourage real people from posting comments to a blog. If you choose to turn word verification off, be aware that the number of spam comments you receive from autobots may increase over time. Word verification is also referred to online as a "CAPTCHA" (an acronym for Completely Automated Public Turing test to tell Computers and Humans Apart), and we've all see what these look like: funky-looking words that appear as part of your secure log-in, account creation, or contact form submission on many online properties.

Turn off word verification from the Settings tab. You modify this setting by selecting Comments from the upper navigation menu. Scroll down to the section labeled Show Word Verification for Comments, and tick No. Click Save Settings at the bottom of the page.

It's true that turning off word verification will eventually increase the amount of spam comments made to your blog, but you can use other settings to help protect your blog and your readers.

One thing you can do to minimize spam comments with word verification off is to limit who can post comments. This option is on the Settings tab, toward the top of the Comments page. The options are

- ▶ **Anyone**—This includes anonymous users. I recommend using this setting only with word verification turned on.

- ▶ **Registered users**—This includes users who use OpenID. This is probably the best choice for most blogs, and it is the default setting.

- ▶ **Users with Google Accounts**—Although this is more effective at reducing spam comments, it bars anyone who does not have a Google account from commenting on your blog.

- ▶ **Only Members of This Blog**—This is the most limiting setting. It's appropriate for private blogs only.

Moderating comments is another option for reducing spam, although this one requires a lot more of your time. Comment Moderation requires that you approve each and every comment before it's posted to your blog. You can choose to always moderate posts, never moderate posts, or choose to moderate only those posts that are older than specified number of days.

When comments require your attention a link appears on your Blogger Dashboard labeled Moderate Comments.

By default, you are automatically notified at the e-mail address you used to sign up for Blogger anytime someone leaves a comment on your blog. You can change this address, or add up to nine other e-mail addresses for notification. You'll find the Comment Notification Email section at the bottom of the Comments page of the Settings menu.

Changing the Appearance of the Comment Page

By default, the box readers use to enter their comments is embedded in the page, but you have the ability to change this. From the Blogger Dashboard, select Settings and then Comments. Look for the section entitled Comment Form Placement. It is three sections down from the top.

You can choose to keep the default method of commenting via an embedded form below each blog post, but you do have the ability to allow readers to type in their comments in a full web page or a pop-up window.

Highlighting Author Comments

If you receive a lot of comments on your blog, you, and your readers, will find it helpful if comments made by you, the blog author, stand out in some way. A few tweaks to the HTML will leave your comments highlighted and easy for your readers to locate.

From the Dashboard, go to the Design tab. Click Edit HTML. As always, download the template to your computer before you begin editing so you have a backup in case things go wrong.

Check the box labeled Expand Widget Templates to make widget HTML visible.

Use your browser's search tool to locate the following:

```
<dd class='comment-body'>.
```

Immediately above this line of code, type the following:

```
<b:if cond='data:comment.author == data:post.author'>
<dd class='comment-body-author'>
<p><data:comment.body/></p>
</dd>
<b:else/>
```

Now, locate the following block of HTML:

```
<dd class='comment-body'>
<b:if cond='data:comment.isDeleted'>
<span class='deleted-comment'><data:comment.body/>
</span>
<b:else/>
<p><data:comment.body/></p>
</b:if>
</dd>
```

On the line immediately after this type the following:

```
</b:if>
```

Use your browser's search function again to find the following:

```
]]></b:skin>
```

Immediately above this line enter the following:

```
.comment-body-author {
background: #00FF00;
border: 2px solid #006400;
padding: 5px;
}
```

> **NOTE** The color of the highlighting is defined in the line that reads **background:** #00FF00. You can change the value #00FF00 to the hexadecimal color value of your choice. The same is true of the border value in the line that defines the highlight border color. That line reads **border: 2px solid #006400**.

Save your changes. See Figure 13-1 to see what the highlighted author comments look like.

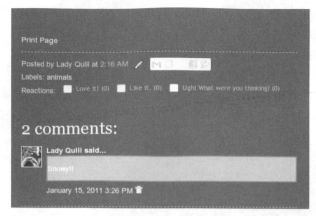

FIGURE 13-1: Highlighted author comments.

IMPROVING USABILITY

Usability is as much about ease of use for you, the owner and author of your blog, as it is for your users. Blogger offers settings to make posting to your blog simpler, so you're more likely to post more often.

Adding Authors

Many blogs host the occasional guest blogger. Maybe you have a friend who has a really interesting hobby you want to share with your readers, or perhaps your blog is business related and you regularly bring in guest bloggers to help increase readership. Or, maybe you're going on vacation and asked Aunt Matilda to write for your blog while you're gone. Whatever the reason, you can give your guest bloggers special access to your blogger account so they can publish without your presence.

To add a guest blogger to the Settings tab, click Permissions. Click the button labeled Add Authors, and type an e-mail address for each guest blogger in the box. When you're finished, click Invite.

TIP You can add up to 100 guest bloggers.

▶ *The guest blogger does not need a Blogger account, but is required to have a Google account. If the user does not have a Google account he will be guided in creating one.*

Blogger sends your guest blogger an e-mail notifying him of his guest blogger status. The guest blogger needs to click the link provided in the e-mail and enter his Google account username and password to accept the invitation.

After your guest blogger accepts your invitation, he has limited access to your blog. Guest bloggers can access the Posting tab and the Settings tab.

Under the Posting tab, guest bloggers can create new posts and edit only those posts they write.

The Settings tab gives guest bloggers the ability to post via e-mail or mobile device. Guest bloggers may also remove themselves from the blog.

NOTE Guest bloggers only have access to the blog to which they were invited. So, if you own more than one blog under the same Blogger account a guest invited to one blog does not have access to the others.

Creating Sticky Posts

Sticky posts are a lot like the front page you created in Chapter 12. The real difference is that readers have the ability to leave comments on a sticky post but they cannot on a front page.

Go to the Design tab and select Page Elements. Add a new Sticky Note gadget. After the gadget is created, grab it from the sidebar (or whichever gadget creation box you used) and use drag and drop to place it at the top of the box labeled Blog Posts. Click Edit to add text or other content.

That's it. Now, that box displays above your blog posts until you remove it.

Creating Selective Expandable Entries

Sometimes, if you post a particularly long blog entry you may want to provide readers with a short blurb and a link to expand the post, if they choose. Doing this gives readers the ability to scan through short posts and expand the long ones as they choose.

The following code shows readers a summary of your long posts, along with a link to the full version of the post.

From the Design tab, click Edit HTML. Click the box in front of Expand Widget Templates.

Type the following code immediately above the `</head>` tag:

```
<style>
<b:if cond='data:blog.pageType =="item">
span.fullpost {display;inline}
span.fullpost {display:none:}
</b:if>
</style>
```

Find the line that reads `<data:post.body/>` and type the following directly after this line:

```
<b:if cond='data:blog.pageType != "item">
<a expr:href- 'data:post.url' target='_blank'>Read more!</a>
</b:if>
```

The final step in this process is to change the post template to include a separation between the part of the post that is visible on the blog's front page and the portion of the post after the Read More button. From the Settings tab, click Formatting. Scroll to the bottom of the page and look for the section titled Post Template. Type the following into the box:

```
This is the beginning of the blog post. <span class="fullpost">
This is the rest of the post.</span>.
```

Now, when you type your post, replace the words "here is the beginning of my blog post" with the section of the post you want to be visible on the front page. Likewise, replace the words, "And here is the rest of it" with the remainder of your post. Figure 13-2 shows the visible blog post.

FIGURE 13-2: The shortened version of the blog post.

SETTING UP RSS FEEDS AND SYNDICATION

RSS, or Real Simple Syndication, feeds are an easy way for readers to receive automatic updates to your blog from their RSS reader, or iGoogle page. Your readers will appreciate the simplicity of being able to follow your blog through RSS. And, as a blog reader yourself, you will appreciate the time you save from reading all your blogs in one place. You do read your friends' blogs, right? Remember, reading and commenting on other blogs regularly helps you build relationships and increase your readership.

Using RSS Feeds

Include the feeds of other blogs directly on your blog. This is useful if you want your readers to see news headlines, fitness tips, or anything else available through a feed.

From your Blogger Dashboard, click Design. From the Page Elements tab, choose one of your designated gadget areas and click Add a Gadget. Don't forget to hit the Save button immediately afterward! Look for the gadget named Feed, shown in Figure 13-3. Click the blue plus sign and then enter the feed URL in the box labeled Feed URL. Click Continue. Give the feed a title, and use the drop-down menu to select how many posts should be shown and how those posts should be organized. The preview box shows how the feed will look on your blog.

FIGURE 13-3: Use the Feed gadget to quickly and easily add someone else's feed to your blog for RSS.

Syndicating Your Blog

You have many ways to get your blog on a feed. The simplest is to use the tools provided by Google-owned Feedburner.

First, if you haven't already, sign up for a Feedburner account, as discussed in Chapter 11.

▶ You can find Feedburner at feedburner.google.com.

Type your blog's web address into the space shown in Figure 13-4 and click Next. On the next screen choose between an RSS or Atom feed. Click Next.

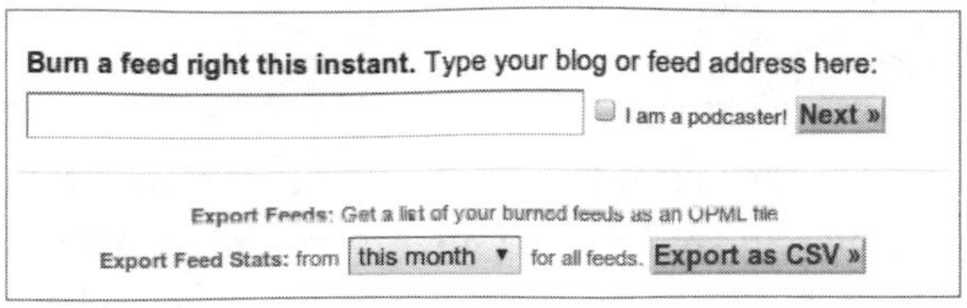

FIGURE 13-4: Enter your blog's URL in the box.

The following screen lets you customize both the name of your feed and the feed's URL. Make any desired changes. Be sure to record both the name of your feed and your feed address. Click Next.

You've now created a basic syndication feed that readers can use to subscribe to your blog. You have the option of stopping here, or continuing and adding free options for tracking your blog's readership.

Now, you need to display a feed icon on your blog so readers can subscribe with one click. From the Feedburner homepage, click the feed you want to work with. This takes you to the Feed Stats Dashboard. From the top navigation, click the Publicize tab. Now, in the left navigation, click Chicklet Chooser. Chose your favorite feed icon by clicking the radio button in front of the one you want to display on your blog. You can also add buttons for My Yahoo!, Google Reader, Newsgator, Bitty Browser, fwicki, and other web aggregators from this page.

When you've selected your desired button, scroll to the bottom of the page. Use the drop-down menu to select Blogger. Click Go. Blogger opens a confirmation window, shown in Figure 13-5, in a new tab or window. Confirm that the button is being added to the correct blog and click Add Widget.

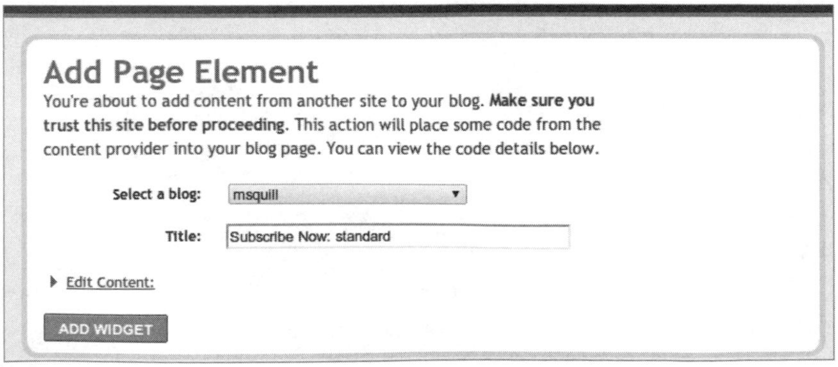

FIGURE 13-5: Confirm that you want to add the button to your blog.

That's it. Users can now subscribe to your blog feed with the click of a button.

SUMMARY

The tools described in this chapter help you communicate with your readers more effectively, making your blog as much of a community as an outlet for information sharing. Feeds are the gold standard of blog and news sharing in today's electronically based world. You'll reach more people, and get more enjoyment from your blog, by taking advantage of this technology.

CHAPTER 14

Getting More from YouTube

YouTube provides video uploading and viewing services. Users upload their own videos to share with the world. By using a few tricks, and a couple of independent programs, you can download videos uploaded by others, or convert an entire movie to MP3 and download it to your computer. Use URL controls to improve movie quality and start a movie at the exact minute and second you want to see. Share movies or use your mobile device to upload and view videos. Even enable parental controls with ease.

UPLOADING AND DOWNLOADING VIDEOS

Uploading video to YouTube (www.youtube.com) is easy. Log in to your YouTube account, click the Upload link to the right of the YouTube search bar, and click the yellow button labeled Upload Video. Use your computer's file navigation to locate the file you want to upload, and YouTube does the rest. Or, if you have a webcam, take advantage of the link that enables you to Record From Webcam.

Use the form provided to give your video a title, description, and tags. The drop-down menu lets you specify an interest category, and the privacy settings give you the options you need to keep questionable videos from younger eyes.

There are two reliable ways to download a video from YouTube. Download a small program to handle it for you, or use the new homepage discussed later in this chapter.

▶ You can find YouTube Downloader at http://download.cnet.com/YouTube-Downloader/3000-2071_4-10647340.html.

For Windows machines, YouTube Downloader is a good choice. It downloads YouTube videos quickly and with little hassle. However, some virus scanners tag the toolbar as a low-risk malware, and some people have reported problems with the toolbar. When installing YouTube Downloader, it may be wise to opt out of toolbar installation. It won't affect the function of the program.

Mac users can find free YouTube downloading software at www.applemacvideo.com/free-mac-youtube-downloader.html. This software gives you drag-and-drop downloading capabilities and enables you to download in a batch. It also includes a video player for viewing your downloaded videos, and enables you to share your videos from within the program with Facebook and Twitter.

For the Linux users, there's FatRat, SlimRat, and youtube-dl. Each gives users efficient downloading abilities. Youtube-dl offers other features such as entire playlist downloading, and the ability to choose video quality. However, youtube-dl is suitable only for those who are comfortable using the command line. Access these programs from the software utility included with your distribution.

Downloading Audio from Video

Did you know it's possible to download only the audio from your favorite YouTube video? With the help of a small online app, you can. Head to www.getaudiofromvideo.com/index.php. You should know that you can download only one video for free with this program. After that you have to either fill out a survey or become a paid member.

Enter the URL of the video from which you want to extract the audio and click Search. This web app, shown in Figure 14-1, finds your YouTube video and displays it in the box on the right. Use the drop-down menu in the Download Options section to set the type of file you want. Choose between MP3, MP4 (ringtone), MP4 (ipod video), G3P (cell phone video), FLV (Adobe Flash Video), AVI (Audio Video Interleave), and WMV (Windows Media Video).

Read the terms of service (TOS) and check the box stating you have done so. The TOS are in the upper navigation under the Terms of Use Tab. Now, click the red Download button. The program converts your video to the file type you selected. After the video is converted, you are given the option to preview the audio file or simply download it to your local computer.

FIGURE 14-1: Use this simple tool to download your favorite YouTube video as an audio file.

INCREASING CONTROL WITH YOUTUBE URL TRICKS

Not all videos are recorded equally. That is, there are ways that you can manipulate the YouTube system to get the most out of any video, regardless whether the video was recorded using your phone's camera, a desktop webcam, or the most expensive, highest-definition professional video camera on Earth.

Additionally, if you're linking to a video on social media or on your website, you can add a query parameter at the end of the URL so that the video starts at a certain spot (instead of being forced to have the video play from the beginning).

Forcing Your Way into High-Quality Videos

Some videos enable you to change the play quality with a menu in the lower-right corner of the video screen. This menu is shown in Figure 14-2. For videos that don't contain a quality menu, you can change video quality by adding the following codes to the end of the video URL.

- **&fmt=6**—Resolution 448 × 336; Flash 7 video at 900kbps; audio 44.1 Khz 96Kbsx; Mono CBR

- **&fmt=18**—Resolution 480 × 360; H.264 video at 512 Kbps; audio 44.1 Khz 96 Kbps; Mono CBR

- **&fmt=22**—If the video was uploaded a high resolution, this setting gives you 720p HDV

It looks like this: www.youtube.com/watch?v=videonumber&fmt=18.

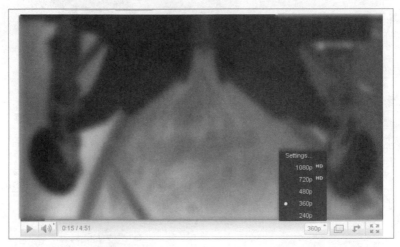

FIGURE 14-2: Video quality control menu.

Advancing Through Videos

YouTube videos can be as long as fifteen minutes. Granted, fifteen minutes isn't a super long time, but it can seem like forever if you're only interested in watching thirty seconds of that fifteen-minute video. You can always use the slider to fast forward to the part of the video you want to watch. But that's imprecise and finding what you're looking for can take more time than watching the video.

Instead of scrolling through the video, simply add the following to the end of the video's URL

`#t=XmYs`

where X equals the number of minutes, and Y equals the number of seconds into the video you want playback to start.

For example, `www.youtube.com/watch?v=videonumber#t=2m5s` starts the selected video at the 2-minute, 5-second mark.

SHARING YOUTUBE CONTENT MORE FREELY

YouTube content is meant to be viewed and shared. You can share any YouTube video by simply e-mailing or otherwise sharing its URL, but simple shortcuts make it possible to share your playlist or embed a video on your website or blog.

Sharing Video Playlists

YouTube lets you share your video playlists easily. Log in to your YouTube account, and click My Videos & Playlists in the upper navigation bar. In the left navigation, click the button marked +New to create a new playlist.

To share a playlist, click the name of the list you want to share. Click Share. The Tab opens with a playlist URL. Simply e-mail this URL to anyone with whom you want to share your playlist.

Embedding YouTube Videos into Blogs and Websites

Sometimes you want to share video, or even one of your YouTube playlists, on your website. To do this, select the video or playlist you want to share from the My Videos & Playlists page. Click Share in the upper navigation tab. Copy the contents of the box labeled Embed Code to your computer's clipboard, and paste it into the HTML of your website.

USING YOUTUBE MOBILE

Like most Google Apps, YouTube is available from your mobile device. The type of device you have determines how you access YouTube and what features are available to you.

Android and iPhone users will find a YouTube app preinstalled on their mobile devices, but those who use the Nokia S60 and most other mobile devices running Windows need to download a YouTube app from m.youtube.com/app. Users of other types of mobile devices should check with their carriers for apps or navigate their mobile browsers to m.youtube.com.

When you use Mobile you have full access to your YouTube account, allowing you to use your favorites list, playlists, and even upload video from your phone.

ADDING CAPABILITIES WITH YOUTUBE TOOLS

The great thing about YouTube (other than it being free and wildly successful) is the flexibility you're allowed with your videos, your pages, and even how you share your videos with the world.

When you add intermediate to advanced YouTube video capabilities you help your video's production quality, which could increase its popularity and appeal, and you don't need to hire a professional media company or spend lots of money to do it.

TestTube

▶ You can find TestTube at www.youtube.com/testtube.

TestTube is YouTube's equivalent to Google Labs. Here you can find plenty of YouTube toys to play with. If you find something you love, or something you hate, e-mail the YouTube developers and let them know.

Some of my favorites include Try a New Homepage, YouTube Music Discovery, Insights for Audiences, and Video Editor.

Try a New Homepage changes basic aspects of your YouTube homepage. It merges your friend activities, subscriptions, and video recommendations into one list for easy scanning. New Homepage also gives you an improved inbox, list of videos you've recently "liked," one-click video delete, and improved upload notifications.

YouTube Music Discovery lets you find your favorite music on YouTube and create a playlist. You can find this tool at www.youtube.com/disco. Enter the artist's name, or a song title, and Music Discovery locates music videos that match your search criteria and automatically creates a play list. Controls let you learn more about the group or song you're listening to, load a different playlist, or get more information about the playlist. However, when you select Get More Information About This Playlist, the information page opens in the same tab, stopping the music. When you use Music Discovery while signed in to your YouTube account, you have the ability to save your playlists.

Insights for Audiences helps you see what users of specific demographics are watching on YouTube. Answer basic questions such as gender, age, and the country viewed from, and Insights for Audiences lists the most popular videos in one of 24 interest categories. You can find Insights for Audiences at www.google.com/videotargeting/ifa/buildQuery.

YouTube Video Editor, www.youtube.com/editor, is a simple but effective online video editor. Trim and add music to up to seven videos at a time. Use the included preview window to make sure your video is exactly like you want it. Publish your completed video with one click. Editing video with the YouTube Video Editor saves the video under a new name.

Creator's Corner

Learn everything you need to create and upload interesting, high-quality videos. Creator's Corner at www.youtube.com/creators_corner is a central hub to all things YouTube. Learn the best ways to edit and optimize your video, get help uploading, and even access the user help forum. You can also find cool project ideas from which to glean creative inspiration. But the coolest thing about Creator's Corner is the Feature Kit.

Feature Kit provides links and information to some beta services, such as YouTube Rentals. This is a service that enables content providers to post videos to YouTube that are intended for rental instead of free viewing. YouTube Rentals is intended for content providers who already have a following, and is intended to help those high-traffic videos make a bit of cash. To make your videos available to rent through YouTube, you first need to be approved via its online application.

Picasa3 Video Editing

Google offers its own online tool for photo and video editing: Picasa3. Use it for editing, cutting, and splicing, and even flipping a sideways-facing video to right-side-up.

> CROSSREF Picasa3 is discussed in depth in Chapter 15.

Greasemonkey Scripts

Greasemonkey scripts are small chunks of JavaScript code that you can add to your web browser to change the function or appearance of a website. Greasemonkey was originally developed for use in the Mozilla Firefox web browser, but scripts also work in other browsers. Scripts developed for Google Chrome are called Userscripts.

One such script is called YouTube Enhancer. This script is available on http://userscripts.org/scripts/show/33042 and was written by Userscripts uploader GiJoe.

YouTube Enhancer gives you

- ▶ A link from which to download video
- ▶ Video quality selector
- ▶ Roll-over preview capabilities
- ▶ Media resizer
- ▶ Ability to set YouTube autoplay to Off

Another script for YouTube is Better YouTube, compiled in 2008, by Gina Trapani from LifeHacker. This script is a compilation of popular Greasemonkey scripts, so you have to add only one script to get great YouTube enhancements. You'll find Better YouTube at https://addons.mozilla.org/en-US/firefox/addon/better-youtube/.

Here's what Better YouTube does:

- ▶ Creates a skin for YouTube that resizes the video to fit the size of your browser.
- ▶ Removes the extra page elements so you can concentrate on your video.
- ▶ Replaces the default YouTube video player with FlowPlayer. FlowPlayer does not automatically start videos. You must click the play button. This is helpful if you open many videos at once, or open a video while you're doing something else.
- ▶ Adds a button on every YouTube video that enables you to download the video.

SEARCHING YOUTUBE MORE EFFECTIVELY

Like Google, YouTube has a sophisticated search engine that lets you search through millions of videos to find the media content that you're looking for. You can customize the YouTube search results to return safe (non-explicit) videos, and videos uploaded at a certain time or date.

Safe Search

Exclude video content that you don't want your kids to find while browsing YouTube. Safety Mode filters video content and comments that may be offensive to some people. To turn Safety Mode on, log in to your YouTube account, and scroll down to the very bottom of the page. Under the links for the About Page, Press & Blogs, Copyright, and so on, look for the words Safety Mode. Click Off, to toggle it to ON. In the box that opens, select ON. Click either Save, or Save and Lock Safety Mode in This Browser to ensure that Safety Mode is in effect for all YouTube accounts accessed through the current browser.

Landing Better Search Results

Find the video you're looking for quickly with YouTube search options. To start, enter search criteria into the YouTube search box. Click Search. Above the search results, click the link for Search Options. In each category, click the search criteria you want to use. For example, if you want to locate a short music video that was uploaded in the past week, you should select Videos, Uploaded Date, This Week, Music, and Short to narrow video selections to within those parameters. You also can choose between Closed Captions, High Definition, Partner Videos, Rentals, and WebM (an open, royalty-free media file format: www.webmproject.org).

SUMMARY

YouTube controls are pretty straightforward, but with these tips you can personalize your YouTube experience to enjoy and share playlists and find your favorite artist easily.

Getting the Picture with Picasa and Picnik

With the popularity of digital photography, nearly everyone has a camera. Of course, having a digital camera means lots of photos to edit, store, and share. Picasa gives you local image editing and organization along with online web albums to make sharing a snap. With Picnik, you upload the picture you want to edit and do your photo editing online. When you're finished, the edited image is saved to your computer.

NAVIGATING PICASA

There are two parts to Picasa: the locally installed Picasa, a tool to help you edit and track your photo collection; and the online Picasa Web Albums, where you store your photos on Google's servers and can share them with other people.

> **NOTE** The easiest way to reach your online Picasa web album is to go to **www.google.com**, click on the More drop-down menu on the upper-left navigation menu and choose Photos. Or, to download the Picasa software program directly and install it on your computer, you can type **picasa.google .com** directly into your browser's address bar.

By default, Picasa scans your entire hard drive to find every image on your computer. It then builds a database of thumbnail images that are used in the Picasa display. Because of this image database, you should always use Picasa to move images on your hard drive. If you move images in any other way Picasa is unable to find the images you moved and repeats the hard drive scan. This can be potentially time consuming.

The Picasa interface is divided into three sections. The first section is the left-hand navigation. You use this to navigate the files on your computer. Picasa gives you the choice between Flat view, shown in Figure 15-1, and Tree view, shown in Figure 15-2.

After you've used Picasa's face recognition feature, you can also browse by people. (Read more about the face recognition feature at the end of the "Sharing Your Photos" section.) Expand the People tab to sort photos by the people in them, as shown in Figure 15-3.

The largest section of Picasa, just to the right of the navigation bar, is a thumbnail view of all the images in your collection. Scroll through the thumbnails using the slider "thumb" on the right edge of the window.

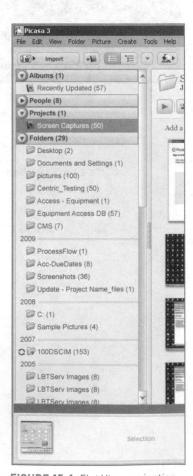

FIGURE 15-1: Flat View navigation.

Click a picture to select it. You can select multiple pictures by holding down the Ctrl key. Selected pictures appear as a thumbnail in the box in the lower-left corner. Right-click a picture and select Properties, and Picasa pulls up a list of all of the EXIF data related to that picture.

Use the filter buttons at the top center of Picasa to control which pictures are displayed. You can filter images based on whether they have faces in them, if they have Geo-Tag information attached (that is, if you've added information about where the picture was taken), or even if they've been flagged with a star. To the right of these buttons is a slider that filters based on the date the picture was taken. By default, it shows all pictures, and by sliding it all the way to the right, you can filter out any picture more than two days old. A green summary stripe, shown in Figure 15-4, appears under the filter buttons when any filter is active.

▶ EXIF, or Exchangeable Image File, data is the information that describes the camera settings used to take the photo. EXIF can show the ISO setting used, what lens was on the camera, whether the flash was used, and a wide variety of other information as well.

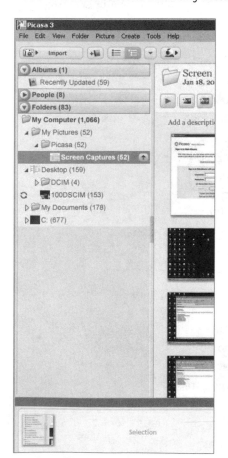

FIGURE 15-2: Tree View navigation.

FIGURE 15-3: Group your pictures by the people in the photos with face recognition.

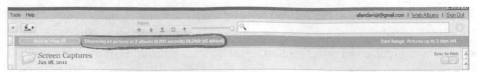

FIGURE 15-4: Summary stripe shows how the photos are filtered.

Using the Photo Editing Tools

The final section of Picasa navigation is along the bottom. This is where you find the photo-editing tools. Use them to rotate, e-mail, blog, print, or even Geo-Tag the selected images.

To edit a picture, first double-click the thumbnail in the main panel. Picasa zooms in on that individual picture and the editing tabs appear on the left, as shown in Figure 15-5.

Use the Basic Fixes tab, shown in Figure 15-6, to crop, auto-adjust color, remove red-eye, and add text to your pictures. Use the gray Caption stripe, just under the picture, to caption the picture. The caption won't print with the picture, but it is stored in the Picasa database. This is also where you find the Picnik link. Picnik is an online photo-editing tool acquired by Google in May 2010. You can move a picture to Picnik, make changes to the photo, and then send it back to Picasa, all with just a couple of mouse clicks. I cover Picnik in more depth later in this chapter.

FIGURE 15-5: Zoom on any picture to use the Picasa editing tools.

The Tuning tab, shown in Figure 15-7, gives you tools to control the lighting and color of your image. The Neutral Color Picker is especially useful for fixing pictures taken under artificial lighting. Simply use the Picker to select a spot in your image that should be white, instead of the purple or orange that ambient lighting caused it to be, and Picasa adjusts the picture accordingly.

The Effects tab, shown in Figure 15-8, is a collection of visual effects you can apply to your pictures, such as changing it to black and white or softening the overall focus.

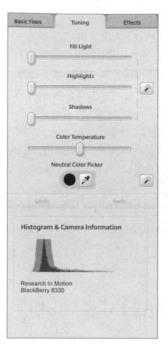

FIGURE 15-6: Access commonly used editing tools with the Basic Fixes tab.

FIGURE 15-7: Use the Tuning tab to adjust the color and lighting of your image.

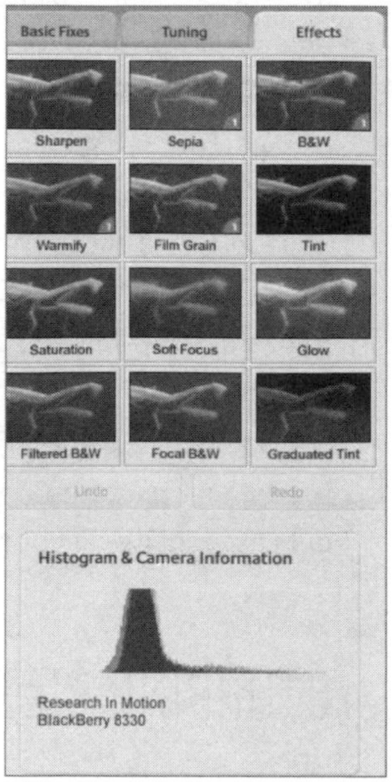

FIGURE 15-8: Apply visual effects with the Effects tab.

Storing Your Photos Online

After you're comfortable with the layout and placement of Picasa's controls, it's time to move your photos online. Highlight one or more pictures and pull down the Share list. With a brand-new install, the only available option is Enable Sync. Select it, and a pop-up displays asking for your Google account login information. This tells Picasa where to store your pictures online. After your account is linked, you can copy pictures to the Web with the Share button or the Sync to Web button.

Now, it's time to move on to the Web Album navigation. The top three tabs switch between your albums, the photos of people in your albums, and Explore. Explore enables you to see pictures uploaded by other people. These controls are shown in Figure 15-9.

On the right is another collection of the people in your pictures, your favorites, and Picasa suggestions of people you might want to add as favorites.

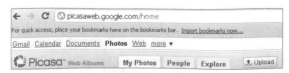

FIGURE 15-9: Navigate your Picasa Web Album.

Click any Gallery to view the pictures inside. From here, you can use the drop-down menu to share images, download to your local version of Picasa, or even order prints. Use the Edit drop-down menu to change the properties of the specific Gallery.

One thing that Picasa does very well is pick out faces from pictures. To try it out, go to Picasa, and hit the People filter near the top center. The left bar is replaced by a list of people, and one of them is named Unknown. Click this Unknown person, and Picasa shows you all of the faces it has managed to find in your pictures. It also groups them as best it can. Click a face to select and type the person's name in the box labeled Add a Name.

If you're logged in to your Google account, Picasa tries to match the name you're typing against your Contacts list. And the more people are named, the better Picasa gets at identifying your friends and family.

STOPPING PICASA FROM LOGGING SCREENSHOTS

Version 3 of Picasa has a feature—or perhaps a known bug—that causes it to take screenshots. For some systems, every time the user takes a screenshot, Picasa shoots a second one simultaneously. On other systems, screenshots happen randomly and frequently. It's a very annoying "feature" and should be fixed, but until the software developers make a fix, you can fix it yourself: Tell the system that Picasa no longer has access rights to the screenshot folder.

First, locate the screenshot folder. If you're using Windows XP, you should find the screenshot folder in C:\Documents and Settings\User.*loginname*\Documents\Pictures\Picasa\Screen Captures (Windows 7 users will find the screenshot folder in C:\users).

In Windows Explorer, right-click the Screen Captures folder and click Properties. From the Properties menu, click the Security tab, then Advanced. Find the checkbox labeled Inherit from Parent.... (See Figure 15-10.) A security alert will appear to verify the change in security settings. Approve it, save changes, and verify that the folder is no longer accessible.

This prevents Picasa from writing to the Screen Captures folder, and without access, Picasa stops taking screenshots.

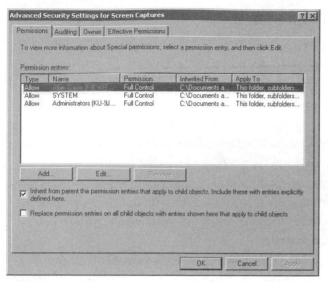

FIGURE 15-10: Change security settings for your Screen Captures folder in Picasa

SHARING YOUR PHOTOS

Editing pictures is only half of the story. You still need to share them to show them off, and that process starts with uploading the pictures. From within your local copy of Picasa, select the pictures or folders you'd like to share. Then click the button marked Share to open the drop-down menu. Select Enable Sync. Now you can click the button labeled Sync to Web in the upper right to upload your photos.

Uploading pictures to the Internet can take a while, especially when it's a very large collection, so don't stress if it doesn't happen immediately. After it's done, it's time to switch programs from Picasa to Picasa Web Albums.

You can find your Picasa Web Album at http://picasaweb.google.com. If you're already logged in to your Google account you go directly to the Web Album, otherwise Picasa Web asks you to log in.

After you've accessed your Picasa Web Album, click any thumbnail to open the album. On the right side of the window you see an information bar with all of the stats for this album. Using these controls, you can share your pictures with specific people or even post to Twitter and Blogger.

Using Picasa on Multiple Computers

Picasa is designed to be a standalone application. All the images you load into Picasa, and the captions, tags, and other notations to those images are stored in local files C:\Users*Your_login_name*\AppData\Local\Google\Picasa2 and C:\Users*Your_login_name*\AppData\Local\Google\Picasa2Albums.

For multiple computers to share the same database, these two files have to be stored in a more public space. Create a new folder that can be designated as a shared folder. Drag and drop the Picasa2 and Picasa2Albums into the shared folder.

▶ You must have administrator rights for this to work.

Now, you need to tell Picasa where to find the files. The best way to do this is with Shortcut. Click the Start button, and in the Run box, type **CMD**. Usually, you press Enter at this point, but if you hold down Ctrl and Shift and press Enter at the same time, an Elevated Command Prompt opens.

After you have your command prompt window open, you need to use the CD command to change your directory to the one where the Picasa database files lived before you moved them. In the Elevated Command Prompt, enter

```
cd \Users\Your_User_Name\AppData\Local\Google
```

Now, create the shortcut with the mklink command:

```
mklink /d Picasa2 C:\Users\Share\PicasaShare\Picasa2
mklink /d Picasa2Albums C:\Users\Share\PicasaShare\Picasa2Albums
```

Although these may look like the original files, they're really shortcuts to the new shared location. Picasa doesn't know the difference and uses the database in the new location.

Don't close the Elevated Command Prompt window yet. You've got a couple more shortcuts to make.

No matter which computer is reading the Picasa database, it expects to see the same drive letter. Remember, Picasa scans the hard drive, looking for new pictures to add to the collection. If some computers on the network use C: and others use, say, R:, then Picasa gets confused and treats the R: drive version as a freshly discovered, brand-new collection of pictures to be added.

To avoid this, you need to create a shortcut to the drive letter. Create the shortcut in the Root directory, C:, and call it drive letter P for Picasa. It connects to the shared directory C:\Users\Share that you created earlier. In the Elevated Command Prompt, enter

```
cd\ \
mklink /d P C:\Users\Share
```

Now, open Picasa. Open the Tools menu and select Folder Manager. De-select everything. Add P:\PicasaShare as the only folder it should watch.

You're done with the server part of this, that is, the computer that hosts the pictures for Picasa. You have to make a change to the client side of this, too. The other computers need a double shortcut to get everything working as it should.

Map the directory *//computername*/users/share, and call it drive letter Q.

In the Elevated Command Prompt, go back to the Root directory, and create a shortcut to link drive letter P to Q:

```
cd \
mklink \d P Q
```

Finally, tell the client computers where to find the Picasa database files. You need to do this on every computer that will share the Picasa database. In the Elevated Command Prompt, set up the following shortcuts in the original Google data directory:

```
cd  \Users\YourLoginNameHere\AppData\Local\Google
mklink /d Picasa2  Q:\PicasaLib\Picasa2
mklink /d Picasa2Albums Q:\PicasaLib\Picasa2Albums
```

Using Picasa with RSS

RSS, or Really Simple Syndication, is an excellent way to keep up-to-date with your favorite blogs and websites. Simply add the link for the RSS feed into your favorite RSS system, and it tracks all new posts for you.

Every Picasa Web Album has an RSS feed included. The link is on the right side of the main Picasa view. Right-click the RSS icon, select Copy Shortcut from the pop-up, and then paste into your RSS reader.

There's another use for RSS photo feeds. From your local Picasa, click Tools and select Configure Screensaver. The standard Windows screensaver interface displays, with Google Photos Screensaver selected by default. Click the Settings button.

As shown in Figure 15-11, there are four sources for images for a Picasa screensaver. The fourth one, Photos from Public Sites, accepts an RSS feed. This gives you total control over the pictures that show in your screensaver. Use photos on your system, photos in your Picasa Web Album, or even photos from other websites via RSS feed.

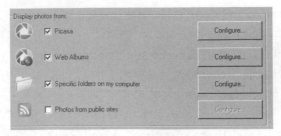

FIGURE 15-11: Use Picasa to create a custom screensaver.

Auto-Watermarking

It's almost always a good idea to use copyright notices on pictures you share online. This shows that the photograph is copyrighted, and the photographer is willing to protect that copyright. The difficulty, of course, lies in the time it takes to add that copyright notice to every one of a large batch of pictures.

Picasa has the perfect solution to this problem. Picasa offers an Automatic Watermark. From the Tools menu, click Options to bring up the dialog box shown in Figure 15-12. Select the Web Albums tab, and activate the last option, Add a Watermark for All Photo Uploads. In the textbox below that, enter the text that you would like added to every picture uploaded. Picasa does not add the watermark to the original—just to the copy that gets uploaded to Picasa Web Albums.

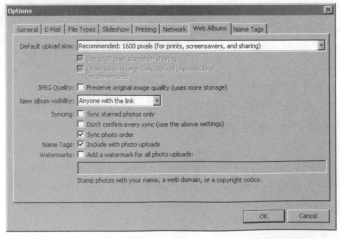

FIGURE 15-12: Use the Options dialog box to add a watermark to all your photos.

CREATING SPECIAL PROJECTS

Picasa has quite a few features that allow you to work with pictures, collections of pictures, and even video clips.

Collages

Most photo-editing programs have a feature that enables you to build a Contact Sheet—that is, a set of tiny thumbnails, one for each picture in your collection. Picasa takes this a step further, enabling you to make full-blown photo collages. To create a collage, click Create in the top toolbar. Select Picture Collage from the menu. With six different collage formats, there's sure to be something that catches your eye.

Movie Presentations

Create a slideshow and turn it into a YouTube video with Picasa Movie Maker.

When you open Picasa, click Movie Maker in the left navigation. Movie Maker enables you to arrange your slideshow however you like.

The first tab, Movie, handles overall formatting, such as the dimensions, transitions between slides, and overall timing. You can even insert an audio track.

The second tab, Slide, controls the formatting of each slide. Change the background color or add text to each slide.

Clips, the third and final tab, holds all slides you've chosen to include in your movie. Use this tab to reorder the images until you have the desired result.

After you've arranged your slideshow save it, and click the YouTube button. Your movie is uploaded to YouTube.

Editing Video

Launching a video file in Picasa opens the Movie Editor. Picasa enables you to do basic editing on video clips. You can rotate the entire video clip 90 degrees, or reset the start and end marks on a clip and save the new shorter version. You can upload your new video to YouTube, and even take snapshots of the clip.

ADVANCED PHOTO EDITING WITH PICNIK

Picasa is not the only option Google offers for editing your images. Google also owns Picnik, an online image-editing program. You can get to it via the link in Picasa, or navigate directly to www.picnik.com.

Registering for a Picnik account is not a requirement, but it does simplify using the site. After you're registered, the Picnik system remembers all the places your images are stored. Without registering, you have to connect your pictures every time you launch the program.

> **NOTE** The free version of Picnik allows only one connection to an outside photo collection. When you store images on both Picasa and Flickr you can connect to only one at a time with the free account. This restriction is lifted with a paid account.

To edit one of your pictures, click the small icon below it, and select Edit from the menu. From here, you can tweak the exposure, adjust the colors, remove red-eye, and sharpen the image. If you're feeling brave, try the Auto-Fix button. It's the first one in the menu. Picnik takes its best guess at what needs to be fixed—which may be exactly what the picture needs, or might leave the image unrecognizable.

The Edit tools in Picnik cover the most common photo adjustments, but the tab where Picnik really shines is the Create tab.

Use the Create tab to add special effects such as stickers and frames, or add a text caption. However, this is also where Picnik wants to convince you to upgrade to a Premium account, because some of the most interesting effects are locked for basic accounts.

Picnik may not have the sheer muscle of Photoshop or Gimp, but it has the most commonly used tools for free. The added benefit of being able to read directly from your Flickr or Picasa Web albums makes it an excellent addition to a digital photographer's bag of tricks.

SUMMARY

Picasa, with related online tools Picasa Web Albums and Picnik, puts a full array of photography tools at the fingertips of a digital photographer. The ability to share photos online rounds out the package perfectly.

Part V

GOOGLE SOCIAL AND COLLABORATION APP SECRETS

Google Talk Secrets

Google Talk is Google's standalone chat program. Use it to chat with or make voice calls to other Google Talk users. Google Talk is compatible with other chat clients, giving you the ability to combine all your chat programs into one client. Inline command parameters and talk registry tweaks give you added power and flexibility.

CHATTING WITH GOOGLE TALK

▶ ICQ (www.icq. com) is one of the early successful Internet chat clients. The acronym is a homophone for "I seek you."

Chat has come a long way since the early days of ICQ. Today's chat programs are integrated and do a lot more than just carry text back and forth between users, and users now expect more out of a chat program. Google Talk lives up to those expectations with a host of features and capabilities.

Downloading Google Talk is rather simple. A visit to www.google.com/talk guides you through the very easy installation process (you can install the video chat plug-in for Gmail, iGoogle, and Orkut, or the desktop Google Talk chat client).

Using Multiple Identities

Some people have several Google accounts. You might have a personal profile address and a business profile address, for example. (Using a personal profile for business purposes isn't professional.) Here is a method for opening multiple instances of Google Talk.

Create a new shortcut on your desktop. Name it Gtalk Personal, and use this for the target:

C:\Program Files\google\google talk\googletalk.exe/nomutex

(Windows 7 users can bring up Windows Explorer, select Computer [OS C:] from the left navigation menu, click the Program Files folder and search for the Google Talk folder.)

Now, make another identical shortcut, but call this one Gtalk Business. The key here is the /nomutex option. Nomutex allows Google Talk to run multiple copies at the same time.

Create a desktop shortcut that uses the nomutex tag, as shown in Figure 16-1, to run multiple Google Talk windows simultaneously.

Now that the two desktop shortcuts have been created, you can choose either one to launch when you need to speak to a client or colleague for business or when you want to chat with a buddy or the significant other for pleasure.

FIGURE 16-1: Create a desktop shortcut using the nomutex tag to run multiple instances of Google Talk.

Using Google Talk in a Web Browser

You aren't limited to using Google Talk solely through the program. It's possible to use Google Talk in a browser—especially if that browser is Firefox!

Type the following link into your Firefox browser, and bookmark it:

```
http://talkgadget.google.com/talkgadget/client
```

Depending on your browser, you may have other options. For example, in Mozilla Firefox, right-click the Google Talk bookmark and select Properties. At the bottom of the Properties window, select Load This Bookmark in the Sidebar. Whenever Google Talk opens, it shows up in the sidebar, making it visible no matter which Firefox tab is open.

Managing Chats

Google Talk has a wide variety of tricks and secrets for use during chats:

- ▶ To change the font size, press and hold the Ctrl key and move the scroll wheel on your mouse up or down.

- ▶ Press Shift+Enter on your keyboard to insert line breaks into a message.

- ▶ Bold a word or phrase by enclosing it in asterisks as I've done with the following phrase: *like this*.

- ▶ Italicize a word or phrase with an underscore on either side like so: _like this_.

- ▶ Add extra space between lines by pressing Ctrl+5 to put 1.5 spaces between lines or Ctrl+2 to put double spaces between lines.

- ▶ Use Ctrl+Shift+L to shift between numbers, letters, capital letters, Roman numerals, and capital Roman numerals.

You can play music to a friend over Google Talk. First, unplug your microphone. Double-click the speaker icon in the lower-right corner to open the volume controls. Select Options and then Properties. Check Recording. Now click OK to save. The Recording Control screen opens. Select Wave Out Mix, and use Google Talk to call a friend so they can hear your music. This music can come from a audio CD or an .mp3 file on your hard drive.

CALLING WITH GOOGLE TALK

Google Talk requires a software download for voice and video. Visit this URL:

`www.google.com/chat/video`

The download and install takes only a few seconds. After the download finishes, restart all browser windows, and Google Talk is ready for both audio and video.

Making Voice Calls

Making a voice call from Google Talk is as easy as browsing through your contacts list. Mouse over the contact you want to call and click the Call button on the resulting pop-up, shown in Figure 16-2. If there's no phone number listed for that contact, the Call button does not appear. You cannot call someone who isn't stored in your contact list, so be sure to add your desired contact before attempting to make a call.

FIGURE 16-2: Place a voice call with Google Talk.

Using Google Talk on Mobile Phones

iGoogle Talk is now available for a wide variety of mobile phones. Previously, only the iPhone was compatible, but over time, Google Talk functions have appeared on most of the major device lines, including Blackberry, Palm Pre, Android, and Nokia. (You should visit your device's app store to download the appropriate Google Talk app.)

The Google Talk Gadget, a Flash-based tool, makes it possible for any mobile device that supports Flash to also support Google Talk.

USING GOOGLE TALK ON OTHER IM NETWORKS

Quite a few chat clients are available. Trillian, Pidgin, iChat, and Kopete are some popular examples. Google's chat client is called Google Talk, and you can download it here: www.google.com/talk/.

Google Talk is a great chat client; it supports standard text chat, along with video chat, audio conferencing, file transfers, and status updates, but if you use a Mac or Linux machine, Google Talk won't work. It runs only on computers and mobile devices running some version of Microsoft Windows.

Those of us who use Linux or Mac have plenty of options, although most chat clients work with only one or two operating systems. For example, iChat works only on Mac OSX, whereas Kopete and Empathy can only be installed on a Linux system. Pidgin is a solid chat client that is installable on Windows, OSX, and Linux systems. Most users may not see the advantages of a chat client that can be installed on any one of the big three operating systems, but if you're like me, and use all three operating systems, it's nice to have one program you can use across all three.

WHERE TO FIND CHAT CLIENTS

If you don't already have a chat client on your computer, visit the following websites to download the client that will work for you:

Google Talk: **www.google.com/talk**

iChat: Comes preloaded with MacOSX

Kopete: Linux repository or **kopete.kde.org/releases.php**

Empathy: Pre-installed in some Linux distros or **live.gnome.org/Empathy**

Pidgin: **www.pidgin.im**

Trillian: **www.trillian.im**

Here are some of the more popular chat clients:

▶ **iChat**—iChat is compatible with Google Talk, provided you have the Mac OSX Tiger operating system. Older versions do not connect.

▶ **Trillian**—The free version of Trillian does not connect with Google Talk but Trillian Pro does.

▶ **Pidgin**—Pidgin is fully compatible with Google Talk.

▶ **Other Clients**—Google Talk is compatible with any other chat clients that use the Jabber/XMPP (Extensible Messaging and Presence Protocol) protocol, including Miranda (Windows), Psi (Windows, OSX, Linux), Adium (OSX), and Kopete (Linux).

TWEAKING GOOGLE TALK'S REGISTRY FOR ADDITIONAL POWER

Google Talk has a few hidden features that can be reached only through the Windows Registry.

> **NOTE**   Before you make any Registry changes, back up your Registry. Changes to the Registry can lock up your computer, cause it to refuse to boot, or even damage your operating system installation and require a hard drive reformat. Visit **http://support.microsoft.com/kb/322756** for assistance on backing up your Windows computer's Registry.

Google Talk registry keys are located at HKEY_CURRENT_USER\Software\Google\ Google Talk\Options. Open Regedit and browse to this section. You can modify the following features of Google Talk:

▶ **Away inactive**—Used to set the status to Away after a certain number of minutes.
HKEY_CURRENT_USER\Software\Google\Google Talk\Options\away_inactive

▶ **Away screensaver**—Used to set the status to Away after a period with the screensaver active.
HKEY_CURRENT_USER\Software\Google\Google Talk\Options\ away_screensaver

▶ **Away screensaver minutes**—Used to set the status to Away after a certain number of minutes have passed.
HKEY_CURRENT_USER\Software\Google\Google Talk\Options\ away_inactive_minutes

MAKING THE MOST OF INLINE COMMAND PARAMETERS

You can also change Google Talk's command-line parameters to change the way it functions. Go to C:\Program Files\google\google talk\googletalk.exe on Windows XP platforms and C:\Users\Your-Name\AppData\Roaming\Google\Google Talk\googletalk.exe. Right-click the filename and add the parameter you want to use after .exe. Here are a few:

- ► /nomutex—Opens more than one instance of Google Talk.

- ► /factoryreset—Returns Google Talk to default settings.

- ► /diag—Starts Google Talk in diagnostic mode.

- ► /mailto email@host.com—Sends e-mail with Gmail.

- ► /plaintextauth—Uses plain authentication instead of the standard GAIA mechanism. This is used for testing.

SUMMARY

Google Talk gives you one more way to effectively communicate so you can keep in touch with the latest family news, or just share your favorite music with friends far away. Using Google Talk for voice calls helps bring you even closer to your friends and family.

CHAPTER 17

Staying Connected with Google Voice

Sure, you can make telephone calls from Google Chat on your Gmail page, but Google Voice gives you all the features of a paid VoIP (Voice over Internet Protocol) service, including custom phone numbers and the ability to change your phone number without any hassles. Plus, Google Voice lets you send SMS, and you can use your Google Voice number on your cell phone for calls or text messaging. Let's see your home VoIP service do that!

VOICE OVER INTERNET PROTOCOL (VOIP)

Voice Over Internet Protocol (VoIP) is essentially a way for someone to call someone else using a computer instead of using a landline or mobile phone. Google has integrated VoIP with Google Talk and within Gmail's chat feature. With VoIP services, callers use headphone and microphone combinations instead of traditional phones to communicate with one another.

TAKING ADVANTAGE OF CALL FEATURES

Google Voice sports all the features of the big paid VoIP services, including the services you've come to rely on such as a text copy of all voicemail sent directly to your Gmail Inbox. But Google's done one better. Because voice-to-text transcription isn't perfect, sometimes you need to hear the voicemail for the message to make sense. Turn on Google Voice player to listen to voicemail from the e-mail notification.

To turn on Google Voice player, log in to your Gmail account and go to Labs. Look for the lab titled Google Voice Player in Mail by Robert D. Click Enable, then save your changes. When you receive a voicemail notification you will still get the text transcription, but, as shown in Figure 17-1, a link to play the message is now included. Click Play Message to open the Google Voice mailbox in a new tab. When the page loads, your voicemail will play automatically.

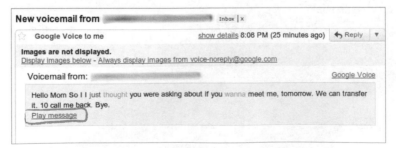

FIGURE 17-1: Google Voice message notification with Play Message link included.

Because Google Voice generates a unique phone number, you can use your Google Voice number to make calls from your mobile device while keeping your actual phone number private. This feature supports Blackberry, Android-powered phones, iPhone, and any mobile device running Palm Web OS. To access this feature, use your phone's web browser, and log on to m.google.com/voice.

From the Google Voice mobile web page, you have access to your Google Voice contact list and voicemail, and can make phone calls using your mobile device using the on-screen keypad.

Text messages you send while logged in to Google Voice are free, just as if you were logged in on your computer. International calls made from within Google Voice Mobile are charged at the Google Voice rate for that country, and charges are deducted from your Google Voice account.

> **NOTE** Blackberry, Android, and iPhone users can download an app to handle Google Voice functions from m.google.com/voice. Other types of phones must access Google Voice via the mobile website.

You can use Google Voice to keep your home or office number private, too. From any phone, dial your Google Voice number. Press the asterisk (*) when the call connects. Enter your Google Voice PIN when directed and press 2 on your telephone keypad. Now, dial the number you want to call. The person you're calling will see your Google Voice number on his or her Caller ID rather than the number of the landline from which you're calling.

When you don't want to be disturbed by phone calls or text messages simply turn them off for a pre-set amount of time with Do Not Disturb. To activate the Do Not Disturb feature, log in to your Google Voice account. From the Google Voice Inbox, go to Voice Settings and select the Calls tab. Check Do Not Disturb. Calls go directly to your voice mail when Do Not Disturb is turned on. To automatically return Google Voice to normal function at a predetermined time, check Ends In. Use the drop-down menu to set the unit in time, and type the amount of time in the box, as shown in Figure 17-2.

If you use Google Voice from your computer often, the keyboard shortcuts in Table 17-1 should come in handy.

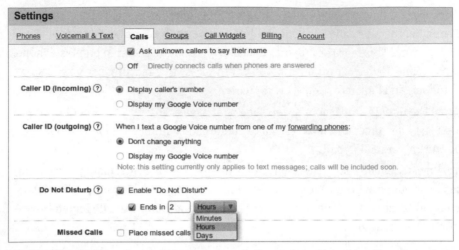

FIGURE 17-2: Program Google Voice to automatically return to normal function.

TABLE 17-1: Keyboard Shortcuts for Google Voice

KEYBOARD	ACTION
C	Open Quick Call
M	Open Quick SMS
Esc	Close Quick Call and/or Quick SMS
/	Go to Search Box
N or Right Arrow	Advance to next page
P or Left Arrow	Back to previous page
#	Move selected message(s) to Trash
!	Mark as SPAM
Shift+I	Mark message as read
Shift+U	Mark message as unread
G then I	Go to Inbox
G then S	See all starred messages
G then H	Open History
G then P	See all placed calls

KEYBOARD	ACTION
G then R	View all received calls
G then M	View all missed calls
G then C	Open Contacts
G then U	View all unread messages
* then A	Select all messages
* then N	De-select all messages
* then R	Select all read messages
* then U	Select all unread messages

ADDING THE POWER OF SMS

SMS messages give you the ability to get a message of up to 160 characters to some-one's cell phone quickly and easily.

Send SMS messages to up to five people at once with Google Voice. From within Google Voice click Text. Enter the phone numbers to which you want to send an SMS message. Separate each phone number with a comma. Enter your message of up to 160 characters in the textbox and click Send.

When you use your Google Voice number for text messages, all incoming messages are forwarded only to those phones you've marked as mobile phones in the Phones tab. A copy of the text message stays in your Google Voice Text folder. Text messages are stored using conversation view for easy searching.

An alternative to receiving text messages on your phone is to have them forwarded to your Gmail account. To turn on text message forwarding, log in to Google Voice. Click Settings in the upper right, and select the Voicemail & Text tab. Look for Text Forward-ing, and click the box in front of Forward Text Messages to My Email. The e-mail to which messages should be forwarded is noted at the end of the line.

I don't know about you, but for me, typing on my computer keyboard is a lot easier than typing on any phone keyboard. At the same time it's distracting to stop what I'm doing and log in to Google Voice just to answer a text message. Instead, I use either Gmail or Google Chat on my Gmail page to answer SMS messages sent to my phone while I'm at the computer.

There are two ways to do this. First, compose a new e-mail and type the phone number to which you are sending the text into the address field. Type and send your message like you do any other e-mail. Keep in mind that if your message is longer than 160 characters your message is split up into two or more messages and sent consecutively one after the other.

Or, mouse over the person's ID from your Google Chat list on the left of your Gmail page. From the menu box, select Video & More. Now, click Send SMS as shown in Figure 17-3. Using this feature helps keep you from sending messages that are longer than the 160-character SMS limit.

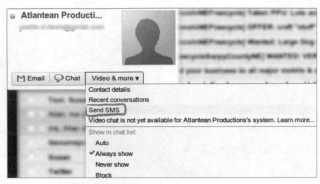

FIGURE 17-3: Use Google Chat in Gmail to send SMS messages.

PERSONALIZING GOOGLE VOICE TO MAKE IT YOUR OWN

▶ There is a one-time $10 fee to change your Google Voice number.

You might need to change your Google Voice number for many reasons. Maybe you've been using the number for your business, and you've sold or closed the business. Or, perhaps you've moved to a different state and want a number local to where you now live. Whatever the reason, you can change your Google Voice number easily. From within Google Voice, go to Settings. Under the Phones tab and next to your Google Voice number, click the link titled Change/Port. From the pop-up, select either I Want to Get a Different Google Voice Number or I Want to Use My Existing Mobile Number Instead. Use the tool to choose your new number, confirm, and pay for the number change. Your old number remains active for three months after you change your number.

Add a Google Voice extension to your Google Chrome web browser so you can keep on top of who is calling you. Extensions do things such as let you see at a glance if you have voicemail or text messages waiting or read messages from your Google Chrome toolbar with just one click.

From the Google Chrome browser, click the wrench icon. Select Tools → Extensions from the menu. Click Get More Extensions at the bottom of the page. Search for Google Voice and select the Google Voice extension you like best. Follow the on-screen instructions for installation. I use the Google Voice extension created by Google Voice, but several others are available. Figure 17-4 shows the extension I use in my Google Chrome toolbar.

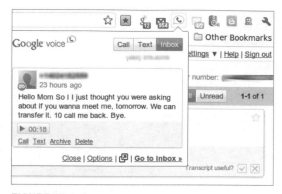

FIGURE 17-4: The Google Voice extension for Chrome. This extension was written by Google Voice.

Annoyed by that salesperson who just won't stop calling? Block them and forget 'em. From your Google Voice Inbox find the caller you want to block. Click the More link and select Block Caller from the drop-down. Now, when that person calls, he or she hears a message saying your number has been disconnected.

Add a Call Widget to your blog or website so readers can call you directly by clicking a button on your blog or website. Your number is not given to the caller, and remains private. From your Google Voice Inbox, click Settings. Go to the Call Widgets tab and click Add a New Call Widget.

Enter a name for the new widget. Then, use the given form to tell Google Talk where to ring you when the Call Widget is used, and which voicemail greeting should be used. Select On to require callers to state their name. Select Off to connect the call right away. Save your changes. Google Voice generates the needed HTML. Copy the HTML to your computer's clipboard and paste it to the appropriate location within your blog's or website's HTML template.

SUMMARY

Whether you want to communicate across town, or across the world, Google Voice gives you the tools you need to get your message through at rates you can afford. Unique calling, SMS, mobile, and keyboard shortcuts help you make Google Voice the one-stop shop for all your telephone needs.

CHAPTER 18

Catching the Buzz: Google Buzz

Buzz is Google's answer to Twitter. Instead of "tweeting" your news you can "buzz" it instead. I find Buzz more convenient than other forms of short message networking because Buzz sits on my Gmail page and I don't have to open up a second window or browser, like I would with Twitter. When you combine Buzz with Gmail, Orkut, Facebook, or Twitter you create a one-stop method of updating all your social media at once.

ADDING SECRET POWERS WITH BROWSER EXTENSIONS

As with most of the Google apps we've discussed, and in fact, any website in existence, Buzz can be improved or enhanced with the use of browser extensions and userscripts.

To locate extensions for the Mozilla Firefox web browser, go to www.mozilla.com and click the Add-Ons tab in the top navigation. Use the search box at the top of the page to search for Google Buzz.

Google Chrome users need to click the wrench on the right side of their Chrome browser. From the drop-down menu, select Tools, then Extensions. Scroll to the bottom of your list of installed extensions and click Get More Extensions. Use the search bar to search for Google Buzz.

Here is a sampling of my favorite extensions for Google Buzz for both Firefox and Chrome.

Buzz Plus, for Chrome, lets you reply to comments made by people other than the Buzz post author, or reply directly to the author of any Buzz post. You'll find Buzz Plus at http://goo.gl/o7v6u.

Buzz any web page with one click, and see how many times that web page has been "buzzed" with the Google Buzz Button for Google Chrome. This button is displayed in your Chrome toolbar. Click it to quickly Buzz any page. Install the Google Buzz Button from http://goo.gl/vkyku.

Hide Buzz posts from those people who are rude or annoying with Buzz Troll Remover for Chrome, found here: http://goo.gl/85B7W.

Shareaholic for Mozilla Firefox gives you one-button sharing for all your social media sites, including Buzz. You can find Shareaholic at https://addons.mozilla.org/en-US/firefox/addon/shareaholic-share-links-with-g/.

Buzz it! makes Buzz status updates via Gmail while shortening the URLs you Buzz with bit.ly. Buzz it! is found here: http://goo.gl/4udmd.

User, or Greasmonkey, scripts are just as easy to use, and are usually much smaller than browser extensions. You'll find a couple good ones in the following list. As always, read the comments, reviews, and discussions of any script before you install it to your browser.

- ▶ The Google Buzz Comment Emoticon adds cool emoticons to your Google Buzz posts. Install it from http://userscripts.org/scripts/show/68749.

- ▶ Search for the five most recent buzz posts on any topic with Buzz Search Results on Google, by Mark Carey. You can get this script here: http://userscripts.org/scripts/show/70491.

BUZZING BY RSS

If you already use an RSS feed to keep on top of your favorite news and entertainment sites, you might want to consider following your Buzz contacts through RSS as well.

To follow a Buzz contact through RSS, go to that person's Google Profile. Look for the orange RSS icon in your browser's address bar, as shown in Figure 18-1. Click the icon to add the person to your favorite RSS reader.

▶ Find anyone's Google profile with this web address: www.google.com / profiles?q=Name_ of_Person.

RSS icon

FIGURE 18-1: Click the RSS reader icon to follow someone's Buzz from your favorite RSS reader.

CREATING E-MAIL BUZZ

Use the drop-down menu to the right of your Buzz screen to follow that person's Buzz by e-mail, or to e-mail a Buzz post to someone else. Use this menu to mute that Buzz post, mute all Twitter posts from the person, link to the post, or stop following the person. Figure 18-2 shows the menu options.

Update your own Buzz via e-mail. Before you can post text and images to Buzz from your Gmail account, you need to connect Buzz to Gmail. To do this, head to your Buzz homepage. Click (Number) Connected Sites. (You can find this link to the right of your name.) In the box that opens, shown in Figure 18-3, find Posted via buzz@gmail. Click Add on the right. Click Next Step. Verify your profile information, and click Save Profile and Continue.

FIGURE 18-2: Use the drop-down menu for added Buzz options, including Buzz by e-mail.

Now you can send text and images to your Buzz account from your connected Gmail account. Type your Buzz status update into the subject of an e-mail and sent it to buzz@gmail.com. To post images, add them to the e-mail as an attachment. Gmail sends you an e-mail when your Buzz post is live.

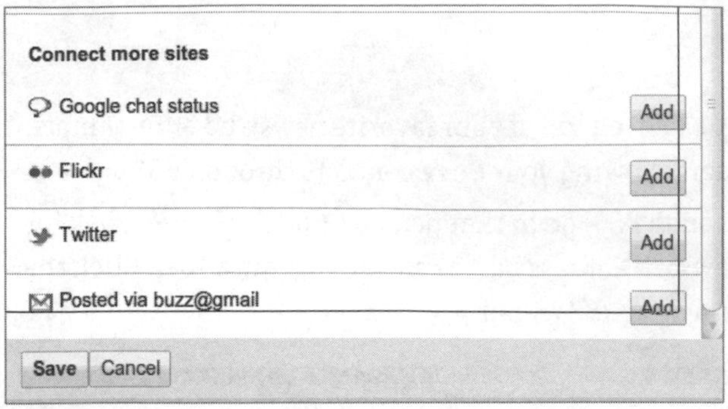

FIGURE 18-3: Connect Gmail to Buzz.

FILTERING BUZZ

If you're overwhelmed by too many Buzz posts, you can turn it off. When you turn off Google Buzz, you won't be able to receive or make Buzz updates. To turn Google Buzz off, go to your Google profile page and click Edit Profile in the upper right of the screen. Now, scroll all the way to the bottom and look for the words Delete Profile and Disable Google Buzz Completely in red letters. Click this link. On the verification page, click Yes, Delete my Profile and Posts. This is a permanent action, and cannot be undone.

Some people don't like others to see their friends list. You can make your Buzz list private so that only you know who you're following. To make your Buzz list private, sign in to your Google account, and go to your profile page. Click Edit Profile at the top-right of the screen. Uncheck the box marked Display the List of People I'm Following. Save your changes.

BUZZZY—THE SECRET BUZZ SEARCH ENGINE

Buzzzy searches Google Buzz for the latest, greatest information on any topic. Use Buzzzy, `http://buzzzy.com`, to find out what everyone is talking about on Buzz. Search for text, videos, and images uploaded to Google Buzz.

When you search for a term on Buzzzy, results are listed by relevance, by default. Use the options on the left to refine your search by country, date, source, media, or even language, as shown in Figure 18-4.

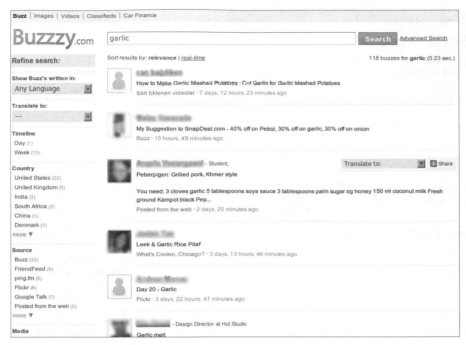

FIGURE 18-4: Use Buzzzy.com to find out what's happening on Google Buzz.

After you find the results you're looking for, use the integrated Share button to rebroadcast the post through your Buzz, Facebook, or Twitter account.

CONNECTING BUZZ SITES

Connect your Buzz to other services, like Flickr, Blogger, Chat, Google Reader, or Twitter so you can post Buzz directly from those websites. From your Buzz homepage, click (Number) Connected Sites, to the right of your name. Find the site you want to connect to your Buzz and click Add. What you post is then pushed over to Google Buzz after you've added a site.

After the site is added, you can control sharing settings through the Edit button. Choose between Public Buzz, when everyone on your Buzz list can view the post, or Private. When you set a site to Private share, you can designate a group of contacts the post is to be shared with. Figure 18-5 shows the Private share options.

Web developers and programmers can connect any website to Buzz through Buzz API. Developers can find in-depth information on this, along with code libraries for Java, Python, and PHP at www.code.google.com/apis/buzz/v1/getting_started.html.

FIGURE 18-5: Private Buzz options.

USING BUZZ WITH OTHER SOCIAL MEDIA

Connect Buzz with your other social media networks so you only have to update once. There a several options for this.

The easiest way is to use one of the social media–updating applications discussed in the "Adding Secret Powers with Browser Extensions" section of this chapter.

The next simplest is to take advantage of a social networking distributor program, such as Gwibber for Linux. Enter your social media information, grant the program access rights, and you can update all your social media networks without ever leaving your desktop.

Barring those options, I suggest connecting your Buzz account to your Twitter account using the site connection tools discussed in the section titled "Connecting Buzz Sites" earlier in this chapter. When you post to your Twitter account, you'll be posting to Buzz, too.

Or, you can use an outside application, such as https://posterous.com, to update all your social media at once from your e-mail.

USING BUZZ TOOLS

Having a way for users to share your content via Google Buzz enhances your social media experience. Adding content to your own Google Buzz account continues to add to the social media experience with Google. There are a couple of tools that can make this possible for you.

BuzzThis

BuzzThis adds a button to your website, blog, or page that enables users to share your site through their Buzz with one click. This works exactly like the Digg, Facebook, or TwitThis buttons you've seen on many websites. You can download BuzzThis from the creator's website: http://drupal.org/project/buzzthis. Because download and install procedures vary depending on the operating system you use, be sure to read the online installation instructions for your operating system.

Buzz It!

Buzz It! is a browser add-on for Mozilla Firefox. It automatically shares the web page you are viewing with your Buzz via e-mail. So, if you want to share a news story on your Buzz account simply click the Buzz It button in your Firefox browser and Buzz It! uses your e-mail to send the link to your Buzz account. You can find Buzz It! at https://addons.mozilla.org/en-US/firefox/addon/buzz-it/.

SUMMARY

Google Buzz is a powerful social media tool that allows you to spread your message quickly to your Google friends, and throughout the world. Browser add-ons and userscripts extend the function of Buzz, making it truly a social media outlet worthy of notice.

Socializing with Orkut

Orkut is Google's answer to social networking. See friends'
update statuses, post messages, upload pictures and video of last night's party—Orkut
has it all. You can even use video chat from within Orkut. And unlike some of the big
guys, with Orkut, you have complete control over how your page looks. Use Orkut Apps on
your homepage so you can keep track of world news, the stock market, convert currency,
play games, listen to music, and more, right from your Orkut page. Orkut's privacy settings ensure that you are in complete control of your personal information.

SOCIAL NETWORKING WITH ORKUT

▶ Services are listed in categories according to function, and in alphabetical order within those categories.

Everyone who has a Google account can use Orkut. If this is your first time using Orkut, the first thing you need to do is activate it within your Google services. Log in to your Google account, and go to Google Account Settings. Scroll down to the section titled Try Something New. If Orkut is not listed there, click More for the complete list of Google services. Orkut is listed on the right side of the page, under the heading Communicate, Show & Share. Click Orkut on the list, then enter, or confirm, your Google login information.

As shown in Figure 19-1, Orkut asks if it may sign you out of Google. Click Yes to continue with the setup.

FIGURE 19-1: Log out of Google to set up your Orkut account.

On the next page, enter the name you want displayed on your Orkut page. If you're concerned about privacy you can use your initial or a nickname. Use the drop-down menus to enter your birth date. By default, Orkut does not show your birth date to anyone. Click Display My Age for My Future Orkut Friends to display your birth date. Use the radio buttons to select your gender. Finally, read the Terms of Service, and click I Accept.

The next screen asks you to create a Google account to use with Orkut. You can simply use your existing Google account. Enter and re-enter your password, and complete the word verification. Click Create My Google Account. That's it; your Orkut account is now active.

Of course, after you activate your account, you want to add friends with whom to socialize. Use Orkut friend suggestions to quickly see which of your Gmail contacts uses Orkut. Click Add under the person's image to add them to your network, or click the X in the right corner of their image to remove the person from your suggested friends list. To add people not on your suggested friends list, use the search tool in the box labeled Friends. Type the name or e-mail address of the person you want to add in the search box. Click the Search for on Orkut link, as shown in Figure 19-2.

Orkut gives you full control over your personal information. From your Orkut homepage, click the Profile tab in the upper navigation. Click Edit My Profile Info. You can find this link in the header, to the right of your name. Click the Privacy tab. As you can see in Figure 19-3, Orkut gives you full control over the following:

FIGURE 19-2: Search for friends on Orkut.

► Who sees your profile

► Who can send you friend requests

► Who can write you

► How you are tagged in photos

► Who may view your e-mail address

► Who may find you on Orkut

Orkut even gives you the ability to see who visits your profile. Be sure to save your settings when you're finished.

Posting to Orkut is as simple as typing in the status update box. When you click the status update box to type, icons appear at the top of the box to enable you to insert emoticons, change the text color, and add bold, underlined, and italicized text to your status updates. You can also add images, videos, and maps directly within your status update. Figure 19-4 shows a status update that includes an image, colored text, and an emoticon.

Personalize your status update even further with HTML. To the right of the status update box toolbar, click the HTML link to customize your update using HTML.

Social networking is, by definition, about being involved in groups that interest you and doing fun things with friends. For this, Orkut offers communities and online games.

To join an Orkut community, click the Communities tab in the upper navigation. Choose a category to find the exact group you're looking for. From the category homepage, either scroll through all the groups until you find the one you want, or use the search bar in the upper right to find a group on your topic quickly. Group information is shown on the homepage. The information provided varies by group, but in general the group's homepage may include information on group rules, language of the group, group owner, group creation date, number of members, sample forum posts, and open polls. To join a group, click Join in the left navigation.

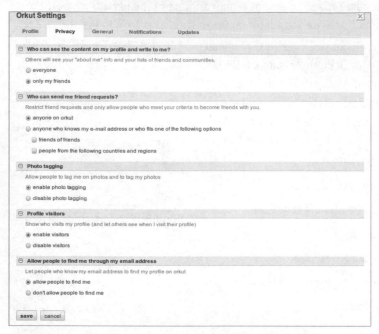

FIGURE 19-3: Use privacy settings to control who may see your account, tag you in photos, and find you on Orkut.

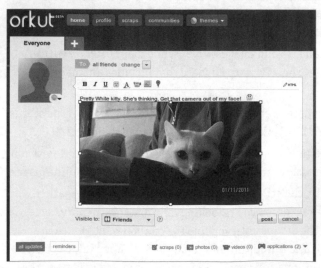

FIGURE 19-4: Include photos, emoticons, colored text, and video in your status updates.

INTEGRATING ORKUT WITH OTHER GOOGLE APPLICATIONS

Google hosts many apps that help you communicate faster, and Orkut is no different. Integrated Google Chat lets you see when people in your Chat list are online.

In the lower-right corner of every profile picture, there is a small circle. This circle indicates the person's online status. The online status dots are color-coded in the same manner as Google Chat within Gmail, so there's never any confusion. To start chatting with a friend, click his/her online status dot to open the chat window.

To control whether your friends see you online, click the online status dot in the lower-right corner of your profile image. As shown in Figure 19-5, a menu displays to give you the option of showing yourself as Available, Busy, Invisible, or Offline. Click your desired status from the menu.

FIGURE 19-5: Set your online chat status from Orkut.

Orkut is also integrated with Picasa for easy photo display.

To share your Picasa photos, click the Photos link, then Add from Picasa, in the blue highlighted area. Choose the photos you want to display on your Orkut page, and click Done. You can also access Picasa navigation from the link labeled Import from Picasa, to the right of the button labeled Create Album.

YouTube is also integrated with Orkut, so you can add any YouTube video with two clicks. To add a YouTube video, click Videos as shown in Figure 19-6. Enter the URL of the YouTube video you want to add, and click Post.

Bring your favorite web apps to your Orkut page. Click Applications. From the drop-down menu, select Add Applications. Use the categories to the left to navigate the applications list. You'll find useful apps such as Google News, Facebook, Article of the Day, political updates, BooksiRead, and others in the offerings. When you find an app you want to add, click Add.

FIGURE 19-6: Clicking the videos link enables you to add YouTube videos to your Orkut account.

If you can't find the app you want, you can submit your own. Click Submit Your Application at the bottom of the category list. Enter the URL and category information, as shown in Figure 19-7. Click Submit. Google notifies you when your application request is approved.

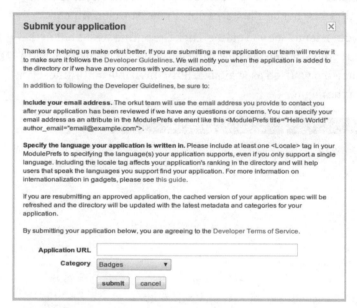

FIGURE 19-7: Enter the URL and Category of the application you want Google to add to Orkut.

Add functionality to Orkut with Greasemonkey or userscripts. My favorites are

▶ **Orkut Manager Plus**—Adds SPAM checker and on-screen keyboard. Enables you to bookmark communities, set chat topics, and add menu items. Available on userscripts.org.

▶ **Orkut Community Manager**—Lets you mass delete and mass ban so you can easily remove spammers from Orkut communities you manage. Available on userscripts.org.

ADDING A PICASA SLIDESHOW TO ORKUT

Orkut automatically turns uploaded photos into a slideshow. To view photos as a slideshow, first click any of the displayed photos to open it. Click the movie screen icon in the lower right of the photo, as shown in Figure 19-8, to view photos as a slideshow.

FIGURE 19-8: View photos on Orkut as a slideshow.

If you want to create a slideshow using images you've saved in many different places, www.slide.com gives you that ability. Follow the on-screen directions to create your slideshow. When you're finished, click the ORKUT tab on the left. Copy the code provided to your computer's clipboard. Log in to your Orkut account, and from the homepage, click the Scrapbook link. Paste code into the box, and click Post Scrap.

> **NOTE** This only works with the older version of Orkut. To switch from the new version to the old version, click the link to Older Version at the top of the page, between the Settings and Sign Out links. Slideshows added in the older version of Orkut are visible when you switch back to the new version. It's unknown for how long the older version of Orkut will be around.

SUMMARY

Orkut is social networking, Google style. Keep in touch with friends, and add images, video, and slideshows easily. Even add functionality by adding useful applications, or have fun playing games with friends from your Orkut page. Orkut brings great social networking right to your Google account.

CHAPTER 20

Expanding Knowledge on the Web with Knol

When Google released Knol, many people assumed it was a competitor to Wikipedia. However, that's not the case. Knol is a different type of information sharing medium.

Knol incorporates Google's philosophy of information sharing, and as such, it is intended for openly sharing information and collaboration. Knol permits multiple articles on the same topic. Articles are written and edited by one person or a group of people. By contrast, Wikipedia is designed as an encyclopedia, with only one article permitted for each topic.

These differences make Knol a great place to collaborate and share a variety of opinions and viewpoints, instead of reading only one opinion written by a ruling group.

COLLABORATING WITH OTHERS

To create a knol, go to `knol.google.com`. Click Write a Knol in the blue highlighted area, just below the search bar. In the pop-up that appears (usually after you log in to your Google account), use the radio buttons to indicate how you want to start your knol. Choose between the default setting of Create a New Knol, Copy an Existing Knol, Create a New Collection of Knols, or Import a File as a New Knol. These options are shown in Figure 20-1. When you're finished, click Create Knol.

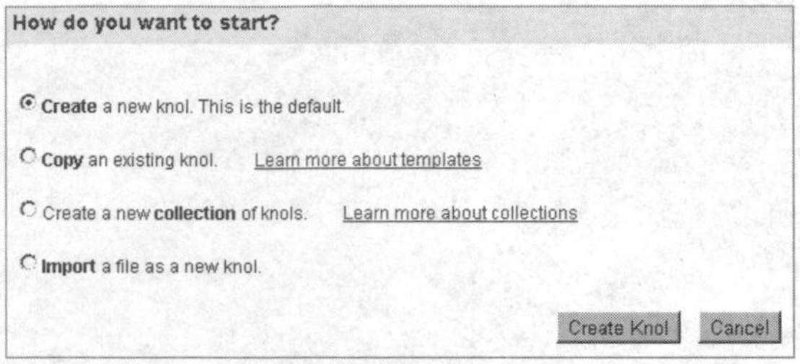

FIGURE 20-1: Use these options to create a new knol.

If you select Copy an Existing Knol, you get a pop-up with a search box. Use the search box to enter keywords that relate to the knol you plan to write. Click Search. Use the search results to find a knol with a look and feel you want to emulate. If you know the URL of the knol you'd like to use as a template, enter the URL into the search box. Use the View link, to the right as shown in Figure 20-2, to see the selected knol.

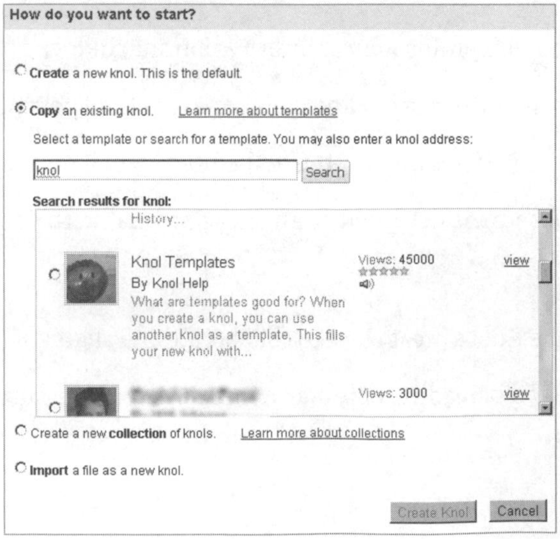

FIGURE 20-2: Viewing your selected Knol

WARNING Even though most knols are published under the Creative Commons license, you can't copy another person's work directly. You must change the work in some substantial way, and provide a link to the original work. You can use the formatting freely, but the text must be changed.

The Knol editor works a lot like Google Docs and Gmail with the addition of the Citation link. Click Citation, shown at the bottom of Figure 20-3, to see a link to your knol formatted for use in formal research papers.

FIGURE 20-3: Use the Citation link to format your knol link for use in research papers.

TIP As you are writing your knol, be sure to save often. Knol does not save automatically like Google Docs or Gmail does.

You can find the Edit Preferences link at the top right of the page. Use it to control the default copyright, collaboration, and e-mail settings for new knols. There are also tabs for Google Adsense and Google Analytics, as well as a control for blocking users.

The basic collaboration settings are under the General tab in Preferences, shown in Figure 20-4.

There are three collaboration settings for a knol:

▶ **Open Collaboration**—Open knols can be modified by anyone, as long as they are logged in to Google.

▶ **Moderated Collaboration**—Anyone can suggest changes to a moderated knol, but only the author can actually make those changes permanent.

▶ **Closed Collaboration**—When a knol is closed, only the author (and approved moderators) can edit the document.

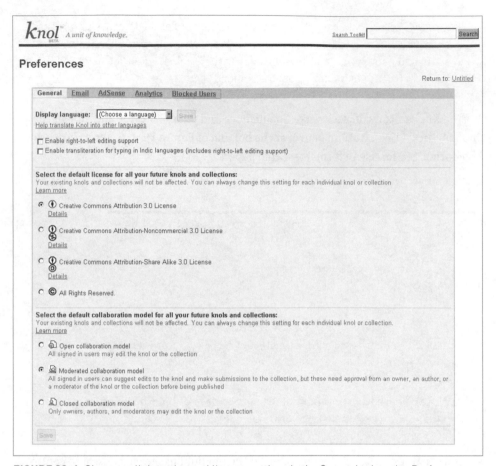

FIGURE 20-4: Change collaboration and license settings in the General tab under Preferences.

This same tab has the license settings for your knols, including Creative Commons and All Rights Reserved.

The Email tab controls how often you receive notifications about changes and updates to your knols. You can set a frequency of immediately, daily, or weekly.

Knol also enables you to lock out specific people. The last tab in the Preferences screen is Blocked Users, which is perfect for weeding out troublemakers and preventing graffiti from appearing all over your knol.

The settings in Preferences are the defaults for any new knols written, but each individual knol also has its own Settings tab. This tab is shown in Figure 20-5. The link is on the right edge of the page, about halfway down, but you have to make your way back to the knol to find it.

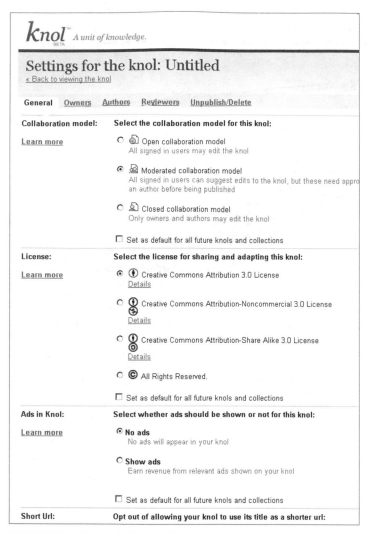

FIGURE 20-5: Change collaboration rules for the knol in its own Settings screen.

One thing that can make your knol stand out is a well-organized and linked Table of Contents. To create one automatically, highlight the Chapter Heading, and click the Format menu, as shown in Figure 20-6. Select Heading H2. After all the Chapter Headings have been formatted, click the Save button and then the Close button. Knol automatically creates a link in the Table of Contents for each of the Chapter Headings.

Use the Insert menu in the toolbar to add images, equations, special characters, or to link to documents hosted in your other Google services. You can even add Google Gadgets to your knol.

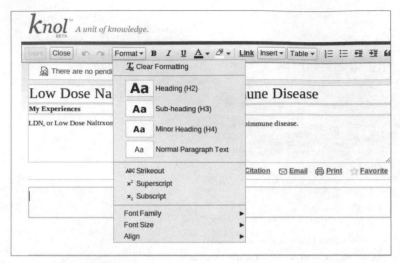

FIGURE 20-6: Use the Format menu to automatically create a Table of Contents.

> **NOTE** Services such as Knol and Wikipedia have generally been accepted as being reliable (or, at least, reliable enough) for basic research and as a good starting point for any official research project. However, because the information on Knol and Wikipedia is user-generated, you should always proceed with caution when reading articles and consuming content; these articles aren't peer-reviewed or officially fact-checked.

SHARING YOUR KNOL

Your knol is written, and you're ready to share your knowledge with the world. Now what?

Click the Share and Invite link on the right side of the page. You can invite other people as either authors or reviewers; authors have the ability to edit your knol, but reviewers do not.

Google suggests that you assign categories to your knol, to make it easier for people to find your knol in their searches. You can find the link to Add a Category on the right side of the page between Knol Translations and Activity for This Knol, as shown in Figure 20-7.

Unfortunately, the Category system doesn't work as well as it should. First, although Google recommends you use existing categories, it doesn't offer a list of them in the Add Categories box. You have to type your categories in by hand, which makes it difficult to know which categories your knol is best suited for. And that brings us to problem number two.

FIGURE 20-7: Add categories to your knol in the box, but remember to use categories that already exist.

Knol uses an algorithm to determine which categories appear in the Category Browser. Only categories that have enough articles associated with them will appear. So, if your category is specific enough that it applies only to a handful of knols, it may never show up—making the Category Browser useless for finding your knol.

USING KNOL TO BUILD A BRAND

Knol is perfectly suited to establishing an Internet presence. Here are some suggestions on how you can use Knol to build your brand:

- ▶ Write a series of knols around a central topic. For each one, follow the usual SEO for web articles.

- ▶ Use titles and text that are heavy with keywords. The more keywords, the more likely search engines will be able to find and catalog it.

- ▶ Write clear and concise summaries that attract readers to the full knol. Keep the summary clean and straightforward so that your readers get a sense of the content, and they will want to see more.

- ▶ Add clear and illuminating images and graphics to illustrate your points. Not every knol needs illustrations, of course, but they break up the text and make the knol easier to read, as well as clarify your points.

- ▶ Invite reviewers to comment and suggest material, keeping your knol growing with new material. New posts and active discussion is one of the things that attracts both viewers and search engines.

- ▶ Cover your topic well from a variety of viewpoints—remember, a knol is not a blog. Readers come to Google Knol for information on a topic, not opinions. A knol should be informational and scholarly.

- ▶ Link to your products and services within your knols. If you're an expert on a topic, there's no reason why your knols cannot link to your own material.

SUMMARY

Google Knol is definitely not the "Wikipedia Killer" that some pundits claimed it would be upon release. It also still has flaws, like the Category system, but, despite the flaws, Knol still does an excellent job of providing a place for authors to write, share, comment, and collaborate on a tremendous selection of topics.

CHAPTER 21

Getting Involved in Google Groups

IN THIS CHAPTER

▶ Using Google Groups to build a community or network of peers
▶ Socializing on Google Groups online
▶ Building your Google Groups with quality content to attract new users

First there was Usenet, then egroups, then Yahoo! Groups took the reins, now Google Groups is making its presence known. E-mail groups have become a vital means of communication. For many people an e-mail group is their first stop for information and support. Whether you're looking for low-carb recipes, help with the latest open source software, or strategies to cope with a major life stressor, you can find real-life solutions from real people in an e-mail group.

CREATING COMMUNITIES IN GOOGLE GROUPS

Creating a new Google Group is as simple as filling out a form.

To build your own Google Group, visit the Groups homepage, at `groups.google.com`, shown in Figure 21-1. The Create button is at the top of the right-hand column, next to the My Groups heading.

FIGURE 21-1: From the Google Groups homepage browse existing groups or create one of your own.

Click the Create button to move to the Create a Group screen, as shown in Figure 21-2.

Name your group. Note that your name has to be unique, because it can't duplicate any existing Google Group. As you enter the group name, Groups automatically populates the group e-mail address in the next box down with the same name. If you want the group name and the e-mail address to be the same, accept the default; otherwise, enter a group e-mail address also. The e-mail address is used to create the group web address. (The group's web address is the URL that appears in the browser's address bar, which you can bookmark for later use.)

In the Group Description box, write something about the group, such as favorite subjects of conversation or, perhaps, ground rules for joining and posting.

Below the group description is the adult content warning. If your group will contain adult or potentially offensive content, check the box to prevent any visits by people younger than eighteen.

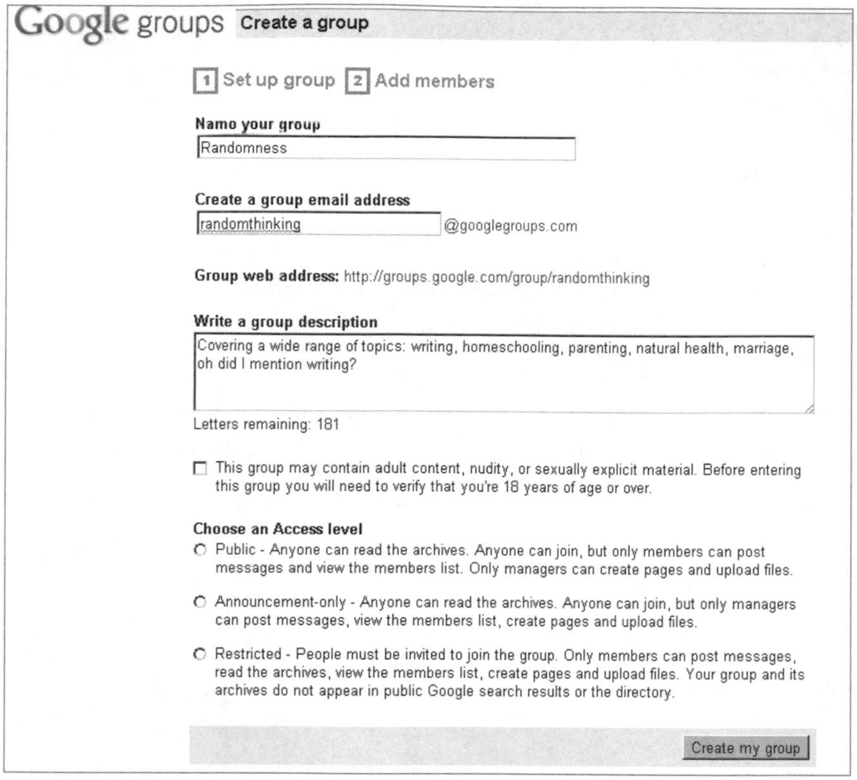

FIGURE 21-2: Use the Create a Group screen to enter all of the information for a new group.

> **WARNING** Failure to flag your group for adult or offensive content, if appropriate, results in Google shutting down your group and possibly suspending your account. Don't try to beat the system—if your group is explicit in nature flag it as such.

Finally, choose the group's Access Level. This controls who can join, post to, or even see your new group.

Click Create My Group. To keep spammer programs from creating hundreds of new, randomly named groups, Google requires that you type in a verification word. Click Create My Group again after you have done so. When your group has been made active, you receive a confirmation e-mail.

THE HISTORY OF GOOGLE GROUPS

Usenet was invented in 1979 by Tom Truscott and Jim Ellis. They designed it as a bulletin board system to enable users to share messages across a network. That network became the World Wide Web a decade later.

Discussion areas were divided into logical groups based on topic. Discussions about the Apple computer and its software were classified as comp.software .appleiigs, while a discussion on heavy metal music was labeled rec.music .heavymetal.

For nearly ten years Usenet was the Internet. Then the World Wide Web was developed, and it opened the previously closed Internet for the general public.

In 1995 DejaNews offered its customers access to a huge library of old Usenet posts, and in 2001, Google acquired DejaNews. Google took the DejaNews archives, and the archives of several other services, and incorporated them into Google Groups.

Because of this, Google Groups contains a wealth of information from more than 800 million Usenet messages dating back to 1981.

GROWING COMMUNITY SIZE AND CONTENT

As soon as you've created your group, Google Groups assumes you would like to add some members, so the next screen you see is an invitation page, as shown in Figure 21-3. Enter any e-mail addresses, along with a description of the group, so that Google can build a list of invitations to send out. Click Invite Members to send out the e-mails.

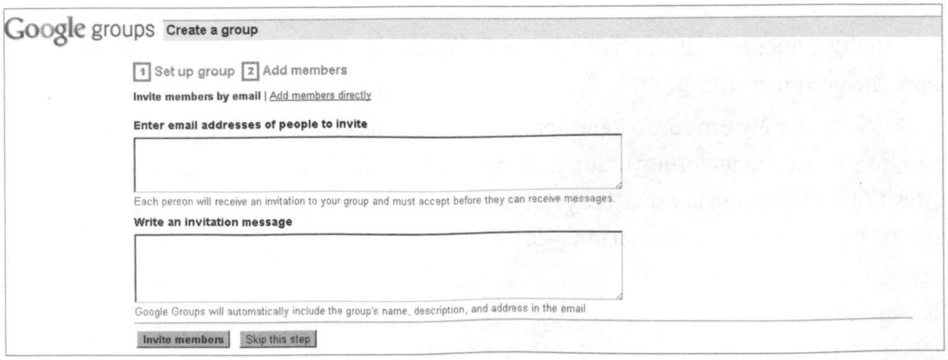

FIGURE 21-3: After the group has been created, it's time to send out invitations.

It's also a good idea to use your social networking systems to get the word out. Post a link to your new group in such places as Facebook and Twitter. Also, consider adding a link to your group in your e-mail signature line.

But the most effective way to bring more people to your group is content. An active group, with interesting messages and a lot of useful information is the surest way to attract members. However, you might get lucky and receive new members via traditional Google search. If a person's search is filtered by groups on Google, she might find your group if your group's content is aligned with the person's search query.

PARTICIPATING IN GROUPS FROM THE WEB

Google has redesigned the Groups interface to make it more like Google Reader. Besides the standard Google banner across the top, the rest of the page is split into two panels. As you can see in Figure 21-4, a group navigation bar sits on the left side of the screen.

FIGURE 21-4: Google Groups uses two panels—a navigation bar on the left and a large panel on the right.

The three main links necessary for navigating through Google Groups are My Groups, Browse All, and New Group. You can return to this menu screen at any time by clicking the word Home at the top of the left navigation bar.

My Groups leads to the list of groups you have created or subscribed to, as shown in Figure 21-5.

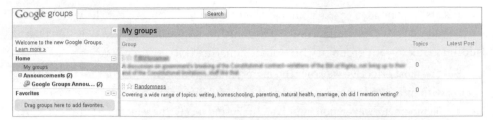

FIGURE 21-5: Click the My Groups link to find any groups you have created or joined.

Browse All leads to the entire Google Groups directory. Choose your group by working your way down through the categories. For example, to find a group discussing the programming language C++, start with the Computers category, and then Programming, as shown in Figure 21-6.

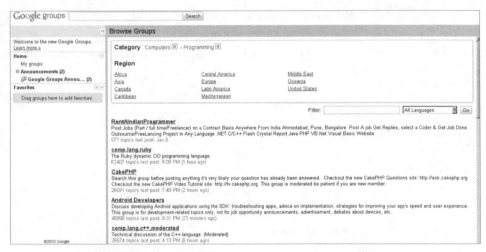

FIGURE 21-6: The subcategories display across the top of the Browse panel as you search through the list.

You can browse the postings in a group without joining that group. Simply click the group name in the Browse screen to see recent postings. Figure 21-7 shows some posts regarding the Ruby programming language. The number of posts in the conversation is at the end of the line.

Click a conversation to read it. You'll find a Reply link at the bottom of each post, so you can join in a conversation at any point, even months in the past.

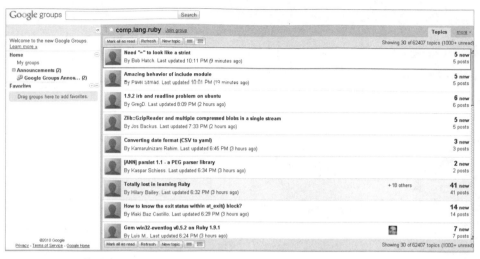

FIGURE 21-7: Recent postings in the comp.lang.ruby group.

As you explore different groups, your navigation bar helps you keep track by listing the groups you've visited most recently, as shown in Figure 21-8.

As a user, you can add your own threads of discussion to existing groups, provided that the group to which you are trying to add a thread is one with settings that allow anyone to start a new thread. When you can add a thread, you see a +Add Post link on the top right of any Group's homepage.

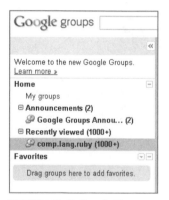

FIGURE 21-8: Google Groups tracks your most recently visited groups.

SUMMARY

Thanks to the Usenet archives, Google Groups is a treasure trove of information, both common and obscure, dating all the way back to 1981. It's quite possibly the best record of the early days of the Internet, online or off, and it continues to grow even today, as new groups and new postings are constantly added.

Part VI

GOOGLE PRODUCTIVITY APPS SECRETS

CHAPTER 22

Creating More with Google Docs

IN THIS CHAPTER

▶ Uploading, importing, and converting Google Docs
▶ Adding links and images and creating text styles
▶ Managing Google Docs templates
▶ Document collaboration with Google

Google Docs is a powerful, full-featured word processing application by Google. It combines your favorite word processing features with push-button publishing and sharing capability, even allowing others to view and edit your work easily. The new search features make finding your work a snap.

IMPORTING DOCS

One of my favorite things about Google Docs is the ability to upload and store my locally created documents. When you import to Docs, you have a choice between leaving the document in its original file format and simply storing it on Docs, or you can convert the document to Google Docs and work with it online.

If you're simply using Docs as storage, the document you upload can be in any file type, provided that file is no bigger than 1024MB. If the file you want to store is larger than 1024MB, try compressing it to a ZIP, SITX, 7Z, GZ, or RAR file with one of the many file compression applications available.

▶ ZIP, 7Z, and RAR are only a few popular compression formats. For a complete list of available compression formats, and the applications that produce them, go to www.fileinfo.com/filetypes/compressed.

> **TIP** Use Google Docs to store your photos or music in compressed files. Instead of uploading each music or photo individually, create a folder on your hard drive that contains the music or photos. Compress the folder and upload the compressed file to Docs.

If you want to upload a document to Google Docs so you can share, collaborate, or work on it, the file needs to be of a format and size Google Docs supports. Supported file types include the following:

Text files up to 1MB	.doc, .docx, .odt, .swx, .rtf, .txt, .htm, .html
Slide presentations up to 10MB	ppt, .pps
Spreadsheets up to 1MB	.xls, .xlsx, .ods, .csv
Drawings up to 2MB	.wmf

To import any file into Google Docs click the button labeled Upload in the left corner, as shown in Figure 22-1.

FIGURE 22-1: Click the Upload button to import a file to Google Docs from your computer.

The old Google Docs interface let you drag and drop files from your computer into the download area with Firefox, Chrome, Chromium, or Safari, whether you use Windows, Linux, or Mac. At this time the new interface supports drag and drop only for those users running Mozilla Firefox, Google Chrome, or Safari web browsers on the Windows operating system. Drag & Drop no longer works for those users running Mozilla Firefox on Linux. It's assumed that Firefox will update the Linux version of the browser soon to support the changes on Google Docs.

If you want to work with the file after it's been uploaded, click the box labeled Convert Documents, Presentations, Spreadsheets and Drawings to the corresponding Google Docs formats. Or, if you're uploading a PDF, select Convert Text from PDF or Image Files to Google Docs Documents. If you are only storing the file on Docs as a backup, and don't intend to access the file on Docs, you can leave the file in its original format.

> **NOTE** Google uses Optical Character Recognition (OCR) technology to extract text from images. OCR algorithms can also process JPG, GIF, and PNG files, so that Google Docs can "read" those file types as well. This lets you upload PDF files created from a PDF converter application, like Adobe Distiller, or those PDFs created by flatbed scanners. Google Docs OCR also lets you upload images from your digital camera or mobile phone. OCR extracts the text from these images for use in Google Docs. Allow up to one minute for these files to extract and upload. Image files must be 2MB or smaller, and OCR scans only the first 10 pages of the document for text to extract. Do note that OCR technology is not 100% accurate; some words or punctuation may not come out as expected.

Not converting the file is a convenient way to move files from one computer to another. Simply upload the file in its original format, and then log in to your Docs account from the receiving computer, and download the unchanged file.

Use the menu to select a Destination Collection, if appropriate.

Use the Private menu shown in Figure 22-2 to select who may view the document. When you're finished, click Start Upload.

> **NOTE** Google rolled out a new interface and updated features in the beginning of February 2011.

▶ Collections are what Google Docs used to call Folders. The name has been changed from Folders to Collections throughout Google Docs.

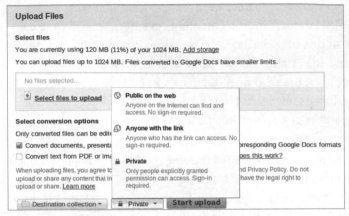

FIGURE 22-2: Set whether your document should be private, shared with anyone with the link, or shared with the entire Internet.

DOCUMENT STYLE SECRETS

Sure, your documents are all about your content, but an attractive, easy to navigate layout is as important as the information you're presenting. If your document is cluttered and difficult to read, it's likely your intended audience won't bother.

Working with Text Styles

One of the best ways to create separation within a written document is to use headings. Google Docs makes headings easily accessible through the text drop-down, shown in Figure 22-3. Click the menu and select the heading size you want to use. Or, use the keyboard shortcuts, as defined in Table 22-1. Figure 22-4 shows an example of each available heading.

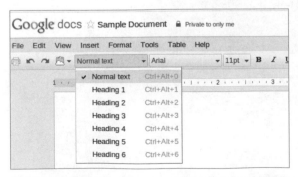

FIGURE 22-3: Use the menu to select your desired heading size.

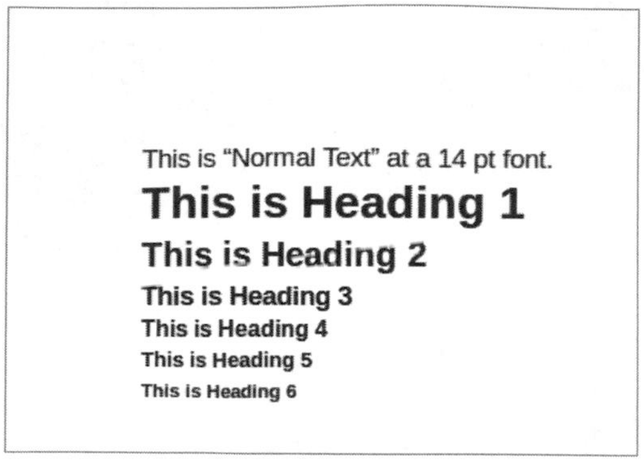

This is "Normal Text" at a 14 pt font.

This is Heading 1

This is Heading 2

This is Heading 3

This is Heading 4

This is Heading 5

This is Heading 6

FIGURE 22-4: Each heading designation gives a different result.

TABLE 22-1: Keyboard Shortcuts to Create Headings

KEYBOARD	HEADING
Ctrl+Alt+0	Normal Text
Ctrl+Alt+1	Heading 1
Ctrl+Alt+2	Heading 2
Ctrl+Alt+3	Heading 3
Ctrl+Alt+4	Heading 4
Ctrl+Alt+5	Heading 5
Ctrl+Alt+6	Heading 6

The second best way to draw your reader's eye to a specific piece of text is by formatting the text itself using bold, italic, or underlined text. These are available from the toolbar, or through keyboard shortcuts. Google Docs also enables you to use strikethrough, superscripts, and subscripts, which are located under the Format menu, and through keyboard shortcuts. Table 22-2 gives the keyboard shortcuts for text formatting.

TABLE 22-2: Keyboard Shortcuts for Text Formatting

KEYBOARD SHORTCUT	ACTION
Ctrl+B	Bold Text
Ctrl+I	Italicize Text

continues

TABLE 22-2: *(continued)*

KEYBOARD SHORTCUT	ACTION
Ctrl+U	Underline Text
Ctrl+. (period)	Superscript
Ctrl+, (comma)	Subscript
Ctrl+L	Align text to Left side
Ctrl+C	Align text to Center
Ctrl+R	Align text to Right side
Ctrl+Shift+J	Justify text
Ctrl+Shift+C	Word Count dialog box

Use the toolbar or the Format menu to create lists and line spacing.

Use the Insert menu to add page breaks, tables of contents, headers, footers, horizontal lines, special characters, and bookmarks in your document.

For even more flexibility in formatting, go to the Preferences tab. Here you can designate keyboard combinations to be turned into symbols. For example, by default when you enter (C) into a Google Doc, it automatically turns into the copyright symbol—©. Look under the Preferences menu to see the list of default symbols. Click the X to right of the symbol to permanently remove it from your list; click the checkbox to disable the symbol temporarily. You can enter your own custom symbols into any blank set of boxes.

Adding Links and Images

Images in a document add a visual that helps many people understand complicated material. Links inside or outside a document connect two or more sections of the material or provide further information.

Add images to your Google Docs document from the Insert menu. Click Insert → Image, as shown in Figure 22-5. Use the upload tool provided to either upload the image from your local hard drive, enter the URL of the image you want to use, use Google Image Search to locate an appropriate image on the Web, or select an image from your Picasa Web Albums. When you've selected the image, click Upload.

To add a link in a Google Docs document, select Insert → Link from the navigation menu, or press Ctrl+K on your keyboard to open the link editor shown in Figure 22-6. In the box labeled Text to Display, type the text on which you want to user to click to open the link. Now select whether the link should take the reader to a website, open an e-mail, or land at a specific point within the document. Enter the website URL or e-mail address, or select the bookmark, as appropriate. Click OK when you are finished.

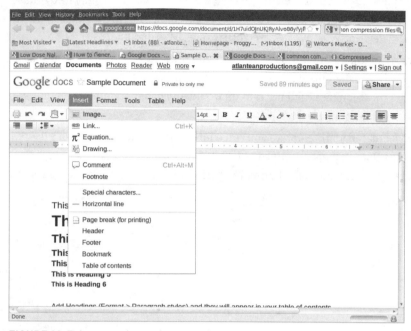

FIGURE 22-5: Insert an image into your document.

TIP If you are linking within your document, you have to create the bookmarks first. Then, use the link editor to create the links.

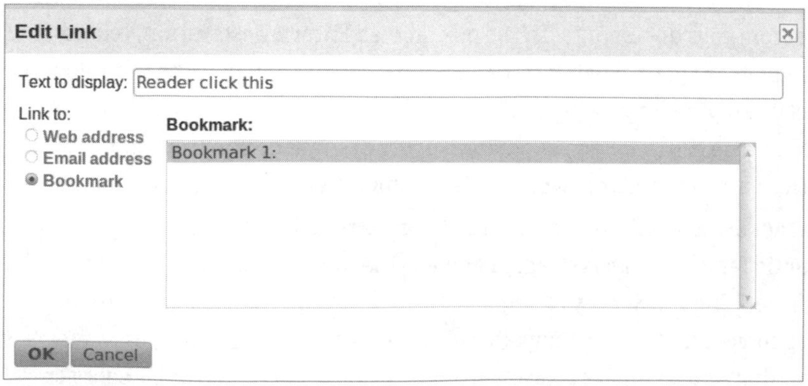

FIGURE 22-6: Use the link editor to create links to websites, e-mails, or within the document.

CREATING TEMPLATES

After you have your document formatted just the way you want it, you may find it useful to create a template so you don't have to do it again. Templates are especially useful for work reports, newsletters, invoices, and other repetitive documents.

Create a new document and format it the way you want it. Be sure to include the word "template" in the document's name. When you want to use that template, search your documents for "template." Fill it in as you would any other document template and save it under a new name.

After you've created your template you can share it with other Google Docs users. From your Google Docs homepage, click the link titled Browse Template Gallery, or click the Create New menu and select From Template. Both are shown in Figure 22-7.

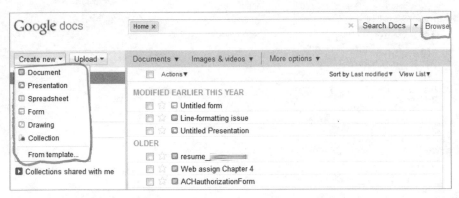

FIGURE 22-7: Access the Template Gallery to submit your template.

Click the link titled Submit a Template on the right side of your screen to access the template submission form, shown in Figure 22-8. Use the tool to select your newly created template from your documents. In the box labeled Enter a Description, tell users about your template. Explain what it's for and how to use it. Then, use the drop-down menu to select a category for your template. If applicable, use the second category drop-down. Next, use the language menu to select the language your template is written in. Read the warnings and terms of template submission. Click Submit Template.

If you'd rather use a template created by someone else, access the Template Gallery. Ensure the Public Templates tab is selected and use the tools on the right to find the template you're looking for. Sort by rating, most users, or "hottest" templates. Or, narrow down your choices and sort by templates for documents, spreadsheets, presentations, forms, or drawings. Further concentrate your efforts and search by category or language. If you know exactly what you want, use the search bar at the top of the page.

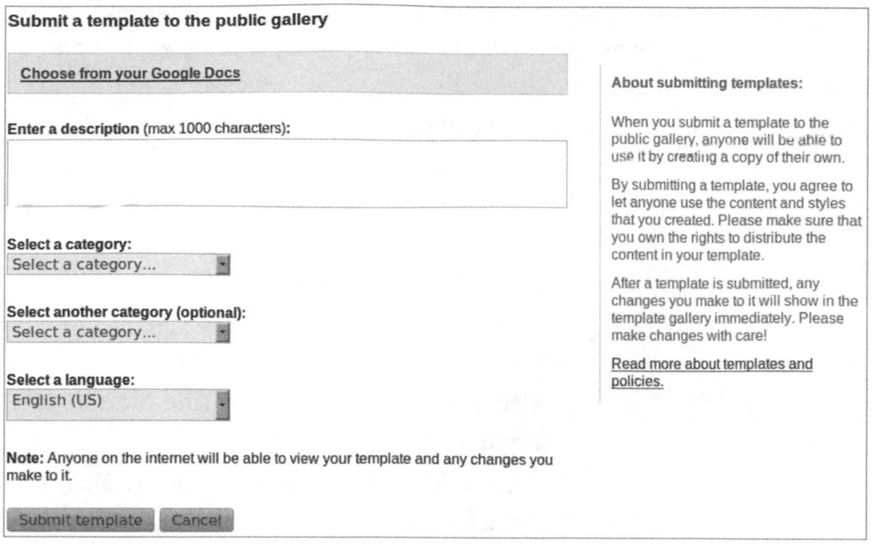

Submit a template to the public gallery

Choose from your Google Docs

Enter a description (max 1000 characters):

Select a category:
Select a category...

Select another category (optional):
Select a category...

Select a language:
English (US)

Note: Anyone on the internet will be able to view your template and any changes you make to it.

Submit template   Cancel

About submitting templates:

When you submit a template to the public gallery, anyone will be able to use it by creating a copy of their own.

By submitting a template, you agree to let anyone use the content and styles that you created. Please make sure that you own the rights to distribute the content in your template.

After a template is submitted, any changes you make to it will show in the template gallery immediately. Please make changes with care!

Read more about templates and policies.

FIGURE 22-8: Use this form to submit your template to Google.

When you locate a template you'd like to use, click Preview to make sure it's exactly what you want. Then, when you're convinced, click Use This Template.

When you click Use This Template, it is automatically saved to your Google Docs document list under the name Copy of Template Name.

Any template can be embedded to your website or blog. Click Embed, and copy the given code to your computer clipboard. Paste that code in the correct place in the HTML of your website or blog.

FINDING DOCUMENTS

Effective February 2011, Google rolled out a new interface for Google Docs. It's very different from what you're used to, but makes it easier to locate your files, especially if you use Google Docs a lot.

The top center of the screen now has three menu options: Documents, Images & Videos, and More Options, as shown in Figure 22-9. Use these menus to sort your documents so you can find the one you're looking for.

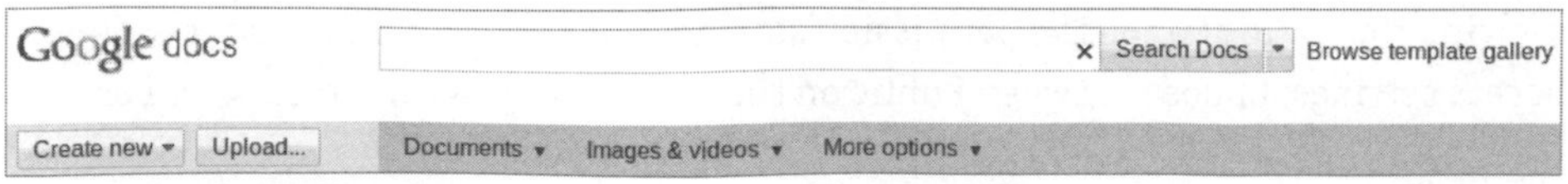

Google docs .... x Search Docs ▾ Browse template gallery

Create new ▾ Upload...   Documents ▾ Images & videos ▾ More options ▾

FIGURE 22-9: Use the upper navigation menu to sort documents.

The Documents menu lets you sort by type of document. Select either Text Documents, PDF Files, Presentations, Spreadsheets, or Drawings. The selected file type displays in the center of your screen.

The Images & Videos menu lets you see all your video files, all your image files, or both.

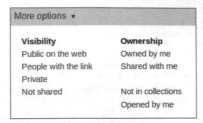

FIGURE 22-10: More Options sorting menu.

The More Options menu shown in Figure 22-10 lets you sort files by how they are shared and by ownership of the file.

Use the Sort By menu, located on the right, directly under the sorting options toolbar to sort visible documents by Priority, Title, Starred, Last Modified, or Last Opened.

Click the document name to open it. Mouse over the document to see the Action Menu for the document. Click the blue highlighted area, but not on the document title, to see a preview of the document in the preview window on the right. This also enables you to view the share settings. See Figure 22-11.

FIGURE 22-11: Navigate each document by clicking the title, mousing over, or clicking in the blue area.

To change the share settings of any document in your list, select the desired document, scroll down until you see Sharing on the left. Click Settings, as shown in Figure 22-12.

The Sharing Settings page, shown in Figure 22-13, gives you sharing options for Gmail, Facebook, Buzz, and Twitter, along with a URL you can paste in e-mail, send as an IM, or link to on your website.

The Permissions box gives you a list of people who have been given editing and viewing rights. To change the permission settings click Change. Select your desired access settings. Choose between Public on the Web, Anyone with the Link, or Private.

There is also a checkbox to allow anyone to edit the document without signing in. When you're finished, click Save.

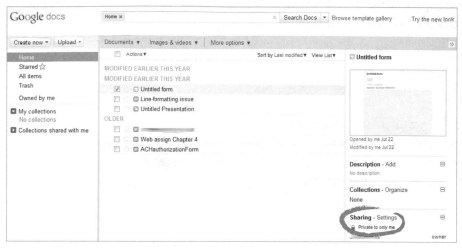

FIGURE 22-12: Access the Sharing Settings for any document in your list.

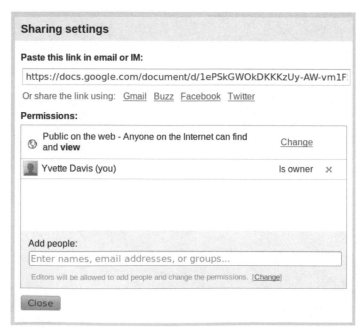

FIGURE 22-13: Sharing a link with options for Gmail, Facebook, Buzz, and Twitter.

For all documents not freely available on the Web, use the Add People box to grant access to specific individuals or groups. When you enter an e-mail into the box a small menu appears to the right. Select either Can Edit or Can View to grant the appropriate permissions. Click Share when you are finished.

SUMMARY

Google Docs offers anyone with a Google account the ability to create and share documents. The new interface makes finding and sharing your documents fast and easy. What's more, Docs is fully compatible with other Google services, making it even easier to embed documents in your blog or website.

CHAPTER 23

Designing Better Presentations

Slide presentations add interest and variety to your website, meeting, or in-person topic discussion. The key to a good presentation is to include images, graphs, and short videos along with limited text. You can either present your presentation verbally (in-person) or record a voice-over (online) to deliver your content.

Google Presentation makes it easy to add graphs, images, and video to your presentation, and it also gives you control of the order elements appear within the same slide.

ADDING AND REMOVING SLIDES

When you first open Presentation (at docs.google.com/, within the Documents drop-down menu, which is found directly underneath the search bar within Google Docs), the application presents you with a title page, and no other slides. In the main area of the screen, click the words Click to Add Title, and type the title of your presentation. Add a subtitle, if appropriate. If you do not want to add a subtitle, don't do anything.

To move the title and subtitle elements around the page, click the desired element so the textbox appears, as shown in Figure 23-1. Grab any gray line around the textbox, and move the element to the desired location.

▶ The title and subtitle won't show if you do not enter text for those elements.

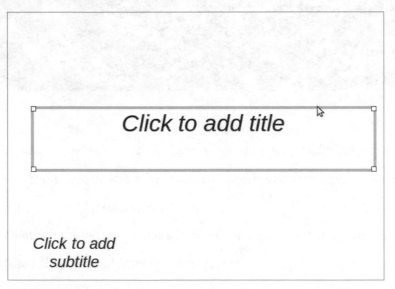

FIGURE 23-1: Use the gray lines to move the textboxes around the slide.

Use the corner points to resize the title and subtitle textboxes as needed.

To add additional text shapes to this, or any other slide, click the text button, shown in Figure 23-2, on the toolbar.

FIGURE 23-2: The text button adds new textbox to any slide.

You have three ways to add slides to your slide presentation. With all three methods, the new slide is added to the end of your presentation, unless you first select a slide from the left navigation bar.

▶ From the top navigation menu, click Slide and then New Slide.

▶ Click the plus sign (+) located in the slide control toolbar, above the left navigation bar. This is shown in Figure 23-3.

▶ Use the Ctrl+M keyboard shortcut to add a new slide.

FIGURE 23-3: Use this toolbar to add, duplicate, or delete slides.

To make an exact copy of an already existing slide, first select the slide you want to duplicate. Then, select Slide and then Duplicate from the top navigation menu, or click the middle of three very small icons next to the slide count (Directly underneath the left-hand side of the navigation menu).

Remove a slide from your presentation by using the Slide menu in the top navigation. Or, select the slide you want to delete from the side navigation, and click the X in the slide control toolbar, as shown in Figure 23-3. Alternatively, select the slide to be deleted from the left navigation, and press the Delete key on your keyboard.

Import slides from other Google presentations or from your local hard drive. Click Insert from the top navigation and then click Import. Use the navigation tools to locate the slide or slides on the presentation you want to import. To select a slide in another Google presentation, click the box under the desired slide. To select a slide on your local computer, click the slide title in your file navigation. On most systems, Ctrl+click enables you to select multiple files.

> **TIP** You can copy and paste slides from one Google presentation to another within the same Google account using the Web Clipboard, discussed in Chapter 25.

▶ If you select a slide from the left navigation and then insert a slide, the new slide is added directly after the selected slide.

▶ You can import other document types, such as .ppt, .pdf, and .jpg, to Google Presentation, but Google only imports the actual slide content for each slide; animations and other elements such as pivot tables or footnotes are not imported.

CREATING SLIDE TEMPLATES

If you're going to use a particular slide many times, it makes sense to create a template so you don't have to re-create the slide each time you need it. You can either import the slide into your current slide show, or use the Google template creation protocol as described in Chapter 22.

To use a template created by another user, browse the Template Gallery as explained in Chapter 22. Use the side navigation to select templates for Google Presentation.

> **CROSSREF** Template creation and use is discussed in depth in Chapter 22.

The keyboard shortcuts you're used to for cutting, copying, pasting, and formatting text also work in Presentation, so you can use them while you're creating slides and slide templates. If you want to insert a new slide, use Ctrl+M.

BUILDING INTEREST WITH THEMES

Let's face it, no matter how interesting your topic is, staring at slide after slide of black text on a white background is just boring. Break the visual monotony with themes and colored backgrounds.

To access the pre-installed themes, click Format → Presentation Settings from the top navigation, as shown in Figure 23-4. Select Change Theme from the menu. When you click a theme, it is automatically applied throughout your current presentation. If you add slides to the current presentation the chosen theme is applied to those as well.

Themes are a great way to add some color to your presentation, but every slide is still the same. Mix it up a little by changing the background color of slides individually. From the Format menu, click Presentation Settings, and then Change Background. Use the tool shown in Figure 23-5 to place an image or solid color as the slide background.

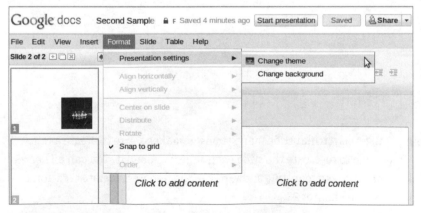

FIGURE 23-4: Use Format → Presentation Settings to access preinstalled themes.

To use an image as the background, click Insert Image. Use the file navigation to browse to the image file on your computer. Select the file and click Open. The image you select is uploaded and displayed in the preview as the background, as shown in Figure 23-6.

Fill the background with a solid color by using the color-picker. First, click the paint bucket found under the Insert Image link. Click the color you want to use as the background color. The color you pick displays in the preview window.

When you're satisfied with your slide background, indicate whether you want to apply the new background to all slides in this presentation, and click Save. Figure 23-7 shows a slide show with many different background images.

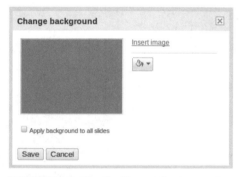

FIGURE 23-5: Use the Change Background tool to create custom slides.

FIGURE 23-6: Use any image on your computer as a slide background.

FIGURE 23-7: Use several different slide backgrounds to add interest to your presentation.

> **NOTE** Please note that you can save a presentation including backgrounds as a template. (Simply configure your template with your desired background and save it). By saving your own template, you can avoid repeating the same work over and over again.

INSERTING IMAGES, VIDEOS, AND OTHER ELEMENTS

Now that you have the background set, it's time to add images, video, charts, and other items that help you get your message across.

To add an image, click Insert in the top navigation. Select Image from the menu. Use the Insert Image tool shown in Figure 23-8 to navigate to an image on your computer, or enter the URL of the image online. When you've selected your image, click OK.

> ▶ You can also drag and drop images from one slide to another within a presentation, or copy an image from the Web Clipboard discussed in Chapter 25.

FIGURE 23-8: Insert an image from your computer or the Internet.

When you select Insert Drawing, a Google Drawing window opens. Create your image and then click Save & Close at the top of the page. Use the bounding box to enlarge, shrink, and position the drawing on the slide.

Insert any video from YouTube. Click Insert and then Video from the top navigation. Type keywords for the video you want to add. Click over the video text of the video you want to add to select it. Click Select Video. Resize and position the video by using the handles and bounding box. You can also add a video from your hard drive as long as it's smaller than 10GB.

> **TIP** If you're unsure whether you have the correct video, click within the video frame to watch the video.

Tables help organize and present information in a logical format. To insert a table into your Google Presentation, select Table from the Insert menu. As shown in Figure 23-9 a grid displays to the right. Use this grid to select the number of rows and columns that should appear in the table and then add your data to the newly created table.

Sometimes you might want to show your viewers a little bit of information at a time. Use images, drawings, text, and video together on one slide and implement an incremental reveal to show the images in succession. Right-click the image you want shown first. Select Incremental Reveal from the menu options. A small clock and the number 1 display in the bottom-left corner of the image to indicate this is the first image to be shown. Next, right-click the second image to be shown and then select Incremental Reveal. This image displays the same clock and the number 2 in the lower-left corner. Repeat for each image in the slide. Figure 23-10 shows images 1 and 2, along with the menu.

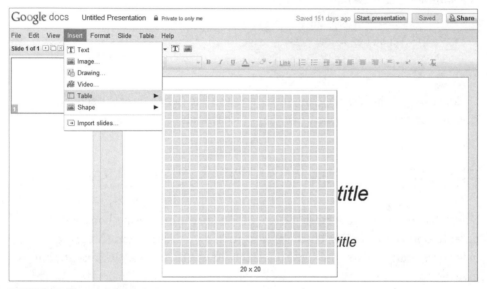

FIGURE 23-9: Use the grid to set the number of columns and rows in the table.

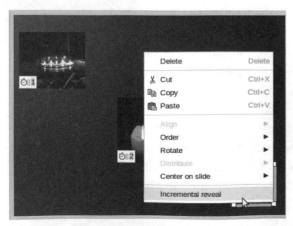

FIGURE 23-10: Applying Incremental Reveal.

PREVIEWING YOUR PRESENTATION

Before you release your presentation for all to see, it's a good idea to preview it to make sure it runs smoothly and looks good.

Click the Start Presentation button at the top of the screen. Your presentation opens in a new, full-sized browser window. Use the controls in the Action menu at the bottom of the screen to Pause, Print, Download, Edit, or Copy your presentation. Use the Slide menu to view individual slides.

> **TIP** You can also start the preview from the View menu. Click View → Start Presentation. Or, press Ctrl+F5 on your keyboard to start the preview.

You can find the URL for your presentation on the right side of the screen. Copy this to your computer's clipboard to share with friends or co-workers.

PRODUCING AND SHARING PRESENTATIONS

Now it's time to share your presentation. Of course, you can always hook your computer to a projector and display the presentation on a large screen. This is great for meetings, family events, and other in-person functions, but Google Presentation gives you more than that.

Use the Share menu, located in the upper right, to embed your presentation into a website or blog, publish it to the Web, or e-mail it to those people who need to view the presentation. Figure 23-11 shows the Share menu choices. The Share menu in Google Presentation holds the same options, and functions in the same manner, as the Share menu in other Google Docs applications.

FIGURE 23-11: Use the Share menu to distribute your slide presentation.

One of the truly great things about Google Presentation, and in fact all apps offered in Google Docs, is the ability to share the document with others for the purpose of collaboration. Add a collaborator from the Share menu. Click Share, and then Share Settings. Add the name or e-mail address of those people you want to collaborate with in the textbox labeled Add People. Use the menu to the right to set permission to Can Edit. Click Share.

> **NOTE** If you're sharing your presentation with a group of people pay close attention to the permissions you give. E-mail addresses entered together receive the same permission settings. So, if you're sharing with collaborators be sure to add only collaborators to the e-mail box. You can share with viewers separately.

HAVING FUN WITH SPECIAL PROJECTS

Create a photo slide show on your website using Google Presentation. Log in to Google Presentation. Create one slide for each photo. Or, use fewer slides and use Incremental Reveal to show multiple photos in a specified order on each slide. Use the chalkboard theme, or set all slide backgrounds to black. Select the first slide. Click Insert → Image from the top navigation. Select the photo you want to add. Continue until you've added all desired photos. To add interest, layer photos using Incremental Reveal.

When you're finished, use the Share menu to access the Publish/Embed screen. Copy the HTML given and paste it in the source code of your blog or website to share the photo slide show outside of Google Presentation. This is a simple, yet effective way to share family photos with Grandma on a private blog, or to share the photos of the latest company picnic or awards ceremony on the corporate website.

For a more interesting photo display, access the template gallery from your Google Docs homepage. In the right navigation, select Presentations. Use the search box to locate the presentation template named Scrapbook Album. Use this template as a starting point for your own scrapbook. To add your own photos, simply click the photo you want to replace and press Delete on your keyboard. Insert and place your own photo in its place.

Add music to your slide shows by combining a blank YouTube video with Google Presentation. First, record a YouTube video with the music you want to use in your presentation. It's best if you shoot the video in a dark room or use little to no movement in the video.

Next insert the video in to every slide where you want the music to be heard. Now, create your slides as you normally would. When you run the presentation the music plays.

SUMMARY

Google Presentation can help you build professional-looking slide presentations easily. Sharing and collaboration abilities let you work with colleagues and share with friends.

CHAPTER 24

Calculating Answers with Spreadsheet

IN THIS CHAPTER

▶ Using finance, math, economics, accounting, and spreadsheet formulas
▶ Representing data visually using charts and illustrations
▶ Integrating forms with Google Spreadsheets
▶ Designing and developing templates

Spreadsheets have long been the workhorse of bookkeepers and accountants. Columns and rows can be totaled and averaged, and values can be referenced from other sections of the page.

Google has added a new level of functionality to spreadsheets. You can convert the contents of a cell to Roman numerals, or use a gadget to convert your project and goal information into a Gantt chart. The finance-minded can even program a cell to get live, up-to-the-second stock market data from Google Finance. All without ever leaving Google Spreadsheets.

ADVANCED FORMULA SECRETS

Google Spreadsheets is a component of Google Docs. From your Google Docs homepage, select Create New and select Spreadsheet from the drop-down menu. At its most basic level, Google Spreadsheets functions like any other spreadsheet program. It stores data in rows and columns. Use functions to complete mathematical calculations. Where Google Spreadsheets really stands out is with some of its specialized formulas and gadgets.

Use the Roman function to convert a number to Roman numerals. For the function to work, the number must be between 1 and 4,000.

Enter the following function directly in the cell where you want the Roman numerals to appear:

```
=ROMAN(number, 0)
```

The tag ROMAN tells the spreadsheet to convert the following number into Roman numerals, and the 0 indicates the traditional standard Roman numeral format.

> **NOTE** In traditional, standard-form Roman numerals, when a smaller number appears before a larger number, the smaller number is subtracted from the larger number. For example, Roman numeral IV is equal to number 4. By contrast the number 6 is written as VI in Roman numerals.
>
>
> In Google Spreadsheets, if the number following the numeral to be converted is anything other than 0, the standard Roman numeral rules are not applied as strictly. For example, when you enter =Roman(999,0) into a cell you get the traditional Roman numeral of CMXCIX. But when you change it to =Roman(999,4) the output is IM. This difference is shown in Figure 24-1.
>
> **FIGURE 24-1:** Change the format of the number to change the way Roman numerals are displayed in the cell.

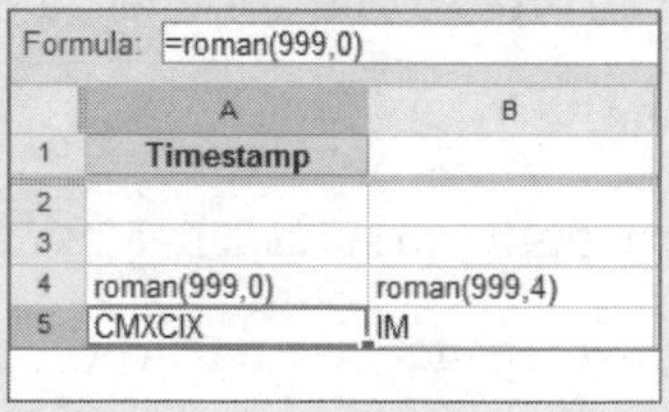

Google Spreadsheets has back-door access to other Google apps, giving Spreadsheets a huge library of functions not available in any spreadsheet program you can use on your local computer.

For example, to use Google Translate within a cell, enter =GoogleTranslate("phrase to be translated", "language 1", "language 2"). For example,

```
=GoogleTranslate("Hello World!", "en", "de")
```

tells Google Spreadsheets to use Google Translate to translate the phrase Hello World! from English into German.

Google Spreadsheets can also identify the language in which a phrase is written with the DetectLanguage function. In an open cell, enter the following:

```
=DetectLanguage("phrase in question")
```

Google Spreadsheets returns the code for the language used.

Table 24-1 shows some of the more popular and interesting languages available in Google Translate and their associated codes.

TABLE 24-1: Google Translate Language Codes

LANGUAGE	CODE	LANGUAGE	CODE
Africaans	Af	Arabic	Ar
Chinese, Simplified	Zh-CH	Chinese, Traditional	Zh-TW
Danish	Da	English	En
French	Fr	German	De
Greek	El	Hebrew	Iw
Italian	It	Japanese	Ja
Korean	Ko	Latin	La
Nepali	Ne	Persian	Fa
Polish	Pl	Portuguese	Pt
Russian	Ru	Scots, Gaelic	Gd
Spanish	Es	Yiddish	Yi

Another useful function, especially if you follow or invest on the stock market, is the GoogleFinance function, shown in Figure 24-2. Enter **=GoogleFinance("ticker code";"price")** into the cell where you want stock information displayed.

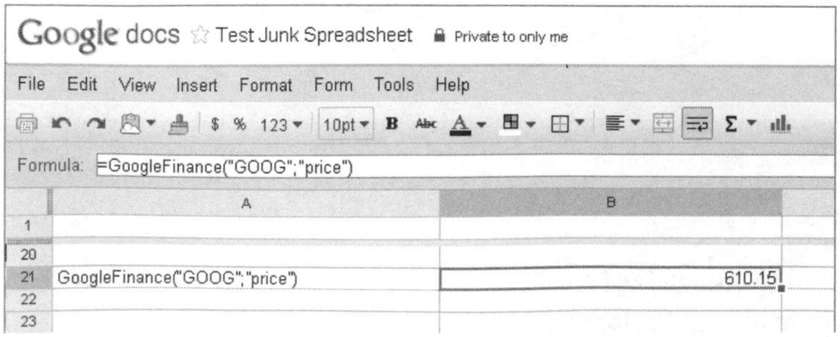

FIGURE 24-2: Use **GoogleFinance** to pull stock information.

If you leave the second element blank, the GoogleFinance function assumes you want the current stock price, so =GoogleFinance("ticker code") gives the same results as the first function.

However, GoogleFinance can accept date ranges and intervals, as well. Enter **=GoogleFinance("stockticker"; "price"; "1/1/2011"; "31"; "DAILY")** to return the daily price of the designated stock over the days indicated.

GADGETS, CHARTS, AND ILLUSTRATIONS

A spreadsheet is only as good as the data it contains. But if you can't present the data in a way your reader can understand, even the best data becomes useless. This is one area where Google Spreadsheets can really help you.

To add a chart to your spreadsheet, first highlight the block of data you would like to include in the chart. Now click Insert from the upper navigation menu, and select Chart. Google Spreadsheet opens the Chart interface, with three tabs. The first tab lets you change and control which cells are included in the chart. The second tab, shown in Figure 24-3, is where you choose which type of chart you want to use to present your information. Click your desired chart type from the first column, and choose the format of that chart in the second column. The third column shows a pre-view of the chart you've selected.

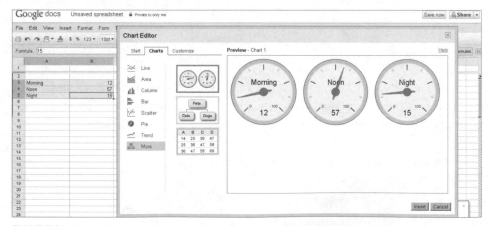

FIGURE 24-3: Use the Chart Setup tabs to preview your Chart.

The third tab is used to customize the chart. You can name the chart, change the sort order, adjust pagination, and color alternating rows.

The functionality of Google Gadgets can also be used in Spreadsheets.

Use Gadgets to bring even greater functionality to your spreadsheets. Like charts, gadgets can help you organize and present your information. In addition, use gadgets to link to other websites and bring their data into Google Spreadsheets. To access gadgets for Spreadsheets, click Insert → Gadget.

For example, link a spreadsheet to Google Maps and provide readers with a color-coded map of the world. Or, show users the location of your business. Figure 24-4 shows some of the gadgets available for Google Spreadsheets.

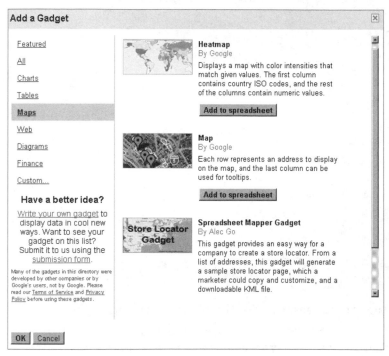

FIGURE 24-4: Use gadgets for Spreadsheets to add more functionality to your spreadsheet.

Finally, if you have programming knowledge, you can create your own gadget using the Google Spreadsheets API. Programming a gadget is beyond the scope of this book, but after you have your gadget ready, use the Insert menu to navigate to gadgets. Click Custom at the bottom of the gadget type list. Now enter your gadget's URL in the textbox, as shown in Figure 24-5. Click Add to use the gadget you developed.

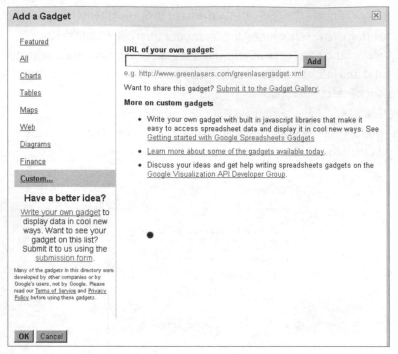

FIGURE 24-5: Enter the URL for your custom gadget.

DATA VALIDATION WITH GOOGLE SPREADSHEET

Validating your data—that is, ensuring that the information entered matches the format and range that makes sense—is key to ensuring data gets entered correctly. One method of doing this is to display a reminder that tells the user what the data should be. For example, if the data should be a number between 1 and 10, a small tip instructing the user to enter a number in that range is displayed.

To create instruction tips in Google Spreadsheets, first highlight the cells to which you are adding the validation. In the upper navigation, click Tools and then select Data Validation from the menu. In the Data Validation pop-up, shown in Figure 24-6, use the first drop-down menu to select the type of data. Choose between Text, Numbers, Date, or Items from a list. The second drop-down changes depending on your choice in the first. This menu helps you define your data even further. Use it to designate a range of numbers, type and contents of text entered by the user, or range of acceptable dates. If you choose Items from a List as your first criteria, the box changes so that you can enter the list terms.

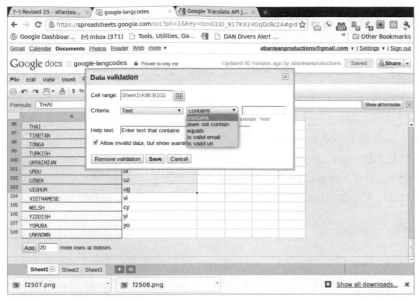

FIGURE 24-6: Select the requirements of data to be entered.

With data validation enabled, users are prompted if they enter data outside the designated range, as shown in Figure 24-7.

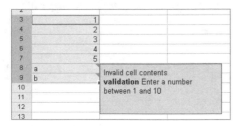

FIGURE 24-7: Google Spreadsheets reporting that the contents of a cell violate data validation rules.

CREATING A TEMPLATE

Because Spreadsheets is a subsection of the larger Google Docs, you can take advantage of all the great template capabilities discussed in Chapter 22.

> **CROSSREF** Finding, building, and submitting templates for all Google Docs products is covered in depth in Chapter 22.

FINISHING YOUR SPREADSHEET

When you're finished creating your spreadsheet you can publish it to the Web to allow people to use it.

To share a spreadsheet on the Web, click the Share menu. You can find it at the top right of the page. Select Publish as a Web Page. If you haven't saved your spreadsheet yet, you are prompted to save and name it now. On the page entitled Publish to the Web, use the drop-down menu to determine whether all sheets or only one sheet from your spreadsheet should be published. When you've made your selection, click Start Publishing, and the bottom half of the window activates, as shown in Figure 24-8.

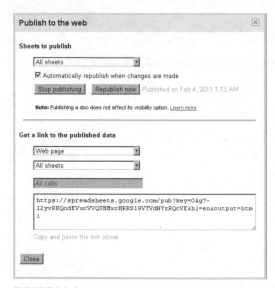

FIGURE 24-8: After you click the Start Publishing button, the bottom half of the form activates.

Use the drop-downs in the bottom half of the form to designate the file type in which the spreadsheet should be saved. When you've made your selection, copy the link in the box to share or embed your spreadsheet.

SUMMARY

Thanks to Google, the plain old color-coded spreadsheet is a thing of the past. A Google Spreadsheet can cross-reference with other Google products and present data clearly and dynamically—which not only makes the data easier to understand, but makes it more interesting and fun to look at.

CHAPTER 25

Demystifying Google Forms and Drawing

You've been asked to survey your classmates or co-workers. You must get responses to one hundred questions from at least fifty people. And you have only one week in which to do it. Don't get overwhelmed, just turn to Google Forms. With Google Forms, you can create a survey of any size. Create a series of multiple-choice questions, or give respondents a textbox for open-ended questions.

Google Drawing lets you take a break from creating forms or editing spreadsheets to allow your creative juices to flow. With Google Drawing, you can enjoy easy keyboard shortcuts, online integration, and tools that make your forget all about your sketch-pad.

DOING MORE WITH GOOGLE FORMS

To access Google Forms navigate to your Google Docs homepage. Open the Create New menu and select Form. Figure 25-1 shows a blank form.

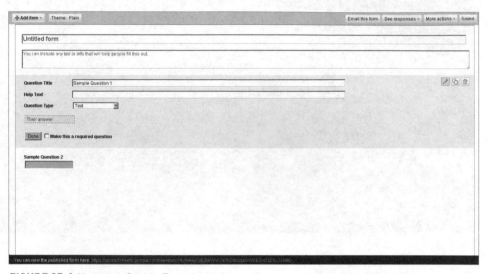

FIGURE 25-1: Your new Google Form is ready.

Use the first textbox to give your form a title. In the second textbox, give users directions or any information they need to answer your questions accurately.

Now, enter your survey question in the box labeled Question Title. Use the Help Text box to enter any additional information the user may need. Use the Question Type drop-down menu, shown in Figure 25-2, to stipulate the type of question. You can choose from Text, Paragraph Text, Multiple Choice, Checkboxes, Choose from a List, Scale, or Grid. These question types are defined in Table 25-1.

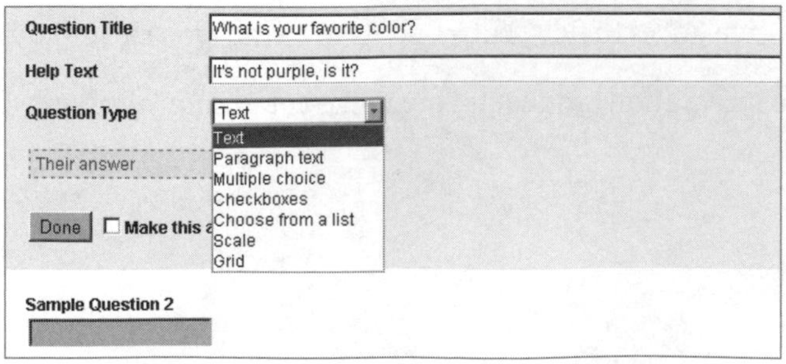

FIGURE 25-2: Google Forms offers a variety of question types, including Text, Multiple Choice, and Checkbox.

TABLE 25-1: Question Types Defined

QUESTION TYPE	DATA REQUIRED
Text	Standard text entry field
Paragraph Text	Long text entry
Multiple Choice	Select only one from the list
Checkboxes	Select one or more from the list
Choose from a List	Select only one from the list
Scale	Rank your answer on a scale
Grid	Rank your answer on two scales, x and y

The area below the Question Type menu changes based on the type of question you choose. For example, if you choose Multiple Choice, an area displays in which you can enter those choices. If you choose Scale, you see menus and textboxes with which to define that scale. This is shown in Figure 25-3.

▶ When you select Multiple Choice, Google Forms gives you the option of allowing the respondent to skip to a specific question based on the answer.

FIGURE 25-3: Question Type menu options

Next, decide if respondents may skip this question. If the question may remain unanswered, click the checkbox. When you are finished with this question, click Done. You have an opportunity to preview your questions after creating each of them and before completing the form. After you preview your question, mouse over the heading of Sample Question 2 to highlight it, and click the Edit button (the pencil) to the right, as shown in Figure 25-4.

FIGURE 25-4: The Edit, Duplicate, and Delete buttons appear to the right of every question.

When you select a multiple-choice question, you have the option to route the respondent to a specific set of questions based on the answer to the multiple-choice question. To use this feature, click the box labeled Go to Page Based on Answer. You can find it immediately to the right of the Question Type drop-down.

> **TIP** This box appears only if you are using multiple-choice questions.

For example, if your survey questions respondents about their pets' habits, the first question might be, "What kind of pet do you own," with multiple-choice answers of Cat, Dog, Fish, Horse, Bird, More Than One Type, and None.

As shown in Figure 25-5, each potential response for this question now shows a menu to the right. Use this menu to tell Forms which set of question to use.

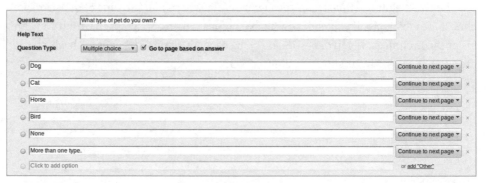

FIGURE 25-5: Use the menu to the right to tell Forms which page of questions corresponds to each answer.

For each question that leads to its own question set you need to add a new page. To do this, click Add Item at the top of the page. Select Page Break from the menu, as shown in Figure 25-6.

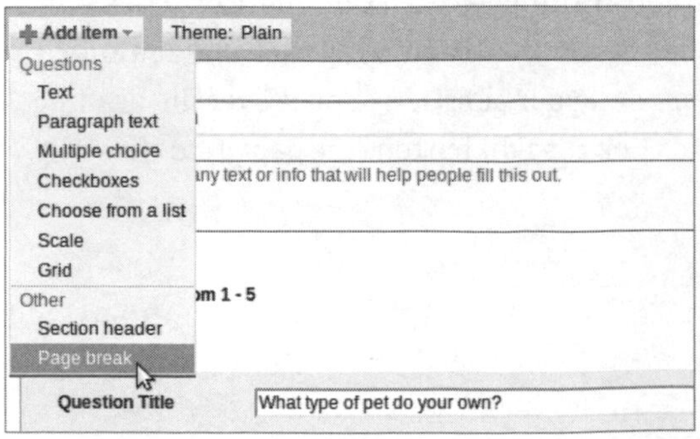

FIGURE 25-6: Use the Add Item menu to add a new page to your survey.

As you can see in Figure 25-7, a new section appears below your multiple-choice question. Use the boxes provided to name the page, and enter a description of the page. To add questions to this page, click Add Item at the top of the page, and select the type of question you want to add from the menu. When you're finished adding questions to this page, click Done.

FIGURE 25-7: Name and describe your page.

Now, click Edit on the original multiple-choice question, in this case Question 2, so you can work with it again.

Use the drop-down menu to the right of the appropriate question to direct the survey to use questions from the form you just created. See Figure 25-8. Continue this process for each multiple-choice answer that leads to a custom question set.

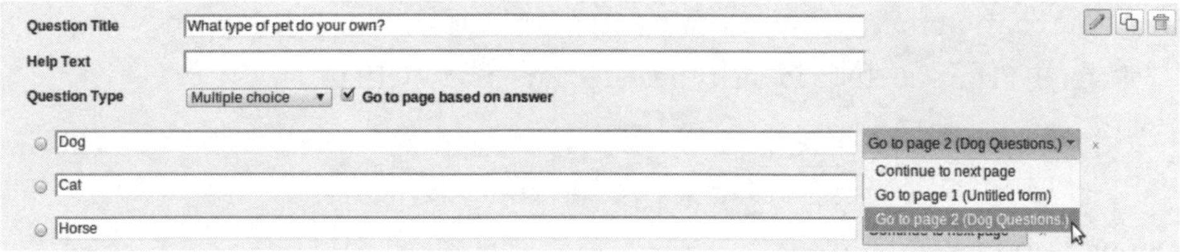

FIGURE 25-8: Use the menu to direct the survey to use the appropriate questions.

After your form is complete, it's time to write the confirmation response. In the top right of your screen, click the More Actions menu. Select Edit Confirmation. Use the box provided, shown in Figure 25-9, to type a message to your respondents. If you want respondents to see a summary of the survey results, click Publish Response Summary. Click Save when you're done.

Now you're ready to distribute your survey. Use the Email This Form button at the top of the page to e-mail the survey to specific people. To embed the survey in your blog or website, click More Actions → Embed. Copy the link and paste it in the HTML of your blog or website.

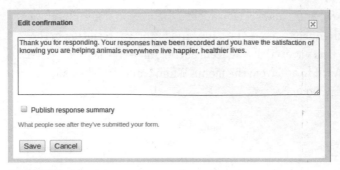

FIGURE 25-9: Insert a message to your respondents.

As responses come in, use the See Responses button to view them. Responses can be viewed in spreadsheet or line graph form. When you select spreadsheet form, survey results open in a full-functioning Google Spreadsheet. Use the spreadsheet to manipulate or chart data as needed.

▶ If viewing results in a line graph, click See Complete Response to switch to spreadsheet form without having to backtrack.

CREATING AND COLLABORATING WITH DRAWING

Google Drawing gives you complete online image creation capabilities. From your Google homepage, click Create New and select Drawing from the menu. The blank drawing page looks pretty similar to any other drawing program you may be familiar with. The controls for Drawing are fairly standard and work as you expect.

Refer to Figure 25-10 to identify each tool and its function.

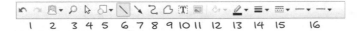

FIGURE 25-10: The Google Drawing toolbar.

1—Use these tools to "undo" or "redo" and action. You can also use the keyboard shortcut Ctrl+Z to Undo or Ctrl+Y to redo a change.

2—Web Clipboard

3—Zoom

4—Select

5—Shape Creator

6—Line Tool

7—Arrow Tool

8—Curve Tool

9—Polyline Tool

10—Text Tool

11—Insert Image Tool

12—Paint Bucket

13—Color Selector, for lines

14—Line Width Tool

15—Dashed or Solid Line

16—Select Arrowhead

Select the tool you want to use by clicking it. Move your mouse over the drawing area, hold down the left mouse button, and create the desired shape. To edit a previously created shape, click the Arrow button in the toolbar and then click the shape you want to edit. Use the handles to move, stretch, or shrink the shape, as shown in Figure 25-11.

Some tools deserve special attention. For example, the Shape Creator (tool 5 in Figure 25-10) contains an interesting collection of small ready-to-use shapes. Available shapes are shown in Figure 25-12.

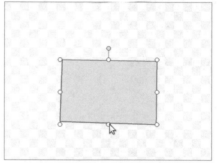

FIGURE 25-11: Use the handles around each object to move, stretch, adjust, or shrink it.

The Web Clipboard tool (tool 2 in Figure 25-10) enables you to copy and paste between Google Docs applications. Copy an image from Drawing and paste it into Presentations, Documents, or Spreadsheets. But the real power of the Web Clipboard lies in its ability to remember what you copied even after you've signed out of your account. It stores the copied data in the cloud—that is, with your Google account—and not with the drawing. You can copy an image to Web Clipboard, sign out of your Google account, and when you sign back into your Google account from any computer, your image is still saved to Web Clipboard.

The Web Clipboard even remembers multiple items. As shown in Figure 25-13, save different drawings into the Web Clipboard, and they will all be available to paste into other documents.

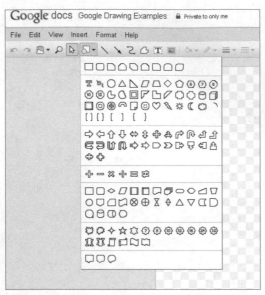

FIGURE 25-12: Add interesting shapes to your drawing with just a click.

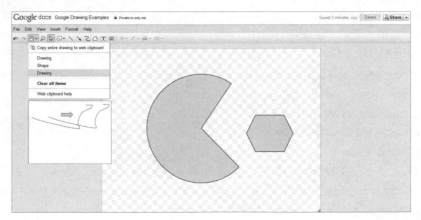

FIGURE 25-13: The Web Clipboard remembers multiple shapes and drawings at once.

SUMMARY

Google Forms and Google Drawings are two of Google's not-so-popular products that can really help you with your education or business. You can use either tool without too much effort or too much learning time involved.

CHAPTER 26

Scheduling Better with Google Calendar

Google Calendar is a great tool. Not only can you use it to keep track of your appointments and events, but multiple calendars and calendar sharing mean you can see where everyone is at a glance, which makes it easier to schedule meetings, family events, or even just a quiet weekend away. With Gmail integration, Google Task list, the ability to handle gadgets, userscripts, and printing, Google Calendar is truly the best calendar application anywhere.

SCHEDULING EVENTS FASTER

We all know that keeping track of appointments, events, and tasks is a huge time saver. And, let's face it: Keeping track of when things are supposed to happen is a huge part of managing your time effectively. But when you're really busy, stopping work to enter events into a calendar can feel like a waste of time. Google Calendar (www .google.com/calendar) provides lots of ways to enter your event in seconds, and get back to what you were doing. It's so fast, you can do it while waiting for the next pot of coffee to brew.

▶ Quick Add only adds events to your default calendar.

The most straightforward way to enter events quickly is to use Quick Add, in the upper left, directly under the Google Calendar log. When you use Quick Add, a small pop-up appears that gives you a single textbox in which to add information.

To get the most from Quick Add, phrase your event information exactly. Enter the name of the event, date, time, and location or name of the person who will be joining you. See Figure 26-1 for an example.

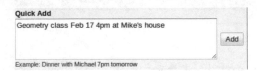

FIGURE 26-1: Form your Quick Add entry carefully to get the best result.

Quick Add recognizes time-sensitive words such as today and yesterday. Use **2 days** to add events that span several days. For example, entering **Rob's birthday party 3 days** gives the result shown in Figure 26-2.

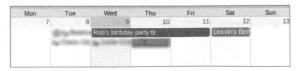

FIGURE 26-2: Select the start date, and include the number of days an event spans in your Quick Add entry.

I often receive notification of upcoming appointments and events through my Gmail account. As discussed in Chapter 11, there are several ways to add events directly to Google Calendar from Gmail. The most direct way is to click Add, which is located on the right side of the screen. This link, shown in Figure 26-3, appears when you open any e-mail that meets Google's criteria for being a suspected event. Google Calendar opens to the Add Event page in a new tab. Enter any important details, set reminders and privacy settings, share the event, and then click Save.

Some event e-mails don't trip the Gmail event sensor. You can still add them to Google Calendar easily. Click an e-mail to open it. Click More Actions, and select Create Event from the menu. The Google Calendar Add Event page opens in a new window. Type in the event details and click Save. This is a handy tool anytime you need to add an event without taking the time to open Google Calendar.

New window
Print all
Add to calendar
Meeting
Wed Feb 9, 2011 5pm - add

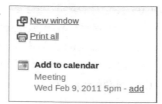

FIGURE 26-3: Click Add to automatically add an event to your Google Calendar.

CROSSREF See Chapter 11 for more ways to add events to Google Calendar from Gmail.

You probably have quite a few contacts in your Gmail contact book. If you've taken the time to record the birth date of a contact, you probably want to at least try to remember it. Why not add those dates to a Google Calendar so you always have them at your fingertips? From your Google Calendar homepage, navigate to Calendar Settings. Click Calendars to go to the Calendars tab. On the right side of your screen in the Other Calendars heading section, click the Browse Interesting Calendars link, as shown in Figure 26-4. Click the More tab, and subscribe to the calendar titled Contacts' Birthdays and Events.

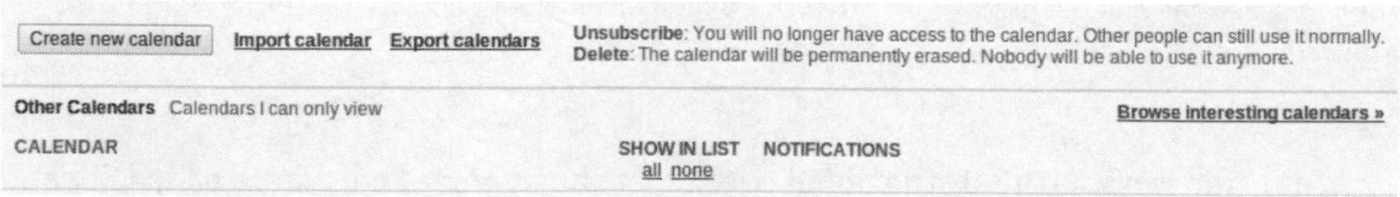

Create new calendar
Import calendar
Export calendars
Unsubscribe: You will no longer have access to the calendar. Other people can still use it normally.
Delete: The calendar will be permanently erased. Nobody will be able to use it anymore.
Other Calendars
Calendars I can only view
Browse interesting calendars »
CALENDAR
SHOW IN LIST
all none
NOTIFICATIONS

FIGURE 26-4: Click Browse Interesting Calendars.

Save time and keystrokes when sending out event invitations by letting Google Calendar do it for you. Click Add Event and enter the event details. On the right, look for the box labeled Add Guests, shown in Figure 26-5. Enter e-mail addresses of invitees in the box. You can either enter each e-mail address individually, or send the invitation to a group you've previously created in Gmail Contacts.

CROSSREF Managing Contacts in Gmail is discussed in Chapter 11.

Meetings are a vital part of every business, but let's face it, not every person invited to a meeting is required for the meeting to be effective. Although it's nice when the whole team can attend every meeting, there are often better uses for your time. That's where Optional Attendees comes in handy. This tool gives you the ability to let every invited team member know at a glance whether or not the success of the meeting hinges on their attendance. To use Optional Attendees, add the meeting or event to your Google Calendar using Add Event. After you've entered the event details, use the Add Guests box to enter e-mail addresses for meeting invitees. Click the link titled Make Some Attendees Optional. Now, click the silhouette in front of the name of the optional invitee, as shown in Figure 26-6. When the invitees receive notification of the event from Google Calendar, their status as optional attendees is noted.

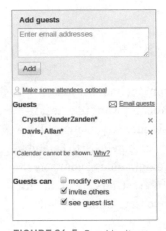

FIGURE 26-5: Send invitations to meetings and events with Add Guests.

FIGURE 26-6: Mark invitees as optional for any event.

When you work with international clients, or the overseas corporate office, it can be a pain to constantly transpose from one time zone to another. Let Google Calendar help you. When you add an event with Quick Add, notice the link titled Time Zone at the end of the date and time entry line. Use this Time Zone link to set the time zone of the event. For example, if you live in New York, but need to call your client at 2:00 p.m. Germany time, set the time zone for Germany using the drop-down menu.

SHARING AND COLLABORATING WITH MULTIPLE CALENDARS

Calendar sharing is a wonderful thing. At a glance you can see when a person or persons are free to attend meetings or appointments, and you can find out where each member of your team or family is on any given day.

If you are charged with scheduling an event for 50 people, finding a time that works for everyone is difficult to say the least. Let Google Calendar make this task a bit easier. First, request that all parties involved share their Google Calendars with you. They don't have to share calendar details, but you do need to see their Free/Busy information.

After you have access to everyone's calendar information you're ready to schedule the event. From your Google Calendar homepage, click Create Event. Next to the Event Details tab, locate the link named Find a Time, shown in Figure 26-7.

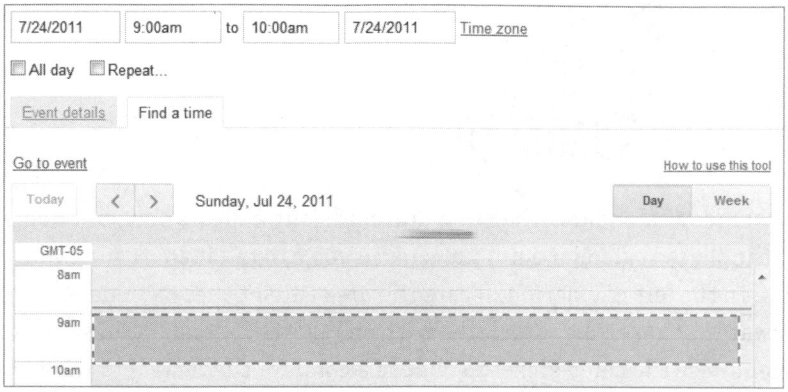

FIGURE 26-7: Use Find a Time to schedule an event that fits into everyone's schedule.

Click this link to open the tab. Use the tool to compare schedules and find a good time for the event. After you've found a time and day agreeable to everyone, enter the event information as you would for any event. Be sure to use the Add Guests box to add the event to everyone's calendar and send invitations.

Shared calendars have other uses, too. For example, let's say you are responsible for allocating company resources such as the conference room, reserved parking spots, or even a shared office assistant. You could track these resources on a spreadsheet, but Google Calendar enables you to automate the process.

First, create a new calendar. Use the name or type of resource as the calendar name. From your Google Calendar homepage, click the downward-facing arrow that corresponds with the calendar you just created. Select Calendar Settings from the menu that appears. Ensure the Calendar Details tab is selected. Look for the section titled Auto-Accept Invitations. It is five headings down from the top. Select Auto-Accept Invitations That Do Not Conflict, as shown in Figure 26-8. Save your changes to return to the Google Calendar homepage.

Now, click the downward-facing arrow associated with this calendar again. This time, select Share This Calendar from the menu. Enter the e-mail addresses of everyone who may need to schedule time with the resource in question. When you set the sharing

▶ To share a calendar, go to Calendar Settings. Click the Calendars tab. Find the calendar you want to share. Click Share This Calendar. Type the e-mail address of the person with whom you're sharing and select the privacy settings. Save your changes.

permissions for this calendar you must, at minimum, give everyone permission to See All Events. Save your changes.

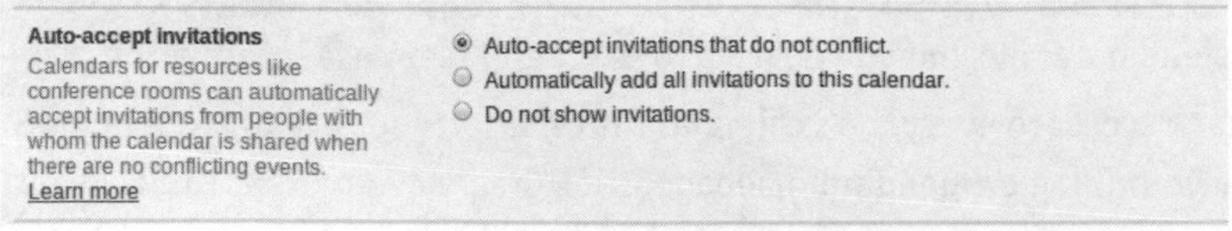

FIGURE 26-8: For an automated resource calendar that does not create scheduling conflicts, set the calendar to Auto-Accept Invitations That Do Not Conflict.

ACCESSING CALENDARS: YOURS AND OTHERS'

When someone shares a calendar with you, it automatically appears on your Google Calendar. Give the shared calendar a unique look so you can tell it apart from your other calendars. In the left navigation, locate the area titled Other Calendars. Click the downward-facing arrow associated with the shared calendar. This opens the calendar menu. Use the color-picker to choose a color for that calendar. Any events from the other calendar that appear on your calendar are highlighted with the chosen color.

If you're using a local calendar program such as Microsoft Outlook, Mozilla Sunbird, Apple Cal, or Evolution for any reason, you may find it helpful to sync that application with your Google calendars. Most of the local applications can sync with only one other calendar. To get around this, move events from all your Google calendars to one, centralized calendar.

First, from your Google Calendar homepage, locate the calendar from which you want to export information. Click the downward-facing arrow associated with that calendar. Select Calendar Settings from the menu.

Ensure the Calendar Details tab is selected, and scroll down to the last section, titled Private Address. Click the ICAL button, as shown in Figure 26-9.

▶ Depending on your browser this may be Save Target As, Download Linked File As, or something similar.

Now, right-click the link that appears in the pop-up. Select Save Link As. Save this file to your desktop under the default name basic.ics.

Repeat this step for each calendar for which you want to move data. Be sure to give each calendar a different name.

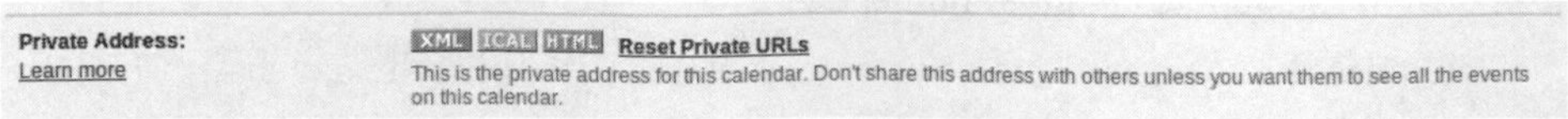

FIGURE 26-9: Get the ICAL link for the calendar you want to import.

Next, go to the Calendars tab on the Calendar Settings page. Click Import Calendar. You can find this link directly between the My Calendars and Other Calendars sections, next to the Create a New Calendar button.

Use the file navigation in the Import Calendar tool, shown in Figure 26-10, to select the ICAL file you just downloaded.

Use the Calendar drop-down to select the calendar to which the ICAL file should be imported. Click Import.

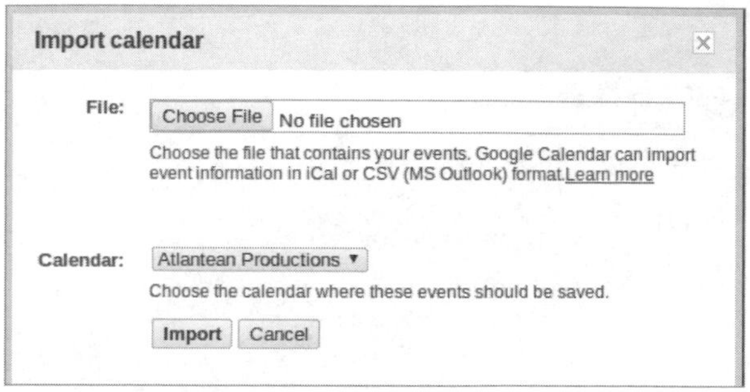

Import calendar   ✕

File: [Choose File] No file chosen

Choose the file that contains your events. Google Calendar can import
event information in iCal or CSV (MS Outlook) format. Learn more

Calendar: [Atlantean Productions ▼]

Choose the calendar where these events should be saved.

[Import] [Cancel]

FIGURE 26-10: Import Calendar tool.

Repeat this process for each calendar to be imported.

Now, configure your local calendar application to sync with the calendar that holds all your data. Every calendar application has a different procedure. If in doubt, consult the help file, FAQ, or other documentation for your program and operating system.

FINDING SECRET CALENDAR SHORTCUTS

Keyboard shortcuts make everything faster. Table 26-1 gives the keyboard shortcuts for Google Calendar.

TABLE 26-1: Google Calendar Keyboard Shortcuts

KEYBOARD	SHORTCUTS
1 or D	Show calendar in Day view
2 or W	Show calendar in Week view
3 or M	Show calendar in Month view
4 or X	Show calendar in Custom view

continues

TABLE 26-1: *(continued)*

KEYBOARD	SHORTCUTS
5 or A	Show Agenda view
C	Create new event
J or N	Jump to next date range
K or P	Show previous date range
Q	Quick Add
R	Refresh calendar
S	Open Calendar Settings
T	View today
/	Move cursor to search box
? or Ctrl+?	Show list of keyboard shortcuts
Z or Ctrl+Z	Undo most recent action
Delete or Backspace	Delete event
Tab	Move cursor to next field

ADDING TOOLS TO BOOST CALENDAR POWER

As with most other Google Apps, you can find add-ons, extensions, and userscripts to expand the power of Google Calendar.

To find and activate Labs for Google Calendar, navigate to Calendar Settings and click the Labs tab.

My favorite Labs for Calendar include the following:

▶ **Event Flair**—Add virtual stickers to any event on your calendar with Event Flair. I use it to help organize kids' activities, remind myself to complete a task, and see at a glance events related to specific people. After you enable Event Flair go back to your Google Calendar and click any event. Flair appears in the right navigation.

▶ **Gentle Reminders**—I love Google's event reminders, and I set pop-up and e-mail reminders for almost every event on my calendar. But when I'm working, the pop-up in the middle of the screen disrupts my concentration and irritates me. Gentle Reminders solves this problem by redirecting the pop-up to appear in the background. Gentle Reminders also triggers a sound, alerting you to its presence.

▶ **Event Attachments**—I use this one at work all the time. Event Attachments lets you attach any file to an event. This is great for including a map, presentation, notes, or even an entire report so everyone attending the meeting has the same information.

▶ **Background Image**—Enable Background Image to load an image of your choice to be the background for your Google Calendar. After Background Image is enabled, the controls appear on the General Calendar Settings page, near the bottom.

▶ **Jump to Date**—This lab enables you to quickly flip to any date in the future or a date in the past using a simple menu. It's easier than turning the page of a paper calendar.

Userscripts are small pieces of JavaScript code that are installed into your browser to change the function of the browser. If you're using Mozilla Firefox, check the website for add-ons for Google Calendar. From within Firefox, click Tools in the navigation bar. Select Add-ons to view the browser extensions you have installed. Click Get Add-ons at the top of the window. This shows a list of the Mozilla-recommended add-ons, as shown in Figure 26-11. Use the search bar directly under the tool buttons to search for Google Calendar. To install an add-on, click Add to Firefox on the right. Then click Install Now in the pop-up.

My favorite Firefox add-on for Google Calendar is Integrated Gmail. This brings Gmail, Google Calendar, Labs, Google Reader, and many other Google Apps together on one page.

If you use the Google Chrome web browser, you can also take advantage of browser extensions for Google Calendar. Click the wrench in the upper right of your Chrome browser. Select Tools → Extensions from the menu to see a list of your installed extensions. Scroll to the bottom of the page and click Get More Extensions to access the Google App Store. Use the search bar at the top right to search for Google Calendar.

> **WARNING** Be sure to read all comments and documentation before you install any extension from the Google App Store. Not all extensions are free. And others give a free trial and then simply shut down if you don't purchase service at the end of the trial. Read the fine print to make sure you know what you're getting into.

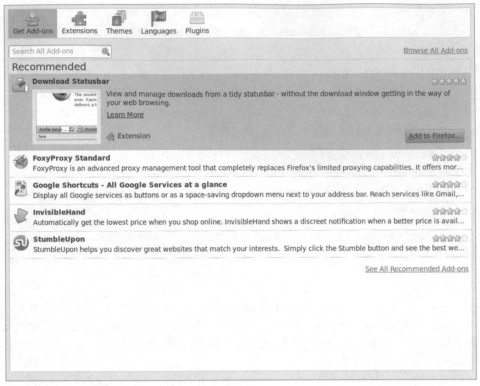

FIGURE 26-11: Recommended add-ons for Mozilla browsers.

Keep up-to-date with what's going on with Google Calendar by subscribing to the Google Calendar Twitter feed. Go to www.twitter.com/googlecalendar to get the latest.

GOOGLE TASKS

Google Tasks gives you an integrated task list to the right of your Google Calendar. Google Tasks is one example of a Lab product that has graduated to become a regular feature. Access your task list in the My Calendars section by clicking the word Tasks. Your task list opens in the right sidebar. Use the tools at the bottom of the task list to add, delete, indent, sort, and clear completed tasks. Enter a due date, set task priority, and enter notes to any task by clicking the arrow to the right of the task. When you enter a task due day, it automatically appears on your Google Calendar on the date due.

Tasks is fully functional from Gmail, too. Click Tasks, located directly above the Compose Mail button. Because Tasks is its own application, it works the same whether you access it from Calendar or Gmail, and entered tasks appear in both applications.

SUMMARY

Google Calendar gives you all the functionality of any standalone or e-mail-integrated scheduling system. Shared calendars, add-ons, and tasks keep all your important information at your fingertips.

CHAPTER 27

Navigating Better with Google Maps

At some point, everyone needs to consult a map. Whether you need directions, are looking for a business, are planning a cross-country road trip, or just need to know where some far-away country lies, maps are one of the most useful reference materials ever invented. Sometimes they're also the most dreaded. Many people have trouble reading maps, or think they do. But with Google Maps, there's no reason to avoid using a map. Google Maps makes finding your way a snap, and with all the cool customizations, mashups, and features, you'll never lose your way again.

CUSTOMIZING GOOGLE MAPS

If you've never used Google Maps (maps.google.com) the first thing you notice is that you don't need a Google account to access the most widely used features. As shown in Figure 27-1, you can set a default location, get directions, print and link to maps, and even view photos, terrain, and live traffic conditions without ever signing into a Google account. However, if you do log in to your Google account, you'll be able to access additional Google Maps features, such walking directions or public transportation directions.

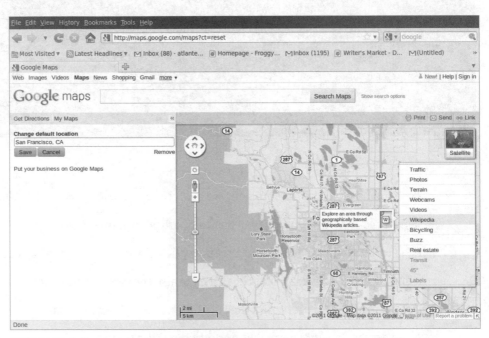

FIGURE 27-1: You don't have to be logged in to a Google account to use Google Maps.

Do you use alternative means of transportation? Use Google Maps to get directions via bike, walking, or even public transportation.

Enter your starting point and your destination. Then click the icon that corresponds to the method of travel you plan to use. If you're using public transportation, use the menus to indicate the time and date you plan to travel, as shown in Figure 27-2.

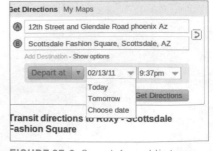

FIGURE 27-2: Search for public transportation routes based on when you want to leave.

Regardless of your method of travel, directions (including times) and routes (if applicable) appear in text on the left and a map of your route and surrounding area is displayed on the right. Use the slider bar on the map to view the area more closely, or widen your view of the area. Many cities are street-view enabled, enabling you to view the map as if you are walking down the middle of the road.

To use Street view, grab the person-shaped icon and drag it to the location you want to view. While in Street view, use the white arrows to navigate through the map, as shown in Figure 27-3. The inset map acts as a guide to the overall area.

FIGURE 27-3: Use the arrows to navigate through Street view and the inset maps to keep track of where you are.

While in Street view, use the plus sign (+) to get closer to an object, and the minus sign (–) to get farther from an object, or to leave street view. To advance the screen as if you are walking forward, place your mouse anywhere along the white line and click.

When you leave Street view, you have many options for customizing the map view.

Switch between Satellite and Street maps by clicking the button in the top-right corner of the map, shown in Figure 27-4. Get an idea of traffic conditions and terrain, find bike routes, see webcam views, and even locate available real estate in the area with the features menu, shown in Figure 27-5. Do note that within Google Maps, the Traffic option is what we're calling Street view in this chapter.

FIGURE 27-4: Use this button to switch between satellite view and street map view.

Use Google Maps to see where the heavy traffic is. Click the feature menu shown in Figure 27-5 and select Traffic to view live traffic conditions. Toggle the drop-down menu and slider in the traffic box shown in Figure 27-6 to see average traffic levels for the day and time you set.

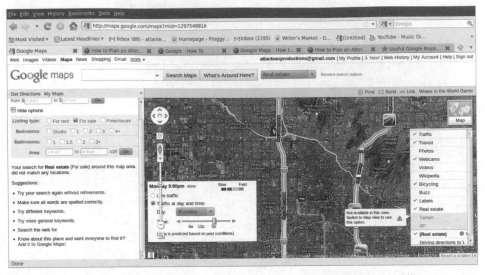

FIGURE 27-5: Use the features menu to see traffic, public transportation routes, bike routes, and more.

Google Map directions are good. I've never had them steer me wrong, but sometimes you might want to use a different route to avoid traffic or construction. You can easily change the route shown. Simply grab the part of the route you want to change and drag it to your preferred route. The map and written directions update instantly to reflect your changes.

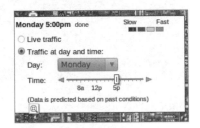

FIGURE 27-6: Use the drop-down menu and slider to set the day and time for which you want to view average traffic levels.

Once in a while, you may find a small error on Google Maps. Granted, it's a rare occurrence, but nothing is perfect and mistakes do happen. Help Google Maps correct errors by editing the location of an ill-placed item. To edit a location, type the address of the location in the Maps search box and click Search Maps. Click the location's marker to open the information bubble associated with the location. Click More and then click Move Marker, as shown in Figure 27-7.

Send any map or directions to your e-mail, cell phone, GPS, or vehicle navigation system. Type the desired destination in the Maps search bar and click Search Maps.

Click the location maker to open the information bubble for that location. Click More and then Send. Use the pop-up shown in Figure 27-8 to choose the device to which you are sending the map (The contents of the pop-up may vary from what's shown, depending on your Google account options). Then enter the device details in the right side of the pop-up.

FIGURE 27-7: Move the marker if a location is incorrect.

FIGURE 27-8: Send maps to e-mail, cell phone, car, or GPS.

ADVERTISING ON GOOGLE MAPS

If you own a business, even a small one, you can improve your visibility by putting yourself on the map. Google Maps encourages business owners to post photos and offer special customer deals through Google Maps. From the Google Maps homepage, click Put Your Business on Google Maps. This takes you to the Google Places homepage, shown in Figure 27-9.

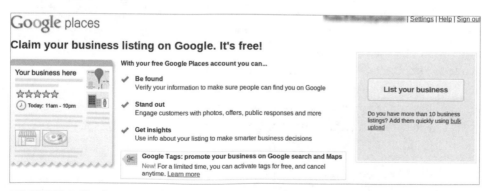

FIGURE 27-9: The Google Places homepage.

Log in to your Google account and click the List Your Business button. Use the drop-down to select your country and enter your business phone number in the indicated box. Click Find Business Information. Google searches to see if there is already information about your business listed.

Use the Google Places form to enter information about your business. Take the time to enter five relevant categories in the spaces provided. Category entries serve as keywords and help potential customers find you in the listing. You can upload images and link to YouTube videos that are associated to your business.

> **TIP** Double-check both the address and phone number you enter for your business. Google requires you verify this information by sending a postcard containing a PIN to your business address. Your business does not appear on Google Maps until you have entered that PIN.

When you finish entering business information, click Submit. Google then sends out a postcard or confirmation letter. This letter or postcard contains a PIN. Navigate to the address shown on the confirmation card and enter your PIN in the designated box. Click Go. Your business is entered on Google Maps.

▶ To create a business listing for your Google Places entry, visit www .google.com/local/ add/businessCenter.

After your Google Maps entry is live, there are quite a few things you can do to increase visibility. Update your Places entry to include current events, new product additions, changes in hours, or special sales and events your business is holding using the update form shown in Figure 27-10.

Use the Offers tab to add coupon offers to your Google Maps listing. From the Offers tab, click Add an Offer now. Use the form provided to define and target your offer. Catch your reader's eye with an attractive photo. Determine an expiration date, and add an offer code to help track offers, if desired. The area on the right is a preview of how the Offer will appear. When you're satisfied, click Continue. A verification screen displays, as shown in Figure 27-11.

FIGURE 27-10: Update your Places entry regularly.

> **TIP** The Headline Details and Expiration Date are required fields.

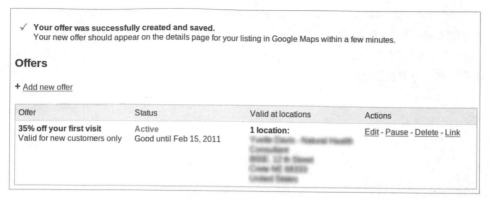

✓ **Your offer was successfully created and saved.**
   Your new offer should appear on the details page for your listing in Google Maps within a few minutes.

Offers

+ Add new offer

Offer	Status	Valid at locations	Actions
35% off your first visit Valid for new customers only	Active Good until Feb 15, 2011	**1 location:**	Edit - Pause - Delete - Link

FIGURE 27-11: Confirmation that your Offer has been created.

USING SPECIAL MAPS FEATURES

In addition to standard map functions, and the ability to mark and advertise your business on a local map, Google Maps gives you a host of special features to help you find your way.

On your next stroll through town, use Google walking directions to find new places to roam. Enter your starting and ending addresses as usual and then click the icon shaped like a person, shown in Figure 27-12, to see walking directions. Google walking directions are compatible with most mobile phones, as well as all computers.

FIGURE 27-12: Walking directions with Google Maps

While you're out and about, share your location with friends via Google Maps Latitude. Latitude is an app that is compatible with most mobile devices using data plans. It enables you to post to your current status and location. Use Latitude with Google Location History, Location badges, and your Google Talk status so that people on your contact list always know where you are and what you're doing. Visit www.google.com/latitude on your computer or mobile device to enable the service.

A bookmarklet (which is cutely referred to as a bookmaplet) called Map That Address enables you to map a location without leaving the web page you are reading. Access the bookmarklet by navigating your browser to www.bookmaplet.com, and click and drag the button shown in Figure 27-13 to the bookmark bar of your web browser. Now, whenever you encounter a location that you're unsure of, simply highlight the address and click Map That Address in your bookmark bar. A map of the selected address opens as a pop-up within your browser window, as shown in Figure 27-14.

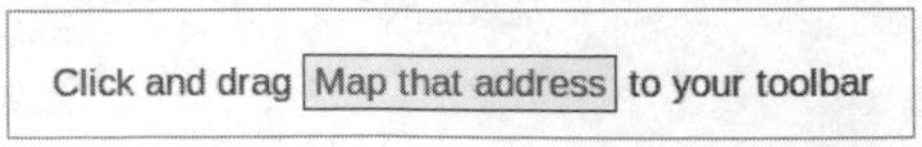

Click and drag Map that address to your toolbar

FIGURE 27-13: Drag the bookmarklet button to your browser's bookmark bar.

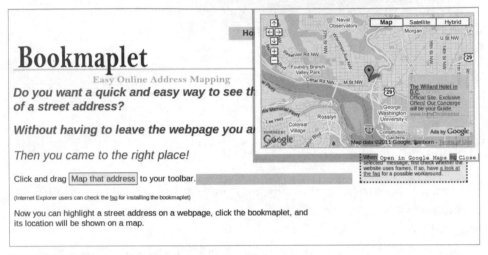

FIGURE 27-14: Open a map within your browser window.

You can also get directions from Google without Internet on your mobile phone using SMS. Send a text message to 466453 containing the words "Directions *starting point* to *destination*." Google auto-sends directions.

USING THE GOOGLE MAPS API

KML, or Keyhole Markup Language, was first developed by Keyhole, Inc., for its Keyhole Earth Viewer. KML is an open source system used to track locations in two and three dimensions. In 2004, Google purchased Keyhole, and renamed it Google Earth. The Google Maps API uses KML and JavaScript.

The Google Maps API is the heart of Google Maps. With only a few lines of code, any website can call up an interactive map. Here is the basic code for a website containing a map:

```
<!DOCTYPE html>
<html>
<head>
```

```
<meta name="viewport" content="initial-scale=1.0, user-scalable=no" />
<style type="text/css">
html { height: 100% }
body { height: 100%; margin: 0px; padding: 0px }
#mapFrame { height: 100% }
</style>
<script type="text/javascript"
src="http://maps.google.com/maps/api/js?sensor=false">
</script>
<script type="text/javascript">
function initialize() {
var latlng = new google.maps.LatLng(44.5891505, -104.6966319);
var mapSettings = {
zoom: 15,
center: latlng,
mapTypeId: google.maps.MapTypeId.HYBRID
};
var map = new google.maps.Map(document.getElementById("mapFrame"),
mapSettings);
}


</script>
</head>
<body onload="initialize()">
<div id="mapFrame" style="width:100%; height:100%"></div>
</body>
</html>
```

The DOCTYPE html line instructs the browser to load this page in Standards mode. This is the best option for browser compatibility; most browsers should be able to display this page.

```
<!DOCTYPE html>
<html>
<head>
```

The meta name line lays out the settings for the frame that holds the Google Map. In this case, fill the entire screen (initial scale), and do not allow the user to resize (user scalable).

```
<meta name="viewport" content="initial-scale=1.0, user-scalable=no" />
```

The style block is CSS code. This code is defining the available styles for this page, which is a height of 100% for the frame, that is, it should completely fill the entire HTML page.

```
<style type="text/css">
html { height: 100% }
```

```
body { height: 100%; margin: 0px; padding: 0px }
#mapFrame { height: 100% }
</style>
```

A script block contains JavaScript code. This block is defining the web address that generates the Google Map. The sensor flag has to be set for either true or false, and it identifies the device that is requesting data from Google. If sensor is true, Google Maps knows that the request is coming from a cell phone or other portable device.

```
<script type="text/javascript"
src="http://maps.google.com/maps/api/js?sensor=false">
</script>
```

The second script block contains all of the data needed to send the request to Google. This map is centered on latitude 44.5891505, longitude –104.6966319, which is the location of Devil's Tower, Wyoming.

```
<script type="text/javascript">
function initialize() {
var latlng = new google.maps.LatLng(44.5891505, -104.6966319);
```

mapSettings contains almost everything needed to generate a Google Map except for the actual latitude and longitude. This map starts with a zoom factor of 15, which is fairly close to the map. The smallest zoom factor is zero, which shows all of planet Earth.

Set the MapTypeId in this section as well. The Hybrid map type shows roads and other features superimposed against a terrain map.

```
var mapSettings = {
zoom: 15,
center: latlng,
mapTypeId: google.maps.MapTypeId.HYBRID
};
```

Now that all of the proper settings are in place, call the code that creates a new map:

```
var map = new google.maps.Map(document.getElementById("mapFrame"),
mapSettings);
}
</script>
</head>
```

Finally, use the OnLoad setting to force the browser to load and display the Google Map before moving on to anything else.

```
<body onload="initialize()">
<div id="mapFrame" style="width:100%; height:100%"></div>
```

```
</body>
</html>
```

As you can see in Figure 27-15, this code opens a Google Map centered on Devils Tower, Wyoming.

FIGURE 27-15: New map centered on Devils Tower Wyoming.

The Google Maps API is actually a family of systems used in Google Maps:

▶ The JavaScript API is the standard tool used to embed Google Maps into web pages.

▶ Use the Flash API for websites designed to run in Flash.

▶ Static Maps use URL encoding, rather than JavaScript, to generate Google Maps images.

▶ The same API that powers Google Maps also controls Google Earth.

▶ The Web Services API is used to request data from other applications.

Using the Search Wizard

The simplest way to add a Google Map to your page is to use the Ajax Search Wizard. You can find it here:

```
www.google.com/uds/solutions/wizards/mapsearch.html
```

To use the Search Wizard, fill in the answers on the page. Set the height and width of the box where the Google Map is to appear. Next, set the default zoom level; Google Maps gives you three options: City Level, Street Level, or Block Level. Enter the name of the location shown in the map, followed by the URL of the website where the map should appear.

The last box before the Preview Center button is the actual location. The Google Maps API understands latitude and longitude. It recognizes a latitude as anything between 90 and –90 and a longitude as anything between 180 and –180. You can also type something in that identifies your target uniquely in the world, and the Google Maps API translates into latitude and longitude as needed.

The last thing you need to do on this page is complete the Tell Us About Your Website section. This box is used to generate a unique API Key. After you've completed the section, click Generate Code. After a couple of minutes, Google Maps delivers your JavaScript code in the bottom of the page. Copy this code to your website to make this particular map appear.

The advantage of using the Map Search Wizard is that no JavaScript coding is necessary, but the disadvantage is that you can't add too many extras to the page.

Using the Static Maps API

For more flexibility than the Search Wizard, use the Static Maps API. Using this system, your website sends a specially encoded HTTP request to the Google Maps Server. The Server reads the information sent by your website and uses it to build an image (formatted either as GIF, JPEG, or PNG) before sending it back to your website for display.

The format of a Static Maps HTTP Request is made up of two parts—the Address and the Parameter List.

The Parameter List determines not only the subject of the map image, but also the size, zoom level, and other attributes. Here are a few sample parameters.

- ▶ Center—Defines the exact center of the map. It must be either a unique identifier (such as "Easter Island") or a latitude-longitude pair.

- ▶ Zoom—Sets the default magnification for the map. This is a number that ranges from zero (the entire earth) to 21.

- ▶ Format—Defines the type of picture that the Google Maps Server generates, either JPG, GIF, or PNG.

- ▶ Size—The Size parameter defines how big the picture will be, in width × height format. 250 × 300 means your map is 250 pixels wide by 300 pixels tall.

▶ Markers—A Marker describes the location of a flag on the map. Markers have their own parameter lists, which are separated with the pipe (|) character. You can define multiple markers in the same list.

▶ MapType—There are four settings for the MapType: Roadmap, Satellite, Terrain, and Hybrid.

▶ Sensor—If the requesting system is a mobile device, Sensor must be set to True.

The following is an example of the HTTP request code. You can see the resulting Google Maps image in Figure 27-16.

```
http://maps.google.com/maps/api/staticmap?center=Easter+Island&zoom=10&
size=700x512&maptype=roadmap&sensor=false
```

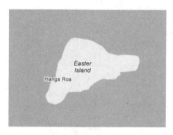

FIGURE 27-16: Static map of Easter Island.

USING GOOGLE MAPS MASHUP

What do you do if you have data you want to show on the map? For example, if you want to build a Google Map that shows every chiropractor in a four-mile radius of your home, you need to create what Google calls a "mashup." The easiest way to do this is with Fusion Tables (www.google.com/fusiontables).

Start your mashup by building a table of information. Fusion Tables accepts Microsoft Excel spreadsheets, Open Document spreadsheets, Keyhole Markup Language sheets, and comma-delimited text files (CSV files), as shown in Figure 27-17. You can also create an empty table from the figure's location as well. If you have a lot of data, use CSV because it can handle as much as 100 megabytes of data, but a standard Excel spreadsheet is limited to only one megabyte of data (as is the Open Document format). Our source data concerns a series of monster attacks in Lincoln, Nebraska, and is stored in a Google Docs spreadsheet, as shown in Figure 27-18.

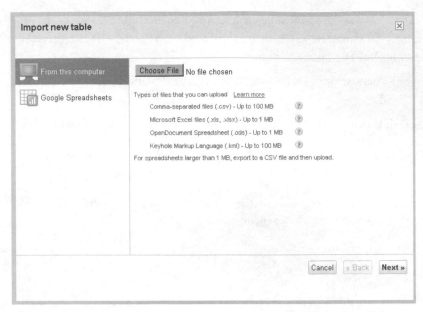

FIGURE 27-17: Open a CSV file.

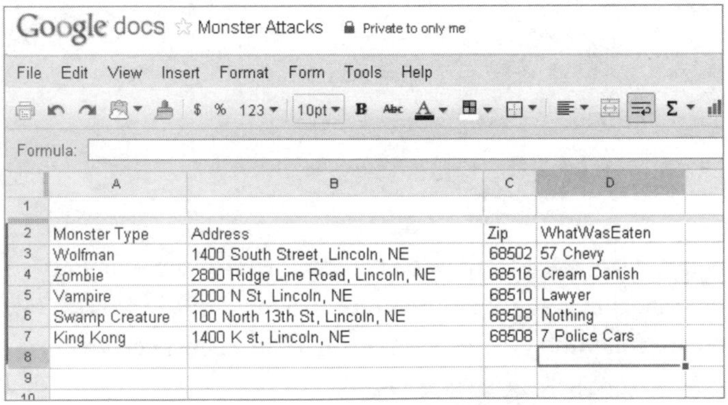

FIGURE 27-18: Enter your data into the spreadsheet.

After you've stored your mashup data in a spreadsheet, log in to Fusion Tables at www.google.com/fusiontables/Home and sign in with your standard Google password. If you have no documents of your own, Fusion Tables shows you a list of public documents instead. These are shown in Figure 27-19.

Import the data from your Google Spreadsheet by clicking the New Table button at the top left. Click Import New Table to open the Import New Table dialog box. Then click the Google Spreadsheets link.

FIGURE 27-19: Public Fusion tables.

Google asks for permission to access your Google Docs account. Click Grant Access to continue and select your spreadsheet from the list of Google Spreadsheets displayed.

Fusion Tables then enables you to adjust the import by selecting which columns to import. This is shown in Figure 27-20. Check the box above each column you want to appear in your Mashup and click Next when you're done.

FIGURE 27-20: Use this screen to select which columns to import.

The last screen in the import process is Attribution and Description. Fill in the fields as you see fit and click Finish. Fusion Tables opens your spreadsheet for you.

Before Fusion Tables can use your data, identify the Location columns. Click Modify Columns under the Edit menu. For each column that contains address or location data, change the Type field to Location, as shown in Figure 27-21.

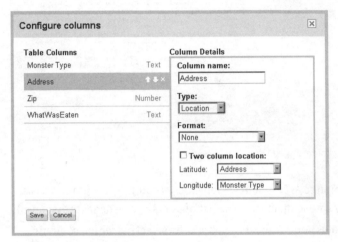

FIGURE 27-21: Change the column type.

Click Save and Fusion Tables highlights the Location columns in bright yellow.

To place your data on the map, click Visualize, and select Map from the menu. You need to zoom in from a view of the entire world, depending on your settings, but as you zoom in closer you should be able to make out your data points. Make your data flags larger by clicking Configure Styles and then choosing large flags from the menu.

This dataset is fictitious monster attacks in the city of Lincoln. Other mashups could include cancer patients near toxic sites, crimes per capita, or even video arcades within a ten mile radius.

SUMMARY

Google Maps is a powerful and revolutionary online application that can clearly meet your basic, intermediate, and advanced needs. You can even advertise on this extremely popular and diverse online tool. Millions of users have migrated from MapQuest and other map applications to use Google Maps because of all the features Google Maps offers.

Part VII

GOOGLE WEBSITE SECRETS

CHAPTER 28

Building Your Home on the Web with Google Sites

IN THIS CHAPTER

▸ Creating a website with Google's platform
▸ Website-editing techniques
▸ Launching your website on the Internet

With Google Sites anyone can create their home on the Web. The website building tools are intuitive and yet there is enough flexibility and power behind them to build an impressive and powerful business website. The provided templates are well thought out and give the non-web designer ample tools. For the experienced web designer, the opportunities are limited only by your imagination!

▶ Markup languages enable the web browser to understand how to format text. They use tags and attributes to create paragraphs, headers, and links on websites for the Internet. Examples of markup languages used for the Internet include HTML, XML, and XHTML.

▶ WYSIWYG stands for "what you see is what you get." These design programs write the HTML for you when you add design elements to a web page. Google Sites is a WYSIWYG web design program.

BUILDING POWER SITES

Have you ever visited a website and been immediately impressed by the site? What makes a "power site" impressive is the combination of graphics, media, text, and information. Power sites bring these components together in a way that makes the site user-friendly and attractive. It's a meeting of form and function.

Many web designers spend two years in school learning design techniques, various markup languages, Adobe Flash, WYSIWYG web design programs, and designing websites. The beauty of Google Sites is that it enables you to include the same design elements without having to learn markup languages or complicated programs.

Google gives you 10GB of combined storage space for every website under your username. If you're using a paid corporate or education account, you will receive an additional 500MB of storage for each Premier or Education user account on top of the 10GB initial storage space.

Using Keyboard Shortcuts

Most people use the mouse to navigate websites and applications. However, it's usually much faster, and easier on the hands, to use keyboard shortcuts. To this end, Google has a fairly extensive list of available keyboard shortcuts for Google Sites. You can't do everything via keyboard, but most functions are keyboard accessible.

Three tables have been created for you: Table 28-1 shows a list of the most popular page-level keyboard shortcuts; Table 28-2 shows a list of the most popular site-level keyboard shortcuts; and Table 28-3 shows a couple of application-level keyboard shortcuts.

TABLE 28-1: Keyboard Shortcut Commands—Page Level

FUNCTION	KEYBOARD SHORTCUT
Cancel	Esc
Edit Page	E
Save Page	Ctrl + S (for Mac use Command key Ð)
Toggle Page Subscription	F
Revision History	G and then R
Move Page	M
Preview Page as Viewer	G then P

FUNCTION	KEYBOARD SHORTCUT
Page Settings	U
Change Page Template	Shift + T
Print Page	Ctrl + P (for Mac use Command key)
Delete Page	Shift +3

TABLE 28-2: Keyboard Shortcut Commands—Site Level

FUNCTION	KEYBOARD SHORTCUT
Create Page	C
Manage Site	G then M
Toggle Site Subscription	Shift + F
Share Site	Shift + S

TABLE 28-3: Keyboard Shortcut Commands—Application Level

FUNCTION	KEYBOARD SHORTCUT
Open Shortcut Help	Ctrl + / (for Mac use Command key)
Search	/

Using the Given Templates

If you've spent any time at all using Google Sites (sites.google.com), you've probably found the built-in templates by now. You should know you can change the site layout, colors, and font of any basic theme from the Site Appearance menu. From the main page of your site select More Actions → Manage Site. On the left, under Site Appearance, there is a link for Themes. Click there to see a page of more than sixty base themes.

As shown in Figure 28-1, Google gives you a choice between building your own theme or browsing more themes. The additional themes, under the Browse More Themes link, are user created. To build your own custom theme, click the Build Your Own Custom Theme link at the top right. To choose from more elaborate, purpose-driven templates click Browse More Themes on the top left.

▶ You can reach these themes directly by going to https://sites .google.com/ sitetemplateinfo/ home.

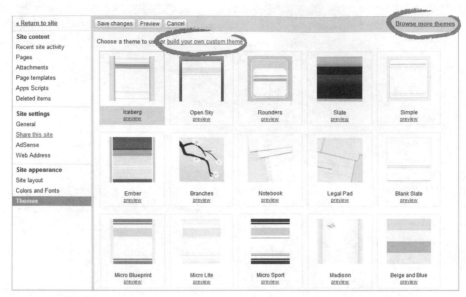

FIGURE 28-1: Choose to build a custom theme, or browse some of the purpose-driven templates provided.

Now that you've chosen your basic theme, it's time to customize it. You have several ways to do this. Your first option is to use the color changing tools under the Build Your Own Custom Theme link. The color changing tools give you the ability to change the background color and font of every component of your chosen theme, as shown in Figure 28-2. This is the tool you use if you want to upload your own photo as a site or header background image. You can also change your basic theme by selecting from the Base Theme drop-down menu at the top of the page.

> **NOTE**   You can reach the same page by selecting Colors and Fonts under Site Appearance in the left navigation menu.

To change the column layout of your chosen basic theme, select Site Layout from the Site Appearance menu in the left navigation bar.

However, if you've chosen your website from one of the featured purpose-driven templates found under the More Themes link or from the Template Tips page (https://sites.google.com/site/sitetemplateinfo/home) then you have the ability to use Adobe Photoshop to edit the template photos. Figure 28-3 shows an example of the templates available for editing in Photoshop.

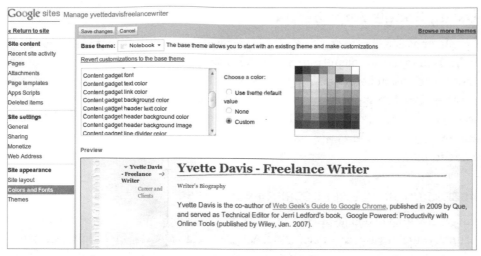

FIGURE 28-2: Change any aspect of your chosen theme with just a few clicks.

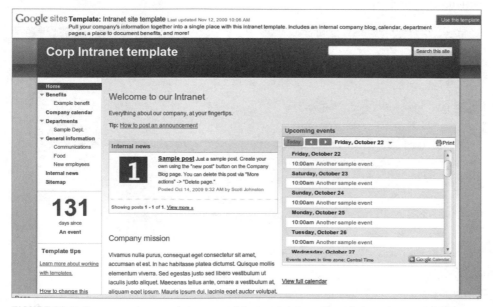

FIGURE 28-3: Corporate Intranet is just one of the many interesting site templates available.

To edit a template photo, select the Template Assets option from the left navigation bar. Here you find the .png and .psd files of the images that are available for editing. Simply select the image you want to edit and click Download.

After you've edited and saved the image, you need to upload it to Google Sites. I talk about how to do that in a minute.

> ▶ .png is an image file format that can be read by most image-editing programs. The .psd file format is proprietary to Adobe Photoshop.

Using Google Apps Script

Google Apps Script is a scripting language based on JavaScript that is intended to be used for cloud computing. Google Apps Script enables all your Google apps to talk to each other behind the scenes, essentially giving you the ability to tie them together into one application. You can also use Google Apps Script to link to other web services. A full tutorial of Google Apps Script is beyond the scope of this book. However, here are a few ways you can use Google Apps Script with your Google Sites account.

ACCESSING GOOGLE APPS SCRIPT FROM SITES

Like everything in Google Sites, finding scripts for Google Apps Script is simple. Launch your Sites account. Select More Actions → Manage Site. In the left navigation bar select **Apps Scripts** to open a list of scripts you've entered. To write a script, select Launch Editor. A window opens that looks like Figure 28-4. This is the window in which you type scripts.

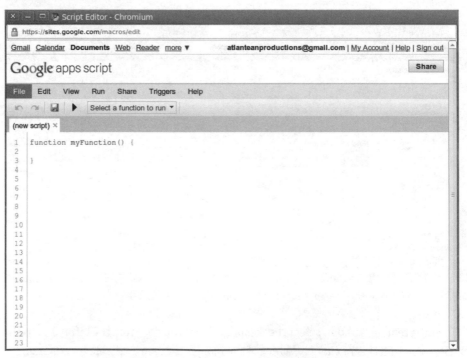

FIGURE 28-4: Use this box to enter Apps Script code.

ADDING A SCRIPT TO YOUR SITE

Say you want visitors to your website to e-mail you with specific information but you don't want to set up a separate e-mail for this purpose. You can use scripts for Google Apps Script to create an automatic e-mail program that is executable by your visitors. Here's how:

```
function sendEmail() {
MailApp.sendEmail('youremail@gmail.com', 'Email Subject Goes Here',
'Enter text you want in the email here');
}
```

Save the code. Use the Play button in the toolbar to test the script.

Now that you've written your script code, you need to activate it so site visitors can use it. Navigate to the page on which you want the script to be active. Click Edit Page. Highlight the text that should link to your script. From the navigation menu select Insert → Link. In the left navigation bar, select **Apps Script**. Highlight the script you want to run when the text you selected is clicked. Click OK.

▶ The Play button is the little triangular icon in the toolbar.

ADDING A SCRIPT FROM THE SCRIPT LIBRARY

Playing Sudoku on your website isn't a very productive thing to do, but this example gives you an idea of what you can do with scripts for Google Apps Script.

Start by opening your Google Docs account and open a new spreadsheet. From the menu, select Tools → Scripts → Insert to see the Script Gallery as shown in Figure 28-5.

All of the App Scripts shown in the Script Gallery have been written specifically for Google Docs files. If you want to use these scripts in Google Sites you need to either tweak the script for Apps, or use it in the appropriate Docs file and embed that file in your site. For the purpose of this example, you're going to embed the spreadsheet.

Using the left navigation of the Script Gallery, select Fun and Games. Scroll down until you find Sudoku. Click Install. A red warning box pops up asking you to authorize this script to run.

When the script has installed, refresh your page. You should now see Sudoku as the last option in the navigation bar. Run the game by selecting Sudoku and then Generate Puzzle. Your Sudoku game should look similar to Figure 28-6. Now that you have the script installed in your document, you need to embed the document in your site, which is discussed in the next section. You can then click Close on the scripts dialog box.

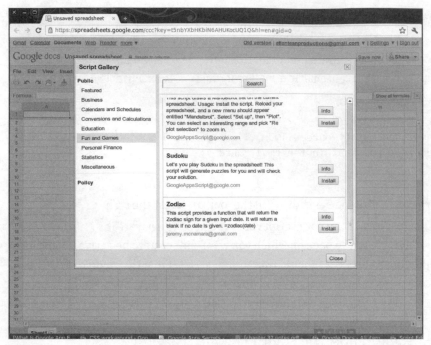

FIGURE 28-5: All the scripts for Google App Script in the Gallery are intended for use in Google Docs.

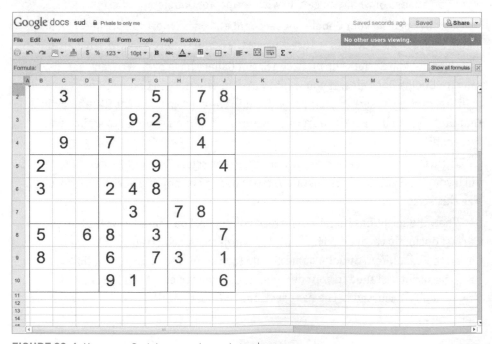

FIGURE 28-6: Your new Sudoku game is ready to play.

MAKING TWEAKS TO WEBSITES

Gone are the days of pure text web pages. To build a site that gets noticed you absolutely must include rich media. Images, video, sound, slideshows, and the like work together with text to deliver your message quickly and efficiently. Remember you're writing for an audience that has a short attention span—sometimes a picture really is worth a thousand words.

It's easy to embed maps hosted on Google Maps, video from Google Video or YouTube, Picasa slideshows, Google Docs documents, or any other media hosted on a Google-owned website. Gadgets are embedded the same way, as well.

When you have obtained media to include on your site, open your Google Sites account and navigate to the page to which you're adding the media. Place the cursor in the location you'd like place the media. Click Edit Page. In the upper navigation bar, select Insert. As you see in Figure 28-7 a menu appears that lists all possible sources of media through your Google accounts. Choose the media you are embedding and Google Sites automatically shows you what is available in your corresponding Google account for that media. For example, if you choose Photos your Picasa photos are available. Highlight the image, map, video, or other file and click Select.

If the file you want to embed is stored on your computer, start at the main Sites page and select More Actions → Manage Site. Now, select Attachments from the navigation menu. Finally, click Upload in the top navigation bar. Choose the file from your computer and upload.

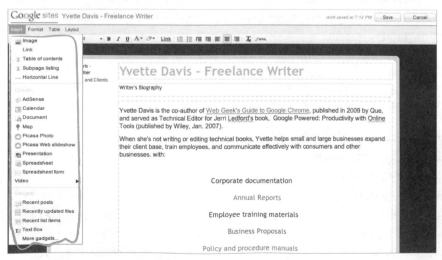

FIGURE 28-7: Embed YouTube, Google Video, Docs, Spreadsheet, or any Google-hosted media with a click.

To embed Flash movies into your Google Sites website, first upload your SWF file to your Google Sites as an attachment.

Navigate to the page where you are embedding your Flash movie. Click HTML on the toolbar. Insert the following HTML:

```
<embed src="http://sites.google.com/site/nameofyoursite/nameofyourmovie
.swf" width="moviewidth" height="movieheight" pluginspage="http://www
.macromedia.com/go/getflashplayer"></embed>
```

An image map is a picture that contains clickable sections that work as links. Google Sites supports image maps through the HTML editor. First tell the browser that the image is intended to be an image map with the following HTML:

```
<img title="name of image"
alt="alternative text"
src="image URL" style="width: xxx;
height:xxx" usemap=#mapid"
```

Now, define the image map and define the clickable areas of the image.

```
<map name="mapid">
<area title="title of area" href="target URL"
shape="rect/circle/poly"
coords="enter coordinates here"
alt="alternate text for area">
</map>
```

Image maps are an easy way to combine beauty with function, and give your website a professionally designed look. And, now you know how easy they are to include in your Google Sites website.

PUBLISHING YOUR SITE

When you're ready to publish your website you have several options, as you see in Figure 28-8. It's easy to make your site available to anyone with Internet access or to invite only a few people to see it.

If you want to share your new site with the whole Internet, simply check the Anyone in the World May View This Site box. To share only with specific people type their e-mail addresses into the textbox and use the radio buttons to declare them as owners, viewers, or collaborators. You can also choose e-mail addresses from your Gmail contacts by clicking the Choose from Contacts link. After you've entered the e-mail addresses of your invitees, click the Invite These People button.

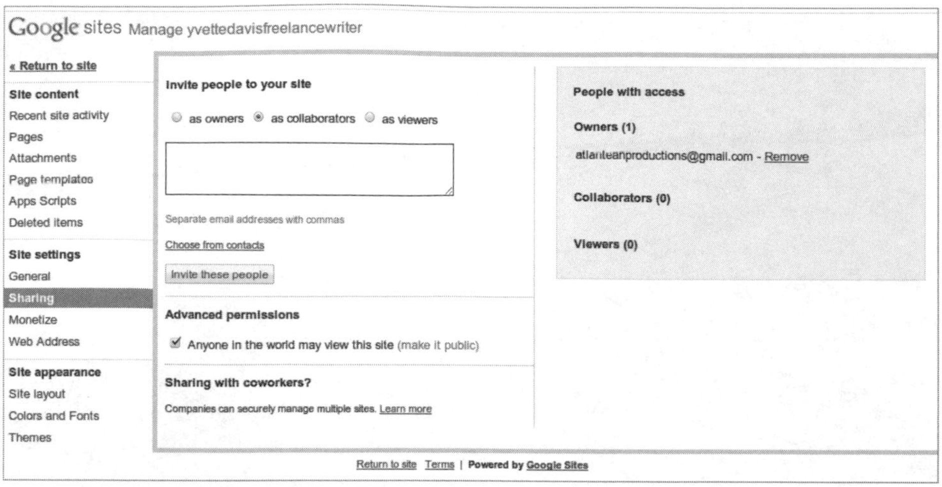

FIGURE 28-8: Share your website with collaborators, co-workers, or the whole world.

NOTE Don't forget that you can give only one type of permission at a time. If you want to add your boss as an owner, your coworkers as collaborators, and your clients as viewers, you need to go through the adding process three times, once for each group.

SUMMARY

Creating a website online isn't too difficult or time-consuming. As long as you have the right tools (such as Google Sites), you can build your business' online presence without needing a large budget, a large agency, or a design studio to build a website for you.

CHAPTER 29

Improving Your Website with Google's Apps

IN THIS CHAPTER

▶ Installing Google Search and customizing it for your website

▶ Google AdSense and Google Search

▶ Strategies on how to appear within Google's search results

Whether you use Google Sites, a different free website service, or pay for hosting and create your own website from scratch, Google offers tools to customize your website and get the word out. Add function to your website with Google search tools or Google Gadgets. When your site is optimized and ready to represent you to the world, submit it to the Google search engine and watch your ranking climb!

ADDING GOOGLE SEARCH TO YOUR SITE

You can add Google search to your website in multiple ways. Which service you use depends on what kind of website you have, the purpose of that website, and your budget. Most Google search capabilities are free, but a couple of options require a paid subscription.

The best way to add search to your website is to use Custom Search. This beta service lets you put a search bar on your website, customize it to match your site design, and gives you the power to customize which websites are searched. Oh, it also makes money for you with AdSense for search.

> **WARNING**   Before you go any further, take a moment to decide if you want to use AdSense with your Custom Search Engine. If you only want to create a Custom Search Engine, continue reading this section. If you want to combine AdSense with your Custom Search Engine go to the next section in this chapter, titled "Using AdSense with Google Search." It is possible to add the two elements separately. However, it is much simpler to set up the combined service as described in the next section.

▶ The links for FAQ, discussion groups, and developer documentation are at the bottom of the page.

To find Custom Search navigate your web browser to www.google.com/cse. As with any new program or application, take the time to read the FAQ and discussion group posts to get a feel for any recurring concerns.

To start using Custom Search, click the big blue button labeled Create a Custom Search Engine. Use the form shown in Figure 29-1 to customize the search engine.

Give your search engine a good descriptive name. This makes it much easier to locate it among other search engines you may create later. Use the Description box to enter a few words about the search engine's purpose and focus. Users won't see this information but it helps you focus your thoughts and further define the purpose of the search engine.

Use the Language drop-down to select the language your search engine should use.

The Sites to Search box is the most important element of this form. This is where you configure the engine to search only the websites or pages you specify. List only one URL per line, and format them as indicated in the box titled Formatting URLs for Search.

Finally, choose between the Standard and Site Search versions of Custom Search. If you choose the Standard Edition, Google places ads on the results page of every search performed. These ads are similar to the ads placed on many websites by Google.

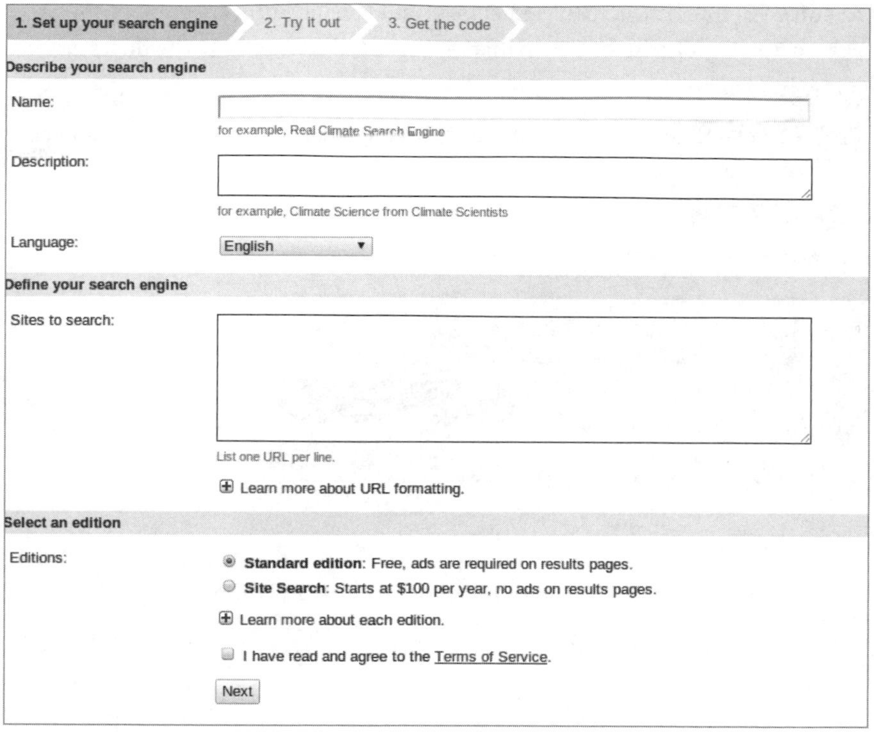

FIGURE 29-1: Define your Custom Search Engine.

If you choose Site Search, you are charged $100 per year for the service. For that money you receive the search engine without ads on the results page, technical support, and greater customization by means of XML and API.

When you have made your selection, click the Terms of Service link to read the TOS, and select the checkbox indicating you have done so. Click Next.

On the next screen, choose an ad style. Hover the mouse over any format to see a description of that style, as shown in Figure 29-2.

Click the Customize button associated with any of the six ad styles to customize. The customization options are shown in Figure 29-3 and described in the following list.

- ▶ **Global Styles**—Change the font, border, and background color of the whole search bar. Most search bars and ads look better and get more traffic with a color and font that matches, or is very close to, the surrounding area of the website, and with no border.

- ▶ **Search Controls**—Set the color of the search input and button.

▶ **Results**—Define link colors, text colors, and the background color of the search results. Choose between displaying a full URL or only the domain name in results.

▶ **Promotions**—Change the color of links, text, and background of ads displayed.

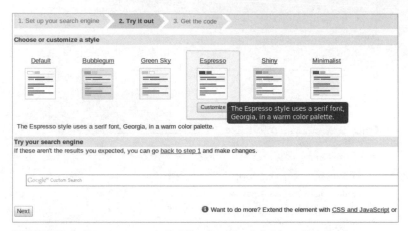

FIGURE 29-2: Hover over any ad style to see the definition of that style.

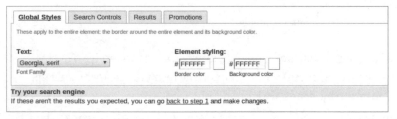

FIGURE 29-3: Use the tabs to change the appearance of the search engine.

When you're finished, click Next.

Copy the given code to your computer's clipboard, and paste it in the HTML of the area of your website where you want the search bar to appear. Figure 29-4 shows a search engine added to a blog.

FIGURE 29-4: Google custom search engine applied to a blog.

> **NOTE** Add a web page or entire website to your Google Custom Search Engine on the fly with Google Marker, found here: **www.google.com/cse/tools/marker**. Drag the bookmark to your browser toolbar, or, if you use IE, right-click the bookmark and add it to your browser favorites. When you find a website you'd like to include in your Custom Search Engine, simply click Google Marker. Use the drop-down to indicate to which Custom Search Engine this change applies and indicate if you are including just the page you are on or the entire website, add a label, if desired, and click Save.

If you're running an online retail sales website you can give customers the ability to search by item, cost, brand, or other feature with Google Commerce Search. This is a paid service from Google. You can find Google Commerce Search here: **www.google.com/commercesearch/**.

FORMATTING URLS FOR SEARCH

www.sitename.com/* to search every page on the designated website.

www.sitename.com/designatepage.html to search only the page you specify on the website.

*.domainname.com to search an entire domain.

www.sitename.com/*word* to search only those page or section titles that contain the word you specify.

You can also add search functions to your website with Google Gadgets. As discussed in Chapter 2, Google Gadgets are small apps that enable you to add specific and limited functions to a web page. Use gadgets to bring relevant search gadgets to your website. Some available search gadgets are:

- ▶ **ebay.com Search**—Search eBay from your website.

- ▶ **ubuntu Search**—Search the Ubuntu community.

- ▶ **Sparknotes Search**—Search for study guides on Sparknotes.

- ▶ **Google Map Search**—Search for and display location or directions with Google Maps.

- ▶ **Google Custom Search Console**—Access all your Custom Search Engines from one place.

▶ **Cnn.com**—Search CNN from your website.

▶ **Google Image Search**—Search for images.

▶ **Google Directory Search**—Search Google Directories for a keyword.

USING ADSENSE WITH GOOGLE SEARCH

If you've decided to use AdSense in conjunction with your Custom Search Engine you need to configure AdSense for your website. From the Google Custom Search homepage click the link that reads AdSense for Search, or navigate your browser directly to www.google.com/adsense.

If you've never used AdSense before, sign up for an account. Enter the URL of the website to which you are applying AdSense. Use the drop-down menu to indicate the primary language used in your website and fill out all contact information.

If you already have an AdSense account, you may need to review and accept the new AdSense TOS. When you've done so, you are taken to your AdSense account.

Currently you have a choice between the old AdSense interface and the new beta interface. If you're using the old interface, select the AdSense Setup tab from the top navigation. Click the link for AdSense for Search, shown in Figure 29-5. On the following page, click Get Started at the bottom of the page.

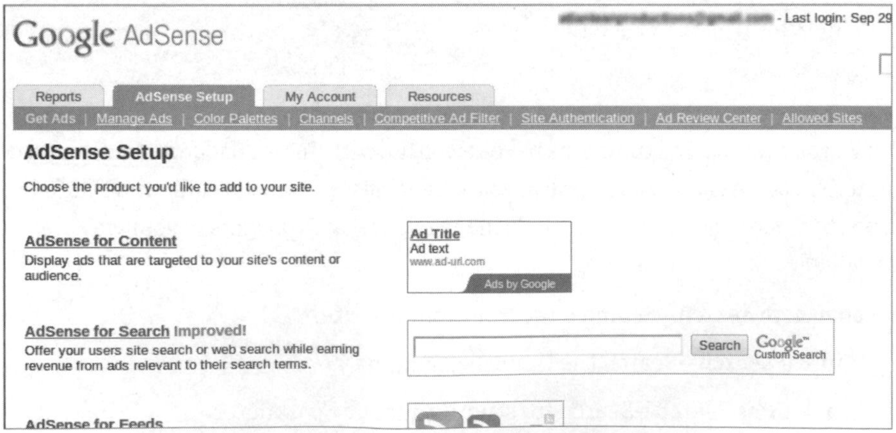

FIGURE 29-5: AdSense for Search setup link in the old interface.

If you're using the new interface click the My Ads tab in the top navigation. Now, click Search in the left navigation to open the menu and then click the button labeled New Custom Search Engine, as shown in Figure 29-6.

At the top of the next screen, under the AdSense for Search heading, choose between single-page entry format and a wizard format, shown in Figure 29-7. It really does not matter which you choose. It's faster and requires fewer clicks to use the single-page format.

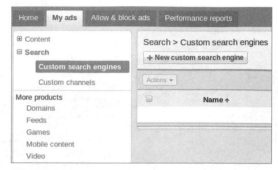

FIGURE 29-6: Find Custom Search in the new interface.

FIGURE 29-7: Define your search engine using a single page or the wizard.

First, define your search engine. Determine whether you want users to search just your website, a selection of websites, or the entire Internet.

Specify websites, web pages, parts of pages, or whole domains to be searched. Use the URL formatting as shown in the box titled Formatting URLs for Search.

Enter keywords that describe your website. This helps focus the search engine, and fine tune the displayed ads so they are relevant to your website.

Now, complete the section titled More Options. Use the drop-down to define the primary language of your website, and select the page encoding used on your site, if different than the default. Select the country to which your website is primarily targeted. If you are a new AdSense user, use the default setting for Custom Channel. Decide if you want your Custom Search Engine to use Safe Search. For most websites, it's recommended to leave Safe Search turned on.

The third section is where you set the font, color, and size of your search box. It's best to try to match the background of the search box to your website as much as possible. Pay close attention to the sample at the top of this section. It accurately reflects how the search bar appears on your website.

In the next section, determine how search results should be displayed. The best method is to have results displayed within your own website. This helps keep users on your site when they have completed their search.

Specify the location of ads in relation to the search results.

Set the ad colors. This is important. People click your ads more readily if the ads stand out from your website background in an attractive manner. Don't be afraid to experiment or edit the given colors. Change the color of any ad element by clicking the color swatch to the right of the element's line, as shown in Figure 29-8.

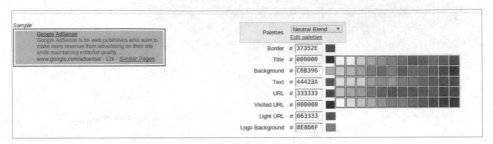

FIGURE 29-8: Change the color of any element with the color-picker.

Finally, read and agree to the additional terms, name your search engine, and click Submit and Get Code.

Copy the code to your computer's clipboard and paste it into the HTML in the section you want the search and ads to appear.

GETTING YOUR SITE LISTED IN GOOGLE'S RESULTS

When your website is complete, it's time to get listed with Google. Sure, you can sit back and wait for the Google spiders to find it on their own, but you get better results faster if you follow Google's recommendations for submitting your site. Site submission helps get your content on Google Search, Map, iGoogle, and Product Search.

Submit your URL to the Google Index. Point your browser to www.google.com/addurl/?continue=/addurl and enter the URL of your homepage in the box provided. In the Comments section enter a short description of your site or simply type the keywords associated with your website. (The comments you enter are not that relevant for Google to index your site; all you really need here is the full URL and you're good.) Enter the security word in the box provided and click Add URL. The security word can be difficult to read, because the letters display as a flowing script. If the confirmation screen does not appear, you did not enter the security word correctly. Reenter your URL and comments and then enter the new security word. When you're finished you see the screen shown in Figure 29-9.

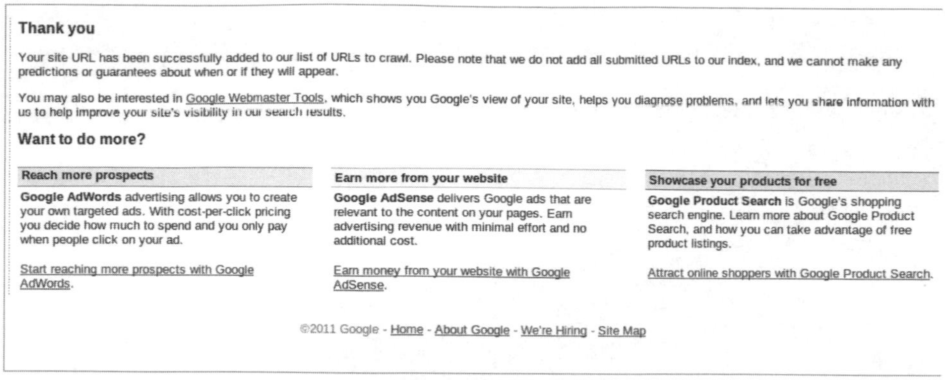

FIGURE 29-9: Confirmation that your URL was accepted for consideration.

IMPROVING YOUR PLACEMENT RESULTS

There's no magic way to earn a good Google Search ranking. The best ways are to provide users with relevant content that is frequently updated and to use keywords in your website content. Keywords should fall naturally in your text, and your topics should be timely. Use Google Analytics, which we'll introduce later in this book, to track the effectiveness of your keywords. AdWords, also to be introduced later, helps you target ad campaigns to specific keywords and geographical locations. Also, use the RSS techniques discussed in relation to blogs in Chapter 13 to create an RSS feed to let users know when your website has been updated. Ask related websites to link to your site, and include multimedia elements when possible.

An excellent resource for improving your website comes from the Google Webmaster Tools help section. These are as close to "official guidelines" as you can find online, so definitely avail yourself of this resource:

```
http://goo.gl/tz2RN
```

SUMMARY

Adding Custom Search to your website provides users with a quick and simple way to find what they need, either within your website or outside of it. When you combine Custom Search with AdSense it creates a winning situation for both you and your users. With some time and attention to content, your website will climb in the Google rankings.

Implementing Google Analytics

For those of you who want to know many fruitful and insightful details about the visitors to your website, Google has an amazing (and free) tool called Google Analytics. With this easy-to-use program, you not only learn how many visits your website receives each day, each week, or each year, you also learn what pages people land on, what goals visitors accomplish, what was purchased from your online store, and much more!

The next few chapters go into the details of what's involved with opening a Google Analytics account and ensuring that your website is configured to track visitor behavior. In this particular chapter, you learn how to customize your Dashboard (you learn what that means shortly), how to perform common tasks, such as editing the date-range tool and using advanced segments, and you see how to create goals, goal funnels, and filters.

> **NOTE** Before visitor data can appear in your Google Analytics account, you must install a small snippet of JavaScript tracking code on all the pages of your website that you wish to track. This tracking code is the mechanism that sets a group of first-party cookies on your visitors' computers, which are required in order for Google to collect and process visitor data. The tracking codes are available within your Google Analytics account, and you can find a few examples in Chapter 31's "Installing the Tracking Code" section.

CUSTOMIZING ANALYTICS DASHBOARDS AND REPORTS

As soon as your Google Analytics account is created (which you can do at www .google.com/analytics) and after you've installed the necessary JavaScript tracking code on all of your website's pages, visitor data begins to appear on your Dashboard and throughout your account.

The Dashboard is the first screen you see when you click your profile's View Reports link, immediately after logging in to your Google Analytics account with your Google account login credentials. The Dashboard is a broad, "30,000-foot" view of your website's visitor statistics, and as you will read in the next few pages, a view that can be customized to fit your specific needs.

An annotation is a 160-character note that you can insert so that you can incorporate offline information (such as a launch date of a traditional print advertising piece) into the Google Analytics platform.

Figure 30-1 shows a Google Analytics Dashboard screen. Although the Dashboard is purposely designed to not be granular, you can do many different things on the Dashboard screen, including modifying the date-range slider (which is set by default to show you the last 30 days of activity), applying an advanced segment, e-mailing and exporting the screen, adding an annotation, and managing the moveable modules.

▶ An advanced segment enables you to view a subset of the analytics data. For example, the "Paid Traffic" advanced segment enables you to view data from a paid traffic initiative, such as Google AdWords. See the "Segmenting Data" section for more information.

Creating Custom Dashboards

You can create a custom Dashboard in Google Analytics using any combination of three different methods: adding a report to your Dashboard, moving Dashboard reports, and deleting reports from your Dashboard. You should know that Dashboard customizations are login-dependent, meaning that your Dashboard is viewable only to you under your login. Another user with access to your Google Analytics account and profile sees the default Dashboard design shown in Figure 30-1.

FIGURE 30-1: The Google Analytics Dashboard.

Google Analytics features more than 100 different reports, all of which can be added to your profile's Dashboard. The neat thing about adding reports to your Dashboard is that your report settings are also saved. Every report in Google Analytics has a default view (the standard report table), a default number of rows that are displayed (10 rows), and a default sort (the first metric of the report—quite often this is the visits metric). If you change any of the default report views before adding the report to your Dashboard and click the Add to Dashboard button (located at the top of every report screen), your changes are also saved. In a way, adding reports to your Dashboard is like saving your work—you don't have to re-create the report to your liking each time when you click the Add to Dashboard button. Figure 30-2 shows where the Add to Dashboard button is located within every report in Google Analytics, using the New vs. Returning report as the example. Add to Dashboard is the third button from the left on the top-left of the screen, immediately to the right of the Email button.

FIGURE 30-2: Location of the Add to Dashboard button.

When you add a report to your Dashboard, a new module is added below your default Dashboard modules and below any other added modules that you may have previously added. You won't see a lot of data in these added modules—only the first five rows and three columns, but you have enough data to be able to recognize that it's your custom module. Each module on the Dashboard is equipped with a View Report link, which you can find on the bottom of each module. Remember that you can add to your Dashboard any report you find within the Google Analytics Dashboard. This includes any custom reports that you create (custom reports are available from the left navigation menu, and they enable Google Analytics users to create their own reports with their own metrics and dimensions).

Speaking of custom reports, there is an additional piece of information that you should know about adding reports to your Dashboard and how what you add affects what you see in the form of Dashboard modules. The heading of the module itself cannot be edited within the Dashboard. If you add the All Traffic Sources report to your Dashboard, for example, the heading reads, exactly, *All Traffic Sources*. Depending on how significantly you modify your report before adding it to your Dashboard, that module heading may look bizarre (something like "Campaign 01" may appear, for example). However, if you add a custom report to your Dashboard, the title of your custom report is the module heading. Figure 30-3 shows the bottom of my Dashboard screen, where you can see that I've added two modules: on the bottom left of Figure 30-3, you can see the All Traffic Sources report, which is filtered by organic traffic and segmented by Connection Speed. On the bottom right of Figure 30-3, you see the exact same report, but with a different module heading (Yvette's Favorite Report). The different module heading comes from the title of the custom report that I created, where I re-created the All Traffic Sources report.

For most people, it's probably too much trouble to go through creating a custom report just to have a custom module heading title, but you can do it.

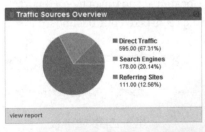

FIGURE 30-3: Two new modules on my Dashboard screen.

There isn't a set limit to the number of reports that you can add to your Dashboard—you can add as many reports as you'd like. Keep in mind that if you ever decide to export or e-mail your Dashboard screen, the recipient of your e-mailed report not only sees your Dashboard modules, but the full reports that were saved to the Dashboard also appear.

You can move Dashboard modules and organize them at your convenience very simply. All you have to do is drag-and-drop the modules by the dark-gray module header from their default positions to whatever positions you see fit. The only module that you can't move is the wider Site Usage module—that one remains in its position directly below the trending graph area.

Lastly, you can easily remove unwanted or accidental Dashboard additions by clicking the black X symbol on the top right of any Dashboard module. You are prompted with a warning message before the module is actually deleted; you have to click Yes to actually delete the module.

Segmenting Data

One of the most powerful features in Google Analytics is the Advanced Segments drop-down menu, located at the top right of the Dashboard and in that same location throughout your account's profile. Segments are slices of data—specific, drilled-down views that enable you to obtain insights from a very specific group of data.

By default, Google Analytics shows you data on all visits to your website. Every piece of data that Google Analytics collects from every visitor is automatically shown throughout the interface. However, if you want to see only your New Visitors or your Mobile Traffic or if you want to create your own view, you need to click the drop-down menu labeled All Visits.

When you click All Visits, the menu shown in Figure 30-4 appears. You see All Visits checked, as it should be. You can, for example, uncheck All Visits and check New Visitors to see data on only your new website visitors whom have never visited your site before.

One of the nicer features of advanced segments with Google Analytics is that you can apply up to four advanced segments at any one time. In Figure 30-5, I have applied the All Visits, the New Visitors, the Non-paid Search Traffic, and the Mobile Traffic segments simultaneously. This changes the way my Dashboard presents my data to me and changes the way other reports display data to others as well.

You can remove or "un-apply" advanced segments at any time by returning to the drop-down menu on the top right of the screen and unchecking the default advanced segments. This returns your Dashboard—and any other report that you're viewing—back to show you data on All Visits.

FIGURE 30-4: The Advanced Segments drop-down menu.

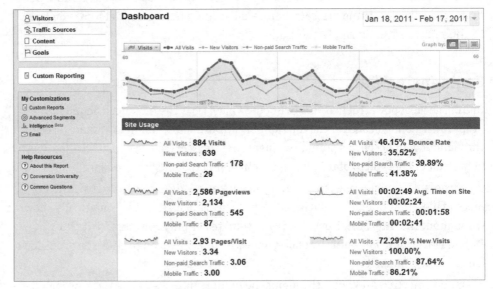

FIGURE 30-5: Applying four advanced segments simultaneously.

Creating a custom advanced segment is similar to the process of creating a custom report, which I discussed briefly earlier in this chapter. You choose the metrics or the dimensions (the rules) that your advanced segment follows, and you can save it for future use. The custom advanced segments you create appear in the corresponding column within the Advanced Segments menu.

Manipulating Date Ranges

Another nice and useful feature available on your Dashboard and every other report within Google Analytics is the date-range slider. As mentioned earlier, by default, Google Analytics shows you the last 30 days of activity on your website, excluding the present day. By clicking the date-range slider, which is below the Advanced Segments drop-down menu, you are able to select your own date range. The menu you see in Figure 30-6 appears when you try to modify the date range.

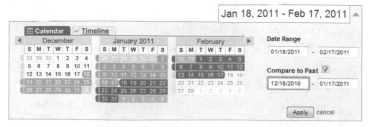

FIGURE 30-6: The date-range slider.

Notice in Figure 30-6 that the Compare to Past checkbox has been clicked, and a second date range is selected. Comparing your data to a previous time period is essential to understanding how your website performance is progressing, and an integral component of the Google Analytics system. When you apply the Comparison to Past function, all your Dashboard data is compared to the previous time period, as you can see in Figure 30-7.

Like advanced segments, date-range modifications and date-range comparisons appear throughout all of the other reports in Google Analytics, and you can disable them at any time.

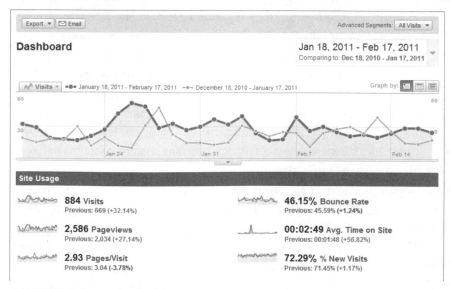

FIGURE 30-7: Comparing Dashboard data to a previous time period.

CREATING GOALS AND FILTERS

Receiving valuable data on the activity of your website is great on its own, but your Google Analytics account profiles can be greatly augmented by the creation of goals and filters.

Goals are desired outcomes that you want visitors to act upon while they are on your website. Contact forms, "RFQ" or Request for Quote forms, online applications, purchases from your online shopping cart, and even views of key pages are excellent examples of things that you want visitors to do. The pages that a visitor ultimately reaches after successfully performing these tasks are the pages that you should set up as a goal in your Google Analytics profile. Each profile in Google Analytics can hold up to 20 goals, and each goal can have a corresponding goal funnel (a path from a starting point to the final goal page). You can also define goals as a certain number of page views per visit, or as a time spent on your website per visit.

Filters are the rules that your profile has to abide by when Google Analytics servers process data to display to you. As you know from advanced segments, Google Analytics defaults to show you data for all visits to your website. A filter can enable you to exclude data, only include data, or modify the way that the data looks. Filters in Google Analytics need to be written in a language known as Regular Expressions, or RegEx for short. Therefore, you need to know how to write in Regular Expression format to properly create filters for your profile (Google Analytics offers help links on the subject as you create a filter). You cannot retroactively apply filters to a profile—they cannot change any historical data. You can apply them only to any future data. Normally, filters only start working about a full day after they're created, so don't worry if the filter you apply today doesn't change today's data.

To create a goal or to create a filter, you must have Administrative access to your Google Analytics account—chances are that you already have this access. If for some reason you do not, you need to contact the administrator (the person who gave you access to Google Analytics) and ask for Administrative access. If the person is knowledgeable with Google Analytics, you may wish to enlist his or her services and expertise before continuing.

To create your first goal, click your profile's Edit link from your account Overview screen (the screen you first see after logging in to Google Analytics, before your Dashboard screen). After clicking Edit, you see a table labeled Goals; this should be the second table from the top, under the first table labeled Main Website Profile Information. From here, click Add Goal, where you are able to enter in this first goal's information.

On the following screen, enter a name for your goal that appears throughout your Google Analytics profile. Ensure that the On radio button is selected for Active Goal and that the Goal Position drop-down menu is set to Set 1, Goal 1 (you can change this if desired, but leave it alone if it's your first goal in the profile). Next, you need to select a Goal Type. If you want to set a page as a goal, choose the URL Destination option. If you want to use either a Time on Site or a Pages/Visit as a goal, choose the appropriate radio button to do so. The example I've used is for a URL Destination goal—the other two goals are extremely easy to configure and are too self-explanatory for this book.

When you select a URL Destination goal, a new set of options appears. You need to define your goal's Match Type and set your Goal URL. A goal on Head Match matches any unique page view of a page containing your Goal URL; a goal on Exact Match only matches unique page views for the URL that you insert into the field. Regular Expression Match allows you to write in Regular Expression format, enabling you to do more complex functions, such as matching multiple pages in one goal at the same time, or matching anything starting with or ending with a specific string of characters.

Next, choose whether your goal URL should be Case Sensitive (almost always, this checkbox should not be clicked), and set a Goal Value for your goal, which Google Analytics uses to augment your goal conversion data in reports. Finally, you have the opportunity to create a Goal Funnel for your goal, where you can define up to 10 pages that lead up to your goal URL. Please note that the Required Step checkbox that you see appear next to step 1 of your goal affects only the Funnel Visualization report in Google Analytics, which is contrary to the popular belief that Required Step affects the count of goals matched (it doesn't).

When you are finished creating your goal, don't forget to hit Save, which is at the very bottom of the screen.

Figure 30-8 shows the goal creation screen with some values filled in, to give you a visual representation of the past few paragraphs.

To create a filter for your profile, you also need to click your profile's Edit link, just like you did when you started the process of creating a goal for your profile. Scroll down below the table labeled Goals and find a table labeled Filters Applied to Profile. Click the white-colored Add Filter link to begin.

You can go about creating a filter for your Google Analytics profile in many, many different ways—there have been entire manuals and online books written that are dedicated entirely to filters and Regular Expressions. To wrap up this first chapter on Google Analytics, you learn how to write a filter to block or remove your own traffic from appearing in reports. Blocking one's traffic is quite possibly the most popular type of filter that Google Analytics administrators make.

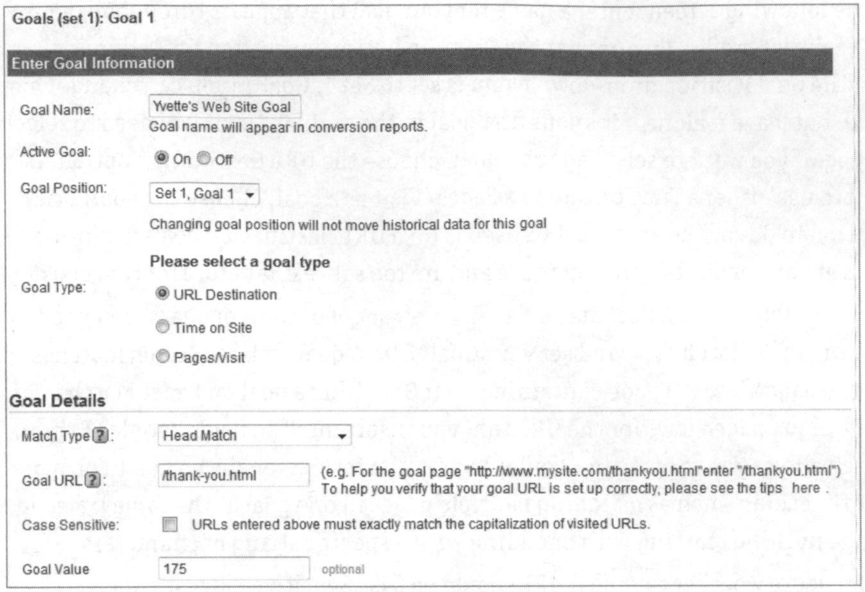

FIGURE 30-8: Creating a goal in Google Analytics.

After you click Add Filter, enter a name for your filter and choose your filter type. This example uses a Custom filter, so, select that option if you are following along in your own Google Analytics account. After you do, you see a list of Filter Types to choose from (you should see Exclude, Include, Lowercase, Uppercase, Search and Replace, and Advanced options). Leave the Exclude option enabled, and select Visitor IP Address within the Filter Field drop-down menu. Next, in the Filter Pattern box, you need to place your IP address in Regular Expression format. Let's say that your IP address is 192.168.1.5—the filter pattern needs to look like this:

```
^192\.168\.1\.5$
```

The ^, $, and \ symbols in and around the IP address are Regular Expression characters that ensure your filter is processed appropriately. The \ symbol is the most important one, because it tells Google Analytics that the periods in the IP address are not Regular Expression characters themselves; they are a part of the filter pattern and not to be processed as Regular Expression characters. The ^ and $ symbols ensure that the Google Analytics servers are looking specifically for that IP address, and when they find it, they process the filter type (exclude) before allowing the data to be served in your profile.

Figure 30-9 shows the filter creation screen for your visual reference.

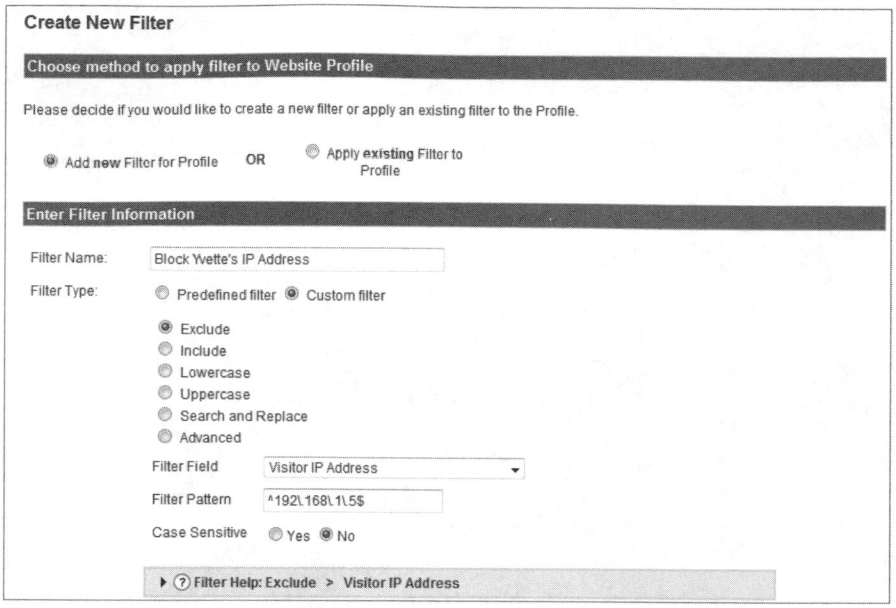

FIGURE 30-9: Excluding an IP address with a filter in Regular Expression format.

Keep in mind that multiple filters applied to one profile in Google Analytics are processed in sequential order. If you have two Exclude filters, the filter in the first position is processed first, and with the remaining data, the second filter is processed. This is critical piece of information to keep in mind when you need to use an Include filter, because Include filters essentially exclude everything *except* your filter pattern. After you create your second filter and return to the profile settings screen, you see a link to Assign Filter Order, which lets you organize the sequence of filters to be processed in your Google Analytics profile.

SUMMARY

Google Analytics is a powerful, robust web analytics package that enables website owners and marketers to learn about their website's visitors and important actions that they're taking. Dashboards, Goals, and Filters are customizable options within the Google Analytics platform that enable you to understand, refine, and glean insights from your website's data so that your website, your marketing efforts, and your business model are the best that they can be.

Using Google Analytics for eCommerce

Online merchants need to be able to evaluate how their online store fronts are performing, and most merchants who don't use a web analytics tool such as Google Analytics cannot tell you much more beyond the number of sales their websites generated. Merchants who do use Google Analytics and whom have installed and configured their websites with the eCommerce tracking component enjoy the rewards of being able to match ordered product SKUs and transaction IDs to a visitor's landing page, marketing campaign information, keyword, geographical location, and much more.

In this chapter, you see some code examples, but you also see some reports in the Google Analytics platform that become available after you install the necessary eCommerce tracking component.

ENABLING ECOMMERCE

The first action item that you need to complete is a rather simple one, but one that gets skipped over by many. You need to enable eCommerce data collection in your Google Analytics account profile.

Log in to your Google Analytics account (www.google.com/analytics), and ensure that you have administrative access (if not, contact the person that provided you with access). On the Overview screen, click your profile's Edit link, which you find all the way on the right-hand side of the screen under the Actions column. Then you should see a table labeled Main Website Profile Information—it may be difficult to pick out due to its white-colored font, but it is the first table on your screen at this time. There is a white-colored Edit link on the upper-right of the table—click this link to access your profile's main information.

The next screen that you see looks very much like the screen shot shown in Figure 31-1. Find the E-Commerce Website section in the middle of the page and be sure to change from Not an E-Commerce Site to Yes, an E-Commerce Site. Click Save Changes and your profile is ready to display eCommerce data.

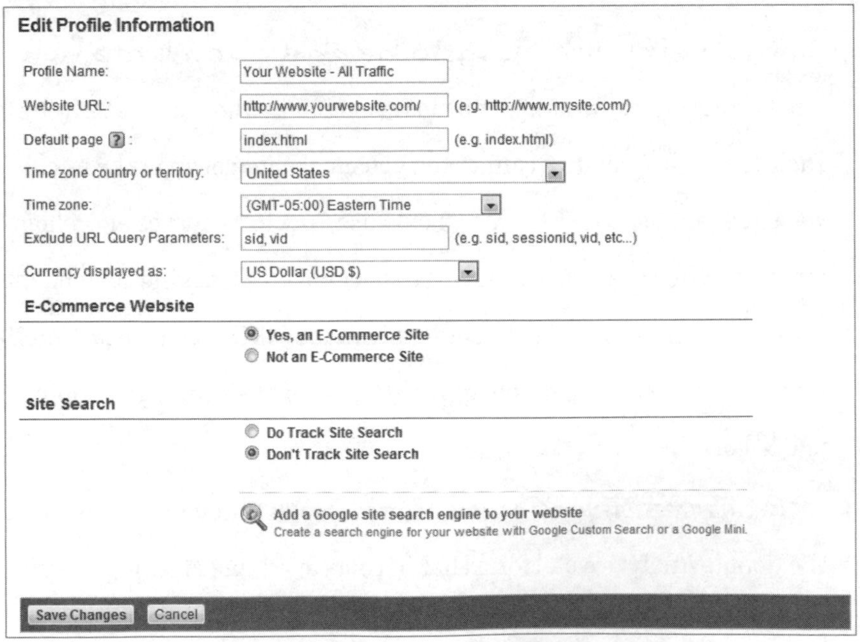

FIGURE 31-1: Enabling eCommerce in a Google Analytics profile.

If you take a sneak peek at most of your reports in Google Analytics after you enable eCommerce, you not only see a new item in the left navigation menu labeled eCommerce, you also see an eCommerce tab integrated into the reporting table. Hopefully soon after you implement the necessary tracking component, you will see actual transaction and product data fill in your now blank reports.

INSTALLING THE TRACKING CODE

Chapter 30 discussed a JavaScript tracking code that you need to place on every page of a website in order for Google Analytics to track visitor data properly. Because you're going to be working closely with the Google Analytics tracking code to implement eCommerce tracking, it's a good idea for you to see it here. Figure 31-2 shows where you can fetch your website's Google Analytics tracking code from within your profile. To get to the page shown in Figure 31-2, you need to go back to your profile's settings and click the Check Status link, which is on the top-right of the Main Website Profile Information table.

FIGURE 31-2: The Google Analytics tracking code from within a Google Analytics account.

Although the JavaScript snippet that you see in Figure 31-2 is placed on every page of your website, a modified version (containing the eCommerce tracking component) is only placed on your shopping cart's receipt page, which is also known colloquially as your Thank You page. When a visitor reaches this receipt page, Google Analytics executes the eCommerce tracking component and sends the additional pieces of information back to Google's servers for processing. This code needs to be added manually with the Google Analytics tracking code that you are using on the pages that you want to track.

The Google Analytics eCommerce tracking method is comprised of three methods— all of which are required for eCommerce tracking to work. You need to integrate these three methods within the standard JavaScript tracking snippet and you need to integrate them in the following order:

1. **The Transaction Object:** For this method, you initialize the _addTrans() method, which stores information about the transaction that occurred. Information like the Order ID, the transaction total, and the shopper's geographic location are collected with this method.

2. **The Item Object:** For the item object, the _addItem() function is initialized. This stores data on the individual items purchased, such as the item name, the SKU, the individual item price, and the quantity ordered.

3. **The "trackTrans" Method:** The _trackTrans() function, which appears at the very end of the Google Analytics eCommerce component, is the method that lets Google Analytics know that the transaction is successful and that all transaction data for this visitor has been collected.

Let's continue to build on this and show the different values that both the _addTrans() and _addItem() methods take. The _trackTrans() method stands alone at the very bottom of the eCommerce tracking component (there is a full example later in this chapter).

Within the _addTrans() method are eight separate values, which are as follows (in the exact order in which they need to be processed):

Order ID: The order's ID number

Affiliation: The store or affiliate name

Total: The transaction total

Tax: The tax charged on the transaction

Shipping: The shipping costs of the transaction

City: The shopper's city

State: The shopper's state

Country: The shopper's country

Within the _addItem() method are six separate values, which are as follows (in the exact order in which they need to be processed):

Order ID: The order's ID number (this must match the order ID in the _addTrans() method)

SKU: The item's SKU number

Name: The product name

Category: The product category

Price: The item's price

Quantity: The unit quantity

Even for the most experienced programmers and web developers, reading this material for the first time can be difficult to digest. However, seeing a full code example as shown in Figure 31-3 should nicely bring everything together that you've read in this section of the chapter. Remember that the eCommerce tracking component is nested within the standard Google Analytics tracking code, and that this modified code should appear only on your shopping cart's receipt or Thank You page.

```
<script type="text/javascript">

 var _gaq = _gaq || [];
 _gaq.push(['_setAccount', 'UA-XXXXX-X']);
 _gaq.push(['_trackPageview']);
 _gaq.push(['_addTrans',
   '1234',             // order ID - required
   'Acme Clothing',    // affiliation or store name
   '11.99',            // total - required
   '1.29',             // tax
   '5',                // shipping
   'San Jose',         // city
   'California',       // state or province
   'USA'               // country
 ]);

 // add item might be called for every item in the shopping cart
 // where your ecommerce engine loops through each item in the cart and
 // prints out _addItem for each
 _gaq.push(['_addItem',
   '1234',             // order ID - required
   'DD44',             // SKU/code - required
   'T-Shirt',          // product name
   'Green Medium',     // category or variation
   '11.99',            // unit price - required
   '1'                 // quantity - required
 ]);
 _gaq.push(['_trackTrans']); //submits transaction to the Analytics servers

 (function() {
   var ga = document.createElement('script'); ga.type = 'text/javascript'; ga.async = true;
   ga.src = ('https:' == document.location.protocol ? 'https://ssl' : 'http://www') + '.google-analytic
s.com/ga.js';
   var s = document.getElementsByTagName('script')[0]; s.parentNode.insertBefore(ga, s);
 })();

</script>
```

FIGURE 31-3: A full example of tracking eCommerce data with Google Analytics.

The example in Figure 31-3 comes from the Google Code website (http://code .google.com/apis/analytics/), which is an outstanding resource for all things Google Analytics technical implementation, including code samples for eCommerce and general guidelines.

Speaking of guidelines, you should be fully aware of all of the following tips regarding eCommerce implementation. You can easily make programming errors that can significantly and negatively impact your profile data, so take the necessary time to ensure that your eCommerce data is collected as cleanly and as accurately as possible.

Code Positioning

It's imperative that the Google Analytics tracking code is located within the <head> and </head> tags of all of your website's pages, including (and especially) the confirmation page on your shopping cart that generates the eCommerce tracking component.

Placing the Google Analytics tracking code outside of the <head> and </head> tags can greatly reduce the volume of data collected. Some users who frequent online forums report as much as a 30 percent difference between actual orders from their shopping cart database and the Google Analytics eCommerce reporting section.

The _addTrans Method

Two required fields in _addTrans method must be used. These are Order ID and Total. The other six fields (Affiliation, Tax, Shipping, City, State, and Country) are optional fields. You can use them, but you're not required to do so. However, if you can pull those fields in from a visitor's order, you may want to do so—especially the geographical data.

The _addItem Method

Three required fields in the _addItem method must also be filled in for proper item data to be sent to Google Analytics. These four required fields are the Order ID (which must be identical to the Order ID in the _addTrans method), the SKU, the Unit Price, and the Quantity. In the _addItem method, Product Name and Category are the optional fields. Again, you aren't required to use the optional fields, but you probably should use at least the Product Name field (in fact, if you don't, the Google Code website informs you that you won't see any product-level data without a Product Name entry, even though that field is not a required one).

The SKU Field

The SKU field (or, as you can see in Figure 33-3, the SKU/Code field) must be populated for every _addItem method that you print. If you have an order with multiple _addItem methods, and the SKU field is not used for every item, only the last item with the SKU field filled in is recorded, which causes big data discrepancies on the reporting side.

"Special" Characters

Avoid using any "special" characters in the names or values for every field. Characters such as currency symbols ($ and €, for example) cause missing data or unrealistic data in your reports. Other characters that cause problems are quotation marks (" and "); these can cause the entire transaction to not be reported. Characters that can also cause some issues are trademark or copyright symbols, letters from non-English language sets (vowels with tildes, circumflexes, umlauts, and grave or acute signs), and several non-ASCII, non UTF-8 symbols. It's best to steer clear of symbols altogether and stick to just letters, especially in the names of products, where most errors seem to occur.

On some online forums, heavy accuracy discrepancies have been reported by users whom have used these non-ASCII or non UTF-8 symbols in their eCommerce data. Reported discrepancy-to-actual percentages range anywhere from as low as 2 percent to as much as 15 percent.

Zeros in Numerical Fields

Standalone zeros in numerical fields (Total, Tax, Shipping, Unit Price, and Quantity) are to be avoided at all costs, because these can also cause problems. Instead of zeros, simply leave the field blank. *Do not* exclude the field entirely.

The Comma Symbol

The comma is another character that breaks your eCommerce data and causes more headaches for you. Commas are very often used, but these numerical fields support integers with decimal places. Don't separate your thousands places with commas with Google Analytics eCommerce.

▶ ASCII stands for American Standard Code for Information Interchange. ASCII codes represent the text in computer software programs, online applications, and mobile devices. The symbols on your everyday keyboard are a part of the ASCII character group.

▶ UTF-8 stands for Unicode Transformation Format-8. It's a technology used to encode characters on HTML and XML files. Google Analytics servers use UTF-8 encoding to process data and display the data within the Google Analytics report suite.

The Country Field

The Country field in the _addTrans method supports the two-letter country code (US), the three-letter country code (USA), or the full name of the country (United States). Using any of these options enables you to see country-level data for shoppers.

Do note that this may not necessarily match the Map Overlay report that is found within the Visitors section in Google Analytics. If a shopper enters Canada as his country in your shopping cart, then Canada appears as that visitor's country even if the person was identified by Google Analytics as originating from the United States.

Multiplication of Price and Quantity

Keep in mind that the last two fields in the _addItem method—Unit Price and Quantity—should not be multiplied together. Google Analytics does the math for you here, so if, for example, you multiply a unit price of 1.25 with a quantity of 3, it appears as 3.75 in the eCommerce source code, which is then multiplied again by 3 by Google for a whopping 11.25, which, obviously, makes your product revenue data highly inaccurate.

Currency Conversions

Currency conversions (dollar to euro, euro to yen, and so on) are not handled by Google Analytics, so they must happen on your end. Again, remember that the Total, Tax, Shipping, and Unit Price are integer fields.

In case your curiosity is piqued, or in the event that you want to set up eCommerce in an international currency (a currency other than the U.S. dollar), you need to log in to your Google Analytics account, find the profile that you want to track eCommerce data for, and find the Currency Displayed As drop-down menu. At present, you have the following currency options to select from:

- ▶ U.S. dollar
- ▶ Japanese yen
- ▶ Euro
- ▶ British pound sterling
- ▶ Australian dollar
- ▶ South Korean won
- ▶ Brazilian real
- ▶ Chinese yuan

- Danish krone
- Russian ruble
- Swedish krona
- Norwegian krone
- Polish zloty
- Turkish lira
- New Taiwan dollar
- Hong Kong dollar
- Thai baht
- Indonesian rupiah
- Argentine peso
- Mexican peso
- Vietnamese dong
- Philippine peso
- Indian rupe
- Swiss franc

Notably absent from the preceding list is the Canadian dollar.

One Final Note Regarding Installing the Tracking Code

One item that you haven't read about yet is how these eCommerce data fields are populated. In other words, how do your visitors' transactions and product details appear within the Google Analytics tracking code? The answer to that question is that it's up to you how the data appears.

A programmer can choose from so many methods and so many techniques to employ that it's outside the scope of this book to cover them all. PHP, .NET, Cold Fusion, ASP, XML, and JSP are just some of the languages that can be used.

What you definitely do not want to do is copy the full example from the Google Code website and paste it directly on to your website without removing the example values! Believe it or not, this actually happens, and if you make this grave error, any visitor that visits your confirmation page shares the same transaction and product information as every other visitor.

If you are using a third-party shopping cart application, chances are good that your vendor has a native, built-in integration with Google Analytics where all you have to do is provide your Google Analytics account number to get eCommerce data to track in your account. There are far too many eCommerce providers to list here; reach out to your platform's company and ask if it provides Google Analytics integration.

USING GOOGLE ANALYTICS WITH SHOPPING CARTS

The good news: Google Analytics works with most shopping carts.

The not-so-good news: Google Checkout does not use the latest version of the Google Analytics tracking code.

The bad news: The most popular payment processing company doesn't allow for Google Analytics (or any JavaScript tags, for that matter).

It's a shame that PayPal—the most popular online payment processing company—does not allow for JavaScript tags. This means that Google Analytics—or any web analytics program dependent upon JavaScript technology—cannot capture transaction and product data. If you use PayPal and Google Analytics, you are "in the dark" and not able to collect transaction or product data.

The Google Shopping Cart (Google Checkout) does have integration with Google Analytics, but as of the time of this writing (and for quite some time now), Google Checkout has not been upgraded to the newest Google Analytics tracking code. Therefore, if you use Google Checkout, you need to become familiar with what is known as the "ga.js" tracking code version.

Other shopping carts and payment processors are finally beginning to understand that the majority of their customers use a web analytics tool like Google Analytics to understand visitor behavior and collect visitor data. Little by little, the major shopping cart players have been providing link-ups, documentation, and guidelines for Google Analytics eCommerce integration. Hopefully, it is only a matter of time before the PayPals of the world follow suit.

Google Shopping Cart

Google Checkout offers two types of requests for its shopping cart product, so before you go cracking open source code, you need to figure out if you're using *Digitally Signed Checkout XML Requests* or if you're using *Server-to-Server Checkout XML Requests*.

If you're using Digitally Signed Checkout XML Requests, encoded shopping data is posted to Google Checkout directly after the visitor clicks the Google Checkout button that you have on your website.

If you're using Server-to-Server Checkout XML Requests, your website calls the Google Checkout API and forwards the visitor to another page on your website before the visitor clicks a unique link to be taken to Google Checkout for payment processing.

You can find all documentation regarding Google Checkout at `http://code.google`
`.com/apis/checkout/developer/checkout_analytics_integration.html`.

DIGITALLY SIGNED CHECKOUT XML REQUESTS

The following steps should integrate your Google Checkout shopping cart with your Google Analytics account if you're using Digitally Signed Checkout XML Requests. Remember that you're going to be dealing with an older version of the Google Analytics tracking code, so be flexible.

1. Ensure that the Google Analytics tracking code is present on every page of your website.

2. On every page that displays a Google Checkout button, add the following JavaScript snippet below the Google Analytics tracking code:

```
<script src="http://checkout.google.com/files/digital/ga_post.js"
   type="text/javascript">
</script>
```

3. On each form on your website that displays a Google Checkout button, add the following hidden input field:

```
<input type="hidden" name="analyticsdata" value="">
```

4. On each form on your website that displays a Google Checkout button, you also need to add the following onSubmit attribute within the <form> tag:

```
onsubmit="setUrchinInputCode(pageTracker);"
```

Following these four steps should enable you to see eCommerce data in your Google Analytics account profile. Figure 31-4 shows a full integration example with this type of Google Checkout request. Again, you're looking at an older version of the Google Analytics tracking code, so it looks different than the code that you might have on your website.

```
<script type="text/javascript">
  var gaJsHost = (("https:" == document.location.protocol) ? "https://ssl." : "http://www.");
  document.write(unescape("%3Cscript src='" + gaJsHost + "google-analytics.com/ga.js'
type='text/javascript'%3E%3C/script%3E"));
</script>

<script type="text/javascript">
  try {
    var pageTracker = _gat._getTracker("UA-XXXXXXX-X");
    pageTracker._trackPageview();
  } catch(err) {
  }
</script>

<script src="http://checkout.google.com/files/digital/ga_post.js"
  type="text/javascript">
</script>


<form action="..." method="POST" onsubmit="setUrchinInputCode(pageTracker);">
    <input type="hidden" name="cart" value="...">
    <input type="hidden" name="signature" value="...">
    <input type="hidden" name="analyticsdata" value="">
    <input type="image" name="Google Checkout" alt="Fast checkout through Google"
        src="http://checkout.google.com/buttons/checkout.gif?merchant_id=YOUR_MERCHANT_ID
        &w=180&h=46&style=white&variant=text&loc=en_US" height="46" width="180"/>
</form>
```

FIGURE 31-4: Using Digitally Signed Checkout
XML Requests with Google Analytics.

SERVER-TO-SERVER CHECKOUT XML REQUESTS

The following steps are the ones that you should follow to configure Google Analytics
for Google Checkout if you use Server-to-Server Checkout XML Requests.

1. Follow the exact same instructions for Digitally Signed Checkout XML Requests
   from the preceding section.

2. You need to make a modification on the form handler that executes on your
   site when a visitor clicks the Google Checkout button. The form handler needs
   to be modified to extract the value of analyticsdata, so that this can be
   included in the API request.

3. You need to add the <analytics-data> element to your Checkout API requests.

Following these steps should get you squared away with Google Analytics and
Google Checkout.

Figures 31-5 and 31-6 show you a sample integration for this method.
Figure 31-5 shows you how the Google Analytics tracking code looks on your
checkout page. Figure 31-6 shows the Checkout API request that you integrate
with Google Analytics.

After you successfully integrate your Google Checkout shopping cart with your
Google Analytics account, you should begin to see eCommerce data appear within
your account profile.

If you want to analyze the performance of the Google Checkout pages, you can find three new pages in the Content section of reports:

- ▶ **Login:** /login.html
- ▶ **Place Order:** /placeOrder.html
- ▶ **Order Confirmed:** /purchaseComplete.html

Many merchants create a goal for the Order Confirmed page in their profile when using Google Checkout. Revisit Chapter 30 to learn how to create a goal for your profile.

```
<script type="text/javascript">
  var gaJsHost = (("https:" == document.location.protocol) ? "https://ssl." : "http://www.");
  document.write(unescape("%3Cscript src='" + gaJsHost + "google-analytics.com/ga.js'
type='text/javascript'%3E%3C/script%3E"));
</script>

<script type="text/javascript">
  try {
    var pageTracker = _gat._getTracker("UA-XXXXXXX-X");
    pageTracker._trackPageview();
  } catch(err) {
  }
</script>

<script src="http://checkout.google.com/files/digital/ga_post.js"
  type="text/javascript">
</script>

<form action="..." method="POST" onsubmit="setUrchinInputCode(pageTracker);">
    <input type="hidden" name="analyticsdata" value="">
    <input type="image" name="Google Checkout" alt="Fast checkout through Google"
        src="http://checkout.google.com/buttons/checkout.gif?merchant_id=YOUR_MERCHANT_ID
        &w=180&h=46&style=white&variant=text&loc=en_US" height="46" width="180"/>
</form>
```

FIGURE 31-5: Sample checkout page integration with Google Analytics and Google Checkout.

```
<checkout-shopping-cart xmlns="http://checkout.google.com/schema/2">
    <shopping-cart>
        <items>
            ...
        </items>
    </shopping-cart>
    <checkout-flow-support>
        <merchant-checkout-flow-support>
            <shipping-methods>
                ...
            </shipping-methods>
            <analytics-data>SW5zZXJ0IDxhbmFseXRpY3MtZGF0YT4gdmFsdWUgGVyZS4=</analytics-data>
        </merchant-checkout-flow-support>
    </checkout-flow-support>
</checkout-shopping-cart>
```

FIGURE 31-6: The Google Checkout API request.

Other Shopping Cart Applications

As mentioned earlier, some shopping carts offer customers the luxury of implementing the Google Analytics eCommerce tracking component directly onto their product. However, each shopping cart can be very different, so it's up to you to read up on your own cart's documentation and follow the instructions. Some carts offer one-click installation (where you merely provide the Google Analytics account UA number), and others make you jump through hoops to get eCommerce data in your Google Analytics account.

Following is a short list of some of the more popular shopping carts, with links to their documentation on how to implement Google Analytics. I've shortened the actual links to these sites using Google's URL shortening tool to save you plenty of keystrokes.

DotNetNuke: Several Topics on Google Analytics—http://goo.gl/Eg0FC

Drupal: Google Analytics Documentation—http://goo.gl/MCETR

Joomla!: Adding Google Analytics to your Joomla Site—http://goo.gl/SyZpV

Magento: Google Analytics—http://goo.gl/OxKpg

Miva Merchant: Google Analytics in Miva Merchant 5.5—http://goo.gl/Cml05

osCommerce: Community Add-Ons - Google Analytics Module— http://goo.gl/TbjH8

osCommerce: Support Forum Topic—http://goo.gl/AdAes

Shopify: Google Analytics—http://goo.gl/MjzEu

Volusion: Setting Up Google Analytics in Volusion—http://goo.gl/qrECq

Yahoo! Store: Google Analytics with a Yahoo! Store—http://goo.gl/AmMJj

Zen Cart: Google Analytics Integration—http://goo.gl/qFKCh

SUMMARY

Using Google Analytics for eCommerce requires a mixture of simple edits within your profile as well as (possibly) some advanced programming techniques. All of the hoops that this will make you or your IT department jump through are worth every second of it. The eCommerce data that you are able to collect from your online shoppers enables you to evaluate your marketing efforts, the performance of your website, and the return on investment that you're producing online.

eCommerce data collection with Google Analytics is not tied to a rigid, specific set of instructions. How the shopper's actual values appear within the eCommerce tracking component is entirely up to you.

CHAPTER 32

Integrating Google Analytics with AdWords

IN THIS CHAPTER

▸ Creating a Google account for non-Gmail users

▸ Obtaining administrative access to both AdWords and Google Analytics

▸ Syncing Google AdWords with Google Analytics

▸ AdWords dimensions and metrics in Google Analytics

▸ Reporting opportunities found with a Google Analytics account

Google AdWords is a multi-billion dollar a year industry, and over the past decade it has revolutionized how marketing budgets get structured and how marketers think about advertising in general. Google AdWords started out by offering only basic search advertising with limited options, but has evolved now to the point where you can advertise in just about any medium, any channel, any device type, any region, and with any type of ad.

As AdWords has evolved over the years, and as more money has been allocated to advertising with Google, the need for precise data and reporting in mass quantity has also drastically surged in demand. The AdWords platform itself has seen a huge increase in the availability of reports, forecasts, filtering, and segmentable data. However, all of the data that marketers see when they log in to their AdWords accounts is data regarding their advertising campaigns—how many clicks, what ads ran on what sites, what search terms generated impressions, and so on. What AdWords cannot tell you is what website pages were viewed after someone clicked an ad, what interactions a visitor engaged with on a website after coming from an AdWords effort, or, to some extent, what important revenue or lead-generating actions occurred on a website after a visitor engaged with an AdWords creative.

Enter Google Analytics. By connecting your Google AdWords account with your Google Analytics account, you can tie in your AdWords marketing data with your web analytics data, allowing you the flexibility to extract rich insights that can help you optimize and refine your marketing efforts, while improving your return on investment. This chapter covers how to connect your Google AdWords to your Google Analytics account, what you need to know if you either don't have the necessary access level to sync accounts or if you don't use a Gmail e-mail account, the metrics and dimensions available to you in Google Analytics from AdWords, and finally, the reports that you can find in your account. A proper AdWords-to-Analytics sync, as well as a foundational understanding of what data and reports become available, is a necessary, elementary building block of knowledge for any online marketer or web analyst involved with Google AdWords.

> **NOTE** You can measure on-site success interactions with Google AdWords Conversion Tracking, which is a separate snippet of JavaScript tracking code that you place on a desired page. So, technically, AdWords can tell you when conversions occur, but I won't be dealing with it for the purposes of this chapter.

YOUR GOOGLE ACCOUNT AND YOUR ACCESS LEVEL

Just because you have access to your Google AdWords and your Google Analytics accounts, and just because you spend lots of advertising dollars online, doesn't mean that you can automatically sync your AdWords and your Google Analytics accounts together.

Basically, your log-in e-mail address *must* be an administrator on both accounts in order for you to be able to sync Google AdWords and Google Analytics together. This is very frequently an issue if your account was created by someone else, such as an agency or a contractor.

Taking a step back from that, it's a good idea that you make sure that you have a Google account in the first place, and that your Google account has access to both AdWords and Google Analytics, before you start going into the levels of access and what you need to do to sync the two accounts. If you have a Gmail Email address, you have nothing to worry about (I deal with how to obtain access to your accounts if you don't already have access in a little bit). However, if you don't have Gmail, and would like to use your Yahoo!, AOL, Hotmail, or your company e-mail account for Google products, it must first be a Google account before you can obtain access.

Creating a Google Account

If you already are accessing both Google AdWords and Google Analytics with a non-Gmail Email account, feel free to skip this section and go right to the next subheading where I start talking about administrative access. For everyone else not using Gmail, go through the following steps to get your non-Gmail Email account converted into a Google account:

1. Visit the Google.com homepage, ensuring you are logged-off from any Gmail account.

2. Click Sign In, found on the upper-right hand side of the Google.com homepage.

3. On the following page, click Create an Account Now, located on the right-hand side, as shown here in Figure 32-1.

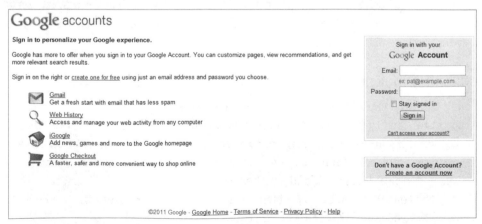

FIGURE 32-1: The Google Accounts log-in screen with the "Create an account now" link on right-hand side.

4. On the Create an Account screen, fill in all the requested information—the field Your Current Email Address is your non-Gmail address. The password that you choose here is your password for both AdWords and Google Analytics. (Choose a separate, more complex password for AdWords and Google Analytics, just to be safe.)

5. When finished, click I Accept. Create My Account.

6. Provided you completed the form accurately, you are then taken to a page that informs you that your e-mail address is being sent an e-mail including a verification link. You must click this verification link before being able to use your Google account.

7. After clicking the verification link, your Google account is created.

Now, you can use your non-Gmail e-mail account to log in to Google AdWords, Google Analytics, or any other Google product that you'd like to use.

Accessing Google AdWords and Google Analytics

Even if you've been accessing Google AdWords or Google Analytics up to now, you may have been doing it without the necessary level of access that you need in order to sync Google AdWords with Google Analytics. If you read the previous page or so that talked about converting your non-Gmail e-mail account into a Google account then this is your next step.

To be able to sync AdWords and Google Analytics, the e-mail address that you use to log in to both accounts must be an administrator on both accounts. It's very possible that you're not an administrator on either account, or on both accounts, so your next step is to get this squared away.

CHECKING YOUR LEVEL OF ACCESS FOR GOOGLE ADWORDS

Log in to your Google AdWords account (www.google.com/adwords), click the **My Account** tab, and then click the **Account access** link that appears in that tab's drop-down menu. If your e-mail address appears with an access level of **Administrative access**, you are all set. If it doesn't, you need to contact the administrator (there always has to be at least one), and ask them to grant you administrative access. Most of the time this won't be a problem—some of the time, the administrator won't know what to do (show them this chapter!).

Figure 32-2 shows what it looks like when an AdWords user has administrative access. Administrative access, by the way, is the highest level of access that a user can obtain to an AdWords account.

> **NOTE** Please note that Google allows an e-mail address access to one (and only one) Google AdWords account at any one time. If in the future you want to access another AdWords account with the same e-mail address, you need to have your e-mail address removed or unassociated with the current AdWords account. This can be a challenging process, especially if you're the lone administrator of the AdWords account.

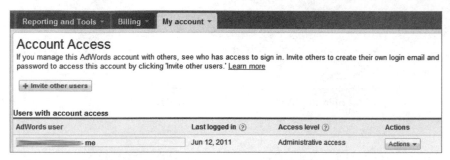

FIGURE 32-2: A user with administrative access to a Google AdWords account.

CHECKING YOUR LEVEL OF ACCESS FOR GOOGLE ANALYTICS

Log in to your Google Analytics account. If you can see links to edit an account or a profile within an account then you have administrative access to your Google Analytics account. If you can't see links to edit the account or profiles within an account, you don't have administrative access. It's as plain and simple as that.

Just like AdWords, if you don't have administrative access, you need to contact your account's administrator. Figure 32-3 shows what it looks like when you have administrative access to a Google Analytics account.

> **NOTE** Unlike Google AdWords, one e-mail address can obtain access to multiple Google Analytics accounts at any one time. The process for obtaining access to a Google Analytics account is much simpler than the process of obtaining access to a Google AdWords account.

It bears repeating: You must have administrative access to both Google AdWords and Google Analytics in order to sync the two accounts.

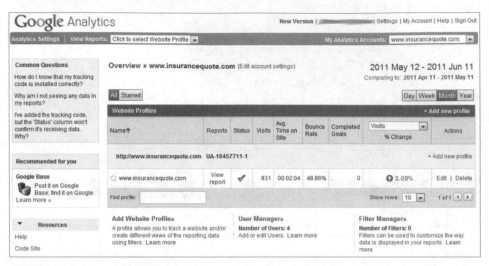

FIGURE 32-3: A user with administrative access to a Google Analytics account.

SYNCING GOOGLE ADWORDS WITH GOOGLE ANALYTICS

Now that you have all of your administrative access issues sorted out, it's time to sync the two accounts together so that you can start to take advantage of your AdWords campaign data in your Google Analytics account.

The process is simple, but you want to make sure that you follow the steps precisely to avoid any errors or mistakes along the way.

First, log in to your Google AdWords account and find the Reporting and Tools tab to see a list of interesting options to choose from, such as Website Optimizer and Conversion Tracking. Select Google Analytics (obviously), to start the syncing process.

Figure 32-4 shows an example of what it looks like if your Google AdWords account is not synced to your Google Analytics account. If you clicked Google Analytics from the Reporting tab, and were taken to your Google Analytics account, then guess what? Your accounts are already synced, and there is nothing else that you need to do. However, because you're reading this, you're probably not being sent directly to Google Analytics, and you are seeing what you see now in Figure 32-4.

Be sure to have the I Already Have radio button checked on before clicking Continue. You don't want to create a new Google Analytics account (but if you did, you would select Create instead).

FIGURE 32-4: The page that you'll see when you attempt to sync your Google AdWords account to your Google Analytics account.

Figure 32-5 shows you what the following screen looks like. The drop-down menu should show your Google Analytics account name. However, if you happen to have administrative access to multiple Google Analytics accounts, you have to be sure to select the correct Google Analytics account from the drop-down menu.

You also need to be sure that the Destination URL Auto-tagging checkbox is checked. This is a key component in being able to see valuable data from AdWords in your Google Analytics account. Data points like the keyword that a visitor searched for, the ad that a visitor clicked to access your website, and the campaign responsible for displaying the ad are sent to your Google Analytics account via Destination URL Auto-tagging.

After you click Link My Account, your Google AdWords account is synced to your Google Analytics account. You can verify that this actually is the case by logging in to Google Analytics and clicking the Data Sources tab. If you see your AdWords account customer ID listed, and applied to at least one profile, then you know you successfully synced the two accounts. Take a quick peek at Figure 32-6 to see what a synced Google AdWords account looks like in Google Analytics.

You may have noticed an Unlink link to the right on Figure 32-6. This is the only place where you can actually unlink or "de-sync" your accounts if the need arises.

Keep in mind that Google AdWords data is not transferred to your Google Analytics account in real time. Wait one to two days before you start seeing AdWords data in your Google Analytics account.

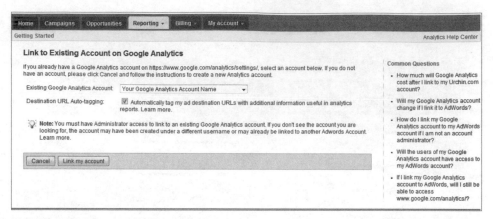

FIGURE 32-5: Selecting the Google Analytics account, and Destination URL Auto-tagging.

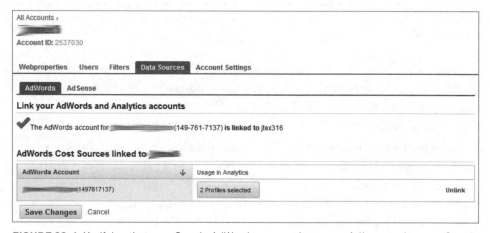

FIGURE 32-6: Verifying that your Google AdWords account is successfully synced to your Google Analytics account.

UNDERSTANDING ADWORDS REPORTS IN GOOGLE ANALYTICS

Not only does Google Analytics provide users with seven different reports that are accessible from the left navigation menu, Google AdWords data is integrated throughout the reporting interface via traffic sources and referral information, as well as advanced segments and other options, including a Clicks metric group.

Let's take a deeper look at the available seven reports, as well as the AdWords-specific Clicks metric group.

Dissecting the "Clicks" Metric Group

Each report in Google Analytics contains metric groups that organize metrics to enhance analysis efforts. For example, most reports in Google Analytics contain the Site Usage metric group, where you find metrics such as Visits, Pages/Visits, and Bounce Rate.

In the AdWords report section, an additional metric group named **Clicks** is available, containing metrics that represent and substantiate your AdWords traffic. Those metrics are the following:

- ▶ **Visits:** The number of sessions to your website (this is the only non-AdWords metric of the group).

- ▶ **Impressions:** The number of views of your ads (the number of times your ad appeared in a search result).

- ▶ **Clicks:** The number of clicks on your ads.

- ▶ **Cost:** The total cost of your AdWords marketing efforts.

- ▶ **CTR:** The click-through rate (the percentage of the number of clicks compared to the number of impressions).

- ▶ **CPC:** The cost-per-click (the average cost for each click).

- ▶ **RPC:** The revenue-per-click (the average revenue—from goals or from ecommerce transactions—for each click).

- ▶ **ROI:** The return-on-investment for your AdWords marketing efforts.

- ▶ **Margin:** Revenue minus cost, divided by revenue.

Figure 32-7 shows the Clicks metric group in a Google Analytics account with reported figures for a particular date range. Go to the AdWords report section within Google Analytics and find a Clicks metric group (which is displayed next to Ecommerce as you see in Figure 32-7).

Explorer								
Site Usage	Goal Set 1	Ecommerce	**Clicks**					
Visits ⑦ ● **19,039**	Impressions **710,839**	Clicks ⑦ **20,880**	Cost ⑦ **$7,333.84**	CTR ⑦ **2.94%**	CPC ⑦ **$0.35**	RPC ⑦ **$3.89**	ROI ⑦ **1,007.79%**	Margin ⑦ **90.97%**
% of Total: 31.82% (59,834)	% of Total: 100.00% (710,839)	% of Total: 100.00% (20,880)	% of Total: 100.00% ($7,333.84)	Site Avg: 2.94% (0.00%)	Site Avg: $0.35 (0.00%)	Site Avg: $15.76 (-75.31%)	Site Avg: 4,387.33% (-77.03%)	Site Avg: 97.77% (-6.95%)

FIGURE 32-7: The "Clicks" metric group (the last three metrics are not available in AdWords—only here).

Understanding AdWords-specific Dimensions

Google understands the need for marketers and web analysts to be able to perform deep segmentation on their AdWords marketing data. To that end, for accounts that are properly synced, Google Analytics enables you to segment your web analytics data by a number of Google AdWords-focused dimensions. Segmenting is quite possibly the most critical component of extracting insights and data mining, and for AdWords marketers, segmentation is the air they breathe.

In a properly AdWords-synced Google Analytics account, you find thirteen different dimensions within the AdWords reporting section, as well as through custom reports or advanced segments. Those dimensions are the following:

▶ **Campaign:** The name of your AdWords marketing campaigns; the first level of hierarchy within an AdWords account.

▶ **Ad Group:** A grouping of ads and keywords; the second level of hierarchy within an AdWords account.

▶ **Keyword:** A term that an advertiser bids on to allow the advertiser's ad to appear in a search result; the third level of hierarchy within an AdWords account.

▶ **Match Type:** The type of matching enabled for each keyword (*Broad, Phrase, or Exact*).

▶ **Matched Search Query:** The actual search query performed by a visitor to your site on Google (*can vary from the keyword that an advertiser bids on*).

▶ **Placement Domain:** The website that the advertiser's ads display on (*Google Display Network only*).

▶ **Placement URL:** The full URL that the advertiser's ads display on (*Google display network only*).

▶ **Display/Content Targeting Option:** The management type for a Display campaign (*Automatic or Managed*).

▶ **Ad Content:** The first line of ad text of each ad.

▶ **Ad Distribution Network:** The distribution network type for an AdWords campaign.

▶ **Ad Format:** The type of ad used (*text, image, video, flash*, or *rich media*).

▶ **Display URL:** The URL used in your AdWords ads.

▶ **Destination URL:** The actual URL where a visitor was taken after clicking an advertiser's ad.

Using a combination of these dimensions, the aforementioned Clicks metric group, and web analytics data, online advertisers can really leverage Google Analytics in a powerful, meaningful, and ROI-focused way.

Viewing the Campaigns Report

The first report in this section mirrors the first tier of hierarchy of an AdWords account, which is the campaign level. Here, you find a listing of all campaigns that have sent you at least one visit during your selected date range. Clicking any campaign name enables you to see the ad groups that have sent you at least one visit during your selected date range, and clicking an ad group name drills the report down into the keyword level.

In this report—as well as in this section and throughout Google Analytics—you may notice a Viewing line resting directly above the reporting table. This enables you to quickly switch dimensions without leaving a report. For example, clicking Ad Group (the second item in the viewing row in this report) toggles the report from your AdWords campaigns to show you your AdWords ad groups. The previous list of AdWords dimensions is also available here for toggling. Figure 32-8 shows a good example of what the Campaigns report looks like. Notice the viewing row right above the reporting table!

		Visits ↓	Impressions	Clicks	Cost	CTR	CPC	RPC	ROI	Margin
1.	2009-▓▓▓▓C-001 ▓▓▓F Adopt An Animal - Search	3,623	78,140	2,917	$1,660.19	3.73%	$0.57	$1.14	100.03%	50.01%
2.	2009-▓▓▓▓C-001 ▓▓▓F Adopt An Animal - Content	216	740,432	243	$160.68	0.03%	$0.66	$0.21	-68.91%	-221.68%
3.	2011-▓▓▓▓C-001 ▓▓▓F Adopt an Animal (Father's Day) - Content	133	713,535	152	$295.08	0.02%	$1.94	$0.00	-100.00%	0.00%
4.	2009-▓▓▓▓C-001 ▓▓▓F Adopt An Animal - Mobile Search	85	8,259	114	$56.01	1.38%	$0.49	$0.44	-10.82%	-12.13%
5.	2011-▓▓▓▓C-001 ▓▓▓F Adopt an Animal (Father's Day) - Search	47	17,896	62	$142.52	0.35%	$2.30	$0.00	-100.00%	0.00%

Viewing: **Campaign** Ad Group Keyword Matched Search Query Other ▾

Secondary dimension: Select... ▾ | advanced | View: | 1 - 10 of 14

FIGURE 32-8: The AdWords → Campaigns report. Each campaign can be clicked on for ad group + keyword data.

Digging through Data within the Keywords Report

The Keywords report essentially shows you data in the same format as you just saw in Figure 32-8, except that instead of starting at the campaign-level data, you start out at the keyword-level data. In the Keywords report, when you click an individual keyword, you view its matched search query—pairing up keywords and matched search queries is a great way for marketers to augment and optimize their paid keywords.

One note of interest here: If you see *(content)* or something like *(Remarketing)* in the keywords list, don't panic too much. This is normal; advertisers running display campaigns or remarketing campaigns (which generally don't use keywords) have entries appear like the previous two examples in their reports.

Analyzing the Day Parts Report

Day parting is becoming increasingly important, especially for advertisers running scheduled campaigns in AdWords. Google Analytics can show you the hour when your campaigns received clicks and other statistics (shown in military time, from "00" to "23"). Clicking an hour shows you the day of week. But be careful here; you see values ranging from 0 to 6, instead of values ranging from Sunday to Saturday. Here, 0 = Sunday, 1 = Monday, and so on.

Reading the Destination URLs Report

The page that an advertiser's visitor is taken to when he clicks on one of the ads is known as the destination page (or the landing page). The destination URL is simply the URL of that destination page, and this report in AdWords breaks down all of your account's statistics grouped by the destination URL.

Be advised that your full, long URL, query parameters and all, appears here in a huge list. Clicking any destination URL reveals the ad distribution network.

Also keep in mind that a destination URL is not necessarily equivalent to a display URL. Google AdWords limits the size of the URL that an advertiser can display on an ad to a maximum of 35 characters, making that space big enough for the domain name of a website. However, your destination URL can lead visitors to an interior page of a website—the searcher on Google never actually sees the longer destination URL unless they click on the advertisement.

Drilling Down into the Placements Report

The Placements report is tailor-made for any advertiser running AdWords campaigns on the Google display network. This report automatically segments all of your AdWords campaigns and shows you only the campaigns that are opted in to the display network. When you access this report, you are first presented with what's known as the content targeting option: You see automatic placements, managed placements, or both of those options together.

Drilling down into a content targeting option reveals its placement domain, which is the domain where the ad was shown. Marketers can go one level deeper and obtain the full placement URL by clicking a desired placement domain. This is great for marketers to see the exact page where their ads are shown (website owners who are a part of the Google display network can modify the shape, size, and location of ads, so marketers rely on this type of report to stay on top of how their message is being spread).

Reviewing the Keyword Positions Report

This report breaks the traditional report barrier and shows you interesting data in a very unique way. First, you're presented with a list of keywords on the left-hand side of where the normal report table would have been located. When you click a keyword, the right-hand side panel refreshes and shows the number of visits per each ad position in a very self-explanatory manner. Figure 32-9 shows what this Keyword Positions report looks like. Notice the two drop-down menus that appear above this report's table. You can use these drop-down menus to change the metric that an advertiser sees here. If someone wanted to see the goal conversions by position or the number of transactions per each position, he could do so by very easily changing the metric on the drop-down menu.

Examining the TV Ads Report

Finally, for the fraction of AdWords advertisers running TV ads through Google's platform, this report pulls in TV impression, ad play, and audience retention metrics that, like every other report outlined so far, can be utilized in conjunction with website statistics to allow advertisers to improve their marketing campaigns and their bottom line.

TV ads with Google is not an offering that has taken off as Google originally expected it to, so the chances that you will ever use this report are extremely small. Expect this report to be blank for your Google Analytics account.

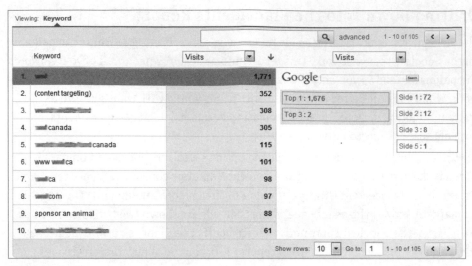

FIGURE 32-9: The Keyword Positions report, showing the number of visits per ad position on Google.

SUMMARY

Integrating your Google AdWords account with your Google Analytics account, and jumping through all of the necessary technical hoops, is only one half of this equation. For marketers to truly take advantage of being able to sync both accounts, they must understand what metrics, dimensions, and reports they have at their disposal. The AdWords report section within Google Analytics enables you to analyze and retrieve insightful pieces of information to improve your cost-per-click marketing efforts.

CHAPTER 33

Tweaking Google Analytics

For most website owners, the standard Google Analytics tracking code (the snippet of JavaScript that is placed on the pages of a website to track visitor activity as reviewed in Chapter 30) is the only item that gets copied and pasted onto a website when a Google Analytics account is involved. Very seldom will account administrators, webmasters, and website owners take the necessary time to customize, tweak, and take into account things such as blogs, subdomains, or shopping carts when configuring their Google Analytics accounts.

This chapter covers some of the more common customizations that need to be considered for a proper, correctly implemented Google Analytics account and website. Depending on your specific situation, you may find that you would like or need to use one, two, or several of the customizations covered in this chapter. Websites using Google Analytics that do not measure social media traffic or file downloads are not getting a complete, accurate picture of everything that is happening on the site. This could be costing their owners valuable pieces of data that could affect how they view their bottom line.

TRACKING SOCIAL MEDIA WITH GOOGLE ANALYTICS

Social media is large—*very* large. If for some odd reason you still don't buy into the power and influence of social media on worldwide Internet users, you definitely have some homework to do. Try checking out www.comscoredatamine.com, www.quantcast.com, or the Press Center section at www.hitwise.com for some factual, hard evidence that social media is dominant today and will be dominant for at least the immediate future.

This being the case, website owners and advertisers with presence or marketing campaigns on social media need to be able to track as much activity as possible with their web analytics tools. If you're using Google Analytics, and if you're doing anything in social media (which you should, because this is where your audience spends most of its time) then we're literally on the same page.

Tracking social media efforts with Google Analytics can be easily and simplistically divided into three subcategories: tracking activity on links you share, tracking paid social media advertising activity, and integrations that social media sites offer with Google Analytics.

Tracking Activity on Links You Share

When you share a link to something on Twitter, you automatically know that you're going to have to shorten that link to fit Twitter's 140-character limit. If you update your status on LinkedIn and share a link, you have to play the same "squeezing a big link into a tight space" game that you do on Twitter. Facebook—out of the three major social media players—is the only one with a limit large enough to accommodate longer links.

All three share something in common—you want to track their activity in Google Analytics. For any of the three situations described in the preceding paragraph, you are really sharing two types of links: links coming to your site and links going everywhere else. For links going anywhere other than your site or a site that you can track, you simply aren't able to integrate that with Google Analytics, or most any other web analytics tool. You need to rely on URL shortening services like bit.ly and goo.gl to provide you with data (which is not a bad thing—they do provide great data on your link's activity).

For links coming to your site, you can either view the data living within the Referring Sites report within the Traffic Sources section (not recommended for this purpose, because this can contain other links shared by others on social media), or you can append some query parameters at the end of your URLs to neatly organize your social media link activity data in your Google Analytics account (recommended).

Here's what you do. Take the following URL as an example of a link to share:

```
http://www.wiley.com/WileyCDA/WileyTitle/productCd-1118026659.html
```

Yes—that's the direct URL to this book on Wiley Publishing's website. It's very close to being too big to use in social media because you'd have very little room for anything else to share. So, you need to shorten this URL. But, wait! Before you shorten it, you need to append those query parameters to the end of it. So your longer URL would then look like this example:

```
http://www.wiley.com/WileyCDA/WileyTitle/productCd-1118026659.html?utm_
source=facebook&utm_medium=social-media&utm_
campaign=shares+june+2011&utm_content=google+secrets
```

Now, using goo.gl, that very long URL would look something like this:

```
http://goo.gl/ClMPL
```

This way, you're not only tracking data on clicks and activity with Google Analytics, but you're also getting data from the goo.gl shortening service because it provides its own stats on shortened URLs.

As far as those query parameters are concerned, you need to know what they mean and how to use them:

- ► **Source** *(shown in the example URL by the utm_source query parameter)*: This represents where someone comes from. For example, Facebook, Twitter, Wiley, Newsletter, and so on.

- ► **Medium** *(shown in the example URL by the utm_medium query parameter)*: This represents the means by which a visitor accesses your site. For example, cpc, cpm, social-media, e-mail, and so on.

- ► **Campaign** *(shown in the example URL by the utm_campaign query parameter)*: This represents the marketing campaign responsible for driving traffic to your site. For example, Branding, March 2012, In-House Mailing, and so on.

▶ **Content** *(shown in the example URL by the* utm_content *query parameter)*: This represents additional information about the link a visitor clicked. For example, red link, blue link, top link, bottom link, 300x250, 160x600, and so on.

The following resource from Google does a great job in going deeper with detail, and offers a URL builder to do the work for you (or, search for "tool URL builder" in Google and click the first result):

```
http://www.google.com/support/googleanalytics/bin/answer.py?answer=55578
```

Tracking Paid Social Media Advertising

Tracking paid advertising on LinkedIn and Facebook happens in much the same way as tracking regularly shared links. The two major differences between tracking paid links and shared links is how you label the utm_medium query parameter in your URL strings, and using an additional query parameter, utm_term.

For the utm_medium query parameter, you should use cpc—using this as a medium (in lowercase lettering) lets Google Analytics know that it is receiving paid traffic so that it knows to group the traffic accordingly.

For the utm_term query parameter, you put in the term (the keyword) that a visitor searched for to find and click on your paid ads. For example, someone searching for the phrase "wiley google secrets book" on LinkedIn could click an ad with a destination URL that could look something like this (note that this is an extension of the previous example using the utm_term query parameter):

```
http://www.wiley.com/WileyCDA/WileyTitle/productCd-1118026659.
html?utm_source=facebook&utm_medium=social-media&utm_
campaign=shares+june+2011&utm_content=google+secrets&utm_
term=wiley+google+secrets+book
```

Social Media Integration with Google Analytics

At the time of this writing, Facebook is the only of the "big three" social media services that offers Google Analytics integration. This subject could be its own separate chapter of this book. If you're interested in deeper integration with Facebook, try reviewing the following resource for great details and user-generated comments:

```
http://www.socialmediaexaminer.com/how-to-add-google-analytics-to-your-
facebook-fan-page/
```

TRACKING BLOGS WITH GOOGLE ANALYTICS

An extension of social media are blogs, which have been around for much longer than Facebook and Twitter and enable website owners to provide valuable content to the World Wide Web.

Sometimes, blogs live as a subdirectory or a subfolder of a website:

```
http://www.website.com/blog
```

Other times, blogs live as a subdomain or separate top-level domain, like the following two examples:

```
http://blog.website.com
http://www.mywebsiteblog.com
```

Blogs can even just live on Blogger, WordPress, or other blog-writing and publishing platforms, generating URLs that look like this:

```
http://atomsofthought.wordpress.com/
```

No matter what the situation is with your blog, there's a very good to excellent chance that you'll be tracking its activity in Google Analytics, just like you would for any other regular web page on your site. If you have access to your Google Analytics tracking code you can simply copy and paste that tracking code on your blog's subdirectory, your blog's website, or your blog publishing software's template files or content management system (CMS).

You might be thinking, "What about tracking between domains with blogs that live off of the main website domain?" For those of you who don't know, Google Analytics is designed, by default, to track activity on only one domain. When you place the Google Analytics tracking code on two or more subdomains or two or more separate domains, any traffic between subdomains or top-level domains is counted as referring traffic, which in many situations is not optimal.

However, you can configure the Google Analytics tracking code to track multiple subdomains (such as the previous example of http://blog.website.com) or multiple domains (such as the previous example of http://www.mywebsiteblog .com/) with the same snippet of JavaScript. In just a few pages, you see how you can do this for not only your blog, but your shopping cart, your client portal, or any other separate domain that you want to track.

TRACKING DIRECT DOWNLOADS WITH GOOGLE ANALYTICS

One of the most common ways that Google Analytics is customized is by configuring the tracking of file downloads. Almost every website today contains some type of non-page view interaction, such as PDF files, podcast downloads, instruction manuals in Microsoft Word, spreadsheets, and many other things. The interactions with all of these can be tracked with your Google Analytics account.

By default, non–page view interactions like the examples just covered are not tracked by Google Analytics; the standard Google Analytics tracking code is basically designed to be executed upon the user's request to view a page of a website. Downloading white papers or PDF "how-to" manuals aren't requesting website page views from a web server, so these downloads must be tracked another way.

Fortunately, Google Analytics offers two basic ways in which you can track direct file downloads: using *virtual* page views and using event tracking. Both methods are executed using a JavaScript onClick action.

▶ **Virtual page views:** To track a direct download as a virtual page view, the following JavaScript onClick action needs to be installed within the desired file's <a href> tag:

```
onClick="_gaq.push(['_trackPageview', '/pdf/name-of-file.pdf']);"
```

▶ **Event tracking:** To track a direct download as an event, the following JavaScript onClick action needs to be installed within the desired file's <a href> tag:

```
onClick="_gaq.push(['_trackEvent', 'PDF-Files', 'Downloads', 'Name-of-File', 375]);"
```

The parameters for Event tracking are (from left to right) the Category (I used PDF-Files in the previous example, Category being a top-level name or grouping for your Event); Action (the action taken by the visitor), Label (a description of the Event, such as the file name); and Value (a numerical value for the Event).

Not only are there obvious technical differences between virtual page view tracking and event tracking, but there are reporting differences as well. Using virtual page view tracking is essentially like adding a new page to your site—if anyone "views" that page (downloads the file), that data is recorded as a page view. This means that you would find a listing for any downloads of your files within the Content report section in Google Analytics, mixed right in with other actual pages. Using event tracking does not count

▶ /pdf/name-of-file.pdf can and should be changed to better reflect the type and name of file being downloaded.

▶ PDF-Files, Downloads, Name-of-File, and 375 can and should be changed to more appropriately categorize your information.

file download data as a page view, but rather as an event, whose data is housed in a separate subsection of the Content report section in Google Analytics, not mixed in with any other data. Also, with virtual page view tracking, you simply name your page within the JavaScript onClick event, and you're done. With event tracking, you need to define a Category (in the preceding example, *PDF-Files*), an Action (*Downloads*), an optional Label (*Name-of-File*), and an optional Value (*375*).

Which method you use is entirely up to you. Interactions with your files using either method do not count your sessions as bounces (if your sessions view only one actual page), and either method can be configured as a conversion goal.

COMMON GOOGLE ANALYTICS CUSTOMIZATIONS

You can employ many other possible customizations with your Google Analytics tracking code to obtain your desired results. Many other resources are also available online and published by Wiley that can further assist you if your needs are deep and complex. However, the remainder of this chapter covers some of the more common, often-used possibilities with Google Analytics.

You already know all about one very common customization: tracking direct downloads. You were promised a few pages ago to be shown two of the most popular and common customizations: subdomain tracking and cross-domain tracking.

All of the following examples use the standard Google Analytics tracking code snippet. For your reference, this is it:

```
<script type="text/javascript">

  var _gaq = _gaq || [];
  _gaq.push(['_setAccount', 'UA-XXXXX-X']);
  _gaq.push(['_trackPageview']);

  (function() {
    var ga = document.createElement('script'); ga.type =
'text/javascript'; ga.async = true;
    ga.src = ('https:' == document.location.protocol ? 'https://ssl' :
'http://www') + '.google-analytics.com/ga.js';
    var s = document.getElementsByTagName('script')[0];
s.parentNode.insertBefore(ga, s);
  })();

</script>
```

Customization: Subdomain Tracking

▶ Change .website.com to the root-level domain name of your website. Also, don't forget to use the leading period.

If you want to track two or more subdomains simultaneously (for example, www.*website.com* and http://blog.*website.com*), add the following line of JavaScript within the Google Analytics tracking code immediately after the _setAccount line and immediately before the _trackPageview line:

```
_gaq.push(['_setDomainName', '.website.com']);
```

Customization: Cross-Domain Tracking

Tracking between domains is a bit more involved than tracking between subdomains. Say that you want to track website traffic between two domains: www.websiteone.com/ and www.websitetwo.com/. First, the Google Analytics tracking code on both websites needs to have the following two lines of code installed, immediately after the _setAccount line and immediately before the _trackPageview line:

```
_gaq.push(['_setDomainName', 'none']);
_gaq.push(['_setAllowLinker', true]);
```

But that's not all you need to do. You also need to install a JavaScript onClick action on each link or each form that takes a visitor from one domain to the other domain. This needs to happen on all links of both websites that you want to track.

For any links, use the following _link command within the link's <a href> tag:

▶ You need to change the URL within the _link function to reflect the full URL path of where a visitor is being taken.

```
onclick="_gaq.push
(['_link', 'http://www.websitetwo.com/page.html']); return false;"
```

For any forms, use the following _linkByPost command within the form's <form> tag:

```
onsubmit="_gaq.push(['_linkByPost', this]);"
```

Not following these instructions precisely (especially not using _link or _linkByPost correctly) results in significant visitor tracking issues (for example, inaccurate data).

Customization: Ecommerce Tracking

Google Analytics can track purchase information from the confirmation/receipt page that a visitor sees when she successfully completes her online order. This collected data is populated into the Ecommerce report section within the Google Analytics platform.

Following is the template of the Ecommerce tracking component for Google Analytics. This must be placed immediately after the _trackPageview command and should appear only on the confirmation/receipt page of your shopping cart system. The actual values that you are going to see need to be dynamically generated by either your shopping cart platform or a piece of logic that you or a web developer writes to pull in the actual shopper's data. There are many, many ways to do this, and it's not possible to cover them all here.

```
_gaq.push(['_addTrans',
'1234',              // order ID - required
'Mountain View',     // affiliation or store name
'11.99',             // total - required
'1.29',              // tax
'5',                 // shipping
'San Jose',          // city
'California',        // state or province
'USA'                // country
]);
_gaq.push(['_addItem',
'1234',              // order ID - required
'DD44',              // SKU/code
'T-Shirt',           // product name
'Green Medium',      // category or variation
'11.99',             // unit price - required
'1'                  // quantity - required
]);
_gaq.push(['_trackTrans']);
```

Customization: Session Time-Outs

With Google Analytics, any period of visitor inactivity lasting more than 30 minutes "times out," which ends that visitor's session. You can modify this time-out period with the _setSessionCookieTimeout command. You can modify the number of seconds that a session lasts (3600000 is the default setting). If you use this customization, you should install it on all website pages that you're tracking, and you should place it immediately after the _setAccount line and immediately before the _trackPageview line:

```
_gaq.push(['_setSessionCookieTimeout', 3600000]);
```

Customization: Campaign Cookie Duration

The default duration for AdWords campaign cookie data is automatically set for six months. Depending on your specific situation, you can change the campaign duration for AdWords marketing initiatives using the _setCampaignCookieTimeout method. Unlike the session time-out customization, this one is set in milliseconds! However, just like most customizations, this one is also installed immediately after the _setAccount line and immediately before the _trackPageview line:

```
_gaq.push(['_setCampaignCookieTimeout',  31536000000]);
```

Customization: Visitor Cookie Duration

The Google Analytics visitor lifetime cookie (the __utma cookie, to be precise) lasts for two years, and you can modify it with the _setVisitorCookieTimeout command. It's also configured by milliseconds, but one neat thing about that is that if you set this command to 0, the visitor cookie expires as soon as the session expires, the browser is closed, or the day ends.

Install _setVisitorCookieTimeout immediately after the _setAccount line and immediately before the _trackPageview line:

```
_gaq.push(['_setVisitorCookieTimeout', 63072000000]);
```

Customization: Site Speed Tracking

One of the newer customizations that Google Analytics offers is the ability to measure a page's loading speed. This is a critical metric for anyone in pay-per-click marketing or doing search engine optimization work on his website. The faster a page loads, the better for both your visitors and the search engines, so the _trackPageLoadTime command really comes in handy.

This additional line of JavaScript gets installed *after* the _trackPageview line:

```
_gaq.push(['_trackPageLoadTime']);
```

> **NOTE** Google Analytics provides many more customization possibilities—too many to mention here. The best online resource that you could use is the Google Code website, which has its own Google Analytics section: http://code.google.com/apis/analytics/.

SUMMARY

Clearly, there are many ways to tweak and customize Google Analytics for your specific needs. Whether you're tracking blogs, downloadable files, social media traffic, or have the need for further customizations, Google Analytics can most likely accommodate.

The best advice in regard to customizing Google Analytics for your needs is to follow to the letter the instructions from this book as well as official online resources. This is the best insurance policy against making a mistake and breaking your tracking code, which can cause serious data consequences.

Part VIII

ANDROID SECRETS

CHAPTER 34

Getting More Done with Android

Android is Google's operating system for mobile devices.
Whether you're running Android on your mobile phone or on your tablet, you'll find Android gives you full customization and lots of features. Whatever it is you want to do with your mobile device, you will find an App that can do it.

CUSTOMIZING MOBILE PHONE FUNCTIONALITY

Most cell phones are simply phones with a built-in contact list, calculator, and a few games. There really isn't much you can do to customize the basic cell phone outside of adding a new faceplate or using a cool cell phone case. But, Android OS for mobile phones gives you control over the look and function of your phone, and you control the functionality of your phone with the apps you choose to download.

Using Apps and Widgets to Customize Your Device

▶ There are two types of Apps for the Android. Standard Apps run on the out-of-the-box Android OS. Apps for rooted phones need special permissions to run correctly. Rooting your phone is explained later in this chapter.

You can customize your Android device in two ways. First, you can use the built-in options configuration. You can also download an App that provides customization abilities. Downloading an App is most likely the easiest way for you to be able to customize your Android device, but there are other ways to do it, as you discover very shortly.

One example of an App you can download to get customization features is LockBot. LockBot is an App that lets you replace your lock screen with custom skins. First, you choose from several screen styles including X10, iPhone, Hero, and others. Then you further customize your screen by using downloadable backgrounds or using pictures from your Flickr, Picasa, or Wretch accounts, or even from your SD card.

Of course, you don't need an App to simply change your wallpaper. All versions of Android include different wallpapers, and all versions after 1.5 enable you to use an image from your SD card as wallpaper as well. To change your wallpaper start at your home screen and long-press any open area. Tap Wallpapers and select the image source. Browse the images until you locate the one you want, and tap Set Wallpaper. When you select a homemade photo you can crop the image before you save it to your wallpaper.

Another great Android App that has been receiving a decent amount of positive online feedback for customizing your device is LauncherPro. LauncherPro replaces the default Android launcher and enables you to customize the number of home screens for widgets (anywhere from one to seven). LauncherPro also lets you create a dock that enables you to put any App or contact directly on it, which makes accessing that App or contact much easier. There is a paid version of LauncherPro with many more features than the free version, so you should try out the free version first before you decide to buy.

An Android-customizing App that you might not know about is called Go Launcher EX. The paid version of Go Launcher was very successful, but not many people are aware that there is a free, "lite" version, which is perfect for Android customization. Go Launcher EX runs when you press your Android phone's Home key, supporting functions that are useful and skins that are plentiful. This great (and free) App also comes with a folder and task manager in the App drawer, smooth scrolling, and gesture support.

Further Customizing Android with Widgets

Further customize the look and functionality of your Android with widgets. Widgets on the Android are exactly like widgets on your iGoogle page, or anywhere else. Use them to bring the time, weather, news, music, RSS feeds, stock information, or just about any other info directly to your Android home screen. Depending on your phone, many customization widgets may be included on your phone. In case they aren't, here is a list of some of the more popular widgets:

▶ Battery Widget, available in the Android Market, accurately displays how much battery power you have left. Power readings appear as an icon on your home screen. Toggle between battery, GPS, Wi-Fi, and Bluetooth readings with a finger touch.

▶ Evernote is a free widget that puts note taking at your fingertips. Simply tap the icon and start typing your note.

▶ 3G Watchdog lets you keep track of the amount of bandwidth you use. Never pay overage charges again.

▶ Pure Calendar is a calendar widget that is more detailed and more customizable than the calendar that may have come installed on your Android device.

▶ Last Call never lets you forget that your Android phone is, well, still a phone. This widget displays your last phone call so you can see the call you missed at a glance.

▶ If you or a loved one travels a lot, then FlightView is indispensable. Enter flight information into the widget and it tracks the flight right on your home screen.

▶ If you follow sports, bring scores to your home screen with Scoreboard. Never again wonder who won that big game.

▶ Pandora is a fairly popular music streaming program. Use the Pandora widget to stream your music directly to your Android device. The Pandora widget enables you to choose your custom station, play and pause music, give a thumbs-up or thumbs down rating, and skip tracks.

Android's "Ice Cream Sandwich"

▶ Why Ice Cream Sandwich? Thus far Google has named every Android release after a sweet dessert item, in alphabetical order. Previous versions were named Donut, Eclair, Froyo, Gingerbread, and Honeycomb.

The next version of Android, called Ice Cream Sandwich is due to be released sometime during the fourth quarter of 2011. It's speculated that Android Ice Cream Sandwich will run on both tablets and smartphones, and it's being regarded online as Google's most aggressive, ambitious update yet. Essentially, Ice Cream Sandwich will help put a stop to "Android Fragmentation," which will help all Android users everywhere consolidate their devices to all use the same version of Android's operating system.

Android Ice Cream Sandwich blazes yet another new trail with features never before seen on a phone. With the next version of Android, you will be able to rent movies to watch directly on your device of choice through the Android Market. This comes on the heels of major deals struck between Google, Sony Pictures, NBC Universal, and Warner Brothers for rights to allow movie rentals, much like you can currently rent movies via Apple iTunes or Apple TV. You'll have access to your rented movies for 24 hours after you start the movie, and unwatched movies are good for 30 days. Movie rental will support downloading the movie to watch offline on your Android device.

The biggest changes with Android Ice Cream Sandwich are face-tracking abilities, camera focus control via voice recognition, and 3D capabilities. The current available documentation suggests that Android devices running Ice Cream Sandwich will enable you to control certain functions with eye and facial movements. Ice Cream Sandwich will also give you the ability to stream music from the cloud instead of storing your music on the local device, without the need to download additional Apps, such as Pandora, Rhapsody, or Slacker.

Rooting Your Device

If you're adventurous you can gain complete control over your Android phone by hacking into the operating system and taking root control. This process, called "rooting," is similar to logging in to a Linux computer as the root user. It gives you administrator rights to every application and process on the system.

> **WARNING** Although rooting your phone gives you greater control over the features and functionality of your phone, it also makes it more likely that you will do something to make your phone unusable. If you make a mistake and accidentally brick your phone, you're on your own. The minute you root your Android phone is the same minute your warranty becomes void.

You should know that as of March 2011 many phone carriers, such as Verizon, are keeping lists of those Android accounts that don't accept the standard OS updates. Not accepting updates is a major clue to a rooted phone. New versions of Android will include a tracking code of some sort. If the tracking code is removed, the phone could lose voice and/or data ability. Nobody seems sure what phone carriers are doing with the lists of rooted phones. The general consensus is that phone companies are trying to block users from rooting most phones. Then phone providers will offer a developer's model phone at a higher price.

Rooting your phone also increases the number of Apps you can use on your Android. Because Android is open source, a large number of open source Apps are available for rooted phones. Just remember that if you use a rooted App there is a possibility you can get malicious software. Be sure to use a good malware detection App, such as Lookout Mobile Security (one of the best available Apps) or Anti-Virus Free from AVG.

After you root your phone you need to find and install Apps designed for altered phones. Some of the most popular Apps include the following:

- **SetCPU:** Gives you the ability to change the speed of the phone's processing chip, which is called overclocking and makes the device run faster. However—as you may already be aware from any desktop PC experience you may have—when you overclock a processor, you always run the risk of burning it out and damaging the chip (even on a mobile device or tablet). When you set the phone to run slower, or underclock it, when you're not using the device, the battery life of the phone is extended. 800Mghz seems to be a solid, safe overclock speed for many Android phones.

- **ShootMe:** Enables you to take screenshots of your phone's screen.

- **JuiceDefender:** By far the absolute best way to manage your phone's battery life. This program lets you turn off programs and features when they're not being used to allow the phone to use less power.

- **Cachemate:** Just like on your home computer, your phone's cache can get full and bog down the system. Cachemate lets you clear out the cache of your Android without having to restart the phone.

- **Titanium Backup:** If you're going to hack your Android phone and install open source Apps, then it's vital to back up your working system often. Accidents happen; protect yourself with an App that backs up everything on your phone, instead of just a few select things.

▶ **ROM Manager:** Makes the process of adding Apps, kernel changes, and radio images easier.

▶ **Root Explorer:** Gives you full access to your phone's file directory. Be careful with this; when you have access to every single folder and file it's very easy to accidentally mess up your system. Do your research before altering unfamiliar folders.

▶ **Shark for Root:** Enables you to see exactly what kind of network activity is going on behind the scenes, so you always know who and what your Apps are talking to when you're not looking.

▶ **Adfree:** Blocks ads from being downloaded while you're surfing on your phone.

Rooting your phone can be as simple as running a program on your computer, or it can be a complicated process that requires a bit of programming knowledge. It depends on which version of Android is installed on your phone, and which phone you own. Developers are always coming up with new ways to root your phone. Because the best rooting methods change so frequently, Lifehacker keeps an updated list of the latest and greatest way to root most phones on `http://lifehacker.com/5789397/the-always-up+to+date-guide-to-rooting-any-android-phone`.

FINDING NEW APPS

With all this cool technology in your phone or tablet device, you may be wondering where to find Apps that make the most of your Android. Well, finding Apps is easy.

The first place to look, although not necessarily the best if you're into open source, is the Android Market. Available at the press of the screen from your Android device, or at `https://market.android.com/apps` from a standard browser, the Android Market is your one-stop shopping place for approved Android Apps. You can find everything from games to productivity Apps. Apps are sortable by price—either free or paid Apps—and by category—games or applications. You can also browse through lists of the most popular, best-selling, or top trending Apps. You can find books and movies for purchase or rent that you can download to your Android device from the menu shown in Figure 34-1.

FIGURE 34-1: Use the menu at the top of your screen to choose between Android Apps, movies, or books.

After you've exhausted your options on the official Android Market, try some other, unofficial sources. Just remember that like with any other unofficial software the potential for viruses, spyware, and other malware exists. Protect yourself (install the aforementioned Lookout Mobile Security or AVG's Anti-Virus Free), your data, and your device by doing your research before installing any software on your Android device. Also, try to search for user-generated reviews and discussion online before installing any unofficial App—you never want to install an App that would be sharing your information with third parties or Apps that seemingly do nothing else but crash, so put your online ear to the ground and find out the true scoop before installing any unofficial App.

One way you can do research to keep your device protected is to use Cyrket. Cyrket is the end all and be all of websites for the advanced Android user, and you can find it at www.cyrket.com. It gives in-depth information about each application, enabling you to analyze user experiences to find the applications that are a great fit for the way you use your Android device. You can find in-depth descriptions, application screen shots, Quick Response (QR) codes, graphs that give a quick visual representation of user rating breakdowns, and lots of user comments. Sort applications by price, rating, popularity, application function, or alphabetical order, or use the search tool to quickly locate the application you're looking for. The search menu is shown in Figure 34-2, and the description page for Google Maps is shown in Figure 34-3.

▶ A QR code is an encoded image you use to access information, much like bar codes on any supermarket product. You use a mobile app to take a picture of and process the QR code. Normally, the QR code leads a visitor to a website.

FIGURE 34-2: Sort applications listed on Cyrket by market, price, rating, alphabetically, and other criteria.

FIGURE 34-3: Use the graphs, comments, feature listings, screen shots, and recent changes listings to determine if the App is a good fit for you.

Androlib (www.androlib.com) lists a lot of the same Apps you'll find on the official Android Market, but you'll find a lot of Apps that are not on the official site, as well. Androlib uses the same five-star rating system used by the official Android Market, information on the App's popularity, QR codes, user reviews, and developer descriptions. The landing page, along with potential search options, are shown in Figure 34-4.

FIGURE 34-4: The landing page of Androlib.com. Notice the search options at the top of the page.

AppBrain not only helps you find Apps for your Android device, it helps you manage them, too. AppBrain, found at www.appbrain.com, gives the same information as the other App sites, plus it includes info on what changes were made to the App with the latest upgrades. It also includes the added ability to create an account with your Google login. Creating an account lets you keep track of which Apps you've installed and your opinion of each App, which is great for people who try a lot of Apps.

These are some of the best places to find Apps for your Android device on the Web, but there are many more. Some of the others are

- ▶ **AndBOT:** www.andbot.com
- ▶ **App Store HQ:** http://android.appstorehq.com
- ▶ **AndroidZoom:** www.androidzoom.com
- ▶ **Phandroid:** http://androidapplications.com

Of course, because Android is open source, you can always write your own Apps and share them with the world. Creating Apps for the Android is covered in Chapter 35.

SUMMARY

Android is changing quickly. It started as a simple operating system for smartphones and tablets and is evolving to enable you to bring your cloud applications with you wherever you go. With Android Ice Cream Sandwich, the possibilities for users on Google's mobile operating system seem endless. For those brave enough to root their Android phones, the possibilities really are endless!

Creating Android Apps

When you hear "Android" you immediately think "Google," but Android is actually developed and released through the Open Handset Alliance. Google Android is a branded version of the Open Android operating system. What this means for the Android developer is that there is an even bigger developing community out there to help you develop the Android App of your dreams. Android Apps are written in Java, so if you're already comfortable with Java, half your battle is won. And, if you're not a Java programmer, lots of resources are available to help you.

> NOTE The Open Handset Alliance (www.openhandsetalliance.com) is a group of companies dedicated to making mobile computing faster, better, and easier for users worldwide.

THE DEVELOPMENT STACK

To make a computer or gadget work and interpret commands given by the user, several programs are layered on top of each other. The purpose of these programs is to facilitate communication between the user and the computer chip.

Detailed information about developing apps is something that is outside of the scope of this book, but this section provides a general overview of the Android development stack. In a device running Android, the layer closest to the chip is a Linux Kernel without all the extra software you find in a distribution intended for your home PC or personal laptop. The Linux Kernel is then optimized to run smoothly with the exact hardware of the device. So, each Android device (such as the HTC Evo, Nexus One, Motorola Droid X, and others) has a slightly different version of the Linux Kernel.

On top of the Linux layer are the native libraries. These are programs with the ability to talk to and interpret between Linux and programs that run basic device functions. This layer is specific to the device hardware. For example, you can find a library for keyboard controls, touchscreen operation, and 2D and 3D graphics. Webkit and SQLite are also in this level.

The next layer consists of the applications that enable your device to understand Java. In Android devices these are Java Runtime and Dalvik Virtual Machine (DVM). Dalvik was written by a Google employee to allow Android devices to run Java code more efficiently using less memory and processing power than is needed by larger devices, such as desktop computers.

The layers are vital for the function of the device, but they run in the background, behind your interaction with Android. The upper layers are the parts you interact with when you build an Android app.

Now we come to the Android Framework layer. This layer of Android is found in the Android SDK and it includes all the Java classes that provide specific functionality to Android devices. Functions such as finding a location via GPS, working with Webkit, communicating with the contacts database, and showing notifications on the screen are part of the Framework.

Finally, on top of the Framework are the System Apps. These are the applications you use to do things. The applications you use to fetch and view e-mail, make a phone call, view or use the contact list—whatever actions you perform with your Android device—are the System Apps. And these are what you learn to build in this chapter. For a visual representation of how this all fits together, see the diagram in Figure 35-1.

▶ SDK is short for Software Development Kit. It's covered in-depth later in this chapter.

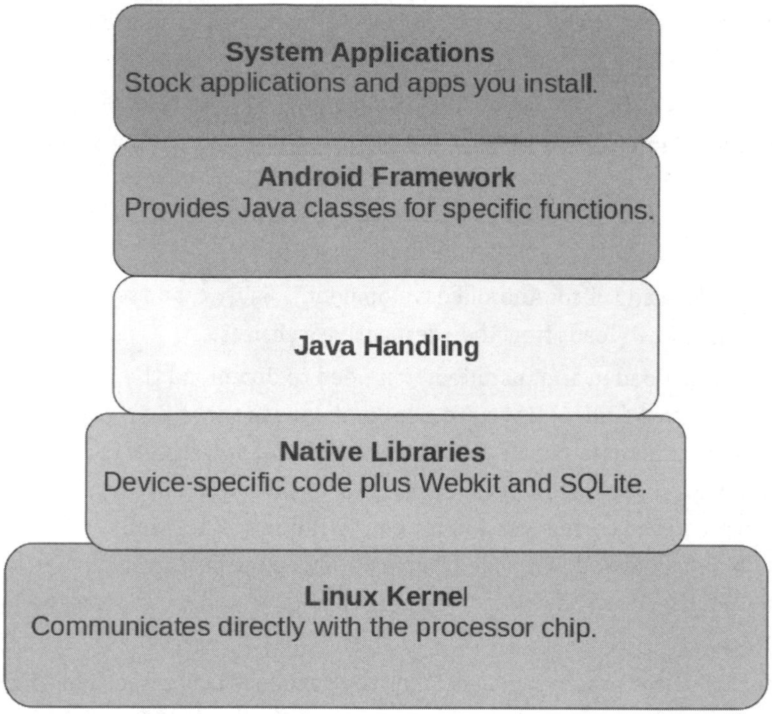

FIGURE 35-1: The Android Development Stack.

NOTE One of the truly great things about Android devices is that the user has complete control over the Apps used to perform every function of the device. If you don't like the e-mail app that came with your device out of the box, you have the freedom to download, or build, an app to meet your needs. You can remove the factory installed app without harm to your system.

THE ENVIRONMENT

You can create Apps for Android in two ways. The first method is to use the Google App Inventor. This is the simple and straightforward way to build basic, uncomplicated apps. This is comparable to an object-oriented programing environment in which to build apps. You lay out the app design and use the code library to tell each piece what to do. The Google App Inventor is covered in more detail in the "Creating a Basic App" section later in this chapter.

▶ You can find Eclipse for Windows or Mac at www.eclipse.org/downloads. It's a free download. If you're a Linux user, you can find Eclipse in your Software Package Center, or through Synaptic Package Manager.

For those of you who want to create your apps the old-fashioned way here's what you need to know.

Android apps are written in Java, so the first thing you need is an integrated development environment, or IDE. IDEs are language-specific programming areas that include tools such as a source code editor, debugger, complier, and so on. It's like a little room on your computer devoted specifically to the programming language you're using.

The most commonly used IDE for Android development is Eclipse, and second is NetBeans. Both are free downloads from their respective websites.

After Eclipse is downloaded and installed, you need to download the Java Development Kit, Version 6 (JDK 6). If you're a current Java programmer, you probably already have this installed on your computer. But if you're new to Java programming, go to www.oracle.com/technetwork/java/javase/downloads/index.html to download the correct version for your Windows, Mac, Linux, or Solaris system. If you've never downloaded from the Java page before, it can be a little confusing. Figure 35-2 shows exactly where to click in order to access the Java Development Kit.

▶ You can download NetBeans for Windows, Mac, or Solaris from http://netbeans.org.

Read and accept the license agreement and click the download link associated with your operating system and your desired install type on the page shown in Figure 35-3.

▶ You can find the Android SDK at developer.android.com/sdk/index.html.

Finally, install the Android SDK Tools from Google. This is the Software Development Kit I talked about in the previous section of this chapter.

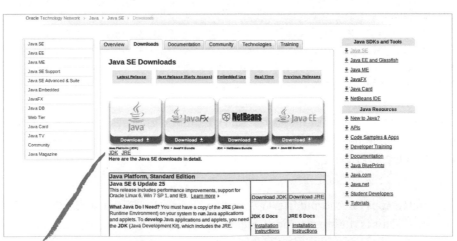

Click JDK to find the Development Kits.

FIGURE 35-2: Click JDK to download the correct Java Development Kit for your operating system.

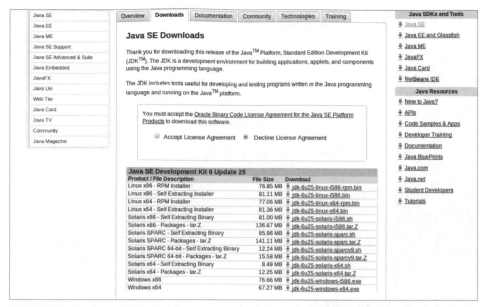

FIGURE 35-3: Choose your operating system and desired package type from the list.

If it seems like a complex set of pieces to download and install, you're right, it is. But, each piece adds a vital component to your development stack.

Now, it's time to configure these pieces into the development environment.

First, open Eclipse. Click Help → Install New Software. Click Add. In the box labeled Name, type **Android**. In the box labeled Location, type **https://dl-ssl.google.com/ android/eclipse/**. Your screen should look like Figure 35-4. Click OK.

> **NOTE** Some systems may require you to change the https to http.

Eclipse then fetches current information on Android libraries and updated development tools from the site you entered. When it's finished your screen looks like the image in Figure 35-5.

Tick each of the available boxes and click Next to install the most recent Android development tools to Eclipse. If the Review Licenses screen appears, as in Figure 35-6, tick the I Accept button and click Finish.

Next, you need to configure the Android SDK that you downloaded earlier. If you're using a Windows OS, run SDK Setup.exe. Select the items related to the Android version for which you're programming and click Install. Linux users read the information in the sidebar.

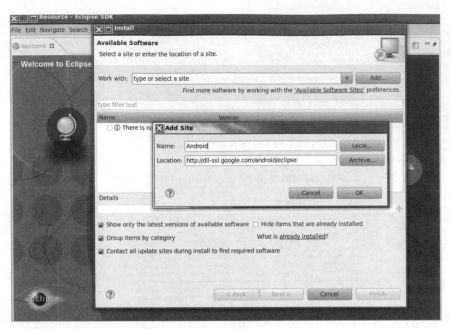

FIGURE 35-4: Eclipse screen after you click Add.

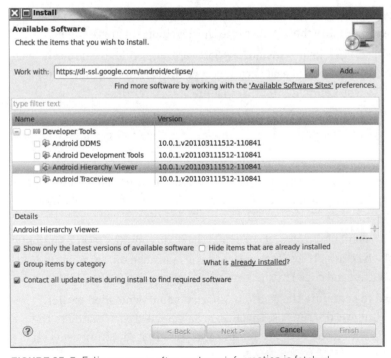

FIGURE 35-5: Eclipse screen after package information is fetched.

FIGURE 35-6: The Review Licenses screen for the Android Development Tools for Eclipse.

INSTALLING THE ANDROID SDK FOR LINUX USERS

First, create a folder named Android SDK. Extract the tarball to this folder with your favorite package extractor. Now, navigate to the folder you created .You see three folders: Add-ons, Platforms, and Tools. Open the Tools folder. Click Android and run the executable file. This opens the screen in Figure 35-7.

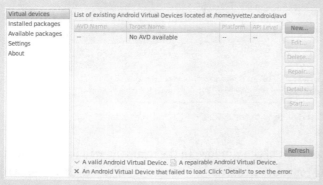

FIGURE 35-7: This is the SDK Manager. Use this to download Android Tools.

Click Available Packages from the list on the left side of the window. Click Android Repository and select the packages that pertain to the Android version for which you are programing. Click the button labeled Install Selected. Accept all packages on the Installation confirmation screen, and click the Install button.

Regardless of your operating system, you should expect this download and installation to take quite a while to complete.

You're almost ready to start creating an app for Android, but first, you need to set up the Android Virtual Device, or AVD. The virtual device acts as testing ground for the programs you write. It's a lot easier to test and debug in a virtual device than it is to compile your program and test it on a real Android device. Besides, if you make a vital programming error, testing on the virtual device may save your real Android device from harm.

To create your virtual device, first select Virtual Devices from the left side of the Android SDK Manager, as shown in Figure 35-8.

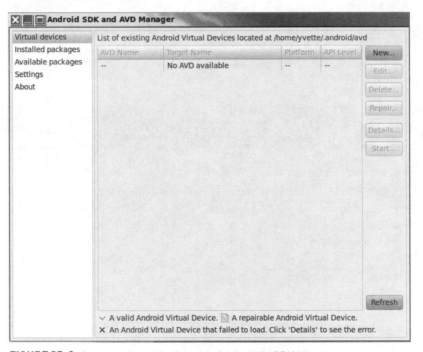

FIGURE 35-8: Create a virtual device with the Android SDK Manager.

Click New on the upper right of the window. In the resulting window, shown in Figure 35-9, enter a name for your virtual device. Then use the drop-down menu to choose the Android release for which you're programming. If you're creating an application for your own personal use, select the version on your device. However, if you intend to release your app for others to download, you may want to program for the latest version of Android (the Android environment is backward compatible).

Configure the remaining settings as closely to your device as possible and then click the button labeled Create AVD. Click OK when the confirmation screen appears. It's a good idea at this point to double-check that your AVD truly does resemble the device you want it to emulate, so click the device you just created from the list and then click Start on the right side of the screen. You can see my AVD in Figure 35-10.

Now you're ready to tell Eclipse where to find the Android SDK so you can start entering code. Open Eclipse, and select Window from the top navigation menu. Now, select Preferences. On the left you see several setting options—General, Android, Ant, Help, and others—select Android. Use the file browser to navigate to the location of the Android SDK on your hard drive. Click Apply. Double-check the settings, and click the OK button.

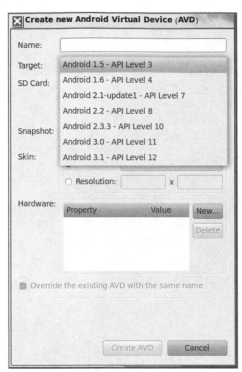

FIGURE 35-9: Name your virtual device and select the Android version your virtual device should emulate.

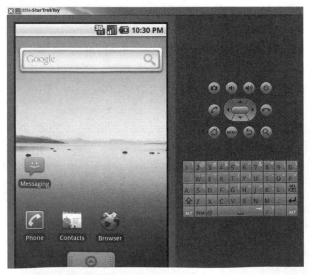

FIGURE 35-10: AVD for Android 2.1.

That's it. You're now ready to create a new project and begin programming!

> ### ANDROID-SPECIFIC VOCABULARY
>
> If you're going to build an app for Android, following are a few words you need to know:
>
> ► **Resource:** Any item that you want the app to interact with that is not code. These are things like text, pictures, video, icons, or sound. Resources are referenced as Class R.
>
> ► **Intent:** Intent is the code you write to complete an action. Examples include call a phone a number, open the contacts database, and open an app.
>
> ► **Activity:** A screen. The code that controls any screen is called an Activity.

CREATING A BASIC APP

For the absolute easiest way to create your own Android apps use Android App Inventor in Google Labs. Remember that because this is a Lab project, it is still in Beta. To start using Google App Inventor, go to appinventor.googlelabs.com, and sign into your Google account. Read the entire Terms of Service page, and if you agree, click the button labeled I Accept the Terms of Service at the top of the page. This takes you to the Setup page, as shown in Figure 35-11.

Follow the onscreen instructions labeled Step 1 to ensure you have the correct version of Java on your computer. If your computer fails the tests, follow the given links to perform the required upgrades.

Now, decide if you are going to hook your Android device up to your computer to test your apps or if you are going to use an emulator similar to the one you created in the previous section of this chapter. Based on your decision, follow the appropriate onscreen instructions for Step 2.

When you're finished, click My Projects in the upper right of the screen to go to the Projects page shown in Figure 35-12.

FIGURE 35-11: Instructions on setting up your computer to work with Google App Inventor.

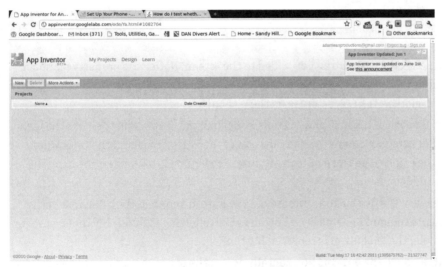

FIGURE 35-12: Projects page. This is the App Inventor homepage.

If you've ever used any type of object-oriented programming environment, such as Microsoft Visual Basic, the environment of Google App Inventor should feel pretty familiar.

Click the button labeled New in the upper left of the screen. Type your project's name in the textbox. Don't use any spaces between words. For the example, you're creating a simple paint program.

First drag five buttons from the Basic menu, and drop them one by one on to the screen view. This is shown in Figure 35-13.

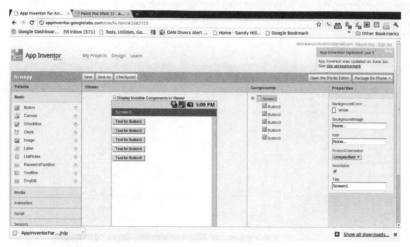

FIGURE 35-13: Five buttons on the screen.

Next, click the first button you added to the screen. Notice the property manager on the right side of the screen. Enter the color name you want to display on the button in the box marked TEXT. Type **Erase** on the last button.

Now, for each of the first four buttons, first click the button and then use the menu labeled BackgroundColor to change the color of the button to match the color word. Change the color of the Erase button to white. See Figure 35-14 for help locating the BackgroundColor menu.

For each of the five buttons, first select the button and then click Rename in the Components column. Rename each button in the following manner: Button*ColorName*. For example, the red button is renamed ButtonRed.

Next, arrange the buttons horizontally across the top of the screen. In the Palette menu on the right, select Screen Arrangement. Click the icon in front of the words Horizontal Arrangement and drag/drop it to the top of the screen view. Now, drag and drop each button into the resulting rectangle, as shown in Figure 35-15.

Now that you have the color buttons on the screen, add the drawing canvas. In the Basic palette, drag the Canvas to the screen. In the Properties section on the right, set Width to Fill Parent and Height to 300px. Rename the canvas to CanvasDraw, or something equally descriptive.

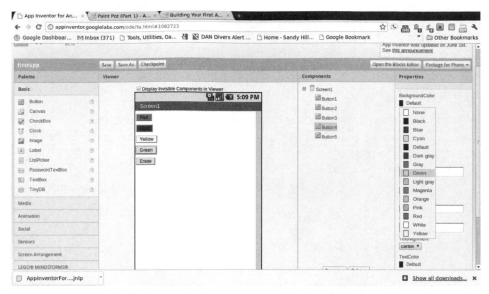

FIGURE 35-14: Use the BackgroundColor menu to set the color of each button.

You've finished designing the screen, now it's time to assign actions to the buttons. To do this, you use the Blocks Editor. You installed this during the initial setup process. If you haven't done so already, click Open Blocks Editor at the top right of the window.

Click My Blocks to switch to the menu for the current project. Your screen should look like the image in Figure 35-16.

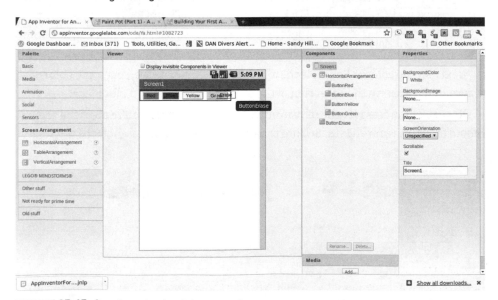

FIGURE 35-15: Creating a horizontal screen view.

FIGURE 35-16: My Blocks menu for the paint program.

First, click ButtonRed. A menu opens to the right side. This menu contains all the possible events related to the button. Apps Inventor calls this a drawer. Drag the piece labeled When ButtonRed.click and drop it to the right of the drawer.

FIGURE 35-17: The DO section with CanvasDraw.PaintColor.

Next, open the drawer for the CanvasDraw button. Drag out the piece labeled Set CanvasDraw.PaintColor to. Place it in the Do section of the when ButtonRed. Click piece as shown in Figure 35-17. The pieces fit together like a jigsaw puzzle, and when you have the piece in correctly you hear a snapping sound.

Next, set the color to Red. Select Built-in from the menu. Then open the Colors drawer and place it in the *To* section of the Set CanvasDraw.PaintColor piece.

Repeat this process for the remaining color buttons. When you're done the screen should look like Figure 35-18. Be sure to save your work often.

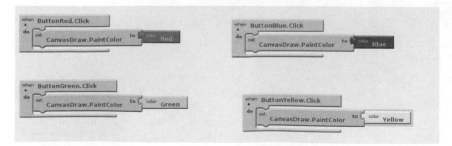

FIGURE 35-18: A completed screen with the chosen color buttons.

Finally, set the Clear button. Select My Blocks. Open the drawer for ButtonErase and drag out When ButtonWipe.Click. Now, go to the CanvasDraw drawer and place the piece labeled Call CanvasDraw.Clear into the Do section of the ButtonErase.Click piece, as shown in Figure 35-19.

FIGURE 35-19: The Canvas-Draw.Clear piece inside the Do section of the Button-Erase.Click piece.

The last step in this process is to make the buttons responsive to screen touch.

Select My Blocks. Open the CanvasDraw drawer and drag out the piece labeled When CanvasDraw.Touched.

Now, open CanvasDraw again. Grab callCanvas.DrawCircle and place it in the Do section of When CanvasDraw.Touched.

Next, open My Definitions. Drag out the value X and value Y pieces and place them in the corresponding spaces of callCanvas.DrawCircle.

Set the circle radius next. Click on any open space in the work area. A floating menu appears. Select Math. Now click 123 to create a number block. Drag this number block to the R slot on the callCanvas.DrawCircle piece. For this tutorial, type the number **5**, to create a 5-pixel radius.

The final version should look like Figure 35-20. Figure 35-21 shows the app working in an Android emulator.

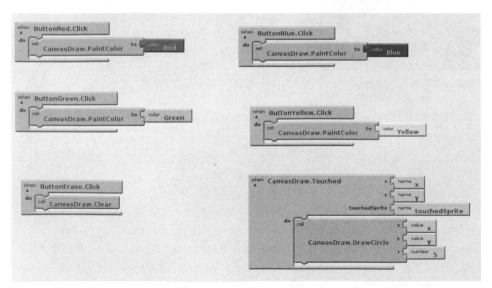

FIGURE 35-20: The final Block Editor screen for your paint program.

The final step is to package the app for your phone. Click Package for Phone in the upper right of your screen. Select from Barcode, Download to This Computer, or Download to Phone. Google App Inventor does the rest.

This simple app gives you an idea of how the Google App Inventor works. Take the time to read through the sample files and tutorials. You can find all the tutorials, FAQ files, and forums by clicking Learn from the menu at the top of the My Projects homepage.

FIGURE 35-21: The paint program in action.

TAPPING THE APPLICATION MARKET

You've already seen what's available on the Android Market, now you can add your own creations to the Market. Point your web browser to the Android Market at market .android.com, scroll to the bottom of the page, and click Developers. That takes you to the Android Developers homepage. The direct link is developer.android.com/index .html. Now, click Learn More in the Publish section to the right. This takes you to the developer sign-up page. Note there is $25.00 registration fee to create a developer profile and upload apps. Of course, you can always upload and sell your apps on your personal website. However, in that event your apps do not appear on the Android Market and might be missed by the majority of users. Some App listing sites do list apps for sale through means other than the official Android Market. Check the requirements of each site.

There are some basic, common-sense things that you should consider doing as you're entering the realm of selling an App within the Android Marketplace. Most of the best-selling apps have clear screenshots, catchy titles and descriptions, are easy to use, and have a competitive price point. Good user reviews (user-generated content) helps, but those only come in if users think your app is worthy of a positive, 5-star review.

SUMMARY

Building Android apps can be as simple as putting together a puzzle, or as complicated as writing your own Java code. The complexity depends on the function of your app, your programming experience, and your personal preference. Google App Inventor lets you build simple to mid-level apps, and with the Android programming environment within Eclipse combined with your Java knowledge, the only limit is your imagination—and the hardware capabilities of your Android device. These tools let you truly customize your Android device and the apps you use.

Index

phrases in searches, 51
Picasa
  collages, 217
  editing tools, 210–211
  face recognition, 208
  filtering, 209
  interface, 208
  local, 208
  movie presentations, 217
  multiple computers, 214–215
  Orkut and, 249
    slideshows, 251
  Picnik, 217
  pictures
    hard drive, 208
    selecting, 209
  RSS feeds, 215–216
  screenshot logging, 212–213
  video editing, 203, 217
  watermarks, 216
Picasa Web Albums, 208, 213
  online storage, 211–212
Picnik, 217
Pidgin, 225, 226
podcasts
  blog posts, 182–185
  searches, 107–108
POP-enabled server messages in Gmail, 140
  sending from Gmail, 140–142
postcard verification for business pages, 68
PowerPoint files in blogs, 181–182
price comparisons, 41
printing from Blogger, 180–181
privacy
  Dashboard, 11
  Google Voice, 231
Profile, 12–13
  About Me page, 13–14
  deleting, 14
  disabling, 14
  hiding, 14
  Public Profile, benefits, 13
  sharing, 14

Psi, 226
public data searches, 42
Public Profile benefits, 13
PureCalendar widget (Android), 417

Q

quotation marks in searches, 41

R

recovering password, 7
Related Places, 64
Related Searches link, 43
restricting results, 58
  domains, 59–60
  pages linked to specific page, 60–61
  specific file types, 61
  websites, 59–60
  words in specific locations, 60
rooting Android
RSS feeds, 194
  Buzz and, 239
  Gears, 33
  Google Reader, keyboard shortcuts, 30–32
  iGoogle, 17
  notifications, 32
  Picasa, 215–216
  sharing, 34–35
  tagging, 33

S

SafeSearch, 54
  enabling, 117
  Google Image Search, 99
  Lock, 117
  SafeSearch Filtering, Search Preferences, 113
  YouTube, 205
Scoreboard widget (Android), 417
Screen Captures folder, 212
screenshots, Picasa and, 212–213
Search Preferences
  access, 112
  auto-complete settings, 115–116
  Google Instant, 113